THE
LIFE AND LETTERS OF
CHARLES DARWIN

Including an Autobiographical Chapter

EDITED BY HIS SON
FRANCIS DARWIN

VOLUME II

Elibron Classics
www.elibron.com

CHARLES DARWIN IN 1881.

THE
LIFE AND LETTERS OF
CHARLES DARWIN

Including an Autobiographical Chapter

EDITED BY HIS SON
FRANCIS DARWIN

IN TWO VOLUMES
VOL. II

NEW YORK
D. APPLETON AND COMPANY
1897

Authorized Edition.

TABLE OF CONTENTS.

CONTENTS.

APPENDICES.

LIST OF ILLUSTRATIONS.

FROM A NOTE-BOOK OF 1837.

led to comprehend true affinities. My theory would give zest to recent & Fossil Comparative Anatomy : it would lead to study of instincts, heredity, & mind heredity, whole metaphysics, it would lead to closest examination of hybridity & generation, causes of change in order to know what we have come from & to what we tend, to what circumstances favour crossing & what prevents it, this & direct examination of direct passages of structure in species, might lead to laws of change, which would then be main object of study, to guide our speculations.

Facsimile of a page from
a note book of 1837
(See transcript opposite)

LIFE AND LETTERS

OF

CHARLES DARWIN.

CHAPTER I.

THE PUBLICATION OF THE 'ORIGIN OF SPECIES.' OCTOBER 3, 1859, TO DECEMBER 31, 1859.

1859.

[UNDER the date of October 1st, 1859, in my father's Diary occurs the entry: "Finished proofs (thirteen months and ten days) of Abstract on 'Origin of Species'; 1250 copies printed. The first edition was published on November 24th, and all copies sold first day."

On October 2d he started for a water-cure establishment at Ilkley, near Leeds, where he remained with his family until December, and on the 9th of that month he was again at Down. The only other entry in the Diary for this year is as follows: "During end of November and beginning of December, employed in correcting for second edition of 3000 copies; multitude of letters."

The first and a few of the subsequent letters refer to proof sheets, and to early copies of the 'Origin' which were sent to friends before the book was published.]

C. Lyell to C. Darwin.*

October 3d, 1859.

My dear Darwin,—I have just finished your volume and right glad I am that I did my best with Hooker to persuade you to publish it without waiting for a time which probably could never have arrived, though you lived till the age of a hundred, when you had prepared all your facts on which you ground so many grand generalizations.

It is a splendid case of close reasoning, and long substantial argument throughout so many pages ; the condensation immense, too great perhaps for the uninitiated, but an effective and important preliminary statement, which will admit, even before your detailed proofs appear, of some occasional useful exemplification, such as your pigeons and cirripedes, of which you make such excellent use.

I mean that, when, as I fully expect, a new edition is soon called for, you may here and there insert an actual case to relieve the vast number of abstract propositions. So far as I am concerned, I am so well prepared to take your statements of facts for granted, that I do not think the " pièces justificatives" when published will make much difference, and I have long seen most clearly that if any concession is made, all that you claim in your concluding pages will follow. It is this which has made me so long hesitate, always feeling that the case of Man and his races, and of other animals, and that of plants is one and the same, and that if a " vera causa" be admitted for one, instead of a purely unknown and imaginary one, such as the word " Creation," all the consequences must follow.

I fear I have not time to-day, as I am just leaving this place, to indulge in a variety of comments, and to say how much I was delighted with Oceanic Islands—Rudimentary Organs—Embryology—the genealogical key to the Natural

---

* Part of this letter is given in the ' Life of Sir Charles Lyell,' vol. ii. p. 325.

System, Geographical Distribution, and if I went on I should be copying the heads of all your chapters. But I will say a word of the Recapitulation, in case some slight alteration, or, at least, omission of a word or two be still possible in that.

In the first place, at p. 480, it cannot surely be said that the most eminent naturalists have rejected the view of the mutability of species? You do not mean to ignore G. St. Hilaire and Lamarck. As to the latter, you may say, that in regard to animals you substitute natural selection for volition to a certain considerable extent, but in his theory of the changes of plants he could not introduce volition ; he may, no doubt, have laid an undue comparative stress on changes in physical conditions, and too little on those of contending organisms. He at least was for the universal mutability of species and for a genealogical link between the first and the present. The men of his school also appealed to domesticated varieties. (Do you mean *living* naturalists?) *

The first page of this most important summary gives the adversary an advantage, by putting forth so abruptly and crudely such a startling objection as the formation of " the eye," not by means analogous to man's reason, or rather by some power immeasurably superior to human reason, but by superinduced variation like those of which a cattle-breeder avails himself. Pages would be required thus to state an objection and remove it. It would be better, as you wish to persuade, to say nothing. Leave out several sentences, and in a future edition bring it out more fully. Between the throwing down of such a stumbling-block in the way of the reader, and the passage to the working ants, in p. 460, there are pages required ; and these ants are a bathos to him before he has recovered from the shock of being called upon to believe the eye to have been brought to perfection, from a state of blindness or purblindness, by such variations as we witness. I think a little omission would greatly lessen the

---

* In the published copies of the first edition, p. 480, the words are " eminent living naturalists."

objectionableness of these sentences if you have not time to recast and amplify.

. . . . But these are small matters, mere spots on the sun. Your comparison of the letters retained in words, when no longer wanted for the sound, to rudimentary organs is excellent, as both are truly genealogical.

The want of peculiar birds in Madeira is a greater difficulty than seemed to me allowed for. I could cite passages where you show that variations are superinduced from the new circumstances of new colonists, which would require some Madeira birds, like those of the Galapagos, to be peculiar. There has been ample time in the case of Madeira and Porto Santo. . . .

You enclose your sheets in old MS., so the Post Office very properly charge them as letters, 2*d.* extra. I wish all their fines on MS. were worth as much. I paid 4*s.* 6*d.* for such wash the other day from Paris, from a man who can prove 300 deluges in the valley of Seine.

With my hearty congratulations to you on your grand work, believe me,

Ever very affectionately yours,
CHAS. LYELL.

C. Darwin to C. Lyell.

Ilkley, Yorkshire,
October 11th [1859].

MY DEAR LYELL,—I thank you cordially for giving me so much of your valuable time in writing me the long letter of 3d, and still longer of 4th. I wrote a line with the missing proof-sheet to Scarborough. I have adopted most thankfully all your minor corrections in the last chapter, and the greater ones as far as I could with little trouble. I damped the opening passage about the eye (in my bigger work I show the gradations in structure of the eye) by putting merely "complex organs." But you are a pretty Lord Chancellor to

tell the barrister on one side how best to win the cause !
The omission of "living" before eminent naturalists was a
dreadful blunder.

Madeira and Bermuda Birds not peculiar.—You are right,
there is a screw out here; I thought no one would have
detected it ; I blundered in omitting a discussion, which I
have written out in full.   But once for all, let me say as an
excuse, that it was most difficult to decide what to omit.
Birds, which have struggled in their own homes, when settled
in a body, nearly simultaneously in a new country, would not
be subject to much modification, for their mutual relations
would not be much disturbed.   But I quite agree with you,
that in time they ought to undergo some.   In Bermuda and
Madeira they have, as I believe, been kept constant by the
frequent arrival, and the crossing with unaltered immigrants
of the same species from the mainland.   In Bermuda this
can be proved, in Madeira highly probable, as shown me by
letters from E. V. Harcourt.   Moreover, there are ample
grounds for believing that the crossed offspring of the new
immigrants (fresh blood as breeders would say), and old
colonists of the same species would be extra vigorous, and
would be the most likely to survive; thus the effects of such
crossing in keeping the old colonists unaltered would be much
aided.

*On Galapagos productions having American type on view of
Creation.*—I cannot agree with you, that species if created
to struggle with American forms, would have to be created on
the American type.   Facts point diametrically the other way.
Look at the unbroken and untilled ground in La Plata,
covered with European products, which have no near affinity
to the indigenous products.   They are not American types
which conquer the aborigines.   So in every island throughout
the world.   Alph. De Candolle's results (though he does not
see its full importance), that thoroughly well naturalised
[plants] are in general very different from the aborigines
(belonging in large proportion of cases to non indigenous
genera) is most important always to bear in mind.   Once for

all, I am sure, you will understand that I thus write dogmatically for brevity sake.

On the continued Creation of Monads.—This doctrine is superfluous (and groundless) on the theory of Natural Selection, which implies no *necessary* tendency to progression. A monad, if no deviation in its structure profitable to it under its *excessively simple* conditions of life occurred, might remain unaltered from long before the Silurian Age to the present day. I grant there will generally be a tendency to advance in complexity of organisation, though in beings fitted for very simple conditions it would be slight and slow. How could a complex organisation profit a monad? if it did not profit it there would be no advance. The Secondary Infusoria differ but little from the living. The parent monad form might perfectly well survive unaltered and fitted for its simple conditions, whilst the offspring of this very monad might become fitted for more complex conditions. The one primordial prototype of all living and extinct creatures may, it is possible, be now alive! Moreover, as you say, higher forms might be occasionally degraded, the snake Typhlops *seems* (?!) to have the habits of earth-worms. So that fresh creatures of simple forms seem to me wholly superfluous.

"*Must you not assume a primeval creative power which does not act with uniformity, or how could man supervene?*"—I am not sure that I understand your remarks which follow the above. We must under present knowledge assume the creation of one or of a few forms in the same manner as philosophers assume the existence of a power of attraction without any explanation. But I entirely reject, as in my judgment quite unnecessary, any subsequent addition "of new powers and attributes and forces;" or of any "principle of improvement," except in so far as every character which is naturally selected or preserved is in some way an advantage or improvement, otherwise it would not have been selected. If I were convinced that I required such additions to the theory of natural selection, I would reject it as rubbish, but I have firm faith in it, as I cannot believe, that if false, it would explain so many whole classes of facts, which, if I am in my senses, it seems to explain. As far as I understand your remarks and illustrations, you doubt the possibility of gradations of intellectual powers. Now, it seems to me, looking to existing animals alone, that we have a very fine gradation in the intellectual powers of the Vertebrata, with one rather wide gap (not half so wide as in many cases of corporeal structure), between say a Hottentot and an Ourang, even if civilised as much mentally as the dog has been from the wolf. I suppose that you do not doubt that the intellectual powers are as important for the welfare of each being as corporeal structure; if so, I can see no difficulty in the most intellectual individuals of a species being continually selected; and the intellect of the new species thus improved, aided probably by effects of inherited mental exercise. I look at this process as now going on with the races of man; the less intellectual races being exterminated. But there is not space to discuss this point. If I understand you, the turning-point in our difference must be, that you think it impossible that the intellectual powers of a species should be much improved by the continued natural selection of the most intellectual individuals. To show how minds graduate, just reflect how impossible every one has yet found it, to define the difference in mind of man and the lower animals; the latter seem to have the very same attributes in a much lower stage of perfection than the lowest savage. I would give absolutely nothing for the theory of Natural Selection, if it requires miraculous additions at any one stage of descent. I think Embryology, Homology, Classification, &c., &c., show us that all vertebrata have descended from one parent; how that parent appeared we know not. If you admit in ever so little a degree, the explanation which I have given of Embryology, Homology and Classification, you will find it difficult to say : thus far the explanation holds good, but no further; here we must call in " the addition of new creative forces." I think you will be driven to reject all or admit all : I fear by your letter it will be the former alternative ; and in that case I shall feel sure it is my fault, and not the theory's fault, and this will certainly comfort me.   With regard to the descent of the great Kingdoms (as Vertebrata, Articulata, &c.) from one parent, I have said in the conclusion, that mere analogy makes me think it probable ; my arguments and facts are sound in my judgment only for each separate kingdom.

The forms which are beaten inheriting some inferiority in common.—I dare say I have not been guarded enough, but might not the term inferiority include less perfect adaptation to physical conditions ?

My remarks apply not to single species, but to groups or genera ; the species of most genera are adapted at least to rather hotter, and rather less hot, to rather damper and dryer climates; and when the several species of a group are beaten and exterminated by the several species of another group, it will not, I think, generally be from *each* new species being adapted to the climate, but from all the new species having some common advantage in obtaining sustenance, or escaping enemies.   As groups are concerned, a fairer illustration than negro and white in Liberia would be the almost certain future extinction of the genus ourang by the genus man, not owing to man being better fitted for the climate, but owing to the inherited intellectual inferiority of the Ourang-genus to Man-genus, by his intellect, inventing fire-arms and cutting down forests.   I believe from reasons given in my discussion, that acclimatisation is readily effected under nature.   It has taken me so many years to disabuse my mind of the *too* great importance of climate—its important influence being so conspicuous, whilst that of a struggle between creature and creature is so hidden—that I am inclined to swear at the North Pole, and, as Sydney Smith said, even to speak disrespectfully of the Equator.   I beg you often to reflect (I have found *nothing* so instructive) on the case of thousands of plants in the middle point of their respective ranges, and which, as we positively know, can perfectly well withstand a little more heat and cold, a little more damp and dry, but which in the metropolis of their range do not exist in vast numbers, although if many of the other inhabitants were destroyed [they] would cover the ground. We thus clearly see that their numbers are kept down, in almost every case, not by climate, but by the struggle with other organisms. All this you will perhaps think very obvious; but, until I repeated it to myself thousands of times, I took, as I believe, a wholly wrong view of the whole economy of nature. . . .

Hybridism.—I am so much pleased that you approve of this chapter; you would be astonished at the labor this cost me; so often was I, on what I believe was, the wrong scent.

Rudimentary Organs.—On the theory of Natural Selection there is a wide distinction between Rudimentary Organs and what you call germs of organs, and what I call in my bigger book "nascent" organs. An organ should not be called rudimentary unless it be useless—as teeth which never cut through the gums—the papillæ, representing the pistil in male flowers, wing of Apteryx, or better, the little wings under soldered elytra. These organs are now plainly useless, and *à fortiori*, they would be useless in a less developed state. Natural Selection acts exclusively by preserving successive slight, *useful* modifications. Hence Natural Selection cannot possibly make a useless or rudimentary organ. Such organs are solely due to inheritance (as explained in my discussion), and plainly bespeak an ancestor having the organ in a useful condition. They may be, and often have been, worked in for other purposes, and then they are only rudimentary for the original function, which is sometimes plainly apparent. A nascent organ, though little developed, as it has to be developed must be useful in every stage of development. As we cannot prophesy, we cannot tell what organs are now nascent; and nascent organs will rarely have been handed down by certain members of a class from a remote period to the present day, for beings with any important organ but little developed, will generally have been supplanted by their descendants with the organ well developed. The mammary glands in Ornithorhynchus may, perhaps, be considered as nascent compared with the udders of a cow—*Ovigerous frena*, in certain cirripedes, are nascent branchiæ—in [illegible] the swim bladder is almost rudimentary for this purpose, and is nascent as a lung. The small wing of penguin, used only as a fin, might be nascent as a wing; not that I think so ; for the whole structure of the bird is adapted for flight, and a penguin so closely re-sembles other birds, that we may infer that its wings have prob-ably been modified, and reduced by natural selection, in ac-cordance with its sub-aquatic habits. Analogy thus often serves as a guide in distinguishing whether an organ is rudi-mentary or nascent. I believe the *Os coccyx* gives attachment to certain muscles, but I can not doubt that it is a rudiment-ary tail. The bastard wing of birds is a rudimentary digit ; and I believe that if fossil birds are found very low down in the series, they will be seen to have a double or bifurcated wing. Here is a bold prophecy !

To admit prophetic germs, is tantamount to rejecting the theory of Natural Selection.

I am very glad you think it worth while to run through my book again, as much, or more, for the subject's sake as for my own sake. But I look at your keeping the subject for some little time before your mind—raising your own diffi-culties and solving them—as far more important than reading my book. If you think enough, I expect you will be per-verted, and if you ever are, I shall know that the theory of Natural Selection is, in the main, safe ; that it includes, as now put forth, many errors, is almost certain, though I can-not see them. Do not, of course, think of answering this ; but if you have other *occasion* to write again, just say whether I have, in ever so slight a degree, shaken any of your objec-tions. Farewell. With my cordial thanks for your long let-ters and valuable remarks,

Believe me, yours most truly,

C. DARWIN.

P. S.—You often allude to Lamarck's work ; I do not know what you think about it, but it appeared to me extremely poor ; I got not a fact or idea from it.

C. Darwin to L. Agassiz.*

Down, November 11th [1859].

MY DEAR SIR,—I have ventured to send you a copy of my book (as yet only an abstract) on the 'Origin of Species.' As the conclusions at which I have arrived on several points differ so widely from yours, I have thought (should you at any time read my volume) that you might think that I had sent it to you out of a spirit of defiance or bravado ; but I assure you that I act under a wholly different frame of mind. I hope that you will at least give me credit, however erroneous you may think my conclusions, for having earnestly endeavoured to arrive at the truth.   With sincere respect, I beg leave to remain,

Yours, very faithfully,

CHARLES DARWIN.

C. Darwin to A. De Candolle.

Down, November 11th [1859].

DEAR SIR,—I have thought that you would permit me to send you (by Messrs. Williams and Norgate, booksellers) a copy of my work (as yet only an abstract) on the 'Origin of Species.'   I wish to do this, as the only, though quite inadequate manner, by which I can testify to you the extreme

---

* Jean Louis Rodolphe Agassiz, born at Mortier, on the lake of Morat in Switzerland, on May 28, 1807.   He emigrated to America in 1846, where he spent the rest of his life, and died Dec. 14, 1873.   His ' Life,' written by his widow, was published in 1885.   The following extract from a letter to Agassiz (1850) is worth giving, as showing how my father regarded him, and it may be added that his cordial feelings towards the great American naturalist remained strong to the end of his life :—

"I have seldom been more deeply gratified than by receiving your most kind present of ' Lake Superior.'   I had heard of it, and had much wished to read it, but I confess that it was the very great honour of having in my possession a work with your autograph as a presentation copy that has given me such lively and sincere pleasure.   I cordially thank you for it.   I have begun to read it with uncommon interest, which I see will increase as I go on."

38

interest which I have felt, and the great advantage which I have derived, from studying your grand and noble work on Geographical Distribution. Should you be induced to read my volume, I venture to remark that it will be intelligible only by reading the whole straight through, as it is very much condensed. It would be a high gratification to me if any portion interested you. But I am perfectly well aware that you will entirely disagree with the conclusion at which I have arrived.

You will probably have quite forgotten me ; but many years ago you did me the honour of dining at my house in London to meet M. and Madame Sismondi,* the uncle and aunt of my wife. With sincere respect, I beg to remain,

Yours, very faithfully,

CHARLES DARWIN.

C. Darwin to Hugh Falconer.

Down, November 11th [1859].

MY DEAR FALCONER,—I have told Murray to send you a copy of my book on the 'Origin of Species,' which as yet is only an abstract.

If you read it, you must read it straight through, otherwise from its extremely condensed state it will be unintelligible.

Lord, how savage you will be, if you read it, and how you will long to crucify me alive ! I fear it will produce no other effect on you ; but if it should stagger you in ever so slight a degree, in this case, I am fully convinced that you will become, year after year, less fixed in your belief in the immutability of species. With this audacious and presumptuous conviction,

I remain, my dear Falconer,

Yours most truly,

CHARLES DARWIN.

---

* Jessie Allen, sister of Mrs Josiah Wedgwood of Maer.

C. Darwin to Asa Gray.

Down, November 11th [1859].

MY DEAR GRAY,—I have directed a copy of my book (as yet only an abstract) on the 'Origin of Species' to be sent you. I know how you are pressed for time; but if you can read it, I shall be infinitely gratified . . . . If ever you do read it, and can screw out time to send me (as I value your opinion so highly), however short a note, telling me what you think its weakest and best parts, I should be extremely grateful. As you are not a geologist, you will excuse my conceit in telling you that Lyell highly approves of the two Geological chapters, and thinks that on the Imperfection of the Geological Record not exaggerated. He is nearly a convert to my views. . . .

Let me add I fully admit that there are very many difficulties not satisfactorily explained by my theory of descent with modification, but I cannot possibly believe that a false theory would explain so many classes of facts as I think it certainly does explain. On these grounds I drop my anchor, and believe that the difficulties will slowly disappear. . . .

C. Darwin to J. S. Henslow.

Down, November 11th, 1859.

MY DEAR HENSLOW,—I have told Murray to send a copy of my book on Species to you, my dear old master in Natural History; I fear, however, that you will not approve of your pupil in this case. The book in its present state does not show the amount of labour which I have bestowed on the subject.

If you have time to read it carefully, and would take the trouble to point out what parts seem weakest to you and what best, it would be a most material aid to me in writing my bigger book, which I hope to commence in a few months. You know also how highly I value your judgment. But I am not so unreasonable as to wish or expect you to write detailed and lengthy criticisms, but merely a few general remarks, pointing out the weakest parts.

If you are *in even so slight a degree* staggered (which I hardly expect) on the immutability of species, then I am convinced with further reflection you will become more and more staggered, for this has been the process through which my mind has gone.   My dear Henslow,

Yours affectionately and gratefully,

C. DARWIN.

C. *Darwin to John Lubbock.**

Ilkley, Yorkshire,
Saturday [November 12th, 1859].

. . . Thank you much for asking me to Brighton. I hope much that you will enjoy your holiday. I have told Murray to send a copy for you to Mansion House Street, and I am surprised that you have not received it.   There so many valid and weighty arguments against my notions, that you, or any one, if you wish on the other side, will easily persuade yourself that I am wholly in error, and no doubt I am in part in error, perhaps wholly so, though I cannot see the blindness of my ways. I dare say when thunder and lightning were first proved to be due to secondary causes, some regretted to give up the idea that each flash was caused by the direct hand of God.

Farewell, I am feeling very unwell to-day, so no more.

Yours very truly,

C. DARWIN.

C. *Darwin to John Lubbock.*

Ilkley, Yorkshire,
Tuesday [November 15th, 1859].

MY DEAR LUBBOCK,—I beg pardon for troubling you again. I do not know how I blundered in expressing myself in making you believe that we accepted your kind invitation

---

* The present Sir John Lubbock.

to Brighton. I meant merely to thank you sincerely for wishing to see such a worn-out old dog as myself. I hardly know when we leave this place,—not under a fortnight, and then we shall wish to rest under our own roof-tree.

I do not think I hardly ever admired a book more than Paley's 'Natural Theology.' I could almost formerly have said it by heart.

I am glad you have got my book, but I fear that you value it far too highly. I should be grateful for any criticisms. I care not for Reviews ; but for the opinion of men like you and Hooker and Huxley and Lyell, &c.

Farewell, with our joint thanks to Mrs. Lubbock and yourself. Adios.

C. DARWIN.

C. Darwin to L. Jenyns.*

Ilkley, Yorkshire,
November 13th, 1859.

MY DEAR JENYNS,—I must thank you for your very kind note forwarded to me from Down. I have been much out of health this summer, and have been hydropathising here for the last six weeks with very little good as yet. I shall stay here for another fortnight at least. Please remember that my book is only an abstract, and very much condensed, and, to be at all intelligible, must be carefully read. I shall be very grateful for any criticisms. But I know perfectly well that you will not at all agree with the lengths which I go. It took long years to convert me. I may, of course, be egregiously wrong ; but I cannot persuade myself that a theory which explains (as I think it certainly does) several large classes of facts, can be wholly wrong ; notwithstanding the several difficulties which have to be surmounted somehow, and which stagger me even to this day.

I wish that my health had allowed me to publish in

---

* Now Rev. L. Blomefield.

extenso; if ever I get strong enough I will do so, as the greater part is written out, and of which MS. the present volume is an abstract.

I fear this note will be almost illegible; but I am poorly, and can hardly sit up. Farewell; with thanks for your kind note and pleasant remembrance of good old days.

Yours very sincerely,

C. DARWIN.

C. Darwin to A. R. Wallace.

Ilkley, November 13th, 1859.

MY DEAR SIR,—I have told Murray to send you by post (if possible) a copy of my book, and I hope that you will receive it at nearly the same time with this note. (N.B. I have got a bad finger, which makes me write extra badly.) If you are so inclined, I should very much like to hear your general impression of the book, as you have thought so profoundly on the subject, and in so nearly the same channel with myself. I hope there will be some little new to you, but I fear not much. Remember it is only an abstract, and very much condensed. God knows what the public will think. No one has read it, except Lyell, with whom I have had much correspondence. Hooker thinks him a complete convert, but he does not seem so in his letters to me ; but is evidently deeply interested in the subject. I do not think your share in the theory will be overlooked by the real judges, as Hooker, Lyell, Asa Gray, &c. I have heard from Mr. Slater that your paper on the Malay Archipelago has been read at the Linnean Society, and that he was *extremely* much interested by it.

I have not seen one naturalist for six or nine months, owing to the state of my health, and therefore I really have no news to tell you. I am writing this at Ilkley Wells, where I have been with my family for the last six weeks, and shall stay for some few weeks longer. As yet I have profited very little. God knows when I shall have strength for my bigger book.

I sincerely hope that you keep your health; I suppose

that you will be thinking of returning * soon with your magnificent collections, and still grander mental materials. You will be puzzled how to publish. The Royal Society fund will be worth your consideration. With every good wish, pray believe me,   Yours very sincerely,
                                        CHARLES DARWIN.

P. S. I think that I told you before that Hooker is a complete convert. If I can convert Huxley I shall be content.

C. Darwin to W. D. Fox.

Ilkley, Yorkshire,
Wednesday [November 16th, 1859].

. . . . . . I like the place very much, and the children have enjoyed it much, and it has done my wife good. It did H. good at first, but she has gone back again. I have had a series of calamities; first a sprained ankle, and then a badly swollen whole leg and face, much rash, and a frightful succession of boils—four or five at once. I have felt quite ill, and have little faith in this " unique crisis," as the doctor calls it, doing me much good. . . . . . You will probably have received, or will very soon receive, my weariful book on species. I naturally believe it mainly includes the truth, but you will not at all agree with me. Dr. Hooker, whom I consider one of the best judges in Europe, is a complete convert, and he thinks Lyell is likewise ; certainly, judging from Lyell's letters to me on the subject, he is deeply staggered. Farewell. If the spirit moves you, let me have a line. . . .

C. Darwin to W. B. Carpenter.

Ilkley, Yorkshire,
November 18th [1859].

MY DEAR CARPENTER,—I must thank you for your letter on my own account, and if I know myself, still more warmly for the subject's sake. As you seem to have understood my

---

* Mr. Wallace was in the Malay Archipelago.

last chapter without reading the previous chapters, you must have maturely and most profoundly self-thought out the subject; for I have found the most extraordinary difficulty in making even able men understand at what I was driving. There will be strong opposition to my views. If I am in the main right (of course including partial errors unseen by me), the admission in my views will depend far more on men, like yourself, with well-established reputations, than on my own writings. Therefore, on the supposition that when you have read my volume you think the view in the main true, I thank and honour you for being willing to run the chance of unpopularity by advocating the view. I know not in the least whether any one will review me in any of the Reviews. I do not see how an author could enquire or interfere; but if you are willing to review me anywhere, I am sure from the admiration which I have long felt and expressed for your ' Comparative Physiology,' that your review will be excellently done, and will do good service in the cause for which I think I am not selfishly deeply interested. I am feeling very unwell to-day, and this note is badly, perhaps hardly intelligibly, expressed; but you must excuse me, for I could not let a post pass, without thanking you for your note. You will have a tough job even to shake in the slightest degree Sir H. Holland. I do not think (privately I say it) that the great man has knowledge enough to enter on the subject. Pray believe me with sincerity, Yours truly obliged,

C. DARWIN.

P. S.—As you are not a practical geologist, let me add that Lyell thinks the chapter on the Imperfection of the Geological Record *not* exaggerated.

C. Darwin to W. B. Carpenter.

Ilkley, Yorkshire,
November 19th [1859].

MY DEAR CARPENTER,—I beg pardon for troubling you again. If, after reading my book, you are able to come to a conclusion in any degree definite, will you think me very un-reasonable in asking you to let me hear from you. I do not ask for a long discussion, but merely for a brief idea of your general impression. From your widely extended knowledge, habit of investigating the truth, and abilities, I should value your opinion in the very highest rank. Though I, of course, believe in the truth of my own doctrine, I suspect that no belief is vivid until shared by others. As yet I know only one believer, but I look at him as of the greatest authority, viz., Hooker. When I think of the many cases of men who have studied one subject for years, and have persuaded them-selves of the truth of the foolishest doctrines, I feel sometimes a little frightened, whether I may not be one of these mono-maniacs.

Again pray excuse this, I fear, unreasonable request. A short note would suffice, and I could bear a hostile verdict, and shall have to bear many a one.

Yours very sincerely,
C. DARWIN.

C. Darwin to J. D. Hooker.

Ilkley, Yorkshire,
Sunday [November, 1859].

MY DEAR HOOKER,—I have just read a review on my book in the *Athenæum*,* and it excites my curiosity much who is the author. If you should hear who writes in the *Athenæum* I wish you would tell me. It seems to me well done, but the reviewer gives no new objections, and, being hostile, passes over every single argument in favour of the doctrine, . . . I fear from the tone of the review, that I have written in a conceited and cocksure style,† which shames me a little. There is another review of which I should like to know the author, viz., of H. C. Watson in the *Gardener's*

---

* Nov. 19, 1859.

† The Reviewer speaks of the author's " evident self-satisfaction," and of his disposing of all difficulties " more or less confidently."

Chronicle. Some of the remarks are like yours, and he does deserve punishment; but surely the review is too severe. Don't you think so?

I hope you got the three copies for Foreign Botanists in time for your parcel, and your own copy. I have heard from Carpenter, who, I think, is likely to be a convert. Also from Quatrefages, who is inclined to go a long way with us. He says that he exhibited in his lecture a diagram closely like mine!

I shall stay here one fortnight more, and then go to Down, staying on the road at Shrewsbury a week. I have been very unfortunate: out of seven weeks I have been confined for five to the house. This has been bad for me, as I have not been able to help thinking to a foolish extent about my book. If some four or five *good* men came round nearly to our view, I shall not fear ultimate success. I long to learn what Huxley thinks. Is your introduction * published? I suppose that you will sell it separately. Please answer this, for I want an extra copy to send away to Wallace. I am very bothersome, farewell.

Yours affectionately,
C. DARWIN.

I was very glad to see the Royal Medal for Mr. Bentham.

C. Darwin to J. D. Hooker.

Down, December 21st, 1859.

MY DEAR HOOKER,—Pray give my thanks to Mrs. Hooker for her extremely kind note, which has pleased me much. We are very sorry she cannot come here, but shall be delighted to see you and W. (our boys will be at home) here in the 2nd week of January, or any other time. I shall much enjoy discussing any points in my book with you. . . .

I hate to hear you abuse your own work. I, on the con-

---

* Introduction to the ' Flora of Australia.'

trary, so sincerely value all that you have written. It is an old and firm conviction of mine, that the Naturalists who accumulate facts and make many partial generalisations are the *real* benefactors of science. Those who merely accumulate facts I cannot very much respect.

I had hoped to have come up for the Club to-morrow, but very much doubt whether I shall be able. Ilkley seems to have done me no essential good. I attended the Bench on Monday, and was detained in adjudicating some troublesome cases 1½ hours longer than usual, and came home utterly knocked up, and cannot rally. I am not worth an old button. . . . . Many thanks for your pleasant note.

Ever yours,
C. DARWIN.

P. S.—I feel confident that for the future progress of the subject of the origin and manner of formation of species, the assent and arguments and facts of working naturalists, like yourself, are far more important than my own book; so for God's sake do not abuse your Introduction.

H. C. Watson to C. Darwin.

Thames Ditton, November 21st [1859].

MY DEAR SIR,—Once commenced to read the 'Origin,' I could not rest till I had galloped through the whole. I shall now begin to re-read it more deliberately. Meantime I am tempted to write you the first impressions, not doubting that they will, in the main, be the permanent impressions :—

1st. Your leading idea will assuredly become recognised as an established truth in science, *i. e.* "Natural Selection." It has the characteristics of all great natural truths, clarifying what was obscure, simplifying what was intricate, adding greatly to previous knowledge. You are the greatest revolutionist in natural history of this century, if not of all centuries.

2nd. You will perhaps need, in some degree, to limit or

modify, possibly in some degree also to extend, your present applications of the principle of natural selection. Without going to matters of more detail, it strikes me that there is one considerable primary inconsistency, by one failure in the analogy between varieties and species; another by a sort of barrier assumed for nature on insufficient grounds and arising from "divergence." These may, however, be faults in my own mind, attributable to yet incomplete perception of your views. And I had better not trouble you about them before again reading the volume.

3rd. Now these novel views are brought fairly before the scientific public, it seems truly remarkable how so many of them could have failed to see their right road sooner. How could Sir C. Lyell, for instance, for thirty years read, write, and think, on the subject of species *and their succession*, and yet constantly look down the wrong road !

A quarter of a century ago, you and I must have been in something like the same state of mind on the main question, But you were able to see and work out the *quo modo* of the succession, the all-important thing, while I failed to grasp it. I send by this post a little controversial pamphlet of old date—Combe and Scott. If you will take the trouble to glance at the passages scored on the margin, you will see that, a quarter of a century ago, I was also one of the few who then doubted the absolute distinctness of species, and special creations of them. Yet I, like the rest, failed to detect the *quo modo* which was reserved for your penetration to *discover*, and your discernment to *apply*.

You answered my query about the hiatus between Satyrus and Homo as was expected. The obvious explanation really never occurred to me till some months after I had read the papers in the 'Linnean Proceedings.' The first species of *Fere-homo* * would soon make direct and exterminating war upon his *Infra-homo* cousins. The gap would thus be made, and then go on increasing, into the present enormous and

---

* " Almost-man."

still widening hiatus. But how greatly this, with your chronology of animal life, will shock the ideas of many men !

Very sincerely,

HEWETT C. WATSON.

J. D. Hooker to C. Darwin.

Athenæum, Monday [Nov. 21st, 1859].

MY DEAR DARWIN,—I am a sinner not to have written
you ere this, if only to thank you for your glorious book—
what a mass of close reasoning on curious facts and fresh
phenomena—it is capitally written, and will be very successful. I say this on the strength of two or three plunges into
as many chapters, for I have not yet attempted to read it.
Lyell, with whom we are staying, is perfectly enchanted, and
is absolutely gloating over it. I must accept your compliment to me, and acknowledgment of supposed assistance
from me, as the warm tribute of affection from an honest
(though deluded) man, and furthermore accept it as very
pleasing to my vanity; but, my dear fellow, neither my name
nor my judgment nor my assistance deserved any such compliments, and if I am dishonest enough to be pleased with
what I don't deserve, it must just pass. How different the
book reads from the MS. I see I shall have much to talk
over with you. Those lazy printers have not finished my
luckless Essay; which, beside your book, will look like a
ragged handkerchief beside a Royal Standard. . . .

All well, ever yours affectionately,

JOS. D. HOOKER.

C. Darwin to J. D. Hooker.

Ilkley, Yorkshire [November, 1859].

MY DEAR HOOKER,—I cannot help it, I must thank you
for your affectionate and most kind note. My head will be
turned. By Jove, I must try and get a bit modest. I was a

little chagrined by the review.*   I hope it was *not* ——   As
advocate, he might think himself justified in giving the argument only on one side.   But the manner in which he drags
in immortality, and sets the priests at me, and leaves me to
their mercies, is base.   He would, on no account, burn me,
but he will get the wood ready, and tell the black beasts how
to catch me. . . . It would be unspeakably grand if Huxley
were to lecture on the subject, but I can see this is a mere
chance ; Faraday might think it too unorthodox.

. . . I had a letter from [Huxley] with such tremendous
praise of my book, that modesty (as I am trying to cultivate
that difficult herb) prevents me sending it to you, which I
should have liked to have done, as he is very modest about
himself.

You have cockered me up to that extent, that I now feel I
can face a score of savage reviewers.   I suppose you are still
with the Lyells.   Give my kindest remembrance to them.   I
triumph to hear that he continues to approve.

Believe me, your would-be modest friend,

C. D.

C. Darwin to C. Lyell.

Ilkley Wells, Yorkshire,
November 23 [1859].

MY DEAR LYELL,—You seemed to have worked admirably on the species question ; there could not have been a
better plan than reading up on the opposite side.   I rejoice
profoundly that you intend admitting the doctrine of modification in your new edition ; † nothing, I am convinced, could
be more important for its success.   I honour you most sincerely.   To have maintained in the position of a master, one

---

* This refers to the review in the *Athenæum*, Nov. 19, 1859, where
the reviewer, after touching on the theological aspects of the book, leaves
the author to " the mercies of the Divinity Hall, the College, the Lecture
Room, and the Museum."

† It appears from Sir Charles Lyell's published letters that he intended
to admit the doctrine of evolution in a new edition of the ' Manual,' but

side of a question for thirty years, and then deliberately give
it up, is a fact to which I much doubt whether the records of
science offer a parallel. For myself, also, I rejoice profoundly ; for, thinking of so many cases of men pursuing an
illusion for years, often and often a cold shudder has run
through me, and I have asked myself whether I may not have
devoted my life to a phantasy. Now I look at it as morally
impossible that investigators of truth, like you and Hooker,
can be wholly wrong, and therefore I rest in peace. Thank
you for criticisms, which, if there be a second edition, I will
attend to. I have been thinking that if I am much execrated
as an atheist, &c., whether the admission of the doctrine of
natural selection could injure your works ; but I hope and
think not, for as far as I can remember, the virulence of
bigotry is expended on the first offender, and those who
adopt his views are only pitied as deluded, by the wise and
cheerful bigots.

I cannot help thinking that you overrate the importance of
the multiple origin of dogs. The only difference is, that in the
case of single origins, all difference of the races has originated since man domesticated the species. In the case of
multiple origins part of the difference was produced under
natural conditions. I should *infinitely* prefer the theory of
single origin in all cases, if facts would permit its reception.
But there seems to me some *à priori* improbability (seeing
how fond savages are of taming animals), that throughout all
times, and throughout all the world, that man should have
domesticated one single species alone, of the widely distributed genus Canis. Besides this, the close resemblance of
at least three kinds of American domestic dogs to wild species still inhabiting the countries where they are now domesticated, seem to almost compel admission that more than one
wild Canis has been domesticated by man.

this was not published till 1865. He was, however, at work on the 'Antiquity of Man' in 1860, and had already determined to discuss the 'Origin' at the end of the book.

I thank you cordially for all the generous zeal and interest you have shown about my book, and I remain, my dear Lyell,
Your affectionate friend and disciple,

CHARLES DARWIN.

Sir J. Herschel, to whom I sent a copy, is going to read my book. He says he leans to the side opposed to me. If you should meet him after he has read me, pray find out what he thinks, for, of course, he will not write ; and I should excessively like to hear whether I produce any effect on such a mind.

T. H. Huxley to C. Darwin.

Jermyn Street, W.,
November 23rd, 1859.

MY DEAR DARWIN,—I finished your book yesterday, a lucky examination having furnished me with a few hours of continuous leisure.

Since I read Von Bär's * essays, nine years ago, no work on Natural History Science I have met with has made so great an impression upon me, and I do most heartily thank you for the great store of new views you have given me. Nothing, I think, can be better than the tone of the book, it impresses those who know nothing about the subject. As for your doctrine, I am prepared to go to the stake, if requisite, in support of Chapter IX., and most parts of Chapters X., XI., XII., and Chapter XIII. contains much that is most admirable, but on one or two points I enter a *caveat* until I can see further into all sides of the question.

As to the first four chapters, I agree thoroughly and fully with all the principles laid down in them. I think you have demonstrated a true cause for the production of species, and have thrown the *onus probandi* that species did not arise in the way you suppose, on your adversaries.

---

* Karl Ernst von Baer, b. 1792, d. at Dorpat 1876—one of the most distinguished biologists of the century. He practically founded the modern science of embryology.

But I feel that I have not yet by any means fully realized the bearings of those most remarkable and original Chapters III., IV. and V., and I will write no more about them just now.

The only objections that have occurred to me are, 1st that you have loaded yourself with an unnecessary difficulty in adopting *Natura non facit saltum* so unreservedly. . . . And 2nd, it is not clear to me why, if continual physical conditions are of so little moment as you suppose, variation should occur at all.

However, I must read the book two or three times more before I presume to begin picking holes.

I trust you will not allow yourself to be in any way disgusted or annoyed by the considerable abuse and misrepresentation which, unless I greatly mistake, is in store for you. Depend upon it you have earned the lasting gratitude of all thoughtful men. And as to the curs which will bark and yelp, you must recollect that some of your friends, at any rate, are endowed with an amount of combativeness which (though you have often and justly rebuked it) may stand you in good stead.

I am sharpening up my claws and beak in readiness.

Looking back over my letter, it really expresses so feebly all I think about you and your noble book that I am half ashamed of it; but you will understand that, like the parrot in the story, " I think the more."

Ever yours faithfully,
T. H. HUXLEY.

C. Darwin to T. H. Huxley.

Ilkley, Nov. 25th [1859].

MY DEAR HUXLEY,—Your letter has been forwarded to me from Down. Like a good Catholic who has received extreme unction, I can now sing " nunc dimittis." I should have been more than contented with one quarter of what you have said. Exactly fifteen months ago, when I put pen to

paper for this volume, I had awful misgivings ; and thought
perhaps I had deluded myself, like so many have done, and
I then fixed in my mind three judges, on whose decision I
determined mentally to abide.   The judges were Lyell,
Hooker, and yourself.   It was this which made me so excessively anxious for your verdict.   I am now contented, and
can sing my nunc dimittis.   What a joke it would be if I
pat you on the back when you attack some immovable creationist !   You have most cleverly hit on one point, which has
greatly troubled me ; if, as I must think, external conditions
produce little *direct* effect, what the devil determines each
particular variation ?   What makes a tuft of feathers come
on a cock's head, or moss on a moss-rose ?   I shall much like
to talk over this with you. . . .

My dear Huxley, I thank you cordially for your letter.

Yours very sincerely,

C. DARWIN.

P. S.—Hereafter I shall be particularly curious to hear
what you think of my explanation of Embryological similarity.   On classification I fear we shall split.   Did you perceive the *argumentum ad hominem* Huxley about kangaroo
and bear ?

Erasmus Darwin * *to C. Darwin.*

November 23rd [1859].

DEAR CHARLES,—I am so much weaker in the head, that
I hardly know if I can write, but at all events I will jot
down a few things that the Dr.† has said.   He has not read
much above half, so as he says he can give no definite conclusion, and it is my private belief he wishes to remain in
that state. . . . He is evidently in a dreadful state of inde-
cision, and keeps stating that he is not tied down to either
view, and that he has always left an escape by the way he
has spoken of varieties.   I happened to speak of the eye be-

---

* His brother.   † Dr., afterwards Sir Henry Holland.

fore he had read that part, and it took away his breath—
utterly impossible—structure—function, &c., &c., &c., but
when he had read it he hummed and hawed, and perhaps it
was partly conceivable, and then he fell back on the bones
of the ear, which were beyond all probability or conceivabil-
ity. He mentioned a slight blot, which I also observed, that
in speaking of the slave-ants carrying one another, you
change the species without giving notice first, and it makes
one turn back. . . .

. . . For myself I really think it is the most interesting
book I ever read, and can only compare it to the first
knowledge of chemistry, getting into a new world or rather
behind the scenes. To me the geographical distribution, I
mean the relation of islands to continents, is the most convincing of the proofs, and the relation of the oldest forms to
the existing species. I dare say I don't feel enough the
absence of varieties, but then I don't in the least know if
everything now living were fossilized whether the paleontolo-
gists could distinguish them. In fact the *à priori* reasoning
is so entirely satisfactory to me that if the facts won't fit in,
why so much the worse for the facts is my feeling. My
ague has left me in such a state of torpidity that I wish I
had gone through the process of natural selection.

Yours affectionately,

E. A. D.

C. Darwin to C. Lyell.

Ilkley, November [24th, 1859].

MY DEAR LYELL,—Again I have to thank you for a most
valuable lot of criticisms in a letter dated 22nd.

This morning I heard also from Murray that he sold the
whole edition * the first day to the trade. He wants a new
edition instantly, and this utterly confounds me. Now, under
water-cure, with all nervous power directed to the skin, I

---

* First edition, 1250 copies.

cannot possibly do head-work, and I must make only actually necessary corrections.   But I will, as far as I can without my manuscript, take advantage of your suggestions : I must not attempt much.   Will you send me one line to say whether I must strike out about the secondary whale,* it goes to my heart.   About the rattle-snake, look to my Journal, under Trigonocephalus, and you will see the probable origin of the rattle, and generally in transitions it is the *premier pas qui coute.*

Madame Belloc wants to translate my book into French ; I have offered to look over proofs for *scientific* errors.   Did you ever hear of her ?   I believe Murray has agreed at my urgent advice, but I fear I have been rash and premature. Quatrefages has written to me, saying he agrees largely with my views.   He is an excellent naturalist.   I am pressed for time.   Will you give us one line about the whales ?   Again I thank you for never-tiring advice and assistance ; I do in truth reverence your unselfish and pure love of truth.

My dear Lyell, ever yours,

C. DARWIN.

[With regard to a French translation, he wrote to Mr. Murray in Nov. 1859 : " I am *extremely* anxious, for the subject's sake (and God knows not for mere fame), to have my book translated ; and indirectly its being known abroad will do good to the English sale.   If it depended on me, I should agree without payment, and instantly send a copy, and only beg that she [Mme. Belloc] would get some scientific man to look over the translation. . . . You might say that, though I am a very poor French scholar, I could detect any scientific mistake, and would read over the French proofs."

The proposed translation was not made, and a second plan fell through in the following year.   He wrote to M. de Quatrefages : " The gentleman who wished to translate my

---

* The passage was omitted in the second edition.

'Origin of Species' has failed in getting a publisher. Ballière, Masson, and Hachette all rejected it with contempt. It was foolish and presumptuous in me, hoping to appear in a French dress; but the idea would not have entered my head had it not been suggested to me. It is a great loss. I must console myself with the German edition which Prof. Bronn is bringing out." *

A sentence in another letter to M. de Quatrefages shows how anxious he was to convert one of the greatest of contemporary Zoologists : " How I should like to know whether Milne Edwards had read the copy which I sent him, and whether he thinks I have made a pretty good case on our side of the question. There is no naturalist in the world for whose opinion I have so profound a respect. Of course I am not so silly as to expect to change his opinion."]

C. Darwin to C. Lyell.

Ilkley, [November 26th, 1859].

MY DEAR LYELL,—I have received your letter of the 24th. It is no use trying to thank you ; your kindness is beyond thanks. I will certainly leave out the whale and bear . . .

The edition was 1250 copies. When I was in spirits, I sometimes fancied that my book would be successful, but I never even built a castle in the air of such success as it has met with ; I do not mean the sale, but the impression it has made on you (whom I have always looked at as chief judge) and Hooker and Huxley. The whole has infinitely exceeded my wildest hopes.

Farewell, I am tired, for I have been going over the sheets.

My kind friend, farewell, yours,

C. DARWIN.

---

* See letters to Bronn, p. 70.

C. Darwin to C. Lyell.

Ilkley, Yorkshire,
December 2nd [1859].

MY DEAR LYELL,—Every note which you have sent me
has interested me much.   Pray thank Lady Lyell for her
remark.   In the chapters she refers to, I was unable to modify the passage in accordance with your suggestion ; but in
the final chapter I have modified three or four.   Kingsley, in
a note * to me, had a capital paragraph on such notions as
mine being *not* opposed to a high conception of the Deity.
I have inserted it as an extract from a letter to me from a
celebrated author and divine.   I have put in about nascent
organs.   I had the greatest difficulty in partially making out
Sedgwick's letter, and I dare say I did greatly underrate its
clearness.   Do what I could, I fear I shall be greatly abused.
In answer to Sedgwick's remark that my book would be
" mischievous," I asked him whether truth can be known except by being victorious over all attacks.   But it is no use.
H. C. Watson tells me that one zoologist says he will read
my book, "but I will never believe it."   What a spirit to
read any book in !   Crawford writes to me that his notice †
will be hostile, but that " he will not calumniate the author."
He says he has read my book, " at least such parts as he
could understand."   He sent me some notes and suggestions (quite unimportant), and they show me that I have un-
avoidably done harm to the subject, by publishing an abstract.   He is a real Pallasian ; nearly all our domestic
races descended from a multitude of wild species now com-

---

* The letter is given at p. 82.

† John Crawford, orientalist, ethnologist, &c., b. 1783, d. 1868.   The
review appeared in the *Examiner*, and, though hostile, is free from bigotry,
as the following citation will show :   " We cannot help saying that piety
must be fastidious indeed that objects to a theory the tendency of which
is to show that all organic beings, man included, are in a perpetual progress of amelioration, and that is expounded in the reverential language
which we have quoted."

mingled.   I expected Murchison to be outrageous.   How
little he could ever have grappled with the subject of denudation !   How singular so great a geologist should have so
unphilosophical a mind !   I have had several notes from
——, very civil and less decided.   Says he shall not pronounce
against me without much reflection, *perhaps will say nothing*
on the subject.   X. says —— will go to that part of hell,
which Dante tells us is appointed for those who are neither
on God's side nor on that of the devil.

I fully believe that I owe the comfort of the next few
years of my life to your generous support, and that of a very
few others.   I do not think I am brave enough to have
stood being odious without support ; now I feel as bold as a
lion.   But there is one thing I can see I must learn, viz., to
think less of myself and my book.   Farewell, with cordial
thanks.   Yours most truly,

                                        C. DARWIN.

I return home on the 7th, and shall sleep at Erasmus's.
I will call on you about ten o'clock, on Thursday, the 8th,
and sit with you, as I have so often sat, during your breakfast.

I wish there was any chance of Prestwich being shaken ;
but I fear he is too much of a catastrophist.

[In December there appeared in ' Macmillan's Magazine '
an article, "Time and Life," by Professor Huxley.   It is
mainly occupied by an analysis of the argument of the
' Origin,' but it also gives the substance of a lecture delivered at the Royal Institution before that book was published.
Professor Huxley spoke strongly in favor of evolution in his
Lecture, and explains that in so doing he was to a great
extent resting on a knowledge of " the general tenor of the
researches in which Mr. Darwin had been so long engaged,"
and was supported in so doing by his perfect confidence in
his knowledge, perseverance, and " high-minded love of

truth." My father was evidently deeply pleased by Mr. Huxley's words, and wrote :

"I must thank you for your extremely kind notice of my book in 'Macmillan.' No one could receive a more delightful and honourable compliment. I had not heard of your Lecture, owing to my retired life. You attribute much too much to me from our mutual friendship. You have explained my leading idea with admirable clearness. What a gift you have of writing (or more properly) thinking clearly."]

C. Darwin to W. B. Carpenter.

Ilkley, Yorkshire,
December 3rd [1859].

MY DEAR CARPENTER,—I am perfectly delighted at your letter. It is a great thing to have got a great physiologist on our side. I say "our" for we are now a good and compact body of really good men, and mostly not old men. In the long run we shall conquer. I do not like being abused, but I feel that I can now bear it; and, as I told Lyell, I am well convinced that it is the first offender who reaps the rich harvest of abuse. You have done an essential kindness in checking the odium theologicum in the E. R.* It much pains all one's female relations and injures the cause.

I look at it as immaterial whether we go quite the same lengths ; and I suspect, judging from myself, that you will go further, by thinking of a population of forms like Ornithorhyncus, and by thinking of the common homological and embryological structure of the several vertebrate orders. But this is immaterial. I quite agree that the principle is everything. In my fuller MS. I have discussed a good many instincts; but there will surely be more unfilled gaps here than with corporeal structure, for we have no fossil instincts,

---

* This must refer to Carpenter's critique which would now have been ready to appear in the January number of the *Edinburgh Review*, 1860, and in which the *odium theologicum* is referred to.

and know scarcely any except of European animals. When I reflect how very slowly I came round myself, I am in truth astonished at the candour shown by Lyell, Hooker, Huxley, and yourself. In my opinion it is grand. I thank you cordially for taking the trouble of writing a review for the 'National.' God knows I shall have few enough in any degree favourable.*

C. Darwin to C. Lyell.

Saturday [December 5th, 1859].

. . . I have had a letter from Carpenter this morning. He reviews me in the ' National.' He is a convert, but does not go quite so far as I, but quite far enough, for he admits that all birds are from one progenitor, and probably all fishes and reptiles from another parent. But the last mouthful chokes him. He can hardly admit all vertebrates from one parent. He will surely come to this from Homology and Embryology. I look at it as grand having brought round a great physiologist, for great I think he certainly is in that line. How curious I shall be to know what line Owen will take ; dead against us, I fear ; but he wrote me a most liberal note on the reception of my book, and said he was quite prepared to consider fairly and without prejudice my line of argument.

J. D. Hooker to C. Darwin.

Kew, Monday.

DEAR DARWIN,—You have, I know, been drenched with letters since the publication of your book, and I have hence forborne to add my mite. I hope now that you are well through Edition II., and I have heard that you were flourishing in London. I have not yet got half-through the book, not from want of will, but of time—for it is the very hardest book to read, to full profits, that I ever tried—it is so cram-full of matter and reasoning. I am all the more glad

---

* See a letter to Dr. Carpenter, p. 57.

that you have published in this form, for the three volumes, unprefaced by this, would have choked any Naturalist of the nineteenth century, and certainly have softened my brain in the operation of assimilating their contents. I am perfectly tired of marvelling at the wonderful amount of facts you have brought to bear, and your skill in marshalling them and throwing them on the enemy ; it is also extremely clear as far as I have gone, but very hard to fully appreciate. Somehow it reads very different from the MS., and I often fancy I must have been very stupid not to have more fully followed it in MS. Lyell told me of his criticisms. I did not appreciate them all, and there are many little matters I hope one day to talk over with you. I saw a highly flattering notice in the ' English Churchman,' short and not at all entering into discussion, but praising you and your book, and talking patronizingly of the doctrine ! . . . Bentham and Henslow will still shake their heads I fancy. . . .

Ever yours affectionately,

Jos. D. Hooker.

C. Darwin to C. Lyell.

Down, Saturday [December 12th, 1859].

. . . I had very long interviews with ——, which perhaps you would like to hear about. . . . I infer from several expressions that, at bottom, he goes an immense way with us. . . . .

He said to the effect that my explanation was the best ever published of the manner of formation of species. I said I was very glad to hear it. He took me up short : "You must not at all suppose that I agree with you in all respects." I said I thought it no more likely that I should be right in nearly all points, than that I should toss up a penny and get heads twenty times running. I asked him what he thought the weakest part. He said he had no particular objection to any part. He added :—

"If I must criticise, I should say, ' we do not want to know what Darwin believes and is convinced of, but what he can prove.'" I agreed most fully and truly that I have probably greatly sinned in this line, and defended my general line of argument of inventing a theory and seeing how many classes of facts the theory would explain. I added that I would endeavour to modify the "believes" and "convinceds." He took me up short : "You will then spoil your book, the charm of (!) it is that it is Darwin himself." He added another objection, that the book was too *teres atque rotundus*—that it explained everything, and that it was improbable in the highest degree that I should succeed in this. I quite agree with this rather queer objection, and it comes to this that my book must be very bad or very good. . . .

I have heard, by roundabout channel, that Herschel says my book "is the law of higgledy-piggledy." What this exactly means I do not know, but it is evidently very contemptuous. If true this is a great blow and discouragement.

C. Darwin to John Lubbock.

December 14th [1859].

. . . The latter part of my stay at Ilkley did me much good, but I suppose I never shall be strong, for the work I have had since I came back has knocked me up a little more than once. I have been busy in getting a reprint (with a very few corrections) through the press.

My book has been as yet *very much* more successful than I ever dreamed of : Murray is now printing 3000 copies. Have you finished it ? If so, pray tell me whether you are with me on the *general* issue, or against me. If you are against me, I know well how honourable, fair, and candid an opponent I shall have, and which is a good deal more than I can say of all my opponents. . . .

Pray tell me what you have been doing. Have you had time for any Natural History ? . . .

P. S.—I have got—I wish and hope I might say that *we* have got—a fair number of excellent men on our side of the question on the mutability of species.

C. Darwin to J. D. Hooker.

Down, December 14th [1859].

MY DEAR HOOKER,—Your approval of my book, for many reasons, gives me intense satisfaction; but I must make some allowance for your kindness and sympathy. Any one with ordinary faculties, if he had *patience* enough and plenty of time, could have written my book. You do not know how I admire your and Lyell's generous and unselfish sympathy, I do not believe either of you would have cared so much about your own work. My book, as yet, has been far more successful than I ever even formerly ventured in the wildest daydreams to anticipate. We shall soon be a good body of working men, and shall have, I am convinced, all young and rising naturalists on our side. I shall be intensely interested to hear whether my book produces any effect on A. Gray; from what I heard at Lyell's, I fancy your correspondence has brought him some way already. I fear that there is no chance of Bentham being staggered. Will he read my book? Has he a copy? I would send him one of the reprints if he has not. Old J. E. Gray,* at the British Musuem, attacked me in fine style : "You have just reproduced Lamarck's doctrine and nothing else, and here Lyell and others have been attacking him for twenty years, and because *you* (with a sneer and laugh) say the very same thing, they are all coming round ; it is the most ridiculous inconsistency, &c., &c."

You must be very glad to be settled in your house, and I hope all the improvements satisfy you. As far as my experience goes, improvements are never perfection. I am very

---

* John Edward Gray (born 1800, died 1875) was the son of S. F. Gray, author of the 'Supplement to the Pharmacopœia.' In 1821 he published in his father's name 'The Natural Arrangement of British Plants,' one of the earliest works in English on the natural method. In 1824 he became connected with the Natural History Department of the British Museum, and was appointed Keeper of the Zoological collections in 1840. He was the author of 'Illustrations of Indian Zoology,' 'The Knowsley Menagerie,' &c., and of innumerable descriptive Zoological papers.

sorry to hear that you are still so very busy, and have so much work. And now for the main purport of my note, which is to ask and beg you and Mrs. Hooker (whom it is really an age since I have seen), and all your children, if you like, to come and spend a week here. It would be a great pleasure to me and to my wife. . . . As far as we can see, we shall be at home all the winter ; and all times probably would be equally convenient ; but if you can, do not put it off very late, as it may slip through. Think of this and persuade Mrs. Hooker, and be a good man and come.

Farewell, my kind and dear friend,

Yours affectionately,

C. DARWIN.

P. S.—I shall be very curious to hear what you think of my discussion on Classification in Chap. XIII. ; I believe Huxley demurs to the whole, and says he has nailed his colours to the mast, and I would sooner die than give up ; so that we are in as fine a frame of mind to discuss the point as any two religionists.

Embryology is my pet bit in my book, and, confound my friends, not one has noticed this to me.

C. Darwin to Asa Gray.

Down, December 21st [1859].

MY DEAR GRAY,—I have just received your most kind, long, and valuable letter. I will write again in a few days, for I am at present unwell and much pressed with business : to-day's note is merely personal. I should, for several reasons, be very glad of an American Edition. I have made up my mind to be well abused ; but I think it of importance that my notions should be read by intelligent men, accustomed to scientific argument, though *not* naturalists. It may seem absurd, but I think such men will drag after them those naturalists who have too firmly fixed in their heads that a species is an entity. The first edition of 1250 copies was sold on the first day, and now my publisher is printing off, as *rapidly as possible*, 3000 more copies. I mention this solely because it renders probable a remunerative sale in America. I should be infinitely obliged if you could aid an American reprint ; and could make, for my sake and the publisher's, any arrangement for any profit. The new edition is only a reprint, yet I have made a *few* important corrections. I will have the clean sheets sent over in a few days of as many sheets as are printed off, and the remainder afterwards, and you can do anything you like,—if nothing, there is no harm done. I should be glad for the new edition to be reprinted and not the old.—In great haste, and with hearty thanks,

Yours very sincerely,
C. DARWIN.

I will write soon again.

C. Darwin to C. Lyell.

Down, 22nd [December, 1859].

MY DEAR LYELL,—Thanks about "Bears," * a word of ill-omen to me.

I am too unwell to leave home, so shall not see you.

I am very glad of your remarks on Hooker. † I have not yet got the essay. The parts which I read in sheets seemed to me grand, especially the generalization about the Australian flora itself. How superior to Robert Brown's celebrated essay ! I have not seen Naudin's paper,‡ and shall not be able till I hunt the libraries. I am very anxious

---

* See 'Origin,' ed. i., p. 184.

† Sir C. Lyell wrote to Sir J. D. Hooker, Dec. 19, 1859 (' Life,' ii. p. 327): " I have just finished the reading of your splendid Essay [the ' Flora of Australia '] on the origin of species, as illustrated by your wide botanical experience, and think it goes very far to raise the variety-making hypothesis to the rank of a theory, as accounting for the manner in which new species enter the world."

‡ " Revue Horticole,' 1852   See Historical Sketch in the later edi tions of the ' Origin of Species.'

to see it. Decaisne seems to think he gives my whole theory. I do not know when I shall have time and strength to grapple with Hooker. . . .

P. S.—I have heard from Sir W. Jardine : * his criticisms are quite unimportant ; some of the Galapagos so-called species ought to be called varieties, which I fully expected ; some of the sub-genera, thought to be wholly endemic, have been found on the Continent (not that he gives his authority), but I do not make out that the species are the same. His letter is brief and vague, but he says he will write again.

C. Darwin to J. D. Hooker.

Down [23rd December, 1859].

MY DEAR HOOKER,—I received last night your 'Introduction,' for which very many thanks ; I am surprised to see how big it is : I shall not be able to read it very soon. It was very good of you to send Naudin, for I was very curious to see it. I am surprised that Decaisne should say it was the same as mine. Naudin gives artificial selection, as well as a score of English writers, and when he says species were formed in the same manner, I thought the paper would

---

* Jardine, Sir William, Bart., b. 1800, d. 1874, was the son of Sir A. Jardine of Applegarth, Dumfriesshire. He was educated at Edinburgh, and succeeded to the title on his father's decease in 1821. He published, jointly with Mr. Prideaux J. Selby, Sir Stamford Raffles, Dr. Horsfield, and other ornithologists, ' Illustrations of Ornithology,' and edited the ' Naturalist's Library,' in 40 vols., which included the four branches : Mammalia, Ornithology, Ichnology, and Entomology. Of these 40 vols. 14 were written by himself. In 1836 he became editor of the ' Magazine of Zoology and Botany,' which, two years later, was transformed into ' Annals of Natural History,' but remained under his direction. For Bohn's Standard Library he edited White's ' Natural History of Selborne.' Sir W. Jardine was also joint editor of the ' Edinburgh Philosophical Journal,' and was author of ' British Salmonidae,' ' Ichthyology of Annandale,' ' Memoirs of the late Hugh Strickland,' ' Contributions to Ornithology,' ' Ornithological Synonyms,' &c.—(Taken from Ward, ' Men of the Reign,' and Cates, ' Dictionary of General Biography.')

certainly prove exactly the same as mine. But I cannot find one word like the struggle for existence and natural selection. On the contrary, he brings in his principle (p. 103) of finality (which I do not understand), which, he says, with some authors is fatality, with others providence, and which adapts the forms of every being, and harmonises them all throughout nature.

He assumes like old geologists (who assumed that the forces of nature were formerly greater), that species were at first more plastic. His simile of tree and classification is like mine (and others), but he cannot, I think, have reflected much on the subject, otherwise he would see that genealogy by itself does not give classification; I declare I cannot see a *much* closer approach to Wallace and me in Naudin than in Lamarck—we all agree in modification and descent. If I do not hear from you I will return the 'Revue' in a few days (with the cover). I dare say Lyell would be glad to see it. By the way, I will retain the volume till I hear whether I shall or not send it to Lyell. I should rather like Lyell to see this note, though it is foolish work sticking up for independence or priority.

Ever yours,
C. DARWIN.

A. Sedgwick * *to C. Darwin.*

Cambridge, December 24th, 1859.

My DEAR DARWIN,—I write to thank you for your work on the 'Origin of Species.' It came, I think, in the latter part of last week; but it *may* have come a few days sooner, and been overlooked among my book-parcels, which often remain unopened when I am lazy or busy with any work before me. So soon as I opened it I began to read it, and I finished it, after many interruptions, on Tuesday. Yesterday I was employed—1st, in preparing for my lecture; 2ndly, in attending

---

* Rev. Adam Sedgwick, Woodwardian Professor of Geology in the University of Cambridge. Born 1785, died 1873.

a meeting of my brother Fellows to discuss the final propositions of the Parliamentary Commissioners ; 3rdly, in lecturing ;
4thly, in hearing the conclusion of the discussion and the
College reply, whereby, in conformity with my own wishes,
we accepted the scheme of the Commissioners ; 5thly, in
dining with an old friend at Clare College ; 6thly, in ad-
journing to the weekly meeting of the Ray Club, from which
I returned at 10 P. M., dog-tired, and hardly able to climb my
staircase. Lastly, in looking through the *Times* to see what
was going on in the busy world.

I do not state this to fill space (though I believe that
Nature does abhor a vacuum), but to prove that my reply
and my thanks are sent to you by the earliest leisure I have,
though that is but a very contracted opportunity. If I did
not think you a good-tempered and truth-loving man, I
should not tell you that (spite of the great knowledge, store
of facts, capital views of the correlation of the various parts
of organic nature, admirable hints about the diffusion,
through wide regions, of many related organic beings, &c.,
&c.) I have read your book with more pain than pleasure.
Parts of it I admired greatly, parts I laughed at till my sides
were almost sore ; other parts I read with absolute sorrow,
because I think them utterly false and grievously mischievous. You have *deserted*—after a start in that tram-road of
all solid physical truth—the true method of induction, and
started us in machinery as wild, I think, as Bishop Wilkins's
locomotive that was to sail with us to the moon. Many of
your wide conclusions are based upon assumptions which can
neither be proved nor disproved, why then express them in
the language and arrangement of philosophical induction ?
As to your grand principle—*natural selection*—what is it but
a secondary consequence of supposed, or known, primary
facts ! Development is a better word, because more close to
the cause of the fact ? For you do not deny causation. I
call (in the abstract) causation the will of God ; and I can
prove that He acts for the good of His creatures. He also
acts by laws which we can study and comprehend. Acting

40

by law, and under what is called final causes, comprehends, I
think, your whole principle. You write of "natural selection" as if it were done consciously by the selecting agent.
'Tis but a consequence of the presupposed development, and
the subsequent battle for life. This view of nature you have
stated admirably, though admitted by all naturalists and denied by no one of common sense. We all admit development as a fact of history : but how came it about ? Here, in
language, and still more in logic, we are point-blank at issue.
There is a moral or metaphysical part of nature as well a
physical. A man who denies this is deep in the mire of folly.
'Tis the crown and glory of organic science that it *does*
through *final cause*, link material and moral ; and yet *does
not* allow us to mingle them in our first conception of laws,
and our classification of such laws, whether we consider one
side of nature or the other. You have ignored this link ;
and, if I do not mistake your meaning, you have done your
best in one or two pregnant cases to break it. Were it possible (which, thank God, it is not) to break it, humanity, in
my mind, would suffer a damage that might brutalize it, and
sink the human race into a lower grade of degradation than
any into which it has fallen since its written records tell us of
its history. Take the case of the bee-cells. If your development produced the successive modification of the bee and its
cells (which no mortal can prove), final cause would stand
good as the directing cause under which the successive generations acted and gradually improved. Passages in your
book, like that to which I have alluded (and there are others
almost as bad), greatly shocked my moral taste. I think, in
speculating on organic descent, you *over*-state the evidence
of geology ; and that you *under*-state it while you are talking of the broken links of your natural pedigree : but my
paper is nearly done, and I must go to my lecture-room.
Lastly, then, I greatly dislike the concluding chapter—not as
a summary, for in that light it appears good—but I dislike it
from the tone of triumphant confidence in which you appeal
to the rising generation (in a tone I condemned in the au-

thor of the ' Vestiges ') and prophesy of things not yet in the womb of time, nor (if we are to trust the accumulated experience of human sense and the inferences of its logic) ever likely to be found anywhere but in the fertile womb of man's imagination. And now to say a word about a son of a monkey and an old friend of yours : I am better, far better, than I was last year. I have been lecturing three days a week (formerly I gave six a week) without much fatigue, but I find by the loss of activity and memory, and of all productive powers, that my bodily frame is sinking slowly towards the earth. But I have visions of the future. They are as much a part of myself as my stomach and my heart, and these visions are to have their antitype in solid fruition of what is best and greatest. But on one condition only—that I humbly accept God's revelation of Himself both in his works and in His word, and do my best to act in conformity with that knowledge which He only can give me, and He only can sustain me in doing. If you and I do all this we shall meet in heaven.

I have written in a hurry, and in a spirit of brotherly love, therefore forgive any sentence you happen to dislike; and believe me, spite of any disagreement in some points of the deepest moral interest, your true-hearted old friend,

A. SEDGWICK.

C. Darwin to T. H. Huxley.

Down, Dec. 25th [1859].

MY DEAR HUXLEY,—One part of your note has pleased me so much that I must thank you for it. Not only Sir II. H. [Holland], but several others, have attacked me about analogy leading to belief in one primordial *created* form.* (By which I mean only that we know nothing as yet [of] how life originates.) I thought I was universally condemned on

---

* 'Origin,' edit. i. p. 484.—" Therefore I should infer from analogy that probably all the organic beings which have ever lived on this earth have descended from some one primordial form, into which life was first breathed."

this head.   But I answered that though perhaps it would have been more prudent not to have put it in, I would not strike it out, as it seemed to me probable, and I give it on no other grounds.   You will see in your mind the kind of arguments which made me think it probable, and no one fact had so great an effect on me as your most curious remarks on the apparent homologies of the head of Vertebrata and Articulata.

You have done a real good turn in the Agency business * (I never before heard of a hard-working, unpaid agent besides yourself), in talking with Sir H. H., for he will have great influence over many.   He floored me from my ignorance about the bones of the ear, and I made a mental note to ask you what the facts were.

With hearty thanks and real admiration for your generous zeal for the subject.

Yours most truly,
C. Darwin.

You may smile about the care and precautions I have taken about my ugly MS. ; † it is not so much the value I set on them, but the remembrance of the intolerable labour—for instance, in tracing the history of the breeds of pigeons.

C. Darwin to J. D. Hooker.

Down, 25th [December, 1859].

. . . I shall not write to Decaisne ; ‡ I have always had a strong feeling that no one had better defend his own priority.   I cannot say that I am as indifferent to the subject as I ought to be, but one can avoid doing anything in consequence.

I do not believe one iota about your having assimilated any

---

* "My General Agent" was a sobriquet applied at this time by my father to Mr. Huxley.

† Manuscript left with Mr. Huxley for his perusal.

‡ With regard to Naudin's paper in the 'Revue Horticole,' 1852.

of my notions unconsciously. You have always done me more than justice. But I do think I did you a bad turn by getting you to read the old MS., as it must have checked your own original thoughts. There is one thing I am fully convinced of, that the future progress (which is the really important point) of the subject will have depended on really good and well-known workers, like yourself, Lyell, and Huxley, having taken up the subject, than on my own work. I see plainly it is this that strikes my non-scientific friends.

Last night I said to myself, I would just cut your Introduction, but would not. begin to read, but I broke down, and had a good hour's read.

Farewell, yours affectionately,
C. Darwin.

C. Darwin to J. D. Hooker.

December 28th, 1859.

. . . Have you seen the splendid essay and notice of my book in the *Times*? * I cannot avoid a strong suspicion that it is by Huxley; but I never heard that he wrote in the *Times*. It will do grand service, . . .

C. Darwin to T. H. Huxley.

Down, Dec. 28th [1859].

My dear Huxley,—Yesterday evening, when I read the *Times* of a previous day, I was amazed to find a splendid essay and review of me. Who can the author be? I am intensely curious. It included an eulogium of me which quite touched me, though I am not vain enough to think it all deserved. The author is a literary man, and German scholar. He has read my book very attentively; but, what is very remarkable, it seems that he is a profound naturalist. He knows my Barnacle-book, and appreciates it too highly. Lastly, he writes and thinks with quite uncommon force and

---

* Dec. 26th.

clearness ; and what is even still rarer, his writing is seasoned
with most pleasant wit. We all laughed heartily over some
of the sentences. I was charmed with those unreasonable
mortals, who know anything, all thinking fit to range themselves on one side.* Who can it be? Certainly I should
have said that there was only one man in England who could
have written this essay, and that *you* were the man. But I
suppose I am wrong, and that there is some hidden genius of
great calibre. For how could you influence Jupiter Olympius
and make him give three and a half columns to pure science?
The old fogies will think the world will come to an end.
Well, whoever the man is, he has done great service to the
cause, far more than by a dozen reviews in common periodicals. The grand way he soars above common religious
prejudices, and the admission of such views into the *Times*,
I look at as of the highest importance, quite independently
of the mere question of species. If you should happen to
be *acquainted* with the author, for Heaven-sake tell me who
he is?

My dear Huxley, yours most sincerely,

C. Darwin.

[It is impossible to give in a short space an adequate idea
of Mr. Huxley's article in the *Times* of December 26. It is
admirably planned, so as to claim for the ' Origin ' a respectful hearing, and it abstains from anything like dogmatism in
asserting the truth of the doctrinces therein upheld. A few
passages may be quoted :—" That this most ingenious

---

* The reviewer proposes to pass by the orthodox view, according to
which the phenomena of the organic world are " the immediate product
of a creative fiat, and consequently are out of the domain of science altogether." And he does so "with less hesitation, as it so happens that
those persons who are practically conversant with the facts of the case
(plainly a considerable advantage) have always thought fit to range themselves " in the category of those holding " views which profess to rest on a
scientific basis only, and therefore admit of being argued to their consequences."

hypothesis enables us to give a reason for many apparent anomalies in the distribution of living beings in time and space, and that it is not contradicted by the main phenomena of life and organisation, appear to us to be unquestionable." Mr. Huxley goes on to recommend to the readers of the 'Origin' a condition of "*thätige Skepsis*"—a state of "doubt which so loves truth that it neither dares rest in doubting, nor extinguish itself by unjustified belief." The final paragraph is in a strong contrast to Professor Sedgwick and his "ropes of bubbles" (see p. 92). Mr. Huxley writes: "Mr. Darwin abhors mere speculation as nature abhors a vacuum. He is as greedy of cases and precedents as any constitutional lawyer, and all the principles he lays down are capable of being brought to the test of observation and experiment. The path he bids us follow professes to be not a mere airy track, fabricated of ideal cobwebs, but a solid and broad bridge of facts. If it be so, it will carry us safely over many a chasm in our knowledge, and lead us to a region free from the snares of those fascinating but barren virgins, the Final Causes, against whom a high authority has so justly warned us."

There can be no doubt that this powerful essay, appearing as it did in the leading daily Journal, must have had a strong influence on the reading public. Mr. Huxley allows me to quote from a letter an account of the happy chance that threw into his hands the opportunity of writing it.

"The 'Origin' was sent to Mr. Lucas, one of the staff of the *Times* writers at that day, in what I suppose was the ordinary course of business. Mr. Lucas, though an excellent journalist, and, at a later period, editor of 'Once a Week,' was as innocent of any knowledge of science as a babe, and bewailed himself to an acquaintance on having to deal with such a book. Whereupon he was recommended to ask me to get him out of his difficulty, and he applied to me accordingly, explaining, however, that it would be necessary for him formally to adopt anything I might be disposed to write, by prefacing it with two or three paragraphs of his own.

"I was too anxious to seize upon the opportunity thus

offered of giving the book a fair chance with the multitudinous readers of the *Times* to make any difficulty about conditions; and being then very full of the subject, I wrote the article faster, I think, than I ever wrote anything in my life, and sent it to Mr. Lucas, who duly prefixed his opening sentences.

"When the article appeared, there was much speculation as to its authorship. The secret leaked out in time, as all secrets will, but not by my aid; and then I used to derive a good deal of innocent amusement from the vehement assertions of some of my more acute friends, that they knew it was mine from the first paragraph!

"As the *Times* some years since, referred to my connection with the review, I suppose there will be no breach of confidence in the publication of this little history, if you think it worth the space it will occupy."]

CHAPTER II.

THE 'ORIGIN OF SPECIES'—(*continued*).

1860.

[I EXTRACT a few entries from my father's Diary :—

"Jan. 7th. The second edition, 3000 copies, of 'Origin' was published."

"May 22nd. The first edition of 'Origin' in the United States was 2500 copies."

My father has here noted down the sums received for the 'Origin.'

First Edition	..	..	.. £180	0	0
Second Edition	..	..	.. 636	13	4
			£816	13	4

After the publication of the second edition he began at once, on Jan. 9th, looking over his materials for the 'Variation of Animals and Plants ;' the only other work of the year was on Drosera.

He was at Down during the whole of this year, except for a visit to Dr. Lane's Water-cure Establishment at Sudbrooke, in June, and for visits to Miss Elizabeth Wedgwood's house at Hartfield, in Sussex (July), and to Eastbourne, Sept. 22 to Nov. 16.]

C. Darwin to J. D. Hooker.

Down, January 3rd [1860].

MY DEAR HOOKER,—I have finished your Essay.* As probably you would like to hear my opinion, though a non-

---

* 'Australian Flora.'

botanist, I will give it without any exaggeration. To my judgment it is by far the grandest and most interesting essay, on subjects of the nature discussed, I have ever read. You know how I admired your former essays, but this seems to me far grander. I like all the part after p. xxvi better than the first part, probably because newer to me. I dare say you will demur to this, for I think every author likes the most speculative parts of his own productions. How superior your essay is to the famous one of Brown (here will be sneer 1st from you). You have made all your conclusions so admirably clear, that it would be no use at all to be a botanist (sneer No. 2). By Jove, it would do harm to affix any idea to the long names of outlandish orders. One can look at your conclusions with the philosophic abstraction with which a mathematician looks at his $a \times x + \sqrt{z^2}$, &c. &c. I hardly know which parts have interested me most; for over and over again I exclaimed, "this beats all." The general comparison of the Flora of Australia with the rest of the world, strikes me (as before) as extremely original, good, and suggestive of many reflections.

. . . . The invading Indian Flora is very interesting, but I think the fact you mention towards the close of the essay—that the Indian vegetation, in contradistinction to the Malayan vegetation, is found in low and level parts of the Malay Islands, *greatly* lessens the difficulty which at first (page 1) seemed so great. There is nothing like one's own hobbyhorse. I suspect it is the same case as of glacial migration, and of naturalised production—of production of greater area conquering those of lesser; of course the Indian forms would have a greater difficulty in seizing on the cool parts of Australia. I demur to your remarks (page 1), as not "conceiving anything in soil, climate, or vegetation of India," which could stop the introduction of Australian plants. Towards the close of the essay (page civ), you have admirable remarks on our profound ignorance of the cause of possible naturalisation or introduction; I would answer p. 1, by a later page, viz. p. civ.

Your contrast of the south-west and south-east corners is one of the most wonderful cases I ever heard of. . . . You show the case with wonderful force. Your discussion on mixed invaders of the south-east corner (and of New Zealand) is as curious and intricate a problem as of the races of men in Britain. Your remark on mixed invading Flora keeping down or destroying an original Flora, which was richer in number of species, strikes me as *eminently new and important*. I am not sure whether to me the discussion on the New Zealand Flora is not even more instructive. I cannot too much admire both. But it will require a long time to suck in all the facts. Your case of the largest Australian orders having none, or very few, species in New Zealand, is truly marvellous. Anyhow, you have now *demonstrated* (together with no mammals in New Zealand) (bitter sneer No. 3), that New Zealand has never been continuously, or even nearly continuously, united by land to Australia!! At p. lxxxix, is the only sentence (on this subject) in the whole essay at which I am much inclined to quarrel, viz. that no theory of transoceanic migration can explain, &c. &c. Now I maintain against all the world, that no man knows anything about the power of trans-oceanic migration. You do not know whether or not the absent orders have seeds which are killed by sea-water, like almost all Leguminosæ, and like another order which I forget. Birds do not migrate from Australia to New Zealand, and therefore floatation *seems* the only possible means; but yet I maintain that we do not know enough to argue on the question, especially as we do not know the main fact whether the seeds of Australian orders are killed by sea-water.

The discussion on European Genera is profoundly interesting; but here alone I earnestly beg for more information, viz. to know which of these genera are absent in the Tropics of the world, *i.e.* confined to temperate regions. I excessively wish to know, *on the notion of Glacial Migration,* how much modification has taken place in Australia. I had better explain when we meet, and get you to go over and mark the list.

. . . . The list of naturalised plants is extremely interesting, but why at the end, in the name of all that is good and bad, do you not sum up and comment on your facts? Come, I will have a sneer at you in return for the many which you will have launched at this letter. Should you have remarked on the number of plants naturalised in Australia and the United States *under extremely different climates*, as showing that climate is so important, and [on] the considerable sprinkling of plants from India, North America, and South Africa, as showing that the frequent introduction of seeds is so important? With respect to "abundance of unoccupied ground in Australia," do you believe that European plants introduced by man now grow on spots in Australia which were absolutely bare? But I am an impudent dog, one must defend one's own fancy theories against such cruel men as you. I dare say this letter will appear very conceited, but one must form an opinion on what one reads with attention, and in simple truth, I cannot find words strong enough to express my admiration of your essay.

My dear old friend, yours affectionately,

C. DARWIN.

P. S.—I differ about the *Saturday Review*.* One cannot expect fairness in a reviewer, so I do not complain of all the other arguments besides the 'Geological Record' being omitted. Some of the remarks about the lapse of years are very good, and the reviewer gives me some good and well-deserved raps—confound it. I am sorry to confess the truth: but it does not at all concern the main argument. That was a nice notice in the *Gardeners' Chronicle*. I hope and imagine that Lindley is almost a convert. Do not forget to tell me if Bentham gets all the more staggered.

---

* *Saturday Review*, Dec. 24, 1859. The hostile arguments of the reviewer are geological, and he deals especially with the denudation of the Weald. The reviewer remarks that, "if a million of centuries, more or less, is needed for any part of his argument, he feels no scruple in taking them to suit his purpose."

With respect to tropical plants during the Glacial period, I throw in your teeth your own facts, at the base of the Himalaya, on the possibility of the co-existence of at least forms of the tropical and temperate regions. I can give a parallel case for animals in Mexico. Oh! my dearly beloved puny child, how cruel men are to you! I am very glad you approve of the Geographical chapters. . . .

C. Darwin to C. Lyell.

Down [January 4th, 1860].

MY DEAR L.—*Gardeners' Chronicle* returned safe. Thanks for note. I am beyond measure glad that you get more and more roused on the subject of species, for, as I have always said, I am well convinced that your opinions and writings will do far more to convince the world than mine. You will make a grand discussion on man. You are very bold in this, and I honour you. I have been, like you, quite surprised at the want of originality in opposed arguments and in favour too. Gwyn Jeffreys attacks me justly in his letter about strictly littoral shells not being often embedded at least in Tertiary deposits. I was in a muddle, for I was thinking of Secondary, yet Chthamalus applied to Tertiary. . . . . .

Possibly you might like to see the enclosed note * from Whewell, merely as showing that he is not horrified with us. You can return it whenever you have occasion to write, so as not to waste your time.

C. D.

---

* Dr. Whewell wrote (Jan. 2. 1860): ". . . I cannot, yet at least, become a convert. But there is so much of thought and of fact in what you have written that it is not to be contradicted without careful selection of the ground and manner of the dissent." Dr. Whewell dissented in a practical manner for some years, by refusing to allow a copy of the 'Origin of Species' to be placed in the Library of Trinity College.

C. Darwin to C. Lyell.

Down, [January 4th ? 1860].

. . . . . . I have had a brief note from Keyserling,* but not worth sending you. He believes in change of species, grants that natural selection explains well adaptation of form, but thinks species change too regularly, as if by some chemical law, for natural selection to be the sole cause of change. I can hardly understand his brief note, but this is I think the upshot.

. . . . . I will send A. Murray's paper whenever published.† It includes speculations (which he perhaps will modify) so rash, and without a single fact in support, that had I advanced them he or other reviewers would have hit me very hard. I am sorry to say that I have no "consolatory view" on the dignity of man. I am content that man will probably advance, and care not much whether we are looked at as mere savages in a remotely distant future. Many thanks for your last note.

Yours affectionately,

C. DARWIN.

I have received, in a Manchester newspaper, rather a good squib, showing that I have proved "might is right," and there-

---

* Joint author with Murchison of the 'Geology of Russia,' 1845.

† The late Andrew Murray wrote two papers on the 'Origin' in the Proc. R. Soc. Edin. 1860. The one referred to here is dated Jan. 16, 1860. The following is quoted from p. 6 of the separate copy : "But the second, and, as it appears to me, by much the most important phase of reversion to type (and which is practically, if not altogether ignored by Mr. Darwin), is the instinctive inclination which induces individuals of the same species by preference to intercross with those possessing the qualities which they themselves want, so as to preserve the purity or equilibrium of the breed. . . . It is trite to a proverb, that tall men marry little women . . . a man of genius marries a fool . . . and we are told that this is the result of the charm of contrast, or of qualities admired in others because we do not possess them. I do not so explain it. I imagine it it is the effort of nature to preserve the typical medium of the race."

fore that Napoleon is right, and every cheating tradesman is also right.

C. Darwin to W. B. Carpenter.

Down, January 6th [1860]?

MY DEAR CARPENTER,—I have just read your excellent article in the 'National.' It will do great good; especially if it becomes known as your production. It seems to me to give an excellently clear account of Mr. Wallace's and my views. How capitally you turn the flanks of the theological opposers by opposing to them such men as Bentham and the more philosophical of the systematists! I thank you sincerely for the *extremely* honourable manner in which you mention me. I should have liked to have seen some criticisms or remarks on embryology, on which subject you are so well instructed. I do not think any candid person can read your article without being much impressed with it. The old doctrine of immutability of specific forms will surely but slowly die away. It is a shame to give you trouble, but I should be very much obliged if you could tell me where differently coloured eggs in individuals of the cuckoo have been described, and their laying in twenty-seven kinds of nests. Also do you know from your own observation that the limbs of sheep imported into the West Indies change colour? I have had detailed information about the loss of wool; but my accounts made the change slower than you describe.

With most cordial thanks and respect, believe me, my dear Carpenter, yours very sincerely,

CH. DARWIN.

C. Darwin to L. Jenyns.*

Down, January 7th, 1860.

MY DEAR JENYNS,—I am very much obliged for your letter. It is of great use and interest to me to know what

---

* Rev. L. Blomefield.

impression my book produces on philosophical and instructed minds. I thank you for the kind things which you say ; and you go with me much further than I expected. You will think it presumptuous, but I am convinced, *if circumstances lead you to keep the subject in mind*, that you will go further. No one has yet cast doubts on my explanation of the subordination of group to group, on homologies, embryology, and rudimentary organs ; and if my explanation of these classes of facts be at all right, whole classes of organic beings must be included in one line of descent.

The imperfection of the Geological Record is one of the greatest difficulties. . . . During the earliest period the record would be most imperfect, and this seems to me sufficient to account for our not finding intermediate forms between the classes in the same great kingdoms. It was certainly rash in me putting in my belief of the probability of all beings having descended from *one* primordial form; but as this seems yet to me probable, I am not willing to strike it out. Huxley alone supports me in this, and something could be said in its favour. With respect to man, I am very far from wishing to obtrude my belief; but I thought it dishonest to quite conceal my opinion. Of course it is open to every one to believe that man appeared by a separate miracle, though I do not myself see the necessity or probability.

Pray accept my sincere thanks for your kind note. Your going some way with me gives me great confidence that I am not very wrong. For a very long time I halted half way ; but I do not believe that any enquiring mind will rest half-way. People will have to reject all or admit all ; by *all* I mean only the members of each great kingdom.

My dear Jenyns, yours most sincerely,

C. DARWIN.

C. Darwin to C. Lyell.

Down, January 10th [1860].

. . . . It is perfectly true that I owe nearly all the corrections * to you, and several verbal ones to you and others; I am heartily glad you approve of them, as yet only two things have annoyed me; those confounded millions † of years (not that I think it is probably wrong), and my not having (by inadvertance) mentioned Wallace towards the close of the book in the summary, not that any one has noticed this to me. I have now put in Wallace's name at p. 484 in a conspicuous place. I cannot refer you to tables of mortality of children, &c. &c. I have notes somewhere, but I have not the *least* idea where to hunt, and my notes would now be old. I shall be truly glad to read carefully any MS. on man, and give my opinion. You used to caution me to be cautious about man. I suspect I shall have to return the caution a hundred fold! Yours will, no doubt, be a grand discussion; but it will horrify the world at first more than my whole volume; although by the sentence (p. 489, new edition ‡) I show that I believe man is in the same predicament with other animals. It is, in fact, impossible to doubt it. I have thought (only vaguely) on man. With respect to the races, one of my best chances of truth has broken down from the impossibility of getting facts. I have one good speculative line, but a man must have entire credence in Natural Selection before he will even listen to it. Psychologically, I have done scarcely any-

---

* The second edition of 3000 copies of the 'Origin' was published on January 7th.

† This refers to the passage in the 'Origin of Species' (2nd edit., p. 285), in which the lapse of time implied by the denudation of the Weald is discussed. The discussion closes with the sentence: "So that it is not improbable that a longer period than 300 million years has elapsed since the latter part of the Secondary period." This passage is omitted in the later editions of the 'Origin,' against the advice of some of his friends, as appears from the pencil notes in my father's copy of the 2nd edition.

‡ First edition, p. 488.

thing.   Unless, indeed, expression of countenance can be included, and on that subject I have collected a good many facts, and speculated, but I do not suppose I shall ever publish, but it is an uncommonly curious subject.   By the way, I sent off a lot of questions the day before yesterday to Tierra del Fuego on expression!   I suspect (for I have never read it) that Spencer's 'Psychology' has a bearing on Psychology as we should look at it.   By all means read the Preface, in about 20 pages, of Hensleigh Wedgwood's new Dictionary on the first origin of Language ; Erasmus would lend it.   I agree about Carpenter, a very good article, but with not much original. . . . Andrew Murray has criticised, in an address to the Botanical Society of Edinburg, the notice in the 'Linnean Journal,' and "has disposed of" the whole theory by an ingenious difficulty, which I was very stupid not to have thought of ; for I express surprise at more and analogous cases not being known.   The difficulty is, that amongst the blind insects of the caves in distant parts of the world there are some of the same genus, and yet the genus is not found out of the caves or living in the free world.   I have little doubt that, like the fish Amblyopsis, and like Proteus in Europe, these insects are "wrecks of ancient life," or "living fossils," saved from competition and extermination.   But that formerly *seeing* insects of the same genus roamed over the whole area in which the cases are included.

Farewell, yours affectionately,
C. DARWIN.

P.S.—*Our* ancestor was an animal which breathed water, had a swim bladder, a great swimming tail, an imperfect skull, and undoubtedly was an hermaphrodite !

Here is a pleasant genealogy for mankind.

C. Darwin to C. Lyell.

Down, January 14th [1860].

. . . I shall be much interested in reading your man discussion, and will give my opinion carefully, whatever that may be worth ; but I have so long looked at you as the type of cautious scientific judgment (to my mind one of the highest and most useful qualities), that I suspect my opinion will be superfluous. It makes me laugh to think what a joke it will be if I have to caution you, after your cautions on the same subject to me !

I will order Owen's book ; * I am very glad to hear Huxley's opinion on his classification of man ; without having due knowledge, it seemed to me from the very first absurd ; all classifications founded on single characters I believe have failed.

. . . What a grand, immense benefit you conferred on me by getting Murray to publish my book. I never till to-day realised that it was getting widely distributed ; for in a letter from a lady to-day to E., she says she heard a man enquiring for it at the *Railway Station ! ! !* at Waterloo Bridge ; and the bookseller said that he had none till the new edition was out. The bookseller said he had not read it, but had heard it was a very remarkable book ! ! ! . . . .

C. Darwin to J. D. Hooker.

Down, 14th [January, 1860].

. . . . I heard from Lyell this morning, and he tells me a piece of news. You are a good-for-nothing man ; here you are slaving yourself to death with hardly a minute to spare, and you must write a review of my book ! I thought it † a very good one, and was so much struck with it that I sent it to Lyell. But I assumed, as a matter of course, that it was Lindley's. Now that I know it is yours, I have re-read it, and, my kind and good friend, it has warmed my heart with all the honourable and noble things you say of me and it. I was a good deal surprised at Lindley hitting on some of the remarks, but I never dreamed of you. I admired it chiefly as

---

* 'Classification of the Mammalia,' 1859.

† *Gardeners' Chronicle*, 1860. Referred to above, at p. 54. Sir J. D. Hooker took the line of complete impartiality, so as not to commit Lindley.

so well adapted to tell on the readers of the *Gardeners'
Chronicle ;* but now I admired it in another spirit. Farewell,
with hearty thanks. . . . Lyell is going at man with an audacity that frightens me. It is a good joke ; he used always
to caution me to slip over man.

[In the *Gardeners' Chronicle,* Jan. 21, 1860, appeared a
short letter from my father which was called forth by
Mr. Westwood's communication to the previous number of
the journal, in which certain phenomena of cross-breeding are
discussed in relation to the ' Origin of Species.' Mr. Westwood wrote in reply (Feb. 11) and adduced further evidence
against the doctrine of descent, such as the identity of the
figures of ostriches on the ancient " Egyptian records," with
the bird as we now know it. The correspondence is hardly
worth mentioning, except as one of the very few cases in
which my father was enticed into anything resembling a controversy.]

Asa Gray to J. D. Hooker.

Cambridge, Mass.,
January 5th, 1860.

My dear Hooker,—Your last letter, which reached me
just before Christmas, has got mislaid during the upturnings
in my study which take place at that season, and has not yet
been discovered. I should be very sorry to lose it, for there
were in it some botanical mems. which I had not secured. . . .

The principal part of your letter was high laudation of
Darwin's book.

Well, the book has reached me, and I finished its careful
perusal four days ago ; and I freely say that your laudation
is not out of place.

It is done in a *masterly manner.* It might well have taken
twenty years to produce it. It is crammed full of most interesting matter—thoroughly digested—well expressed—close,
cogent, and taken as a system it makes out a better case than
I had supposed possible. . . .

Agassiz, when I saw him last, had read but a part of it. He says it is *poor—very poor!!* (entre nous). The fact [is] he is very much annoyed by it, ... and I do not wonder at it. To bring all *ideal* systems within the domain of science, and give good physical or natural explanations of all his capital points, is as bad as to have Forbes take the glacier materials . . . and give scientific explanation of all the phenomena.

Tell Darwin all this. I will write to him when I get a chance. As I have promised, he and you shall have fair-play here. . . . I must myself write a review of Darwin's book for 'Silliman's Journal' (the more so that I suspect Agassiz means to come out upon it) for the next (March) No., and I am now setting about it (when I ought to be every moment working the Expl[oring] Expedition Compositæ, which I know far more about). And really it is no easy job, as you may well imagine.

I doubt if I shall please you altogether. I know I shall not please Agassiz at all. I hear another reprint is in the Press, and the book will excite much attention here, and some controversy. . . .

C. Darwin to Asa Gray.

Down, January 28th [1860].

MY DEAR GRAY,—Hooker has forwarded to me your letter to him; and I cannot express how deeply it has gratified me. To receive the approval of a man whom one has long sincerely respected, and whose judgment and knowledge are most universally admitted, is the highest reward an author can possibly wish for; and I thank you heartily for your most kind expressions.

I have been absent from home for a few days, and so could not earlier answer your letter to me of the 10th of January. You have been extremely kind to take so much trouble and interest about the edition. It has been a mistake of my publisher not thinking of sending over the sheets. I had entirely and utterly forgotten your offer of receiving the sheets as printed off. But I must not blame my publisher, for had I remembered your most kind offer I feel pretty sure I should not have taken advantage of it; for I never dreamed of my book being so successful with general readers; I believe I should have laughed at the idea of sending the sheets to America.*

After much consideration, and on the strong advice of Lyell and others, I have resolved to leave the present book as it is (excepting correcting errors, or here and there inserting short sentences) and to use all my strength, *which is but little*, to bring out the first part (forming a separate volume, with index, &c.) of the three volumes which will make my bigger work; so that I am very unwilling to take up time in making corrections for an American edition. I enclose a list of a few corrections in the second reprint, which you will have received by this time complete, and I could send four or five corrections or additions of equally small importance, or rather of equal brevity. I also intend to write a *short* preface with a brief history of the subject. These I will set about, as they must some day be done, and I will send them to you in a short time—the few corrections first, and the preface afterwards, unless I hear that you have given up all idea of a separate edition. You will then be able to judge whether it is worth having the new edition with *your review prefixed*. Whatever be the nature of your review, I assure you I should feel it a *great* honour to have my book thus preceded. . . .

Asa Gray to C. Darwin.

Cambridge, January 23rd, 1860.

My DEAR DARWIN,—You have my hurried letter telling you of the arrival of the remainder of the sheets of the reprint, and of the stir I had made for a reprint in Boston.

* In a letter to Mr. Murray, 1860, my father wrote :—" I am amused by Asa Gray's account of the excitement my book has made amongst naturalists in the U. States. Agassiz has denounced it in a newspaper,

Well, all looked pretty well, when, lo, we found that a second
New York publishing house had announced a reprint also?
I wrote then to both New York publishers, asking them to
give way to the *author* and his reprint of a revised edition.
I got an answer from the Harpers that they withdraw—from
the Appletons that they had got the book *out* (and the next
day I saw a copy); but that, "if the work should have any
considerable sale, we certainly shall be disposed to pay the
author reasonably and liberally."

The Appletons being thus out with their reprint, the Boston house declined to go on. So I wrote to the Appletons
taking them at their word, offering to aid their reprint, to
give them the use of the alterations in the London reprint, as
soon as I find out what they are, &c. &c. And I sent
them the first leaf, and asked them to insert in their future
issue the additional matter from Butler,* which tells just
right. So there the matter stands. If you furnish any matter in advance of the London third edition, I will make them
pay for it.

I may get something for you. All got is clear gain ; but
it will not be very much, I suppose.

Such little notices in the papers here as have yet appeared
are quite handsome and considerate.

I hope next week to get printed sheets of my review from
New Haven, and send [them] to you, and will ask you to
pass them on to Dr. Hooker.

To fulfil your request, I ought to tell you what I think
the weakest, and what the best, part of your book. But this
is not easy, nor to be done in a word or two. The *best part*,
I think, is the *whole*, *i. e.* its *plan* and *treatment*, the vast
amount of facts and acute inferences handled as if you had a

---

but yet in such terms that it is in fact a fine advertisement !" This seems
to refer to a lecture given before the Mercantile Library Association.

* A quotation from Butler's 'Analogy, on the use of the word natural,
which in the second edition is placed with the passages from Whewell and
Bacon on p. ii, opposite the title-page.

perfect mastery of them. I do not think twenty years too much time to produce such a book in.

Style clear and good, but now and then wants revision for little matters (p. 97, self-fertilises *itself*, &c.).

Then your candour is worth everything to your cause. It is refreshing to find a person with a new theory who frankly confesses that he finds difficulties, insurmountable, at least for the present. I know some people who never have any difficulties to speak of.

The moment I understood your premisses, I felt sure you had a real foundation to hold on. Well, if one admits your premisses, I do not see how he is to stop short of your conclusions, as a probable hypothesis at least.

It naturally happens that my review of your book does not exhibit anything like the full force of the impression the book has made upon me. Under the circumstances I suppose I do your theory more good here, by bespeaking for it a fair and favourable consideration, and by standing non-committed as to its full conclusions, than I should if I announced myself a convert; nor could I say the latter, with truth.

Well, what seems to me the weakest point in the book is the attempt to account for the formation of organs, the making of eyes, &c., by natural selection. Some of this reads quite Lamarckian.

The chapter on *Hybridism* is not a *weak*, but a *strong* chapter. You have done wonders there. But still you have not accounted, as you may be held to account, for divergence up to a certain extent producing increased fertility of the crosses, but carried one short almost imperceptible step more, giving rise to sterility, or reversing the tendency. Very likely you are on the right track; but you have something to do yet in that department.

Enough for the present.

. . . . . . I am not insensible to your compliments, the very high compliment which you pay me in valuing my opinion. You evidently think more of it than I do, though from the way I write [to] you, and especially [to] Hooker, this might not be inferred from the reading of my letters.

I am free to say that I never learnt so much from one book as I have from yours. There remain a thousand things I long to say about it.

Ever yours,

ASA GRAY.

C. Darwin to Asa Gray.

[February ? 1860.]

. . . . . Now I will just run through some points in your letter. What you say about my book gratifies me most deeply, and I wish I could feel all was deserved by me. I quite think a review from a man, who is not an entire convert, if fair and moderately favourable, is in all respects the best kind of review. About the weak points I agree. The eye to this day gives me a cold shudder, but when I think of the fine known gradations, my reason tells me I ought to conquer the cold shudder.

Pray kindly remember and tell Prof. Wyman how very grateful I should be for any hints, information, or criticisms. I have the highest respect for his opinion. I am so sorry about Dana's health. I have already asked him to pay me a visit.

Farewell, you have laid me under a load of obligation— not that I feel it a load. It is the highest possible gratification to me to think that you have found my book worth reading and reflection; for you and three others I put down in my own mind as the judges whose opinions I should value most of all.

My dear Gray, yours most sincerely,

C. DARWIN.

P.S.—I feel pretty sure, from my own experience, that if you are led by your studies to keep the subject of the origin of species before your mind, you will go further and further in your belief. It took me long years, and I assure you I am astonished at the impression my book has made on many minds. I fear twenty years ago, I should not have been half as candid and open to conviction.

C. Darwin to J. D. Hooker.

Down [January 31st, 1860].

MY DEAR HOOKER,—I have resolved to publish a little sketch of the progress of opinion on the change of species. Will you or Mrs. Hooker do me the favour to copy *one* sentence out of Naudin's paper in the 'Revue Horticole,' 1852, p. 103, namely, that on his principle of Finalité. Can you let me have it soon, with those confounded dashes over the vowels put in carefully ? Asa Gray, I believe, is going to get a second edition of my book, and I want to send this little preface over to him soon. I did not think of the necessity of having Naudin's sentence on finality, otherwise I would have copied it.

Yours affectionately,

C. DARWIN.

P.S.—I shall end by just alluding to your Australian Flora Introduction. What was the date of publication : December 1859, or January 1860 ? Please answer this.

My preface will also do for the French edition, which, *I believe*, is agreed on.

C. Darwin to J. D. Hooker.

February [1860].

. . . . As the 'Origin' now stands, Harvey's * is a good hit against my talking so much of the insensibly fine grada-

---

* William Henry Harvey was descended from a Quaker family of Youghal, and was born in February, 1811, at Summerville, a country house on the banks of the Shannon. He died at Torquay in 1866. In 1835, Harvey went to Africa (Table Bay) to pursue his botanical studies, the results of which were given in his 'Genera of South African Plants.' In 1838, ill-health compelled him to obtain leave of absence, and return

tions ; and certainly it has astonished me that I should be pelted with the fact, that I had not allowed abrupt and great enough variations under nature. It would take a good deal more evidence to make me admit that forms have often changed by *saltum*.

Have you seen Wollaston's attack in the 'Annals'?* The stones are beginning to fly. But Theology has more to do with these two attacks than Science. . . .

[In the above letter a paper by Harvey in the *Gardeners' Chronicle*, Feb. 18, 1860, is alluded to. He describes a case of monstrosity in *Begonia frigida*, in which the "sport" differed so much from a normal Begonia that it might have served as the type of a distinct natural order. Harvey goes on to argue that such a case is hostile to the theory of natural selection, according to which changes are not supposed to take place *per saltum*, and adds that "a few such cases would overthrow it [Mr. Darwin's hypothesis] altogether." In the following number of the *Gardeners' Chronicle* Sir J. D. Hooker showed that Dr. Harvey had misconceived the bearing of the Begonia case, which he further showed to be by no means calculated to shake the validity of the doctrine of modification by means of natural selection. My father mentions the Begonia case in a letter to Lyell (Feb. 18, 1860) :—

"I send by this post an attack in the *Gardeners' Chronicle*, by Harvey (a first-rate Botanist, as you probably know). It seems to me rather strange ; he assumes the permanence of monsters, whereas, monsters are generally sterile, and not

---

to England for a time ; in 1840 he returned to Cape Town, to be again compelled by illness to leave. In 1843 he obtained the appointment of Botanical Professor at Trinity College, Dublin. In 1854, 1855, and 1856 he visited Australia, New Zealand, the Friendly and Fiji Islands. In 1857 Dr. Harvey reached home, and was appointed the successor of Professor Allman to the Chair of Botany in Dublin University. He was author of several botanical works, principally on Algæ.—(From a Memoir published in 1869.)

* 'Annals and Magazine of Natural History,' 1860.

often inheritable. But grant his case, it comes that I have been too cautious in not admitting great and sudden variations. Here again comes in the mischief of my *abstract*. In the fuller MS. I have discussed a parallel case of a normal fish like the monstrous gold-fish."

With reference to Sir J. D. Hooker's reply, my father wrote:]

Down [February 26th, 1860].

MY DEAR HOOKER,—Your answer to Harvey seems to me *admirably* good. You would have made a gigantic fortune as a barrister. What an omission of Harvey's about the graduated state of the flowers! But what strikes me most is that surely I ought to know my own book best, yet, by Jove, you have brought forward ever so many arguments which I did not think of! Your reference to classification (viz. I presume to such cases as Aspicarpa) is *excellent*, for the monstrous Begonia no doubt in all details would be Begonia. I did not think of this, nor of the *retrograde* step from separated sexes to an hermaphrodite state ; nor of the lessened fertility of the monster. Proh pudor to me.

The world would say what a lawyer has been lost in a *mere* botanist !

Farewell, my dear master in my own subject,

Yours affectionately,

C. DARWIN.

I am so heartily pleased to see that you approve of the chapter on Classification.

I wonder what Harvey will say. But no one hardly, I think, is able at first to see when he is beaten in an argument.

[The following letters refer to the first translation (1860) of the 'Origin of Species' into German, which was superintended by H. G. Bronn, a good zoologist and palæontologist, who was at the time at Freiburg, but afterwards Professor at Heidelberg. I have been told that the translation was not a success, it remained an obvious translation, and was correspondingly unpleasant to read. Bronn added to the translation an appendix of the difficulties that occurred to him. For instance, how can natural selection account for differences between species, when these differences appear to be of no service to their possessors; e. g., the length of the ears and tail, or the folds in the enamel of the teeth of various species of rodents? Krause, in his book, 'Charles Darwin,' p. 91, criticises Bronn's conduct in this matter, but it will be seen that my father actually suggested the addition of Bronn's remarks. A more serious charge against Bronn made by Krause (*op. cit.* p. 87) is that he left out passages of which he did not approve, as, for instance, the passage ('Origin,' first edition, p. 488) "Light will be thrown on the origin of man and his history." I have no evidence as to whether my father did or did not know of these alterations.]

C. Darwin to H. G. Bronn.

Down, Feb. 4 [1860].

DEAR AND MUCH HONOURED SIR,—I thank you sincerely for your most kind letter; I feared that you would much disapprove of the 'Origin,' and I sent it to you merely as a mark of my sincere respect. I shall read with much interest your work on the productions of Islands whenever I receive it. I thank you cordially for the notice in the 'Neues Jahrbuch für Mineralogie,' and still more for speaking to Schweitzerbart about a translation; for I am most anxious that the great and intellectual German people should know something about my book.

I have told my publisher to send immediately a copy of the *new* * edition to Schweitzerbart, and I have written to Schweitzerbart that I gave up all right to profit for myself, so that I hope a translation will appear. I fear that the book will be difficult to translate, and if you could advise Schweitzerbart about a *good* translator, it would be of very great

---

* Second edition.

service. Still more, if you would run your eye over the more difficult parts of the translation; but this is too great a favour to expect. I feel sure that it will be difficult to translate, from being so much condensed.

Again I thank you for your noble and generous sympathy, and I remain, with entire respect,

Yours, truly obliged,

C. DARWIN.

P. S.—The new edition has some few corrections, and I will send in MS. some additional corrections, and a short historical preface, to Schweitzerbart.

How interesting you could make the work by *editing* (I do not mean translating) the work, and appending notes of *refutation* or confirmation. The book has sold so very largely in England, that an editor would, I think, make profit by the translation.

C. Darwin to H. G. Bronn.

Down, Feb. 14 [1860].

MY DEAR AND MUCH HONOURED SIR,—I thank you cordially for your extreme kindness in superintending the translation. I have mentioned this to some eminent scientific men, and they all agree that you have done a noble and generous service. If I am proved quite wrong, yet I comfort myself in thinking that my book may do some good, as truth can only be known by rising victorious from every attack. I thank you also much for the review, and for the kind manner in which you speak of me. I send with this letter some corrections and additions to M. Schweitzerbart, and a short historical preface. I am not much acquainted with German authors, as I read German very slowly; therefore I do not know whether any Germans have advocated similar views with mine; if they have, would you do me the favour to insert a foot-note to the preface? M. Schweitzerbart has now the reprint ready for a translator to begin. Several scientific men have thought the term "Natural Selection" good, because its meaning is *not* obvious, and each man could not put on it his own interpretation, and because it at once connects variation under domestication and nature. Is there any analogous term used by German breeders of animals? "Adelung," ennobling, would, perhaps, be too metaphorical. It is folly in me, but I cannot help doubting whether "Wahl der Lebensweise" expresses my notion. It leaves the impression on my mind of the Lamarckian doctrine (which I reject) of habits of life being all-important. Man has altered, and thus improved the English race-horse by *selecting* successive fleeter individuals; and I believe, owing to the struggle for existence, that similar *slight* variations in a wild horse, *if advantageous to it*, would be *selected* or *preserved* by nature; hence Natural Selection. But I apologise for troubling you with these remarks on the importance of choosing good German terms for "Natural Selection." With my heartfelt thanks, and with sincere respect,

I remain, dear Sir, yours very sincerely,

CHARLES DARWIN.

C. Darwin to H. G. Bronn.

Down, July 14 [1860].

DEAR AND HONOURED SIR,—On my return home, after an absence of some time, I found the translation of the third part * of the 'Origin,' and I have been delighted to see a final chapter of criticisms by yourself. I have read the first few paragraphs and final paragraph, and am perfectly contented, indeed more than contented, with the generous and candid spirit with which you have considered my views. You speak with too much praise of my work. I shall, of course, carefully read the whole chapter; but though I can read descriptive books like Gaertner's pretty easily, when any reasoning comes in, I find German excessively difficult to understand. At some *future* time I should very much like to hear how my

---

* The German translation was published in three pamphlet-like numbers.

book has been received in Germany, and I most sincerely hope M. Schweitzerbart will not lose money by the publication. Most of the reviews have been bitterly opposed to me in England, yet I have made some converts, and *several* naturalists who would not believe in a word of it, are now coming slightly round, and admit that natural selection may have done something. This gives me hope that more will ultimately come round to a certain extent to my views.

I shall ever consider myself deeply indebted to you for the immense service and honour which you have conferred on me in making the excellent translation of my book. Pray believe me, with most sincere respect,

Dear Sir, yours gratefully,

CHARLES DARWIN.

C. Darwin to C. Lyell.

Down [February 12th, 1860].

. . . I think it was a great pity that Huxley wasted so much time in the lecture on the preliminary remarks ; . . . but his lecture seemed to me very fine and very bold. I have remonstrated (and he agrees) against the impression that he would leave, that sterility was a universal and infallible criterion of species.

You will, I am sure, make a grand discussion on man. I am so glad to hear that you and Lady Lyell will come here. Pray fix your own time ; and if it did not suit us we would say so. We could then discuss man well. . . .

How much I owe to you and Hooker ! I do not suppose I should hardly ever have published had it not been for you.

The lecture referred to in the last letter was given at the Royal Institution, February 10, 1860. The following letter was written in reply to Mr. Huxley's request for information about breeding, hybridisation, &c. It is of interest as giving a vivid retrospect of the writer's experience on the subject.]

C. Darwin to T. H. Huxley.

Ilkley, Yorks, Nov. 27 [1859].

MY DEAR HUXLEY,—Gärtner grand, Kölreuter grand, but papers scattered through many volumes and very lengthy. I had to make an abstract of the whole. Herbert's volume on Amaryllidaceæ very good, and two excellent papers in the 'Horticultural Journal.' For animals, no résumé to be trusted at all; facts are to be collected from all original sources.* I fear my MS. for the bigger book (twice or thrice as long as in present book), with all references, would be illegible, but it would save you infinite labour; of course I would gladly lend it, but I have no copy, so care would have to be taken of it. But my accursed handwriting would be fatal, I fear.

About breeding, I know of no one book. I did not think well of Lowe, but I can name none better. Youatt I look at as a far better and *more practical* authority; but then his views and facts are scattered through three or four thick volumes. I have picked up most by reading really numberless special treatises and *all* agricultural and horticultural journals; but it is a work of long years. *The difficulty is to know what to trust.* No one or two statements are worth a farthing; the facts are so complicated. I hope and think I have been really cautious in what I state on this subject, although all

---

* This caution is exemplified in the following extract from an earlier letter to Professor Huxley :—" The inaccuracy of the blessed gang (of which I am one) of compilers passes all bounds. *Monsters* have frequently been described as hybrids without a tittle of evidence. I must give one other case to show how we jolly fellows work. A Belgian Baron (I forget his name at this moment) crossed two distinct geese and got *seven* hybrids, which he proved subsequently to be quite sterile; well, compiler the first, Chevreul, says that the hybrids were propagated for *seven* generations *inter se.* Compiler second (Morton) mistakes the French name, and gives Latin names for two more distinct geese, and says *Chevreul* himself propagated them *inter se* for seven generations; and the latter statement is copied from book to book."

42

that I have given, as yet, is *far* too briefly. I have found it very important associating with fanciers and breeders. For instance, I sat one evening in a gin palace in the Borough amongst a set of pigeon fanciers, when it was hinted that Mr. Bull had crossed his Pouters with Runts to gain size; and if you had seen the solemn, the mysterious, and awful shakes of the head which all the fanciers gave at this scandalous proceeding, you would have recognised how little crossing has had to do with improving breeds, and how dangerous for endless generations the process was. All this was brought home far more vividly than by pages of mere statements, &c. But I am scribbling foolishly. I really do not know how to advise about getting up facts on breeding and improving breeds. Go to Shows is one way. Read *all* treatises on any *one* domestic animal, and believe nothing without largely confirmed. For your lectures I can give you a few amusing anecdotes and sentences, if you want to make the audience laugh.

I thank you particularly for telling me what naturalists think. If we can once make a compact set of believers we shall in time conquer. I am *eminently* glad Ramsey is on our side, for he is, in my opinion, a first-rate geologist. I sent him a copy. I hope he got it. I shall be very curious to hear whether any effect has been produced on Prestwich; I sent him a copy, not as a friend, but owing to a sentence or two in some paper, which made me suspect he was doubting.

Rev. C. Kingsley has a mind to come round. Quatrefages writes that he goes some long way with me; says he exhibited diagrams like mine. With most hearty thanks,

Yours very tired,
C. DARWIN.

[I give the conclusion of Professor Huxley's lecture, as being one of the earliest, as well as one of the most eloquent of his utterances in support of the 'Origin of Species':

"I have said that the man of science is the sworn interpreter of nature in the high court of reason. But of what avail is his honest speech, if ignorance is the assessor of the judge, and prejudice the foreman of the jury? I hardly know of a great physical truth, whose universal reception has not been preceded by an epoch in which most estimable persons have maintained that the phenomena investigated were directly dependent on the Divine Will, and that the attempt to investigate them was not only futile, but blasphemous. And there is a wonderful tenacity of life about this sort of opposition to physical science. Crushed and maimed in every battle, it yet seems never to be slain; and after a hundred defeats it is at this day as rampant, though happily not so mischievous, as in the time of Galileo.

"But to those whose life is spent, to use Newton's noble words, in picking up here a pebble and there a pebble on the shores of the great ocean of truth—who watch, day by day, the slow but sure advance of that mighty tide, bearing on its bosom the thousand treasures wherewith man ennobles and beautifies his life—it would be laughable, if it were not so sad, to see the little Canutes of the hour enthroned in solemn state, bidding that great wave to stay, and threatening to check its beneficent progress. The wave rises and they fly; but, unlike the brave old Dane, they learn no lesson of humility: the throne is pitched at what seems a safe distance, and the folly is repeated.

"Surely it is the duty of the public to discourage anything of this kind, to discredit these foolish meddlers who think they do the Almighty a service by preventing a thorough study of His works.

"The Origin of Species is not the first, and it will not be the last, of the great questions born of science, which will demand settlement from this generation. The general mind is seething strangely, and to those who watch the signs of the times, it seems plain that this nineteenth century will see revolutions of thought and practice as great as those which the sixteenth witnessed   Through what trials and sore contests the civilised world will have to pass in the course of this new reformation, who can tell?

" But I verily believe that come what will, the part which England may play in the battle is a grand and a noble one. She may prove to the world that, for one people, at any rate, despotism and demagogy are not the necessary alternatives of government; that freedom and order are not incompatible ; that reverence is the handmaid of knowledge; that free discussion is the life of truth, and of true unity in a nation.

" Will England play this part ? That depends upon how you, the public, deal with science. Cherish her, venerate her, follow her methods faithfully and implicitly in their application to all branches of human thought, and the future of this people will be greater than the past.

" Listen to those who would silence and crush her, and I fear our children will see the glory of England vanishing like Arthur in the mist ; they will cry too late the woful cry of Guinever:—

> ' It was my duty to have loved the highest ;
> It surely was my profit had I known ;
> It would have been my pleasure had I seen.' "]

C. Darwin to C. Lyell.

Down [February 15th, 1860].

. . . I am perfectly convinced (having read this morning) that the review in the 'Annals'* is by Wollaston ; no one else in the world would have used so many parentheses. I have written to him, and told him that the "pestilent" fellow

---

* Annals and Mag. of Nat. Hist. third series, vol. 5, p. 132. My father has obviously taken the expression " pestilent " from the following passage (p. 138): " But who is this Nature, we have a right to ask, who has such tremendous power, and to whose efficiency such marvellous performances are ascribed ? What are her image and attributes, when dragged from her wordy lurking-place ? Is she aught but a pestilent abstraction, like dust cast in our eyes to obscure the workings of an Intelligent First Cause of all ? " The reviewer pays a tribute to my father's candour, " so manly and outspoken as almost to ' cover a multitude of sins.' " The parentheses (to which allusion is made above) are so frequent as to give a characteristic appearance to Mr. Wollaston's pages.

thanks him for his kind manner of speaking about him. I have also told him that he would be pleased to hear that the Bishop of Oxford says it is the most unphilosophical * work he ever read. The review seems to me clever, and only misinterprets me in a few places. Like all hostile men, he passes over the explanation given of Classification, Morphology, Embryology, and Rudimentary Organs, &c. I read Wallace's paper in MS.,† and thought it admirably good ; he does not know that he has been anticipated about the depth of intervening sea determining distribution. . . . The most curious point in the paper seems to me that about the African character of the Celebes productions, but I should require further confirmation. . . .

Henslow is staying here ; I have had some talk with him ; he is in much the same state as Bunbury, ‡ and will go a very little way with us, but brings up no real argument against going further. He also shudders at the eye ! It is really curious (and perhaps is an argument in our favour) how differently different opposers view the subject. Henslow used to rest his opposition on the imperfection of the Geological Record, but he now thinks nothing of this, and says I have got well out of it ; I wish I could quite agree with him. Baden Powell says he never read anything so conclusive as my statement about the eye ! ! A stranger writes to me about sexual selection, and regrets that I boggle about such a trifle as the brush of hair on the male turkey, and so on. As L. Jenyns has a really philosophical mind, and as you say you like to see everything, I send an old letter of his. In a later letter to Henslow, which I have seen, he is more candid than any opposer I have heard of, for he says, though he *cannot* go so far as I do, yet he can give no good reason why he should not.

---

* Another version of the words is given by Lyell, to whom they were spoken, viz. '' the most illogical book ever written."—' Life,' vol. ii. p. 358.

† '' On the Zoological Geography of the Malay Archipelago."—Linn Soc. Journ. 1860.

‡ The late Sir Charles Bunbury, well known as a Palæo-botanist.

It is funny how each man draws his own imaginary line at which to halt. It reminds me so vividly what I was told* about you when I first commenced geology—to believe a *little*, but on no account to believe all.

Ever yours affectionately,
C. DARWIN.

C. Darwin to Asa Gray.

Down, February 18th [1860].

MY DEAR GRAY,—I received about a week ago two sheets of your Review;† read them, and sent them to Hooker; they are now returned and re-read with care, and to-morrow I send them to Lyell. Your Review seems to me *admirable ;* by far the best which I have read. I thank you from my heart both for myself, but far more for the subject's sake. Your contrast between the views of Agassiz and such as mine is very curious and instructive. ‡ By the way, if Agassiz writes anything on the subject, I hope you will tell me. I am charmed with your metaphor of the streamlet never running against the force of gravitation. Your distinction between an hypothesis and theory seems to me very ingenious ; but I do not think it is ever followed. Every one now speaks of the undulatory *theory* of light; yet the ether is itself hypothetical, and the undulations are inferred only from explaining the phenomena of light. Even in the *theory* of gravitation is the attractive power in any way known, except by explaining the fall of the apple, and the movements of the Planets? It seems to me that an hypothesis is *developed* into a theory solely by explaining an ample lot of facts. Again and again I thank

---

* By Professor Henslow.

† The 'American Journal of Science and Arts,' March, 1860. Reprinted in 'Darwiniana,' 1876.

‡ The contrast is briefly summed up thus : " The theory of Agassiz regards the origin of species and their present general distribution over the world as equally primordial, equally supernatural ; that of Darwin as equally derivative, equally natural."—'Darwiniana,' p. 14.

you for your generous aid in discussing a view, about which you very properly hold yourself unbiassed.

My dear Gray, yours most sincerely,

C. DARWIN.

P.S.—Several clergymen go far with me. Rev. L. Jenyns, a very good naturalist. Henslow will go a very little way with me, and is not shocked with me. He has just been visiting me.

[With regard to the attitude of the more liberal representatives of the Church, the following letter (already referred to) from Charles Kingsley is of interest:]

C. Kingsley to C. Darwin.

Eversley Rectory, Winchfield,
November 18th, 1859.

DEAR SIR,—I have to thank you for the unexpected honour of your book. That the Naturalist whom, of all naturalists living, I most wish to know and to learn from, should have sent a scientist like me his book, encourages me at least to observe more carefully, and think more slowly.

I am so poorly (in brain), that I fear I cannot read your book just now as I ought. All I have seen of it *awes* me; both with the heap of facts and the prestige of your name, and also with the clear intuition, that if you be right, I must give up much that I have believed and written.

In that I care little. Let God be true, and every man a liar! Let us know what *is*, and, as old Socrates has it, ἔπεσθαι τῷ λόγῳ—follow up the villainous shifty fox of an argument, into whatsoever unexpected bogs and brakes he may lead us, if we do but run into him at last.

From two common superstitions, at least, I shall be free while judging of your books:—

(1.) I have long since, from watching the crossing of domesticated animals and plants, learnt to disbelieve the dogma of the permanence of species.

(2.) I have gradually learnt to see that it is just as noble a conception of Deity, to believe that he created primal forms capable of self development into all forms needful *pro tempore* and *pro loco*, as to believe that He required a fresh act of intervention to supply the *lacunas* which He Himself had made. I question whether the former be not the loftier thought.

Be it as it may, I shall prize your book, both for itself, and as a proof that you are aware of the existence of such a person as

Your faithful servant,

C. KINGSLEY.

[My father's old friend, the Rev. J. Brodie Innes, of Milton Brodie, who was for many years Vicar of Down, writes in the same spirit:

"We never attacked each other. Before I knew Mr. Darwin I had adopted, and publicly expressed, the principle that the study of natural history, geology, and science in general, should be pursued without reference to the Bible. That the Book of Nature and Scripture came from the same Divine source, ran in parallel lines, and when properly understood would never cross. . . . . .

"His views on this subject were very much to the same effect from his side. Of course any conversations we may have had on purely religious subjects are as sacredly private now as in his life; but the quaint conclusion of one may be given. We had been speaking of the apparent contradiction of some supposed discoveries with the Book of Genesis; he said, 'you are (it would have been more correct to say you ought to be) a theologian, I am a naturalist, the lines are separate. I endeavour to discover facts without considering what is said in the Book of Genesis. I do not attack Moses, and I think Moses can take care of himself.' To the same effect he wrote more recently, 'I cannot remember that I ever published a word directly against religion or the clergy; but if you were to read a little pamphlet which I received a

couple of days ago by a clergyman, you would laugh, and admit that I had some excuse for bitterness.　After abusing me
for two or three pages, in language sufficiently plain and emphatic to have satisfied any reasonable man, he sums up by
saying that he has vainly searched the English language to
find terms to express his contempt for me and all Darwinians.'　In another letter, after I had left Down, he writes,
' We often differed, but you are one of those rare mortals
from whom one can differ and yet feel no shade of animosity,
and that is a thing [of] which I should feel very proud, if any
one could say [it] of me.'

" On my last visit to Down, Mr. Darwin said, at his din-
ner-table, ' Brodie Innes and I have been fast friends for
thirty years, and we never thoroughly agreed on any subject
but once, and then we stared hard at each other, and thought
one of us must be very ill.' "]

C. Darwin to C. Lyell.

Down, February 23rd [1860].

MY DEAR LYELL,—That is a splendid answer of the
father of Judge Crompton.　How curious that the Judge
should have hit on exactly the same points as yourself.　It
shows me what a capital lawyer you would have made, how
many unjust acts you would have made appear just!　But
how much grander a field has science been than the law,
though the latter might have made you Lord Kinnordy.　I
will, if there be another edition, enlarge on gradation in the
eye, and on all forms coming from one prototype, so as to
try and make both less glaringly improbable. . . .

With respect to Bronn's objection that it cannot be shown
how life arises, and likewise to a certain extent Asa Gray's
remark that natural selection is not a *vera causa*, I was much
interested by finding accidentally in Brewster's ' Life of
Newton,' that Leibnitz objected to the law of gravity because
Newton could not show what gravity itself is.　As it has
chanced, I have used in letters this very same argument,

little knowing that any one had really thus objected to the law of gravity   Newton answers by saying that it is philosophy to make out the movements of a clock, though you do not know why the weight descends to the ground.   Leibnitz further objected that the law of gravity was opposed to Natural Religion !   Is this not curious ?   I really think I shall use the facts for some introductory remarks for my bigger book.

. . . You ask (I see) why we do not have monstrosities in higher animals; but when they live they are almost always sterile (even giants and dwarfs are *generally* sterile), and we do not know that Harvey's monster would have bred.   There is I believe only one case on record of a peloric flower being fertile, and I cannot remember whether this reproduced itself..

To recur to the eye.   I really think it would have been dishonest, not to have faced the difficulty ; and worse (as Talleyrand would have said), it would have been impolitic I think, for it would have been thrown in my teeth, as H. Holland threw the bones of the ear, till Huxley shut him up by showing what a fine gradation occurred amongst living creatures.

I thank you much for your most pleasant letter.

Yours affectionately,
C. DARWIN.

P.S.—I send a letter by Herbert Spencer, which you can read or not as you think fit.   He puts, to my mind, the philosophy of the argument better than almost any one, at the close of the letter.   I could make nothing of Dana's idealistic notions about species; but then, as Wollaston says, I have not a metaphysical head.

By the way, I have thrown at Wollaston's head, a paper by Alexander Jordan, who demonstrates metaphysically that all our cultivated races are God-created species.

Wollaston misrepresents accidentally, to a wonderful extent, some passages in my book.   He reviewed, without relooking at certain passages.

C. Darwin to C. Lyell.

Down, February 25th [1860].

. . . . I cannot help wondering at your zeal about my book. I declare to heaven you seem to care as much about my book as I do myself. You have no right to be so eminently unselfish! I have taken off my spit [*i. e.* file] a letter of Ramsay's, as every geologist convert I think very important. By the way, I saw some time ago a letter from H. D. Rogers * to Huxley, in which he goes very far with us. . . .

C. Darwin to J. D. Hooker.

Down, Saturday, March 3rd, [1860].

MY DEAR HOOKER,—What a day's work you had on that Thursday! I was not able to go to London till Monday, and then I was a fool for going, for, on Tuesday night, I had an attack of fever (with a touch of pleurisy), which came on like a lion, but went off as a lamb, but has shattered me a good bit.

I was much interested by your last note. . . . I think you expect too much in regard to change of opinion on the subject of Species. One large class of men, more especially I suspect of naturalists, never will care about *any* general question, of which old Gray, of the British Museum, may be taken as a type; and secondly, nearly all men past a moderate age, either in actual years or in mind, are, I am fully convinced, incapable of looking at facts under a new point of view. Seriously, I am astonished and rejoiced at the progress which the subject has made; look at the enclosed memorandum.†
—— says my book will be forgotten in ten years, perhaps so; but, with such a list, I feel convinced the subject will not. The outsiders, as you say, are strong.

---

* Professor of Geology in the University of Glasgow. Born in the United States 1809, died 1866.

† See table of names, p. 87.

You say that you think that Benthan is touched, " but, like a wise man, holds his tongue." Perhaps you only mean that he cannot decide, otherwise I should think such silence the reverse of magnanimity ; for if others behaved the same way, how would opinion ever progress ? It is a dereliction of actual duty.*

I am so glad to hear about Thwaites.† . . . I have had an astounding letter from Dr. Boott ; ‡ it might be turned into ridicule against him and me, so I will not send it to any one. He writes in a noble spirit of love of truth.

I wonder what Lindley thinks ; probably too busy to read or think on the question.

I am vexed about Bentham's reticence, for it would have been of real value to know what parts appeared weakest to a man of his powers of observation.

Farewell, my dear Hooker, yours affectionately,

C. DARWIN.

P.S.—Is not Harvey in the class of men who do not at all care for generalities? I remember your saying you could not get him to write on Distribution. I have found his works very unfruitful in every respect.

[Here follows the memorandum referred to :]

---

* In a subsequent letter to Sir J. D. Hooker (March 12th, 1860), my father wrote, " I now quite understand Bentham's silence."

† Dr. G. J. K. Thwaites, who was born in 1811, established a reputation in this country as an expert microscopist, and an acute observer, working especially at cryptogamic botany. On his appointment as Director of the Botanic Gardens at Peradenyia, Ceylon, Dr. Thwaites devoted himself to the flora of Ceylon. As a result of this he has left numerous and valuable collections, a description of which he embodied in his ' Enumeratio Plantarum Zeylaniae' (1864). Dr. Thwaites was a Fellow of the Linnean Society, but beyond the above facts little seems to have been recorded of his life. His death occurred in Ceylon on September 11th, 1882, in his seventy-second year. *Athenæum*, October 14th, 1882, p. 500.

‡ The letter is enthusiastically laudatory, and obviously full of genuine feeling.

Geologists.	Zoologists and Palæontologists.	Physiologists.	Botanists.
Lyell.	Huxley.	Carpenter.	Hooker.
Ramsay.*	J. Lubbock.	Sir H. Holland (to large extent).	H. C. Watson.
Jukes.†	L. Jenyns (to large extent).		Asa Gray (to some extent).
H. D. Rogers.	Searles Wood.‡		Dr. Boott (to large extent),
			Thwaites.

[The following letter is of interest in connection with the mention of Mr. Bentham in the last letter :]

G. Bentham to Francis Darwin.

25 Wilton Place, S. W.,
May 30th, 1882.

MY DEAR SIR,—In compliance with your note which I received last night, I send herewith the letters I have from your father. I should have done so on seeing the general request published in the papers, but that I did not think there were any among them which could be of any use to you. Highly flattered as I was by the kind and friendly notice with which Mr. Darwin occasionally honoured me, I was never admitted into his intimacy, and he therefore never made any communications to me in relation to his views and labours. I have been throughout one of his most sincere admirers, and

---

* Andrew Ramsay, late Director-General of the Geological Survey.

† Joseph Beete Jukes, M. A., F. R. S., born 1811, died 1869. He was educated at Cambridge, and from 1842 to 1846 he acted as naturalist to H. M. S. *Fly*, on an exploring expedition in Australia and New Guinea. He was afterwards appointed Director of the Geological Survey of Ireland. He was the author of many papers, and of more than one good hand-book of geology.

‡ Searles Valentine Wood, born Feb. 14, 1798, died 1880. Chiefly known for his work on the Mollusca of the 'Crag.'

fully adopted his theories and conclusions, notwithstanding the severe pain and disappointment they at first occasioned me. On the day that his celebrated paper was read at the Linnean Society, July 1st, 1858, a long paper of mine had been set down for reading, in which, in commenting on the British Flora, I had collected a number of observations and facts illustrating what I then believed to be a fixity in species, however difficult it might be to assign their limits, and showing a tendency of abnormal forms produced by cultivation or otherwise, to withdraw within those original limits when left to themselves. Most fortunately my paper had to give way to Mr. Darwin's and when once that was read, I felt bound to defer mine for reconsideration ; I ·began to entertain doubts on the subject, and on the appearance of the 'Origin of Species,' I was forced, however reluctantly, to give up my long-cherished convictions, the results of much labour and study, and I cancelled all that part of my paper which urged original fixity, and published only portions of the remainder in another form, chiefly in the ' Natural History Review.' I have since acknowledged on various occasions my full adoption of Mr. Darwin's views, and chiefly in my Presidential Address of 1863, and in my thirteenth and last address, issued in the form of a report to the British Association at its meeting at Belfast in 1874.

I prize so highly the letters that I have of Mr. Darwin's, that I should feel obliged by your returning them to me when you have done with them. Unfortunately I have not kept the envelopes, and Mr. Darwin usually only dated them by the month not by the year, so that they are not in any chronological order.

Yours very sincerely,
GEORGE BENTHAM.

C. Darwin to C. Lyell.

Down [March] 12th [1860].

MY DEAR LYELL,—Thinking over what we talked about, the high state of intellectual development of the old Grecians with the little or no subsequent improvement, being an apparent difficulty, it has just occurred to me that in fact the case harmonises perfectly with our views. The case would be a decided difficulty on the Lamarckian or Vestigian doctrine of necessary progression, but on the view which I hold of progression depending on the conditions, it is no objection at all, and harmonises with the other facts of progression in the corporeal structure of other animals. For in a state of anarchy, or despotism, or bad government, or after irruption of barbarians, force, strength, or ferocity, and not intellect, would be apt to gain the day.

We have so enjoyed your and Lady Lyell's visit.

Good-night.

C. DARWIN.

P.S.—By an odd chance (for I had not alluded even to the subject) the ladies attacked me this evening, and threw the high state of old Grecians into my teeth, as an unanswerable difficulty, but by good chance I had my answer all pat, and silenced them. Hence I have thought it worth scribbling to you. . . .

C. Darwin to J. Prestwich.*

Down, March 12th [1860].

. . . At some future time, when you have a little leisure, and when you have read my 'Origin of Species,' I should esteem it a *singular* favour if you would send me any general criticisms. I do not mean of unreasonable length, but such as you could include in a letter. I have always admired your various memoirs so much that I should be eminently glad to receive your opinion, which might be of real service to me.

Pray do not suppose that I expect to *convert* or *pervert* you ; if I could stagger you in ever so slight a degree I should be satisfied ; nor fear to annoy me by severe criticisms, for I have had some hearty kicks from some of my best

* Now Professor of Geology in the University of Oxford.

friends. If it would not be disagreeable to you to send me your opinion, I certainly should be truly obliged. . . .

C. Darwin to Asa Gray.

Down, April 3rd [1860].

. . . . I remember well the time when the thought of the eye made me cold all over, but I have got over this stage of the complaint, and now small trifling particulars of structure often make me very uncomfortable. The sight of a feather in a peacock's tail, whenever I gaze at it, makes me sick ! . . .

You may like to hear about reviews on my book. Sedgwick (as I and Lyell feel *certain* from internal evidence) has reviewed me savagely and unfairly in the *Spectator*.* The notice includes much abuse, and is hardly fair in several respects. He would actually lead any one, who was ignorant of geology, to suppose that I had invented the great gaps between successive geological formations, instead of its being an almost universally admitted dogma. But my dear old friend Sedgwick, with his noble heart, is old, and is rabid with indignation. It is hard to please every one; you may remember that in my last letter I asked you to leave out about the Weald denudation : I told Jukes this (who is head man of the Irish geological survey), and he blamed me much, for he believed every word of it, and thought it not at all exaggerated ! In fact, geologists have no means of gauging the infinitude of past time. There has been one prodigy of a review, namely, an *opposed* one (by Pictet,† the palæontologist, in the Bib. Universelle of Geneva) which is *perfectly* fair and

---

* See the quotations which follow the present letter.

† François Jules Pictet, in the 'Archives des Sciences de la Bibliothèque Universelle,' Mars 1860. The article is written in a courteous and considerate tone, and concludes by saying that the 'Origin' will be of real value to naturalists, especially if they are not led away by its seductive arguments to believe in the dangerous doctrine of modification. A passage which seems to have struck my father as being valuable, and opposite which he has made double pencil marks and written the word "good," is worth quoting: " La théorie de M. Darwin s'accorde mal avec

just, and I agree to every word he says ; our only difference being that he attaches less weight to arguments in favour, and more to arguments opposed, than I do. Of all the opposed reviews, I think this the only quite fair one, and I never expected to see one. Please observe that I do not class your review by any means as opposed, though you think so yourself! It has done me *much* too good service ever to appear in that rank in my eyes. But I fear I shall weary you with so much about my book. I should rather think there was a good chance of my becoming the most egotistical man in all Europe ! What a proud pre-eminence ! Well, you have helped to make me so and therefore you must forgive me if you can.

My dear Gray, ever yours most gratefully,
C. DARWIN.

[In a letter to Sir Charles Lyell reference is made to Sedgwick's review in the *Spectator*, March 24 :

"I now feel certain that Sedgwick is the author of the article in the *Spectator*. No one else could use such abusive terms. And what a misrepresentation of my notions ! Any ignoramus would suppose that I had *first* broached the doctrine, that the breaks between successive formations marked long intervals of time. It is very unfair. But poor dear old Sedgwick seems rabid on the question. " Demoralised understanding ! " If ever I talk with him I will tell him that I never could believe that an inquisitor could be a good man ; but now I know that a man may roast another, and yet have as kind and noble a heart as Sedgwick's."

The following passages are taken from the review :

"I need hardly go on any further with these objections. But I cannot conclude without expressing my detestation of

---

l'histoire des types à formes bien tranchées et definies qui paraissent n'avoir vécu que pendant un temps limité. On en pourrait citer des centaines d'exemples, tel que les reptiles volants, les ichthyosaures, les bélemnites, les ammonites, &c." Pictet was born in 1809, died 1872 ; he was Professor of Anatomy and Zoology at Geneva.

the theory, because of its unflinching materalism ;—because it has deserted the inductive track, the only track that leads to physical truth ;—because it utterly repudiates final causes, and thereby indicates a demoralised understanding on the part of its advocates."

"Not that I believe that Darwin is an atheist ; though I cannot but regard his materialism as atheistical. I think it untrue, because opposed to the obvious course of nature, and the very opposite of inductive truth. And I think it intensely mischievous."

"Each series of facts is laced together by a series of assumptions, and repetitions of the one false principle. You cannot make a good rope out of a string of air bubbles."

"But any startling and (supposed) novel paradox, maintained very boldly and with something of imposing plausibility, produces in some minds a kind of pleasing excitement which predisposes them in its favour ; and if they are unused to careful reflection, and averse to the labour of accurate investigation, they will be likely to conclude that what is (apparently) *original*, must be a production of original *genius*, and that anything very much opposed to prevailing notions must be a grand *discovery*,—in short, that whatever comes from the 'bottom of a well' must be the 'truth' supposed to be hidden there."

In a review in the December number of 'Macmillan's Magazine,' 1860, Fawcett vigorously defended my father from the charge of employing a false method of reasoning ; a charge which occurs in Sedgwick's review, and was made at the time *ad nauseam*, in such phrases as : "This is not the true Baconian method." Fawcett repeated his defence at the meeting of the British Association in 1861.*]

---

* See an interesting letter from my father in Mr. Stephen's 'Life of Henry Fawcett,' 1886, p. 101.

C. Darwin to W. B. Carpenter.

Down, April 6th [1860].

MY DEAR CARPENTER,—I have this minute finished your review in the 'Med. Chirurg. Review.'* You must let me express my admiration at this most able essay, and I hope to God it will be largely read, for it must produce a great effect. I ought not, however, to express such warm admiration, for you give my book, I fear, far too much praise. But you have gratified me extremely ; and though I hope I do not care very much for the approbation of the non-scientific readers, I cannot say that this is at all so with respect to such few men as yourself. I have not a criticism to make, for I object to not a word ; and I admire all, so that I cannot pick out one part as better than the rest. It is all so well balanced. But it is impossible not to be struck with your extent of knowledge in geology, botany, and zoology. The extracts which you give from Hooker seem to me *excellently* chosen, and most forcible. I am so much pleased in what you say also about Lyell. In fact I am in a fit of enthusiasm, and had better write no more. With cordial thanks,

Yours very sincerely,

C. DARWIN.

C. Darwin to C. Lyell.

Down, April 10th [1860].

MY DEAR LYELL,—Thank you much for your note of the 4th ; I am very glad to hear that you are at Torquay. I should have amused myself earlier by writing to you, but I have had Hooker and Huxley staying here, and they have fully occupied my time, as a little of anything is a full dose for me. . . . There has been a plethora of reviews, and I am really quite sick of myself. There is a very long review by Carpenter in the 'Medical and Chirurg. Review,' very good

---

* April 1860.

and well balanced, but not brilliant. He discusses Hooker's books at as great length as mine, and makes excellent extracts; but I could not get Hooker to feel the least interest in being praised.

Carpenter speaks of you in thoroughly proper terms. There is a *brilliant* review by Huxley,* with capital hits, but I do not know that he much advances the subject. I *think* I have convinced him that he has hardly allowed weight enough to the case of varieties of plants being in some degrees sterile.

To diverge from reviews : Asa Gray sends me from Wyman (who will write), a good case of all the pigs being black in the Everglades of Virginia. On asking about the cause, it seems (I have got capital analogous cases) that when the *black* pigs eat a certain nut their bones become red, and they suffer to a certain extent, but that the *white* pigs lose their hoofs and perish, "and we aid by *selection*, for we kill most of the young white pigs." This was said by men who could hardly read. By the way, it is a great blow to me that you cannot admit the potency of natural selection. The more I think of it, the less I doubt its power for great and small changes. I have just read the 'Edinburgh,' † which without doubt is by ——. It is extremely malignant, clever, and I fear will be very damaging. He is atrociously severe on Huxley's lecture, and very bitter against Hooker. So we three *enjoyed* it together. Not that I really enjoyed it, for it made me uncomfortable for one night; but I have got quite over it to-day. It requires much study to appreciate all the bitter spite of many of the remarks against me ; indeed I did not discover all myself. It scandalously misrepresents many parts. He misquotes some passages, altering words within inverted commas. . . .

It is painful to be hated in the intense degree with which —— hates me.

---

* Westminster Review,' April 1860.

† ' Edinburgh Review,' April 1860.

Now for a curious thing about my book, and then I have done. In last Saturday's *Gardeners' Chronicle*,* a Mr. Patrick Matthew publishes a long extract from his work on 'Naval Timber and Arboriculture,' published in 1831, in which he briefly but completely anticipates the theory of Natural Selection. I have ordered the book, as some few passages are rather obscure, but it is certainly, I think, a complete but not developed anticipation! Erasmus always said that surely this would be shown to be the case some day. Anyhow, one may be excused in not having discovered the fact in a work on Naval Timber.

I heartily hope that your Torquay work may be successful. Give my kindest remembrances to Falconer, and I hope he is pretty well. Hooker and Huxley (with Mrs. Huxley) were extremely pleasant. But poor dear Hooker is tired to death of my book, and it is a marvel and a prodigy if you are not worse tired—if that be possible. Farewell, my dear Lyell,

Yours affectionately,
C. DARWIN.

C. Darwin to J. D. Hooker.

Down [April 13th, 1860].

MY DEAR HOOKER,—Questions of priority so often lead to odious quarrels, that I should esteem it a great favour if you would read the enclosed.† If you think it proper that I

---

* April 7th, 1860.

† My father wrote (*Gardeners' Chronicle*, 1860, p. 362, April 21st): "I have been much interested by Mr. Patrick Matthew's communication in the number of your paper dated April 7th. I freely acknowledge that Mr. Matthew has anticipated by many years the explanation which I have offered of the origin of species, under the name of natural selection. I think that no one will feel surprised that neither I, nor apparently any other naturalist, had heard of Mr. Matthew's views, considering how briefly they are given, and that they appeared in the appendix to a work on Naval Timber and Arboriculture. I can do no more than offer my apologies to Mr. Matthew for my entire ignorance of this publication. If an-

should send it (and of this there can hardly be any question), and if you think it full and ample enough, please alter the date to the day on which you post it, and let that be soon. The case in the *Gardeners' Chronicle* seems a *little* stronger than in Mr. Matthew's book, for the passages are therein scattered in three places ; but it would be mere hair-splitting to notice that.   If you object to my letter, please return it ; but I do not expect that you will, but I thought that you would not object to run your eye over it.   My dear Hooker, it is a great thing for me to have so good, true, and old a friend as you.   I owe much for science to my friends.

Many thanks for Huxley's lecture.   The latter part seemed to be grandly eloquent.

. . . I have gone over [the ' Edinburgh '] review again, and compared passages, and I am astonished at the misrepresentations.   But I am glad I resolved not to answer.   Perhaps it is selfish, but to answer and think more on the subject is too unpleasant.   I am so sorry that Huxley by my means has been thus atrociously attacked.   I do not suppose you much care about the gratuitous attack on you.

Lyell in his letter remarked that you seemed to him as if you were overworked.   Do, pray, be cautious, and remember how many and many a man has done this—who thought it absurd till too late.   I have often thought the same.   You know that you were bad enough before your Indian journey.

C. Darwin to C. Lyell.

Down, April [1860].

MY DEAR LYELL,—I was very glad to get your nice long letter from Torquay.   A press of letters prevented me writing

---

other edition of my work is called for, I will insert to the foregoing effect."   In spite of my father's recognition of his claims, Mr. Matthew remained unsatisfied, and complained that an article in the ' Saturday Analyst and Leader' was " scarcely fair in alluding to Mr. Darwin as the parent of the origin of species, seeing that I published the whole that Mr. Darwin attempts to prove, more than twenty-nine years ago."—*Saturday Analyst and Leader*, Nov. 24, 1860.

to Wells. I was particularly glad to hear what you thought about not noticing [the 'Edinburgh'] review. Hooker and Huxley thought it a sort of duty to point out the alteration of quoted citations, and there is truth in this remark; but I so hated the thought that I resolved not to do so. I shall come up to London on Saturday the 14th, for Sir B. Brodie's party, as I have an accumulation of things to do in London, and will (if I do not hear to the contrary) call about a quarter before ten on Sunday morning, and sit with you at breakfast, but will not sit long, and so take up much of your time. I must say one more word about our quasi-theological controversy about natural selection, and let me have your opinion when we meet in London. Do you consider that the successive variations in the size of the crop of the Pouter Pigeon, which man has accumulated to please his caprice, have been due to "the creative and sustaining powers of Brahma?" In the sense that an omnipotent and omniscient Deity must order and know everything, this must be admitted; yet, in honest truth, I can hardly admit it. It seems preposterous that a maker of a universe should care about the crop of a pigeon solely to please man's silly fancies. But if you agree with me in thinking such an interposition of the Deity uncalled for, I can see no reason whatever for believing in such interpositions in the case of natural beings, in which strange and admirable peculiarities have been naturally selected for the creature's own benefit. Imagine a Pouter in a state of nature wading into the water and then, being buoyed up by its inflated crop, sailing about in search of food. What admiration this would have excited—adaptation to the laws of hydrostatic pressure, &c. &c. For the life of me I cannot see any difficulty in natural selection producing the most exquisite structure, *if such structure can be arrived at by gradation*, and I know from experience how hard it is to name any structure towards which at least some gradations are not known.

Ever yours,

C. DARWIN.

P.S.—The conclusion at which I have come, as I have told Asa Gray, is that such a question, as is touched on in this note, is beyond the human intellect, like " predestination and free will," or the " origin of evil."

C. Darwin to J. D. Hooker.

Down [April 18th, 1860].

MY DEAR HOOKER,—I return ——'s letter. . . . Some of my relations say it cannot *possibly* be ——'s article,* because the reviewer speaks so very highly of —— Poor dear simple folk ! My clever neighbour, Mr. Norman, says the article is so badly written, with no definite object, that no one will read it. . . . Asa Gray has sent me an article † from the United States, clever, and dead against me. But one argument is funny. The reviewer says, that if the doctrine were true, geological strata would be full of monsters which have failed ! A very clear view this writer had of the struggle for existence !

. . . . I am glad you like Adam Bede so much. I was charmed with it. . . .

We think you must by mistake have taken with your own numbers of the ' National Review ' my precious number.‡ I wish you would look.

C. Darwin to Asa Gray.

Down, April 25th [1860].

MY DEAR GRAY,—I have no doubt I have to thank you for the copy of a review on the ' Origin ' in the ' North

---

* The ' Edinburgh Review.'

† ' North American Review,' April, 1860. " By Professor Bowen," is written on my father's copy. The passage referred to occurs at p. 488, where the author says that we ought to find " an infinite number of other varieties—gross, rude, and purposeless—the unmeaning creations of an unconscious cause."

‡ This no doubt refers to the January number, containing Dr. Carpenter's review of the ' Origin.'

American Review.' It seems to me clever, and I do not doubt will damage my book. I had meant to have made some remarks on it ; but Lyell wished much to keep it, and my head is quite confused between the many reviews which I have lately read. I am sure the reviewer is wrong about bees' cells, *i.e.* about the distance ; any lesser distance would do, or even greater distance, but then some of the places would lie outside the generative spheres ; but this would not add much difficulty to the work. The reviewer takes a strange view of instinct : he seems to regard intelligence as a developed instinct ; which I believe to be wholly false. I suspect he has never much attended to instinct and the minds of animals, except perhaps by reading.

My chief object is to ask you if you could procure for me a copy of the *New York Times* for Wednesday, March 28th. It contains *a very striking* review of my book, which I should much like to keep. How curious that the two most striking reviews (*i.e.* yours and this) should have appeared in America. This review is not really useful, but somehow is impressive. There was a good review in the 'Revue des Deux Mondes,' April 1st, by M. Laugel, said to be a very clever man.

Hooker, about a fortnight ago, stayed here a few days, and was very pleasant ; but I think he overworks himself. What a gigantic undertaking, I imagine, his and Bentham's 'Genera Plantarum' will be ! I hope he will not get too much immersed in it, so as not to spare some time for Geographical Distribution and other such questions.

I have begun to work steadily, but very slowly as usual, at details on variation under domestication.

My dear Gray,

Yours always truly and gratefully,

C. DARWIN.

C. Darwin to C. Lyell.

Down [May 8th, 1860].

. . . . . . I have sent for the 'Canadian Naturalist.' If I cannot procure a copy I will borrow yours. I had a letter from Henslow this morning, who says that Sedgwick was, on last Monday night, to open a battery on me at the Cambridge Philosophical Society. Anyhow, I am much honoured by being attacked there, and at the Royal Society of Edinburgh.

I do not think it worth while to contradict single cases, nor is it worth while arguing against those who do not attend to what I state. A moment's reflection will show you that there must be (on our doctrine) large genera not varying (see p. 56 on the subject, in the second edition of the ' Origin '). Though I do not there discuss the case in detail.

It may be sheer bigotry for my own notions, but I prefer to the Atlantis, my notion of plants and animals having migrated from the Old to the New World, or conversely, when the climate was much hotter, by approximately the line of Behring's Straits. It is most important, as you say, to see living forms of plants going back so far in time. I wonder whether we shall ever discover the flora of the dry land of the coal period, and find it not so anomalous as the swamp or coal-making flora. I am working away over the blessed Pigeon Manuscript; but, from one cause or another, I get on very slowly. . . .

This morning I got a letter from the Academy of Natural Sciences of Philadelphia, announcing·that I am elected a correspondent. . . . It shows that some Naturalists there do not think me such a scientific profligate as many think me here.

My dear Lyell, yours gratefully,

C. DARWIN.

P.S.—What a grand fact about the extinct stag's horn worked by man !

C. Darwin to J. D. Hooker.

Down [May 13th, 1860].

MY DEAR HOOKER,—I return Henslow, which I was very glad to see. How good of him to defend me.* I will write and thank him.

---

* Against Sedgwick's attack before the Cambridge Philosophical Society.

As you said you were curious to hear Thomson's * opinion, I send his kind letter. He is evidently a strong opposer to us. . . . . .

C. Darwin to J. D. Hooker.

Down [May 15th, 1860].

. . . . . . How paltry it is in such men as X, Y and Co. not reading your essay. It is incredibly paltry.† They may all attack me to their hearts' content. I am got case-hardened. As for the old fogies in Cambridge, it really signifies nothing. I look at their attacks as a proof that our work is worth the doing. It makes me resolve to buckle on my armour. I see plainly tnat it will be a long uphill fight. But think of Lyell's progress with Geology. One thing I see most plainly, that without Lyell's, yours, Huxley's, and Carpenter's aid, my book would have been a mere flash in the pan. But if we all stick to it, we shall surely gain the day. And I now see that the battle is worth fighting. I deeply hope that you think so. Does Bentham progress at all? I do not know what to say about Oxford.‡ I should like it much with you, but it must depend on health. . . .

Yours most affectionately,

C. DARWIN.

C. Darwin to C. Lyell.

Down, May 18th [1860].

MY DEAR LYELL,—I send a letter from Asa Gray to show how hotly the battle rages there. Also one from Wallace, very just in his remarks, though too laudatory and too modest, and how admirably free from envy or jealousy. He must be

---

* Dr. Thomas Thomson the Indian Botanist. He was a collaborateur in Hooker and Thomson's Flora Indica. 1855.

† These remarks do not apply to Dr. Harvey, who was, however, in a somewhat similar position. See p. 107.

‡ His health prevented him from going to Oxford for the meeting of the British Association.

a good fellow.   Perhaps I will enclose a letter from Thomson of Calcutta; not that it is much, but Hooker thinks so highly of him. . . .

Henslow informs me that Sedgwick * and then Professor Clarke [*sic*] † made a regular and savage onslaught on my book lately at the Cambridge Philosophical Society, but Henslow seems to have defended me well, and maintained that the subject was a legitimate one for investigation.   Since then Phillips ‡ has given lectures at Cambridge on the same subject, but treated it very fairly.   How splendidly Asa Gray is fighting the battle.   The effect on me of these multiplied attacks is simply to show me that the subject is worth fighting for, and assuredly I will do my best. . . .   I hope all the attacks make you keep up your courage, and courage you assuredly will require. . . .

C. Darwin to A. R. Wallace.

Down, May 18th, 1860.

My dear Mr. Wallace,—I received this morning your letter from Amboyna, dated February 16th, containing some remarks and your too high approval of my book.   Your letter has pleased me very much, and I most completely agree with you on the parts which are strongest and which are weakest. The imperfection of the Geological Record is, as you say, the weakest of all; but yet I am pleased to find that there are almost more geological converts than of pursuers of other

---

* Sedgwick's address is given somewhat abbreviated in *The Cambridge Chronicle*, May 19th, 1860.

† The late William Clark, Professor of Anatomy.   My father seems to have misunderstood his informant.   I am assured by Mr. J. W. Clark that his father (Prof. Clark) did not support Sedgwick in the attack.

‡ John Phillips, M. A., F. R. S., born 1800, died 1874, from the effects of a fall.   Professor of Geology at King's College, London, and afterwards at Oxford.   He gave the 'Rede' lecture at Cambridge on May 15th, 1860, on 'The Succession of Life on the earth.'   The Rede Lecturer is appointed annually by the Vice-Chancellor, and is paid by an endowment left in 1524 by Sir Robert Rede, Lord Chief Justice, in the reign of Henry VIII.

branches of natural science. . . . I think geologists are more easily converted than simple naturalists, because more accustomed to reasoning. Before telling you about the progress of opinion on the subject, you must let me say how I admire the generous manner in which you speak of my book. Most persons would in your position have felt some envy or jealousy. How nobly free you seem to be of this common failing of mankind. But you speak far too modestly of yourself. You would, if you had my leisure, have done the work just as well, perhaps better, than I have done it. . . . .

. . . Agassiz sends me a personal civil message, but incessantly attacks me ; but Asa Gray fights like a hero in defence. Lyell keeps as firm as a tower, and this Autumn will publish on the 'Geological History of Man,' and will then declare his conversion, which now is universally known. I hope that you have received Hooker's splendid essay. . . . Yesterday I heard from Lyell that a German, Dr. Schaaffhausen,* has sent him a pamphlet published some years ago, in which the same view is nearly anticipated ; but I have not yet seen this pamphlet. My brother, who is a very sagacious man, always said, "you will find that some one will have been before you." I am at work at my larger work, which I shall publish in a separate volume. But from ill-health and swarms of letters, I get on very very slowly. I hope that I shall not have wearied you with these details. With sincere thanks for your letter, and with most deeply felt wishes for your success in science, and in every way, believe me,

Your sincere well-wisher,

C. DARWIN.

---

* Hermann Schaaffhausen 'Ueber Beständigkeit und Umwandlung der Arten.' Verhandl. d. Naturhist. Vereins, Bonn, 1853. See 'Origin,' Historical Sketch.

C. Darwin to Asa Gray.

Down, May 22nd [1860].

MY DEAR GRAY,—Again I have to thank you for one of
your very pleasant letters of May 7th, enclosing a very pleasant remittance of £22. I am in simple truth astonished at
all the kind trouble you have taken for me. I return Appleton's account. For the chance of your wishing for a formal
acknowledgment I send one. If you have any further communication to the Appletons, pray express my acknowledgment for [their] generosity; for it is generosity in my opinion.
I am not at all surprised at the sale diminishing; my extreme
surprise is at the greatness of the sale. No doubt the public
has been *shamefully* imposed on! for they bought the book
thinking that it would be nice easy reading. I expect the sale
to stop soon in England, yet Lyell wrote to me the other day
that calling at Murray's he heard that fifty copies had gone in
the previous forty-eight hours. I am extremely glad that you
will notice in 'Silliman' the additions in the 'Origin.' Judging from letters (and I have just seen one from Thwaites to
Hooker), and from remarks, the most serious omission in my
book was not explaining how it is, as I believe, that all forms
do not necessarily advance, how there can now be *simple* organisms still existing. . . . I hear there is a *very* severe review
on me in the 'North British,' by a Rev. Mr. Dunns,* a Free
Kirk minister, and dabbler in Natural History. I should be
very glad to see any good American reviews, as they are all
more or less useful. You say that you shall touch on other
reviews. Huxley told me some time ago that after a time he
would write a review on all the reviews, whether he will I
know not. If you allude to the 'Edinburgh,' pray notice *some*
of the points which I will point out on a separate slip. In
the *Saturday Review* (one of our cleverest periodicals) of May
5th, p. 573, there is a nice article on [the 'Edinburgh'] re-

---

* This statement as to authorship was made on the authority of Robert
Chambers.

view, defending Huxley, but not Hooker; and the latter, I think, [the 'Edinburgh' reviewer] treats most ungenerously.* But surely you will get sick unto death of me and my reviewers.

With respect to the theological view of the question. This is always painful to me. I am bewildered. I had no intention to write atheistically. But I own that I cannot see as plainly as others do, and as I should wish to do, evidence of design and beneficence on all sides of us. There seems to me too much misery in the world. I cannot persuade myself that a beneficent and omnipotent God would have designedly created the Ichneumonidæ with the express intention of their feeding within the living bodies of Caterpillars, or that a cat should play with mice. Not believing this, I see no necessity in the belief that the eye was expressly designed. On the other hand, I cannot anyhow be contented to view this wonderful universe, and especially the nature of man, and to conclude that everything is the result of brute force. I am inclined to look at everything as resulting from designed laws, with the details, whether good or bad, left to the working out of what we may call chance. Not that this notion *at all* satisfies me. I feel most deeply that the whole subject is too profound for the human intellect. A dog might as well speculate on the mind of Newton. Let each man hope and believe what he can. Certainly I agree with you that my views are not at all necessarily atheistical. The lightning kills a man, whether a good one or bad one, owing to the excessively complex action of natural laws. A child (who may turn out an idiot) is born by the action of even more complex laws, and I can see no reason why a man, or other animal, may not have been aboriginally produced by other laws, and that all these laws may have been expressly designed by an

---

* In a letter to Mr. Huxley my father wrote : " Have you seen the last *Saturday Review?* I am very glad of the defence of you and of myself. I wish the reviewer had noticed Hooker. The reviewer, whoever he is, is a jolly good fellow, as this review and the last on me showed. He writes capitally, and understands well his subject. I wish he had slapped [the 'Edinburgh' reviewer] a little bit harder."

omniscient Creator, who foresaw every future event and consequence. But the more I think the more bewildered I become ; as indeed I probably have shown by this letter.

Most deeply do I feel your generous kindness and interest.

Yours sincerely and cordially,

CHARLES DARWIN.

[Here follow my father's criticisms on the 'Edinburgh
Review' :

"What a quibble to pretend he did not understand what I
meant by *inhabitants* of South America ; and any one would
suppose that I had not throughout my volume touched on
Geographical Distribution. He ignores also everything
which I have said on Classification, Geological Succession,
Homologies, Embryology, and Rudimentary Organs—p. 496.

He falsely applies what I said (too rudely) about "blindness of preconceived opinions " to those who believe in creation, whereas I exclusively apply the remark to those who give
up multitudes of species as true species, but believe in the
remainder—p. 500.

He slightly alters what I say,—I *ask* whether creationists
really believe that elemental atoms have flashed into life. He
says that I describe them as so believing, and this, surely, is a
difference—p. 501.

He speaks of my "clamouring against" all who believe
in creation, and this seems to me an unjust accusation—
p. 501.

He makes me say that the dorsal vertebræ vary ; this is
simply false : I nowhere say a word about dorsal vertebræ—
p. 522.

What an illiberal sentence that is about my pretension to
candour, and about my rushing through barriers which stopped
Cuvier : such an argument would stop any progress in science
—p. 525.

How disingenuous to quote from my remark to you about
my *brief* letter [published in the ' Linn. Soc. Journal '], as if
it applied to the whole subject—p. 530.

How disingenuous to say that we are called on to accept the theory, from the imperfection of the geological record, when I over and over again [say] how grave a difficulty the imperfection offers—p. 530."]

C. Darwin to J. D. Hooker.

Down, May 30th [1860].

MY DEAR HOOKER,—I return Harvey's letter, I have been very glad to see the reason why he has not read your Essay. I feared it was bigotry, and I am glad to see that he goes a little way (*very much* further than I supposed) with us. . . .

I was not sorry for a natural opportunity of writing to Harvey, just to show that I was not piqued at his turning me and my book into ridicule,* not that I think it was a proceeding which I deserved, or worthy of him. It delights me that you are interested in watching the progress of opinion on the change of Species; I feared that you were weary of the subject; and therefore did not send A. Gray's letters. The battle rages furiously in the United States. Gray says he was preparing a speech, which would take $1\frac{1}{2}$ hours to deliver, and which he "fondly hoped would be a stunner." He is fighting splendidly, and there seems to have been many discussions with Agassiz and others at the meetings. Agassiz pities me much at being so deluded. As for the progress of opinion, I clearly see that it will be excessively slow, almost as slow as the change of species. . . . I am getting wearied at the storm of hostile reviews and hardly any useful. . . .

---

* A "serio-comic squib," read before the 'Dublin University Zoological and Botanical Association,' Feb. 17, 1860, and privately printed. My father's presentation copy is inscribed, "With the writer's *repentance*, Oct. 1860."

C. Darwin to C. Lyell.

Down, Friday night [June 1st, 1860].

. . . Have you seen Hopkins * in the new ' Fraser '? the public will, I should think, find it heavy. He will be dead against me, as you prophesied ; but he is generously civil to me personally.† On his standard of proof, *natural* science would never progress, for without the making of theories I am convinced there would be no observation.

---

* William Hopkins died in 1866, "in his seventy-third year." He began life with a farm in Suffolk, but ultimately entered, comparatively late in life, at Peterhouse, Cambridge ; he took his degree in 1827, and afterward became an Esquire Bedell of the University. He was chiefly known as a mathematical " coach," and was eminently successful in the manufacture of Senior Wranglers. Nevertheless Mr. Stephen says (' Life of Fawcett,' p. 26) that he " was conspicuous for inculcating " a " liberal view of the studies of the place. He endeavored to stimulate a philosophical interest in the mathematical sciences, instead of simply rousing an ardour for competition." He contributed many papers on geological and mathematical subjects to the scientific journals. He had a strong influence for good over the younger men with whom he came in contact. The letter which he wrote to Henry Fawcett on the occasion of his blindness illustrates this. Mr. Stephen says (' Life of Fawcett,' p. 48) that by " this timely word of good cheer," Fawcett was roused from " his temporary prostration," and enabled to take a " more cheerful and resolute tone."

† ' Fraser's Magazine,' June 1860. My father, no doubt, refers to the following passage, p. 752, where the Reviewer expresses his " full participation in the high respect in which the author is universally held, both as a man and a naturalist ; and the more so, because in the remarks which will follow in the second part of this Essay we shall be found to differ widely from him as regards many of his conclusions and the reasonings on which he has founded them, and shall claim the full right to express such differences of opinion with all that freedom which the interests of scientific truth demands, and which we are sure Mr. Darwin would be one of the last to refuse to any one prepared to exercise it with candour and courtesy." Speaking of this review, my father wrote to Dr. Asa Gray: " I have remonstrated with him [Hopkins] for so coolly saying that I base my views on what I reckon as great difficulties. Any one, by taking these difficulties alone, can make a most strong case against me. I could myself write a

. . . . I have begun reading the 'North British,'* which so far strikes me as clever.

Phillips's Lecture at Cambridge is to be published.

All these reiterated attacks will tell heavily; there will be no more converts, and probably some will go back. I hope you do not grow disheartened, I am determined to fight to the last. I hear, however, that the great Buckle highly approves of my book.

I have had a note from poor Blyth, † of Calcutta, who is much disappointed at hearing that Lord Canning will not grant any money; so I much fear that all your great pains will be thrown away. Blyth says (and he is in many respects a very good judge) that his ideas on species are quite revolutionized. . . .

C. Darwin to J. D. Hooker.

Down, June 5th [1860].

MY DEAR HOOKER,—It is a pleasure to me to write to you, as I have no one to talk about such matters as we write

---

more damning review than has as yet appeared!" A second notice by Hopkins appeared in the July number of 'Fraser's Magazine.'

* May 1860.

† Edward Blyth, born 1810, died 1873. His indomitable love of natural history made him neglect the druggist's business with which he started in life, and he soon got into serious difficulties. After supporting himself for a few years as a writer on Field Natural History, he ultimately went out to India as Curator of the Museum of the R. Asiatic Soc. of Bengal, where the greater part of his working life was spent. His chief publications were the monthly reports made as part of his duty to the Society. He had stored in his remarkable memory a wonderful wealth of knowledge, especially with regard to the mammalia and birds of India—knowledge of which he freely gave to those who asked. His letters to my father give evidence of having been carefully studied, and the long list of entries after his name in the index to 'Animals and Plants,' show how much help was received from him. His life was an unprosperous and unhappy one, full of money difficulties and darkened by the death of his wife after a few years of marriage.

on. But I seriously beg you not to write to me unless so inclined ; for busy as you are, and seeing many people, the case is very different between us. . . .

Have you seen ——'s abusive article on me ? . . . It outdoes even the 'North British' and 'Edinburgh' in misapprehension and misrepresentation. I never knew anything so unfair as in discussing cells of bees, his ignoring the case of Melipona, which builds combs almost exactly intermediate between hive and humble bees. What has —— done that he feels so immeasurably superior to all us wretched naturalists, and to all political economists, including that great philosopher Malthus ? This review, however, and Harvey's letter have convinced me that I must be a very bad explainer. Neither really understand what I mean by Natural Selection. I am inclined to give up the attempt as hopeless. Those who do not understand, it seems, cannot be made to understand.

By the way, I think, we entirely agree, except perhaps that I use too forcible language about selection. I entirely agree, indeed would almost go further than you when you say that climate (*i. e.* variability from all unknown causes) is "an active handmaid, influencing its mistress most materially." Indeed, I have never hinted that Natural Selection is "the efficient cause to the exclusion of the other," *i. e.* variability from Climate, &c. The very term *selection* implies something, *i. e.* variation or difference, to be selected. . . .

How does your book progress (I mean your general sort of book on plants), I hope to God you will be more successful than I have been in making people understand your meaning. I should begin to think myself wholly in the wrong, and that I was an utter fool, but then I cannot yet persuade myself, that Lyell, and you and Huxley, Carpenter, Asa Gray, and Watson, &c., are all fools together. Well, time will show, and nothing but time. Farewell. . . .

C. Darwin to C. Lyell.

Down, June 6th [1860].

. . . It consoles me that —— sneers at Malthus, for that clearly shows, mathematician though he may be, he cannot understand common reasoning.   By the way what a discouraging example Malthus is, to show during what long years the plainest case may be misrepresented and misunderstood.   I have read the 'Future'; how curious it is that several of my reviewers should advance such wild arguments, as that varieties of dogs and cats do not mingle ; and should bring up the old exploded doctrine of definite analogies . . . I am beginning to despair of ever making the majority understand my notions.   Even Hopkins does not thoroughly.   By the way, I have been so much pleased by the way he personally alludes to me.   I must be a very bad explainer.   I hope to Heaven that you will succeed better.   Several reviews and several letters have shown me too clearly how little I am understood.   I suppose "natural selection" was a bad term ; but to change it now, I think, would make confusion worse confounded, nor can I think of a better ; "Natural Preservation" would not imply a preservation of particular varieties, and would seem a truism, and would not bring man's and nature's selection under one point of view.   I can only hope by reiterated explanations finally to make the matter clearer. If my MS. spreads out, I think I shall publish one volume exclusively on variation of animals and plants under domestication.   I want to show that I have not been quite so rash as many suppose.

Though weary of reviews, I should like to see Lowell's * some time. . . . I suppose Lowell's difficulty about instinct is the same as Bowen's ; but it seems to me wholly to rest on the assumption that instincts cannot graduate as finely as

---

* The late J. A. Lowell in the 'Christian Examiner' (Boston, U. S., May, 1860.

structures. I have stated in my volume that it is hardly possible to know which, *i. e.* whether instinct or structure, change first by insensible steps. Probably sometimes instinct, sometimes structure. When a British insect feeds on an exotic plant, instinct has changed by very small steps, and their structures might change so as to fully profit by the new food. Or structure might change first, as the direction of tusks in one variety of Indian elephants, which leads it to attack the tiger in a different manner from other kinds of elephants. Thanks for your letter of the 2nd, chiefly about Murray. (N.B. Harvey of Dublin gives me, in a letter, the argument of tall men marrying short women, as one of great weight ! *)

I do not quite understand what you mean by saying, " that the more they prove that you underrate physical conditions, the better for you, as Geology comes in to your aid."

. . . I see in Murray and many others one incessant fallacy, when alluding to slight differences of physical conditions as being very important ; namely, oblivion of the fact that all species, except very local ones, range over a considerable area, and though exposed to what the world calls considerable *diversities*, yet keep constant. I have just alluded to this in the 'Origin' in comparing the productions of the Old and the New Worlds. Farewell, shall you be at Oxford? If H. gets quite well, perhaps I shall go there.

Yours affectionately,

C. DARWIN.

C. Darwin to C. Lyell.

Down [June 14th, 1860].

. . . Lowell's review † is pleasantly written, but it is clear that he is not a naturalist. He quite overlooks the importance of the accumulation of mere individual differences, and which, I think I can show, is the great agency of change

---

* See footnote, *ante*, p. 56.

† J. A. Lowell in the 'Christian Examiner,' May 1860.

under domestication. I have not finished Schaaffhausen, as i read German so badly. I have ordered a copy for myself, and should like to keep yours till my own arrives, but will return it to you instantly if wanted. He admits statements rather rashly, as I dare say I do. I see only one sentence as yet at all approaching natural selection.

There is a notice of me in the penultimate number of 'All the Year Round,' but not worth consulting; chiefly a well-done hash of my own words. Your last note was very interesting and consolatory to me.

I have expressly stated that I believe physical conditions have a more direct effect on plants than on animals. But the more I study, the more I am led to think that natural selection regulates, in a state of nature, most trifling differences. As squared stone, or bricks, or timber, are the indispensable materials for a building, and influence its character, so is variability not only indispensable, but influential. Yet in the same manner as the architect is the *all* important person in a building, so is selection with organic bodies. . . . . .

[The meeting of the British Association at Oxford in 1860 is famous for two pitched battles over the 'Origin of Species.' Both of them originated in unimportant papers. On Thursday, June 28, Dr. Daubeny of Oxford made a communication to Section D : "On the final causes of the sexuality of plants, with particular reference to Mr. Darwin's work on the 'Origin of Species.'" Mr. Huxley was called on by the President, but tried (according to the *Athenæum* report) to avoid a discussion, on the ground "that a general audience, in which sentiment would unduly interfere with intellect, was not the public before which such a discussion should be carried on." However, the subject was not allowed to drop. Sir R. Owen (I quote from the *Athenæum*, July 7, 1860), who "wished to approach this subject in the spirit of the philosopher," expressed his "conviction that there were facts by which the public could come to some conclusion with regard to the probabilities of the truth of Mr. Darwin's theory." He went on to say that the brain of the gorilla "presented more differences, as compared with the brain of man, than it did when compared with the brains of the very lowest and most problematical of the Quadrumana." Mr. Huxley replied, and gave these assertions a "direct and unqualified contradiction," pledging himself to "justify that unusual procedure elsewhere," * a pledge which he amply fulfilled.† On Friday there was peace, but on Saturday 30th, the battle arose with redoubled fury over a paper by Dr. Draper of New York, on the 'Intellectual development of Europe considered with reference to the views of Mr. Darwin.'

The following account is from an eye-witness of the scene.

" The excitement was tremendous. The Lecture-room, in which it had been arranged that the discussion should be held, proved far too small for the audience, and the meeting adjourned to the Library of the Museum, which was crammed to suffocation long before the champions entered the lists. The numbers were estimated at from 700 to 1000. Had it been term-time, or had the general public been admitted, it would have been impossible to have accommodated the rush to hear the oratory of the bold Bishop. Professor Henslow, the President of Section D, occupied the chair and wisely announced *in limine* that none who had not valid arguments to bring forward on one side or the other, would be allowed to address the meeting : a caution that proved necessary, for no fewer than four combatants had their utterances burked by him, because of their indulgence in vague declamation.

" The Bishop was up to time, and spoke for full half-an-hour with inimitable spirit, emptiness and unfairness. It was evident from his handling of the subject that he had been ' crammed ' up to the throat, and that he knew nothing at first hand ; in fact, he used no argument not to be found in his ' Quarterly ' article. He ridiculed Darwin badly, and Huxley savagely, but all in such dulcet tones, so persuasive a manner,

---

* 'Man's Place in Nature,' by T. H. Huxley, 1863, p. 114.
† See the ' Nat. Hist. Review,' 1861.

and in such well-turned periods, that I who had been inclined
to blame the President for allowing a discussion that could
serve no scientific purpose now forgave him from the bottom
of my heart.   Unfortunately the Bishop, hurried along on the
current of his own eloquence, so far forgot himself as to push
his attempted advantage to the verge of personality in a telling passage in which he turned round and addressed Huxley :
I forget the precise words, and quote from Lyell.   'The
Bishop asked whether Huxley was related by his grandfather's or grandmother's side to an ape.' *   Huxley replied
to the scientific argument of his opponent with force and eloquence, and to the personal allusion with a self-restraint, that
gave dignity to his crushing rejoinder."

Many versions of Mr. Huxley's speech were current : the
following report of his conclusion is from a letter addressed
by the late John Richard Green, then an undergraduate, to
a fellow-student, now Professor Boyd Dawkins. " I asserted,
and I repeat, that a man has no reason to be ashamed of
having an ape for his grandfather. If there were an ancestor
whom I should feel shame in recalling, it would be a *man*, a
man of restless and versatile intellect, who, not content with
an equivocal † success in his own sphere of activity, plunges
into scientific questions with which he has no real acquaintance, only to obscure them by an aimless rhetoric, and dis-
tract the attention of his hearers from the real point at issue
by eloquent digressions, and skilled appeals to religious
prejudice."

The letter above quoted continues :

" The excitement was now at its height ; a lady fainted
and had to be carried out, and it was some time before the
discussion was resumed. Some voices called for Hooker, and
his name having been handed up, the President invited him

---

* Lyell's 'Letters,' vol. ii. p. 335.

† Prof. V. Carus, who has a distinct recollection of the scene, does not
remember the word equivocal. He believes too that Lyell's version of the
" ape " sentence is slightly incorrect.

to give his view of the theory from the Botanical side. This
he did, demonstrating that the Bishop, by his own showing,
had never grasped the principles of the 'Origin,' * and that
he was absolutely ignorant of the elements of botanical science. The Bishop made no reply, and the meeting broke up.

"There was a crowded conversazione in the evening at
the rooms of the hospitable and genial Professor of Botany,
Dr. Daubeny, where the almost sole topic was the battle of
the 'Origin,' and I was much struck with the fair and unpre-
judiced way in which the black coats and white cravats of
Oxford discussed the question, and the frankness with which
they offered their congratulations to the winners in the
combat."]

C. Darwin to J. D. Hooker.

Sudbrook Park, Monday night
[July 2nd, 1860].

My dear Hooker,—I have just received your letter.   I
have been very poorly, with almost continuous bad headache
for forty-eight hours, and I was low enough, and thinking
what a useless burthen I was to myself and all others, when
your letter came, and it has so cheered me ; your kindness
and affection brought tears into my eyes. Talk of fame,
honour, pleasure, wealth, all are dirt compared with affection ;
and this is a doctrine with which, I know, from your letter,
that you will agree with from the bottom of your heart.
. . . How I should have liked to have wandered about
Oxford with you, if I had been well enough ; and how still
more I should have liked to have heard you triumphing
over the Bishop. I am astonished at your success and
audacity. It is something unintelligible to me how any one
can argue in public like orators do. I had no idea you had
this power. I have read lately so many hostile views, that I
was beginning to think that perhaps I was wholly in the

---

* With regard to the Bishop's ' Quarterly Review,' my father wrote :
" These very clever men think they can write a review with a very
slight knowledge of the book reviewed or subject in question."

wrong, and that —— was right when he said the whole subject would be forgotten in ten years ; but now that I hear that you and Huxley will fight publicly (which I am sure I never could do), I fully believe that our cause will, in the long-run, prevail. I am glad I was not in Oxford, for I should have been overwhelmed, with my [health] in its present state.

C. Darwin to T. H. Huxley.

Sudbrook Park, Richmond,
July 3rd (1860).

. . . . I had a letter from Oxford, written by Hooker late on Sunday night, giving me some account of the awful battles which have raged about species at Oxford. He tells me you fought nobly with Owen (but I have heard no particulars), and that you answered the B. of O. capitally. I often think that my friends (and you far beyond others) have good cause to hate me, for having stirred up so much mud, and led them into so much odious trouble. If I had been a friend of myself, I should have hated me. (How to make that sentence good English, I know not.) But remember, if I had not stirred up the mud, some one else certainly soon would. I honour your pluck ; I would as soon have died as tried to answer the Bishop in such an assembly. . . .

[On July 20th, my father wrote to Mr. Huxley :

" From all that I hear from several quarters, it seems that Oxford did the subject great good. It is of enormous importance, the showing the world that a few first-rate men are not afraid of expressing their opinion."]

C. Darwin to J. D. Hooker.

[July 1860.]

. . . . I have just read the ' Quarterly.' * It is uncommonly clever ; it picks out with skill all the most conjectural

---

* ' Quarterly Review,' July 1860. The article in question was by Wilberforce, Bishop of Oxford, and was afterwards published in his " Essays

parts, and brings forward well all the difficulties. It quizzes me quite splendidly by quoting the 'Anti-Jacobin' versus my Grandfather. You are not alluded to, nor, strange to say, Huxley; and I can plainly see, here and there, ——'s hand. The concluding pages will make Lyell shake in his shoes. By Jove, if he sticks to us, he will be a real hero. Goodnight. Your well-quizzed, but not sorrowful, and affectionate friend.   C. D.

I can see there has been some queer tampering with the Review, for a page has been cut out and reprinted.

[Writing on July 22 to Dr. Asa Gray my father thus refers to Lyell's position :—

Contributed to the 'Quarterly Review,' 1874." The passage from the 'Anti-Jacobin' gives the history of the evolution of space from the "primæval point or *punctum saliens* of the universe," which is conceived to have moved "forward in a right line, *ad infinitum*, till it grew tired ; after which the right line, which it had generated, would begin to put itself in motion in a lateral direction, describing an area of infinite extent. This area, as soon as it became conscious of its own existence, would begin to ascend or descend according as its specific gravity would determine it, forming an immense solid space filled with vacuum, and capable of containing the present universe."

The following (p. 263) may serve as an example of the passages in which the reviewer refers to Sir Charles Lyell :—" That Mr. Darwin should have wandered from this broad highway of nature's works into the jungle of fanciful assumption is no small evil. We trust that he is mistaken in believing that he may count Sir C. Lyell as one of his converts. We know, indeed, that the strength of the temptations which he can bring to bear upon his geological brother. . . . Yet no man has been more distinct and more logical in the denial of the transmutation of species than Sir C. Lyell, and that not in the infancy of his scientific life, but in its full vigour and maturity." The Bishop goes on to appeal to Lyell, in order that with his help " this flimsy speculation may be as completely put down as was what in spite of all denials we must venture to call its twin though less instructed brother, the 'Vestiges of Creation.'"

With reference to this article, Mr. Brodie Innes, my father's old friend and neighbour, writes :—" Most men would have been annoyed by an article written with the Bishop's accustomed vigour, a mixture of argument

"Considering his age, his former views and position in society, I think his conduct has been heroic on this subject."]

C. Darwin to Asa Gray.

[Hartfield, Sussex] July 22nd [1860].

MY DEAR GRAY,—Owing to absence from home at water-cure and then having to move my sick girl to whence I am now writing, I have only lately read the discussion in Proc. American Acad.,* and now I cannot resist expressing my sincere admiration of your most clear powers of reasoning. As Hooker lately said in a note to me, you are more than *any one* else the thorough master of the subject. I declare that you know my book as well as I do myself; and bring to the question new lines of illustration and argument in a manner which excites my astonishment and almost my envy! I admire these discussions, I think, almost more than your article in Silliman's Journal. Every single word seems weighed carefully, and tells like a 32-pound shot. It makes me much wish (but I know that you have not time) that you could write more in detail, and give, for instance, the facts on the variability of the American wild fruits. The *Athenæum* has the largest circulation, and I have sent my copy to the editor with a request that he would republish the first discussion; I much fear he will not, as he reviewed the subject in so hostile a spirit. . . . I shall be curious [to see] and will order the August number, as soon as I know that it contains your review of Reviews. My conclusion is that

---

and ridicule. Mr. Darwin was writing on some parish matter, and put a postscript—'If you have not seen the last 'Quarterly,' do get it; the Bishop of Oxford has made such capital fun of me and my grandfather.' By a curious coincidence, when I received the letter, I was staying in the same house with the Bishop, and showed it to him. He said, 'I am very glad he takes it in that way, he is such a capital fellow.'"

* April 10, 1860. Dr. Gray criticised in detail "several of the positions taken at the preceding meeting by Mr. [J. A.] Lowell, Prof. Bowen and Prof. Agassiz." It was reprinted in the *Athenæum*, Aug. 4, 1860.

you have made a mistake in being a botanist, you ought
to have been a lawyer.

. . . . Henslow * and Daubeny are shaken.   I hear from
Hooker that he hears from Hochstetter that my views are
making very considerable progress in Germany, and the good
workers are discussing the question.   Bronn at the end of his
translation has a chapter of criticism, but it is such difficult
German that I have not yet read it.   Hopkins's review in
' Fraser' is thought the best which has appeared against us.
I believe that Hopkins is so much opposed because his course
of study has never led him to reflect much on such subjects
as geographical distribution, classification, homologies, &c.,
so that he does not feel it a relief to have some kind of
explanation.

C. Darwin to C. Lyell.

Hartfield [Sussex], July 30th [1860].

. . . . I had lots of pleasant letters about the Brit.
Assoc., and our side seems to have got on very well.   There
has been as much discussion on the other side of the Atlantic
as on this.   No one I think understands the whole case better
than Asa Gray, and he has been fighting nobly.   He is a
capital reasoner.   I have sent one of his printed discussions
to our *Athenæum*, and the editor says he will print it.   The
' Quarterly' has been out some time.   It contains no malice,

---

* Professor Henslow was mentioned in the December number of ' Macmillan's Magazine' as being an adherent of Evolution.   In consequence
of this he published, in the February number of the following year, a letter defining his position.   This he did by means of an extract from a letter addressed to him by the Rev. L. Jenyns (Blomefield) which "very
nearly," as he says, expressed his views.   Mr. Blomefield wrote, " I was
not aware that you had become a convert to his (Darwin's) theory, and can
hardly suppose you have accepted it as a whole, though, like myself, you
may go to the length of imagining that many of the smaller groups, both of
animals and plants, may at some remote period have had a common parentage.   I do not with some say that the whole of his theory cannot be true
—but that it is very far from proved ; and I doubt its ever being possible
to prove it."

which is wonderful. . . . It makes me say many things which I do not say. At the end it quotes all your conclusions against Lamarck, and makes a solemn appeal to you to keep firm in the true faith. I fancy it will make you quake a little. —— has ingeniously primed the Bishop (with Murchison) against you as head of the uniformitarians. The only other review worth mentioning, which I can think of, is in the third No. of the 'London Review,' by some geologist, and favorable for a wonder. It is very ably done, and I should like much to know who is the author. I shall be very curious to hear on your return whether Bronn's German translation of the 'Origin' has drawn any attention to the subject. Huxley is eager about a 'Natural History Review,' which he and others are going to edit, and he has got so many first-rate assistants, that I really believe he will make it a first-rate production. I have been doing nothing, except a little botanical work as amusement. I shall hereafter be very anxious to hear how your tour has answered. I expect your book on the geological history of Man will, with a vengeance, be a bomb-shell. I hope it will not be very long delayed. Our kindest remembrances to Lady Lyell. This is not worth sending, but I have nothing better to say.

Yours affectionately,

C. DARWIN.

C. Darwin to F. Watkins.*

Down, July 30th, [1860?]

MY DEAR WATKINS,—Your note gave me real pleasure. Leading the retired life which I do, with bad health, I oftener think of old times than most men probably do ; and your face now rises before me, with the pleasant old expression, as vividly as if I saw you.

My book has been well abused, praised, and splendidly quizzed by the Bishop of Oxford ; but from what I see of its influence on really good workers in science, I feel confident

---

* See Vol. I. p. 144.

that, *in the main*, I am on the right road. With respect to your question, I think the arguments are valid, showing that all animals have descended from four or five primordial forms ; and that analogy and weak reasons go to show that all have descended from some single prototype.

Farewell, my old friend. I look back to old Cambridge days with unalloyed pleasure.

Believe me, yours most sincerely,
CHARLES DARWIN.

T. H. Huxley to C. Darwin.

August 6th, 1860.

MY DEAR DARWIN,—I have to announce a new and great ally for you. . . . .

Von Bär writes to me thus :—" Et outre cela, je trouve que vous écrivez encore des rédactions. Vous avez écrit sur l'ouvrage de M. Darwin une critique dont je n'ai trouvé que des débris dans un journal allemand. J'ai oublié le nom terrible du journal anglais dans lequel se trouve votre récension. En tout cas aussi je ne peux pas trouver le journal ici. Comme je m'intéresse beaucoup pour les idées de M. Darwin, sur lesquelles j'ai parlé publiquement et sur lesquelles je ferai peut-être imprimer quelque chose—vous m'obligeriez infiniment si vous pourriez me faire parvenir ce que vous avez écrit sur ces idées.

" J'ai énoncé les mêmes idées sur la transformation des types ou origine d'espèces que M. Darwin.* Mais c'est seulement sur la géographie zoologique que je m'appuie. Vous trouve-rez, dans le dernier chapitre du traité ' Ueber Papuas und Alfuren,' que j'en parle très décidément sans savoir que M. Darwin s'occupait de cet objet."

The treatise to which Von Bär refers he gave me when over here, but I have not been able to lay hands on it since this

---

* See footnote, Vol. I. p. 540.

letter reached me two days ago. When I find it I will let you know what there is in it.

Ever yours faithfully,

T. H. HUXLEY.

C. Darwin to T. H. Huxley.

Down, August 8 [1860].

MY DEAR HUXLEY—Your note contained magnificent news, and thank you heartily for sending it me. Von Baer weighs down with a vengeance all the virulence of [the 'Edinburgh' reviewer] and weak arguments of Agassiz. If you write to Von Baer, for heaven's sake tell him that we should think one nod of approbation on our side, of the greatest value ; and if he does write anything, beg him to send us a copy, for I would try and get it translated and published in the *Athenæum* and in 'Silliman' to touch up Agassiz. . . . . Have you seen Agassiz's weak metaphysical and theological attack on the 'Origin' in the last 'Silliman'? * I would send it you, but apprehend it would be less trouble for you to look at it in London than return it to me. R. Wagner has sent me a German pamphlet,† giving an abstract of Agassiz's 'Essay on Classification,' "mit Rücksicht auf Darwins Ansichten," &c. &c. He won't go very "dangerous lengths," but thinks the truth lies half-way between Agassiz and the 'Origin.' As he goes thus far he will, nolens volens, have to go further. He says he is going to review

---

* The 'American Journal of Science and Arts' (commonly called 'Silliman's Journal'), July 1860. Printed from advanced sheets of vol. iii. of 'Contributions to the Nat. Hist. of the U. S.' My father's copy has a pencilled " Truly " opposite the following passage :—" Unless Darwin and his followers succeed in showing that the struggle for life tends to something beyond favouring the existence of certain individuals over that of other individuals, they will soon find that they are following a shadow."

† ' Louis Agassiz's Prinzipien der Classification, &c., mit Rücksicht auf Darwins Ansichten. Separat-Abdruck aus den Göttingischen gelehrten Anzeigen,' 1860.

me in [his] yearly Report.   My good and kind agent for the propagation of the Gospel—*i. e.* the devil's gospel.

Ever yours,
C. DARWIN.

C. Darwin to C. Lyell.

Down, August 11th [1860].

. . . I have laughed at Woodward thinking that you were a man who could be influenced in your judgment by the voice of the public; and yet after mortally sneering at him, I was obliged to confess to myself, that I had had fears, what the effect might be of so many heavy guns fired by great men. As I have (sent by Murray) a spare 'Quarterly Review,' I send it by this post, as it may amuse you.   The Anti-Jacobin part amused me.   It is full of errors, and Hooker is thinking of answering it.   There has been a cancelled page; I should like to know what gigantic blunder it contained.   Hooker says that —— has played on the Bishop, and made him strike whatever note he liked; he has wished to make the article as disagreeable to you as possible.   I will send the *Athenæum* in a day or two.

As you wish to hear what reviews have appeared, I may mention that Agassiz has fired off a shot in the last 'Silliman,' not good at all, denies variations and rests on the perfection of Geological evidence.   Asa Gray tells me that a very clever friend has been almost converted to our side by this review of Agassiz's . . . Professor Parsons * has published in the same 'Silliman' a speculative paper correcting my notions, worth nothing.   In the 'Highland Agricultural Journal' there is a review by some Entomologist, not worth much.   This is all that I can remember. . . . As Huxley says, the platoon firing must soon cease.   Hooker and Huxley, and Asa Gray, I see, are determined to stick to the battle and not give in; I am fully convinced that whenever

---

* Theophilus Parsons, Professsor of Law in Harvard University.

you publish, it will produce a great effect on all *trimmers*, and on many others. By the way I forgot to mention Daubeny's pamphlet,* very liberal and candid, but scientifically weak. I believe Hooker is going nowhere this summer; he is excessively busy . . . He has written me many, most nice letters. I shall be very curious to hear on your return some account of your Geological doings. Talking of Geology, you used to be interested about the "pipes" in the chalk. About three years ago a perfectly circular hole suddenly appeared in a flat grass field to everyone's astonishment, and was filled up with many waggon loads of earth; and now two or three days ago, again it has circularly subsided about two feet more. How clearly this shows what is still slowly going on. This morning I recommenced work, and am at dogs; when I have written my short discussion on them, I will have it copied, and if you like, you can then see how the argument stands, about their multiple origin. As you seemed to think this important, it might be worth your reading; though I do not feel sure that you will come to the same probable conclusion that I have done. By the way, the Bishop makes a very telling case against me, by accumulating several instances where I speak very doubtfully; but this is very unfair, as in such cases as this of the dog, the evidence is and must be very doubtful. . . .

C. Darwin to Asa Gray.

Down, August 11 [1860].

MY DEAR GRAY,—On my return home from Sussex about a week ago, I found several articles sent by you. The first article, from the 'Atlantic Monthly,' I am very glad to possess. By the way, the editor of the *Athenæum* † has inserted your answer to Agassiz, Bowen, and Co., and when

---

* ' Remarks on the final causes of the sexuality of plants with particular reference to Mr. Darwin's work on the "Origin of Species." '—Brit. Assoc. Report, 1860.

† Aug. 4, 1860.

I therein read them, I admired them even more than at first. They really seemed to be admirable in their condensation, force, clearness and novelty.

I am surprised that Agassiz did not succeed in writing something better. How absurd that logical quibble—" if species do not exist, how can they vary?" As if any one doubted their temporary existence. How coolly he assumes that there is some clearly defined distinction between individual differences and varieties. It is no wonder that a man who calls identical forms, when found in two countries, distinct species, cannot find variation in nature. Again, how unreasonable to suppose that domestic varieties selected by man for his own fancy (p. 147) should resemble natural varieties or species. The whole article seems to me poor ; it seems to me hardly worth a detailed answer (even if I could do it, and I much doubt whether I possess your skill in picking out salient points and driving a nail into them), and indeed you have already answered several points. Agassiz's name, no doubt, is a heavy weight against us. . . .

If you see Professor Parsons, will you thank him for the extremely liberal and fair spirit in which his Essay * is written. Please tell him that I reflected much on the chance of favourable monstrosities (*i. e.* great and sudden variation) arising. I have, of course, no objection to this, indeed it would be a great aid, but I did not allude to the subject, for, after much labour, I could find nothing which satisfied me of the probability of such occurrences. There seems to me in almost every case too much, too complex, and too beautiful adaptation, in every structure, to believe in its sudden production. I have alluded under the head of beautifully hooked seeds to such possibility. Monsters are apt to be sterile, or *not* to transmit monstrous peculiarities. Look at the fineness of gradation in the shells of successive *sub-stages* of the same great formation ; I could give many other considerations which made me doubt such view. It holds, to a certain extent, with domestic

---

* ' Silliman's Journal,' July, 1860.

productions no doubt, where man preserves some abrupt change in structure. It amused me to see Sir R. Murchison quoted as a judge of affinities of animals, and it gave me a cold shudder to hear of any one speculating about a true crustacean giving birth to a true fish ! *

Yours most truly,

C. DARWIN.

C. Darwin to C. Lyell.

Down, September 1st [1860].

My DEAR LYELL,—I have been much interested by your letter of the 28th, received this morning. It has *delighted* me, because it demonstrates that you have thought a good deal lately on Natural Selection. Few things have surprised me more than the entire paucity of objections and difficulties new to me in the published reviews. Your remarks are of a different stamp and new to me. I will run through them, and make a few pleadings such as occur to me.

I put in the possibility of the Galapagos having been *continuously* joined to America, out of mere subservience to the many who believe in Forbes's doctrine, and did not see the danger of admission, about small mammals surviving there in such case. The case of the Galapagos, from certain facts on littoral sea-shells (viz. Pacific Ocean and South American littoral species), in fact convinced me more than in any other case of other islands, that the Galapagos had never been continuously united with the mainland ; it was mere base subservience, and terror of Hooker and Co.

With respect to atolls, I think mammals would hardly survive *very long*, even if the main islands (for as I have said in the Coral Book, the outline of groups of atolls do not look

---

* Parson's, *loc. cit.* p. 5, speaking of Pterichthys and Cephalaspis, says —
" Now is it too much to infer from these facts that either of these animals, if a crustacean, was so nearly a fish that some of its ova may have become fish ; or, if itself a fish, was so nearly a crustacean that it may have been born from the ovum of a crustacean ? "

like a former *continent*) had been tenanted by mammals, from the extremely small area, the very peculiar conditions, and the probability that during subsidence all or nearly all atolls have been breached and flooded by the sea many times during their existence as atolls.

I cannot conceive any existing reptile being converted into a mammal. From homologies I should look at it as certain that all mammals had descended from some single progenitor. What its nature was, it is impossible to speculate. More like, probably, the Ornithorhynchus or Echidna than any known form ; as these animals combine reptilian characters (and in a less degree bird character) with mammalian. We must imagine some form as intermediate, as is Lepidosiren now, between reptiles and fish, between mammals and birds on the one hand (for they retain longer the same embryological character) and reptiles on the other hand. With respect to a mammal not being developed on any island, besides want of time for so prodigious a development, there must have arrived on the island the necessary and peculiar progenitor, having a character like the embryo of a mammal; and not an *already developed* reptile, bird or fish.

We might give to a bird the habits of a mammal, but inheritance would retain almost for eternity some of the bird-like structure, and prevent a new creature ranking as a true mammal.

I have often speculated on antiquity of islands, but not with your precision, or at all under the point of view of Natural Selection *not* having done what might have been anticipated. The argument of littoral Miocene shells at the Canary Islands is new to me. I was deeply impressed (from the amount of the denudation) [with the] antiquity of St. Helena, and its age agrees with the peculiarity of the flora. With respect to bats at New Zealand (N. B. There are two or three European bats in Madeira, and I think in the Canary Islands) not having given rise to a group of non-volant bats, it is, now you put the case, surprising ; more especially as the genus of bats in New Zealand is very peculiar, and therefore has probably been long introduced, and they now speak of Cretacean fossils there. But the first necessary step has to be shown, namely, of a bat taking to feed on the ground, or anyhow, and anywhere, except in the air. I am bound to confess I do know one single such fact, viz. of an Indian species killing frogs. Observe, that in my wretched Polar Bear case, I do show the first step by which conversion into a whale " would be easy," " would offer no difficulty " ! ! So with seals, I know of no fact showing any the least incipient variation of seals feeding on the shore. Moreover, seals wander much; I searched in vain, and could not find *one* case of any species of seal confined to any islands. And hence wanderers would be apt to cross with individuals undergoing any change on an island, as in the case of land birds of Madeira and Bermuda. The same remark applies even to bats, as they frequently come to Bermuda from the mainland, though about 600 miles distant. With respect to the Amblyrhynchus of the Galapagos, one may infer as probable, from marine habits being so rare with Saurians, and from the terrestrial species being confined to a few central islets, that its progenitor first arrived at the Galapagos ; from what country it is impossible to say, as its affinity I believe is not very clear to any known species. The offspring of the terrestrial species was probably rendered marine. Now in this case I do not pretend I can show variation in habits; but we have in the terrestrial species a vegetable feeder (in itself a rather unusual circumstance), largely on *lichens*, and it would not be a great change for its offspring to feed first on littoral algæ and then on submarine algæ. I have said what I can in defence, but yours is a good line of attack. We should, however, always remember that no change will ever be effected till a variation in the habits or structure or of both *chance* to occur in the right direction, so as to give the organism in question an advantage over other already established occupants of land or water, and this may be in any particular case indefinitely long. I am very glad you will read my dogs MS., for it will be important to me to see what you think of the balance of evidence. After long pondering on a subject it is often hard to judge. With hearty thanks for your most interesting letter. Farewell.

My dear old master,

C. DARWIN.

C. Darwin to J. D. Hooker.

Down, September 2nd [1860].

MY DEAR HOOKER,—I am astounded at your news received this morning. I am become such an old fogy that I am amazed at your spirit. For God's sake do not go and get your throat cut. Bless my soul, I think you must be a little insane. I must confess it will be a most interesting tour ; and, if you get to the top of Lebanon, I suppose extremely interesting—you ought to collect any beetles under stones there ; but the Entomologists are such slow coaches. I dare say no result could be made out of them. [They] have never worked the Alpines of Britain.

If you come across any Brine lakes, do attend to their minute flora and fauna ; I have often been surprised how little this has been attended to.

I have had a long letter from Lyell, who starts ingenious difficulties opposed to Natural Selection, because it has not done more than it has. This is very good, as it shows that he has thoroughly mastered the subject ; and shows he is in earnest. Very striking letter altogether and it rejoices the cockles of my heart.

. . . . How I shall miss you, my best and kindest of friends. God bless you.

Yours ever affectionately,

C. DARWIN.

C. Darwin to Asa Gray.

Down, Sept. 10 [1860].

. . . . You will be weary of my praise, but it * does strike me as quite admirably argued, and so well and pleasantly

---

* Dr. Gray in the 'Atlantic Monthly' for July, 1860.

written.   Your many metaphors are inimitably good.   I said
in a former letter that you were a lawyer, but I made a gross
mistake, I am sure that you are a poet.   No, by Jove, I will
tell you what you are, a hybrid, a complex cross of lawyer,
poet, naturalist and theologian !   Was there ever such a monster seen before?

I have just looked through the passages which I have
marked as appearing to me extra good, but I see that they
are too numerous to specify, and this is no exaggeration.
My eye just alights on the happy comparison of the colours
of the prism and our artificial groups.   I see one little error
of fossil *cattle* in South America.

It is curious how each one, I suppose, weighs arguments
in a different balance : embryology is to me by far the strongest single class of facts in favour of change of forms, and not
one, I think, of my reviewers has alluded to this.   Variation
not coming on at a very early age, and being inherited at not
a very early corresponding period, explains, as it seems to
me, the grandest of all facts in natural history, or rather in
zoology, viz. the resemblance of embryos.

[Dr. Gray wrote three articles in the 'Atlantic Monthly' for
July, August, and October, which were reprinted as a pamphlet in 1861, and now form chapter iii. in 'Darwiniana'
(1876), with the heading ' Natural Selection not inconsistent
with Natural Theology.']

C. Darwin to C. Lyell.

Down, September 12th [1860].

MY DEAR LYELL,—I never thought of showing your letter
to any one.   I mentioned in a letter to Hooker that I had
been much interested by a letter of yours with original objections, founded chiefly on Natural Selection not having done
so much as might have been expected. . . . . In your letter
just received, you have improved your case versus Natural
Selection ; and it would tell with the public (do not be

tempted by its novelty to make it too strong) ; yet it seems
to me, not *really* very killing, though I cannot answer your
case, especially, why Rodents have not become highly developed in Australia.   You must assume that they have inhabited Australia for a very long period, and this may or may
not be the case.   But I feel that our ignorance is so profound, why one form is preserved with nearly the same structure, or advances in organisation or even retrogrades, or becomes extinct, that I cannot put very great weight on the
difficulty.   Then, as you say often in your letter, we know
not how many geological ages it may have taken to make any
great advance in organisation.   Remember monkeys in the
Eocene formations : but I admit that you have made out an
excellent objection and difficulty, and I can give only unsatisfactory and quite vague answers, such as you have yourself
put ; however, you hardly put weight enough on the absolute necessity of variations first arising in the right direction,
videlicet, of seals beginning to feed on the shore.

I entirely agree with what you say about only one species
of many becoming modified.   I remember this struck me
much when tabulating the varieties of plants, and I have a
discussion somewhere on this point.   It is absolutely implied
in my ideas of classification and divergence that only one or
two species, of even large genera, give birth to new species ;
and many whole genera become *wholly* extinct. . . . . Please
see p. 341 of the 'Origin.'   But I cannot remember that I
have stated in the 'Origin' the fact of only very few species
in each genus varying.   You have put the view much better
in your letter.   Instead of saying, as I often have, that very
few species vary at the same time, I ought to have said, that
very few species of a genus *ever* vary so as to become modified ; for this is the fundamental explanation of classification,
and is shown in my engraved diagram. . . .

I quite agree with you on the strange and inexplicable
fact of Ornithorhynchus having been preserved, and Australian Trigonia, or the Silurian Lingula.   I always repeat to
myself that we hardly know why any one single species is

rare or common in the best-known countries. I have got a set of notes somewhere on the inhabitants of fresh water; and it is singular how many of these are ancient, or intermediate forms; which I think is explained by the competition having been less severe, and the rate of change of organic forms having been slower in small confined areas, such as all the fresh waters make compared with sea or land.

I see that you do allude in the last page, as a difficulty, to Marsupials not having become Placentals in Australia; but this I think you have no right at all to expect; for we ought to look at Marsupials and Placentals as having descended from some intermediate and lower form. The argument of Rodents not having become highly developed in Australia (supposing that they have long existed there) is much stronger. I grieve to see you hint at the creation " of distinct successive types, as well as of a certain number of distinct aboriginal types." Remember, if you admit this, you give up the embryological argument (*the weightiest of all to me*), and the morphological or homological argument. You cut my throat, and your own throat; and I believe will live to be sorry for it. So much for species.

The striking extract which E. copied was your own writing!! in a note to me, many long years ago—which she copied and sent to Mme. Sismondi; and lately my aunt, in sorting her letters, found E.'s and returned them to her. . . . . I have been of late shamefully idle, *i. e.* observing * instead of writing, and how much better fun observing is than writing.

Yours affectionately,

C. DARWIN.

C. Darwin to C. Lyell.

15 Marine Parade, Eastbourne,
Sunday [September 23rd, 1860].

MY DEAR LYELL,—I got your letter of the 18th just before starting here. You speak of saving me trouble in an-

---

* Drosera.

swering. Never think of this, for I look at every letter of
yours as an honor and pleasure, which is a pretty deal more
than I can say of some of the letters which I receive. I have
now one of 13 *closely written folio pages* to answer on species ! . . . .

I have a very decided opinion that all mammals must
have descended from a *single* parent. Reflect on the multitude of details, very many of them of extremely little importance to their habits (as the number of bones of the head, &c.,
covering of hair, identical embryological development, &c.
&c.). Now this large amount of similarity I must look at as
certainly due to inheritance from a common stock. I am
aware that some cases occur in which a similar or nearly
similar organ has been acquired by independent acts of natural selection. But in most of such cases of these apparently so closely similar organs, some important homological difference may be detected. Please read p. 193, beginning,
"The electric organs," and trust me that the sentence, "In
all these cases of two very distinct species," &c. &c., was not
put in rashly, for I went carefully into every case. Apply
this argument to the whole frame, internal and external, of
mammifers, and you will see why I think so strongly that all
have descended from one progenitor. I have just re-read your
letter, and I am not perfectly sure that I understand your point.

I enclose two diagrams showing the sort of manner I *conjecture* that mammals have been developed. I thought a little
on this when writing page 429, beginning, "Mr. Waterhouse."
(Please read the paragraph.) I have not knowledge enough
to choose between these two diagrams. If the brain of Marsupials in embryo closely resembles that of Placentals, I
should strongly prefer No. 2, and this agrees with the antiquity of Microlestes. As a general rule I should prefer No. 1
diagram ; whether or not Marsupials have gone on being
developed, or rising in rank, from a very early period would
depend on circumstances too complex for even a conjecture.
Lingula has not risen since the Silurian epoch, whereas other
molluscs may have risen.

A, in the following diagrams, represents an unknown form, probably intermediate between Mammals, Reptiles, and Birds, as intermediate as Lepidosiren now is between Fish and

DIAGRAM I.

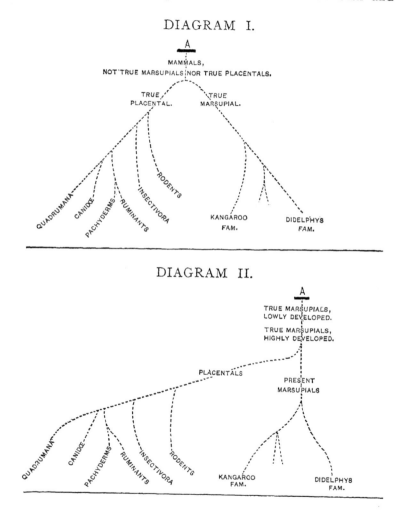

DIAGRAM II.

Batrachians. This unknown form is probably more closely related to Ornithorhynchus than to any other known form.

I do not think that the multiple origin of dogs goes against the single origin of man. . . . . All the races of man are so infinitely closer together than to any ape, that (as in the case of descent of all mammals from one progenitor), I should look at all races of men as having certainly descended from one parent. I should look at it as probable that the races of men were less numerous and less divergent formerly than now, unless, indeed, some lower and more aberrant race even than the Hottentot has become extinct. Supposing, as I do for one believe, that our dogs have descended from two or three wolves, jackals, &c. ; yet these have, on *our view*, descended from a single remote unknown progenitor. With domestic dogs the question is simply whether the whole amount of difference has been produced since man domesticated a single species ; or whether part of the difference arises in the state of nature. Agassiz and Co. think the negro and Caucasian are now distinct species, and it is a mere vain discussion whether, when they were rather less distinct, they would, on this standard of specific value, deserve to be called species.

I agree with your answer which you give to yourself on this point; and the simile of man now keeping down any new man which might be developed, strikes me as good and new. The white man is " improving off the face of the earth " even races nearly his equals. With respect to islands, I think I would trust to want of time alone, and not to bats and Rodents.

N.B.—I know of no rodents on oceanic islands (except my Galapagos mouse, which *may* have been introduced by man) keeping down the development of other classes. Still *much* more weight I should attribute to there being now, neither in islands nor elsewhere, [any] known animals of a grade of organisation intermediate between mammals, fish, reptiles, &c., whence a new mammal could be developed. If every vertebrate were destroyed throughout the world, except our *now well-established* reptiles, millions of ages might elapse before reptiles could become highly developed on a scale equal to mammals ; and, on the principle of inheritance, they would make some quite *new class*, and not mammals; though *possibly* more intellectual! I have not an idea that you will care for this letter, so speculative.

Most truly yours,

C. DARWIN.

C. Darwin to Asa Gray.

Down, Sept. 26 [1860].

. . . . I have had a letter of fourteen folio pages from Harvey against my book, with some ingenious and new remarks; but it is an extraordinary fact that he does not understand at all what I mean by Natural Selection. I have begged him to read the Dialogue in next 'Silliman,' as you never touch the subject without making it clearer. I look at it as even more extraordinary that you never say a word or use an epithet which does not express fully my meaning. Now Lyell, Hooker, and others, who perfectly understand my book, yet sometimes use expressions to which I demur. Well, your extraordinary labour is over; if there is any fair amount of truth in my view, I am well assured that your great labour has not been thrown away. . . .

I yet hope and almost believe, that the time will come when you will go further, in believing a very large amount of modification of species, than you did at first or do now. Can you tell me whether you believe further or more firmly than you did at first? I should really like to know this. I can perceive in my immense correspondence with Lyell, who objected to much at first, that he has, perhaps unconsciously to himself, converted himself very much during the last six months, and I think this is the case even with Hooker. This fact gives me far more confidence than any other fact.

C. Darwin to C. Lyell.

15 Marine Parade, Eastbourne,
Friday evening [September 28th, 1860].

. . . . I am very glad to hear about the Germans reading my book. No one will be converted who has not independently begun to doubt about species. Is not Krohn * a good fellow ? I have long meant to write to him. He has been working at Cirripedes, and has detected two or three gigantic blunders, ... about which, I thank Heaven, I spoke rather doubtfully. Such difficult dissection that even Huxley failed. It is chiefly the interpretation which I put on parts that is so wrong, and not the parts which I describe. But they were gigantic blunders, and why I say all this is because Krohn, instead of crowing at all, pointed out my errors with the utmost gentleness and pleasantness. I have always meant to write to him and thank him. I suppose Dr. Krohn, Bonn, would reach him.

I cannot see yet how the multiple origin of dog can be properly brought as argument for the multiple origin of man. Is not your feeling a remnant of the deeply impressed one on all our minds, that a species is an entity, something quite distinct from a variety ? Is it not that the dog case injures the argument from fertility, so that one main argument that the races of man are varieties and not species—*i.e.*, because they are fertile *inter se*, is much weakened?

I quite agree with what Hooker says, that whatever variation is possible under culture, is *possible* under nature ; not that the same form would ever be accumulated and arrived at by selection for man's pleasure, and by natural selection for the organism's own good.

Talking of "natural selection ; " if I had to commence *de*

---

* There are two papers by Aug. Krohn, one on the Cement Glands, and the other on the development of Cirripedes, 'Wiegmann's Archiv,' xxv. and xxvi. My father has remarked that he "blundered dreadfully about the cement glands," 'Autobiography,' p. 66.

novo, I would have used "natural preservation." For I find men like Harvey of Dublin cannot understand me, though he has read the book twice. Dr. Gray of the British Museum remarked to me that, "*selection* was obviously impossible with plants! No one could tell him how it could be possible!" And he may now add that the author did not attempt it to him!

Yours ever affectionately,
C. DARWIN.

C. Darwin to C. Lyell.

15 Marine Parade, Eastbourne,
October 8th [1860].

MY DEAR LYELL,—I send the [English] translation of Bronn,* the first part of the chapter with generalities and praise is not translated. There are some good hits. He makes an apparently, and in part truly, telling case against me, says that I cannot explain why one rat has a longer tail and another longer ears, &c. But he seems to muddle in assuming that these parts did not all vary together, or one part so insensibly before the other, as to be in fact contemporaneous. I might ask the creationist whether he thinks these differences in the two rats of any use, or as standing in some relation from laws of growth; and if he admits this, selection might come into play. He who thinks that God created animals unlike for mere sport or variety, as man fashions his clothes, will not admit any force in my *argumentum ad hominem.*

Bronn blunders about my supposing several Glacial periods, whether or no such ever did occur.

He blunders about my supposing that development goes on at the same rate in all parts of the world. I presume that he has misunderstood this from the supposed migration into all regions of the more dominant forms.

---

* A MS. translation of Bronn's chapter of objections at the end of his German translation of the 'Origin of Species.'

I have ordered Dr. Bree,* and will lend it to you, if you like, and if it turns out good.

. . . . . I am very glad that I misunderstood you about species not having the capacity to vary, though in fact few do give birth to new species. It seems that I am very apt to misunderstand you ; I suppose I am always fancying objections. Your case of the Red Indian shows me that we agree entirely. . . . .

I had a letter yesterday from Thwaites of Ceylon, who was much opposed to me. He now says, " I find that the more familiar I become with your views in connection with the various phenomena of nature, the more they commend themselves to my mind."

C. Darwin to J. M. Rodwell.†

15 Marine Parade, Eastbourne.
November 5th [1860].

MY DEAR SIR,—I am extremely much obliged for your letter, which I can compare only to a plum-pudding, so full it is of good things. I have been rash about the cats : ‡ yet I spoke on what seemed to me, good authority. The Rev. W. D. Fox gave me a list of cases of various foreign breeds in which he had observed the correlation, and for years he had vainly sought an exception. A French paper also gives numerous cases, and one very curious case of a kitten which *gradually* lost the blue colour in its eyes and as gradually acquired its power of hearing. I had not heard of your uncle, Mr. Kirby's case # (whom I, for as long as I can re-

---

* ' Species not Transmutable,' by C. R. Bree, 1860.

† Rev. J. M. Rodwell, who was at Cambridge with my father, remembers him saying :—" It strikes me that all our knowledge about the structure of our earth is very much like what an old hen would know of a hundred acre field, in a corner of which she is scratching."

‡ " Cats with blue eyes are invariably deaf," ' Origin of Species,' ed. i. p. 12.

William Kirby, joint author with Spence, of the well-known ' Introduction to Entomology,' 1818.

member, have venerated) of care in breeding cats.   I do not
know whether Mr. Kirby was your uncle by marriage, but
your letters show me that you ought to have Kirby blood in
your veins, and that if you had not taken to languages you
would have been a first-rate naturalist.

   I sincerely hope that you will be able to carry out your intention of writing on the " Birth, Life, and Death of Words."
Anyhow, you have a capital title, and some think this the
most difficult part of a book.   I remember years ago at the
Cape of Good Hope, Sir J. Herschel saying to me, I wish
some one would treat language as Lyell has treated geology.
What a linguist you must be to translate the Koran ! Having
a vilely bad head for languages, I feel an awful respect for
linguists.

   I do not know whether my brother-in-law, Hensleigh
Wedgwood's ' Etymological Dictionary ' would be at all in
your line ; but he treats briefly on the genesis of words ; and,
as it seems to me, very ingeniously.   You kindly say that
you would communicate any facts which might occur to you,
and I am sure that I should be most grateful.   Of the multitude of letters which I receive, not one in a thousand is like
yours in value.

   With my cordial thanks, and apologies for this untidy letter written in haste, pray believe me, my dear Sir,

Yours sincerely obliged,

CH. DARWIN.

C. Darwin to C. Lyell.

November 20th [1860].

   . . . . I have not had heart to read Phillips * yet, or a
tremendous long hostile review by Professor Bowen in the
4to Mem. of the American Academy of Sciences.†   (By the

---

   * ' Life on the Earth.'
   † " Remarks on the latest form of the Development Theory." By
Francis Bowen, Professor of Natural Religion and Moral Philosophy, at
Harvard University. ' American Academy of Arts and Sciences,' vol. viii.

way, I hear Agassiz is going to thunder against me in the next part of the 'Contributions.') Thank you for telling me of the sale of the 'Origin,' of which I had not heard. There will be some time, I presume, a new edition, and I especially want your advice on one point, and you know I think you the wisest of men, and I shall be *absolutely guided by your advice*. It has occurred to me, that it would *perhaps* be a good plan to put a set of notes (some twenty to forty or fifty) to the 'Origin,' which now has none, exclusively devoted to errors of my reviewers. It has occurred to me that where a reviewer has erred, a common reader might err. Secondly, it will show the reader that he must not trust implicitly to reviewers. Thirdly, when any special fact has been attacked, I should like to defend it. I would show no sort of anger. I enclose a mere rough specimen, done without any care or accuracy—done from memory alone—to be torn up, just to show the sort of thing that has occurred to me. *Will you do me the great kindness to consider this well?*

It seems to me it would have a good effect, and give some confidence to the reader. It would [be] a horrid bore going through all the reviews.

Yours affectionately,

C. DARWIN.

[Here follow samples of foot-notes, the references to volume and page being left blank. It will be seen that in some cases he seems to have forgotten that he was writing foot-notes, and to have continued as if writing to Lyell :—

* Dr. Bree (p.   ) asserts that I explain the structure of the cells of the Hive Bee by "the exploded doctrine of pressure." But I do not say one word which directly or indirectly can be interpreted into any reference to pressure.

* The 'Edinburgh' Reviewer (vol.   , p.   ) quotes my work as saying that the "dorsal vertebræ of pigeons vary in number, and disputes the fact." I nowhere even allude to the dorsal vertebræ, only to the sacral and caudal vertebræ.

* The 'Edinburgh' Reviewer throws a doubt on these organs being the Branchiæ of Cirripedes. But Professor Owen in 1854 admits,

without hesitation, that they are Branchiæ, as did John Hunter long ago.

* The confounded Wealden Calculation to be struck out, and a note to be inserted to the effect that I am convinced of its inaccuracy from a review in the *Saturday Review*, and from Phillips, as I see in his Table of Contents that he alludes to it.

* Mr. Hopkins (' Fraser,' vol. , p.) states—I am quoting only from vague memory—that, " I argue in favour of my views from the extreme imperfection of the Geological Record," and says this is the first time in the history of Science he has ever heard of ignorance being adduced as an argument. But I repeatedly admit, in the most emphatic language which I can use, that the imperfect evidence which Geology offers in regard to transitorial forms is most strongly opposed to my views. Surely there is a wide difference in fully admitting an objection, and then in endeavoring to show that it is not so strong as it at first appears, and in Mr. Hopkins's assertion that I found my argument on the Objection.

* I would also put a note to " Natural Selection," and show how variously it has been misunderstood.

* A writer in the ' Edinburgh Philosophical Journal' denies my statement that the Woodpecker of La Plata never frequents trees. I observed its habits during two years, but, what is more to the purpose, Azara, whose accuracy all admit, is more emphatic than I am in regard to its never frequenting trees. Mr. A. Murray denies that it ought to be called a woodpecker ; it has two toes in front and two behind, pointed tail feathers, a long pointed tongue, and the same general form of body, the same manner of flight, colouring and voice. It was classed, until recently, in the same genus— Picus—with all other woodpeckers, but now has been ranked as a distinct genus amongst the Picidæ. It differs from the typical Picus only in the beak, not being quite so strong, and in the upper mandible being slightly arched. I think these facts fully justify my statement that it is " in all essential parts of its organisation " a Woodpecker.]

C. Darwin to T. H. Huxley.

Down, Nov. 22 [1860].

MY DEAR HUXLEY,—For heaven's sake don't write an anti-Darwinian article ; you would do it so confoundedly well. I have sometimes amused myself with thinking how I could best pitch into myself, and I believe I could give two or three good digs ; but I will see you —— first before I will try. I shall be very impatient to see the Review.* If it succeeds it may really do much, very much good. . . . .

I heard to-day from Murray that I must set to work at once on a new edition † of the 'Origin.' [Murray] says the Reviews have not improved the sale. I shall always think those early reviews, almost entirely yours, did the subject an *enormous* service. If you have any important suggestions or criticisms to make on any part of the 'Origin,' I should, of course, be very grateful for [them]. For I mean to correct as far as I can, but not enlarge. How you must be wearied with and hate the subject, and it is God's blessing if you do not get to hate me. Adios.

C. Darwin to C. Lyell.

Down, November 24th [1860].

MY DEAR LYELL,—I thank you much for your letter. I had got to take pleasure in thinking how I could best snub my reviewers ; but I was determined, in any case, to follow your advice, and, before I had got to the end of your letter, I was convinced of the wisdom of your advice.‡ What an advantage it is to me to have such friends as you. I shall follow every hint in your letter exactly.

I have just heard from Murray ; he says he sold 700 copies at his sale, and that he has not half the number to supply ; so that I must begin at once.# . . . .

---

* The first number of the new series of the 'Nat. Hist. Review' appeared in 1861.

† The 3rd edition.

‡ "I get on slowly with my new edition. I find that your advice was *excellent*. I can answer all reviews, without any direct notice of them, by a little enlargement here and there, with here and there a new paragraph. Bronn alone I shall treat with the respect of giving his objections with his name. I think I shall improve my book a good deal, and add only some twenty pages."—From a letter to Lyell, December 4th, 1860.

On the third edition of the 'Origin of Species,' published in April 1861.

P.S.—I must tell you one little fact which has pleased me. You may remember that I adduce electrical organs of fish as one of the greatest difficulties which have occurred to me, and —— notices the passage in a singularly disingenuous spirit. Well, McDonnell, of Dublin (a first-rate man), writes to me that he felt the difficulty of the whole case as overwhelming against me. Not only are the fishes which have electric organs very remote in scale, but the organ is near the head in some, and near the tail in others, and supplied by wholly different nerves. It seems impossible that there could be any transition. Some friend, who is much opposed to me, seems to have crowed over McDonnell, who reports that he said to himself, that if Darwin is right, there must be homologous organs both near the head and tail in other non-electric fish. He set to work, and, by Jove, he has found them! * so that some of the difficulty is removed; and is it not satisfactory that my hypothetical notions should have led to pretty discoveries? McDonnell seems very cautious; he says, years must pass before he will venture to call himself a believer in my doctrine, but that on the subjects which he knows well, viz., Morphology and Embryology, my views accord well, and throw light on the whole subject.

C. Darwin to Asa Gray.

Down, November 26th, 1860.

MY DEAR GRAY,—I have to thank you for two letters. The latter with corrections, written before you received my letter asking for an American reprint, and saying that it was hopeless to print your reviews as a pamphlet, owing to the impossibility of getting pamphlets known. I am very glad to say that the August or second 'Atlantic' article has been reprinted in the 'Annals and Magazine of Natural History';

---

* 'On an organ in the Skate, which appears to be the homologue of the electrical organ of the Torpedo,' by R. McDonnell, 'Nat. Hist. Review,' 1861, p. 57.

but I have not yet seen it there.   Yesterday I read over with
care the third article; and it seems to me, as before, *admi-rable*.   But I grieve to say that I cannot honestly go as far
as you do about Design.   I am conscious that I am in an
utterly hopeless muddle.   I cannot think that the world, as
we see it, is the result of chance; and yet I cannot look at
each separate thing as the result of Design.   To take a cru-cial example, you lead me to infer (p. 414) that you believe
"that variation has been led along certain beneficial lines."
I cannot believe this; and I think you would have to believe,
that the tail of the Fantail was led to vary in the number
and direction of its feathers in order to gratify the caprice of
a few men.   Yet if the Fantail had been a wild bird, and had
used its abnormal tail for some special end, as to sail before
the wind, unlike other birds, every one would have said,
"What a beautiful and designed adaptation."   Again, I say
I am, and shall ever remain, in a hopeless muddle.

Thank you much for Bowen's 4to. review.*   The coolness
with which he makes all animals to be destitute of reason is
simply absurd.   It is monstrous at p. 103, that he should
argue against the possibility of accumulative variation, and
actually leave out, entirely, selection!   The chance that an
improved Short-horn, or improved Pouter-pigeon, should
be produced by accumulative variation without man's selec-tion is as almost infinity to nothing; so with natural species
without natural selection.   How capitally in the 'Atlantic' you
show that Geology and Astronomy are, according to Bowen,
Metaphysics; but he leaves out this in the 4to Memoir.

I have not much to tell you about my Book.   I have just
heard that Du Bois-Reymond agrees with me.   The sale of
my book goes on well, and the multitude of reviews has not
stopped the sale . . . ; so I must begin at once on a new
corrected edition.   I will send you a copy for the chance of
your ever re-reading; but, good Heavens, how sick you must
be of it!

---

* 'Memoirs of the American Academy of Arts and Sciences,' vol. viii.

C. Darwin to T. H. Huxley.

Down, Dec. 2nd [1860].

. . . . I have got fairly sick of hostile reviews. Nevertheless, they have been of use in showing me when to expatiate a little and to introduce a few new discussions. *Of course* I will send you a copy of the new edition.

I entirely agree with you, that the difficulties on my notions are terrific, yet having seen what all the Reviews have said against me, I have far more confidence in the *general* truth of the doctrine than I formerly had. Another thing gives me confidence, viz. that some who went half an inch with me now go further, and some who were bitterly opposed are now less bitterly opposed. And this makes me feel a little disappointed that you are not inclined to think the general view in some slight degree more probable than you did at first. This I consider rather ominous. Otherwise I should be more contented with your degree of belief. I can pretty plainly see that, if my view is ever to be generally adopted, it will be by young men growing up and replacing the old workers, and then young ones finding that they can group facts and search out new lines of investigation better on the notion of descent, than on that of creation. But forgive me for running on so egotistically. Living so solitary as I do, one gets to think in a silly manner of one's own work.

Ever yours very sincerely,

C. DARWIN.

C. Darwin to J. D. Hooker.

Down, December 11th [1860].

. . . . . . I heard from A. Gray this morning; at my suggestion he is going to reprint the three 'Atlantic' articles as a pamphlet, and send 250 copies to England, for which I intend to pay half the cost of the whole edition, and shall give away, and try to sell by getting a few advertisements put in, and if possible notices in Periodicals.

. . . . . . David Forbes has been carefully working the Geology of Chile, and as I value praise for accurate observation far higher than for any other quality, forgive (if you can) the *insufferable* vanity of my copying the last sentence in his note : " I regard your Monograph on Chile as, without exception, one of the finest specimens of Geological enquiry." I feel inclined to strut like a Turkey-cock !

CHAPTER III.

Spread of Evolution.

1861–1862.

[The beginning of the year 1861 saw my father with the third chapter of 'The Variation of Animals and Plants' still on his hands. It had been begun in the previous August, and was not finished until March 1861. He was, however, for part of this time (I believe during December 1860 and January 1861) engaged in a new edition (2000 copies) of the 'Origin,' which was largely corrected and added to, and was published in April 1861.

With regard to this, the third edition, he wrote to Mr. Murray in December 1860 :—

"I shall be glad to hear when you have decided how many copies you will print off—the more the better for me in all ways, as far as compatible with safety ; for I hope never again to make so many corrections, or rather additions, which I have made in hopes of making my many rather stupid reviewers at least understand what is meant. I hope and think I shall improve the book considerably."

An interesting feature in the new edition was the "Historical Sketch of the Recent Progress of Opinion on the Origin of Species "* which now appeared for the first time, and was continued in the later editions of the work. It bears a strong

---

* The Historical Sketch had already appeared in the first German edition (1860) and the American edition. Bronn states in the German edition (footnote, p. 1) that it was his critique in the 'N. Jahrbuch für Mineralogie' that suggested the idea of such a sketch to my father.

impress of the author's personal character in the obvious wish
to do full justice to all his predecessors,—though even in
this respect it has not escaped some adverse criticism.

Towards the end of the present year (1861), the final
arrangements for the first French edition of the 'Origin' were
completed, and in September a copy of the third English
edition was despatched to Mdlle. Clémence Royer, who undertook the work of translation. The book was now spreading
on the Continent, a Dutch edition had appeared, and, as we
have seen, a German translation had been published in 1860.
In a letter to Mr. Murray (September 10, 1861), he wrote,
"My book seems exciting much attention in Germany,
judging from the number of discussions sent me." The
silence had been broken, and in a few years the voice of
German science was to become one of the strongest of the
advocates of evolution.

During all the early part of the year (1861) he was working
at the mass of details which are marshalled in order in the early
chapter of 'Animals and Plants.' Thus in his Diary occur
the laconic entries, "May 16, Finished Fowls (eight weeks) ;
May 31, Ducks."

On July 1, he started, with his family, for Torquay, where
he remained until August 27—a holiday which he characteristically enters in his diary as "eight weeks and a day." The
house he occupied was in Hesketh Crescent, a pleasantly
placed row of houses close above the sea, somewhat removed
from what was then the main body of the town, and not far
from the beautiful cliffed coast-line in the neighbourhood of
Anstey's Cove.

During the Torquay holiday, and for the remainder of the
year, he worked at the fertilisation of orchids. This part of
the year 1861 is not dealt with in the present chapter, because
(as explained in the preface) the record of his life, as told in
his letters, seems to become clearer when the whole of his
botanical work is placed together and treated separately.
The present series of chapters will, therefore, include only
the progress of his works in the direction of a general

amplification of the ' Origin of Species '—e.g., the publication of ' Animals and Plants,' ' Descent of Man,' &c.]

C. *Darwin to J. D. Hooker.*

Down, Jan. 15 [1861].

MY DEAR HOOKER,—The sight of your handwriting always rejoices the very cockles of my heart. . . . .

I most fully agree to what you say about Huxley's Article,* and the power of writing. . . . . The whole review seems to me excellent. How capitally Oliver has done the résumé of botanical books. Good Heavens, how he must have read ! . . . .

I quite agree that Phillips † is unreadably dull. You need not attempt Bree.‡ . . . .

---

* ' Natural History Review,' 1861, p. 67, " On the Zoological Relations of Man with the Lower Animals." This memoir had its origin in a discussion at the previous meeting of the British Association, when Professor Huxley felt himself " compelled to give a diametrical contradiction to certain assertions respecting the differences which obtain between the brains of the higher apes and of man, which fell from Professor Owen." But in order that his criticisms might refer to deliberately recorded words, he bases them on Professor Owen's paper, " On the Characters, &c., of the Class Mammalia," read before the Linnean Society in February and April, 1857, in which he proposed to place man not only in a distinct order, but in " a distinct sub-class of the Mammalia "—the Archencephala.

† ' Life on the Earth' (1860), by Prof. Phillips, containing the substance of the Rede Lecture (May 1860).

‡ The following sentence (p. 16) from ' Species not Transmutable,' by Dr. Bree, illustrates the degree in which he understood the ' Origin of Species ' : " The only real difference between Mr. Darwin and his two predecessors " [Lamarck and the ' Vestiges '] " is this :—that while the latter have each given a mode by which they conceive the great changes they believe in have been brought about, Mr. Darwin does no such thing." After this we need not be surprised at a passage in the preface : " No one has derived greater pleasure than I have in past days from the study of Mr. Darwin's other works, and no one has felt a greater degree of regret that he should have imperilled his fame by the publication of his treatise upon the ' Origin of Species.' "

If you come across Dr. Freke on 'Origin of Species by means of Organic Affinity,' read a page here and there. . . . He tells the reader to observe [that his result] has been arrived at by " induction," whereas all my results are arrived at only by "analogy." I see a Mr. Neale has read a paper before the Zoological Society on 'Typical Selection ; ' what it means I know not. I have not read H. Spencer, for I find that I must more and more husband the very little strength which I have. I sometimes suspect I shall soon entirely fail. . . . . As soon as this dreadful weather gets a little milder, I must try a little water cure. Have you read the 'Woman in White' ? the plot is wonderfully interesting. I can recommend a book which has interested me greatly, viz., Olmsted's 'Journey in the Back Country.' It is an admirably lively picture of man and slavery in the Southern States. . . . .

C. Darwin to C. Lyell.

February 2, 1861.

MY DEAR LYELL,—I have thought you would like to read the enclosed passage in a letter from A. Gray (who is printing his reviews as a pamphlet,* and will send copies to England), as I think his account is really favourable in high degree to us :—

" I wish I had time to write you an account of the lengths to which Bowen and Agassiz, each in their own way, are going. The first denying all heredity (all transmission except specific) whatever. The second coming near to deny that we are genetically descended from our great-great-grandfathers ; and insisting that evidently affiliated languages, e. g. Latin, Greek, Sanscrit, owe none of their similarities to a community of origin, are all autochthonal ; Agassiz admits that the derivation of languages, and that of species or forms,

---

* "Natural Selection not inconsistent with Natural Theology," from the ' Atlantic Monthly ' for July, August, and October, 1860 ; published by Trübner.

stand on the same foundation, and that he must allow the latter if he allows the former, which I tell him is perfectly logical."

Is not this marvellous?

Ever yours,
C. DARWIN.

C. Darwin to J. D. Hooker.

Down, Feb. 4 [1861].

MY DEAR HOOKER,—I was delighted to get your long chatty letter, and to hear that you are thawing towards science. I almost wish you had remained frozen rather longer; but do not thaw too quickly and strongly. No one can work long as you used to do. Be idle; but I am a pretty man to preach, for I cannot be idle, much as I wish it, and am never comfortable except when at work. The word holiday is written in a dead language for me, and much I grieve at it. We thank you sincerely for your kind sympathy about poor H. [his daughter]. . . . . She has now come up to her old point, and can sometimes get up for an hour or two twice a day. . . . Never to look to the future or as little as possible is becoming our rule of life. What a different thing life was in youth with no dread in the future; all golden, if baseless, hopes.

. . . . With respect to the 'Natural History Review' I can hardly think that ladies would be so very sensitive about "lizards' guts;" but the publication is at present certainly a sort of hybrid, and original illustrated papers ought hardly to appear in a review. I doubt its ever paying; but I shall much regret if it dies. All that you say seems very sensible, but could a review in the strict sense of the word be filled with readable matter?

I have been doing little, except finishing the new edition of the 'Origin,' and crawling on most slowly with my volume of 'Variation under Domestication.' . . . .

[The following letter refers to Mr. Bates's paper, "Contri-

butions to an Insect Fauna of the Amazon Valley," in the
'Transactions of the Entomological Society,' vol. 5, N.S.*
Mr. Bates points out that with the return, after the glacial
period, of a warmer climate in the equatorial regions, the
"species then living near the equator would retreat north
and south to their former homes, leaving some of their con-
geners, slowly modified subsequently . . . to re-people the
zone they had forsaken." In this case the species now living
at the equator ought to show clear relationship to the species
inhabiting the regions about the 25th parallel, whose distant
relatives they would of course be. But this is not the case,
and this is the difficulty my father refers to. Mr. Belt has
offered an explanation in his 'Naturalist in Nicaragua'
(1874), p. 266. "I believe the answer is that there was much
extermination during the glacial period, that many species
(and some genera, &c., as, for instance, the American horse),
did not survive it . . . . but that a refuge was found for
many species on lands now below the ocean, that were un-
covered by the lowering of the sea, caused by the immense
quantity of water that was locked up in frozen masses on the
land."]

C. Darwin to J. D. Hooker.

Down, 27th [March 1861].

My dear Hooker,—I had intended to have sent you
Bates's article this very day. I am so glad you like it. I
have been extremely much struck with it. How well he
argues, and with what crushing force against the glacial doctrine. I cannot wriggle out of it : I am dumbfounded ; yet
I do believe that some explanation some day will appear, and
I cannot give up equatorial cooling. It explains so much
and harmonises with so much. When you write (and much
interested I shall be in your letter) please say how far floras
are generally uniform in generic character from 0° to 25° N.
and S.

---

* The paper was read Nov. 24, 1860.

Before reading Bates, I had become thoroughly dissatisfied with what I wrote to you. I hope you may get Bates to write in the ' Linnean.'

Here is a good joke: H. C. Watson (who, I fancy and hope, is going to review the new edition * of the 'Origin') says that in the first four paragraphs of the introduction, the words " I," " me," " my," occur forty-three times ! I was dimly conscious of the accursed fact. He says it can be explained phrenologically, which I suppose civilly means, that I am the most egotistically self-sufficient man alive ; perhaps so. I wonder whether he will print this pleasing fact; it beats hollow the parentheses in Wollaston's writing.

I am, *my* dear Hooker, ever yours,

C. DARWIN.

P.S.—Do not spread this pleasing joke ; it is rather too biting.

C. Darwin to J. D. Hooker.

Down, [April] 23 ? [1861.]

. . . . I quite agree with what you say on Lieutenant Hutton's Review † (who he is I know not) ; it struck me as very original. He is one of the very few who see that the change of species cannot be directly proved, and that the doctrine must sink or swim according as it groups and explains phenomena. It is really curious how few judge it in this way, which is clearly the right way. I have been much interested by Bentham's paper ‡ in the N. H. R., but it would not, of course, from familiarity strike you as it did me. I liked the whole ; all the facts on the nature of close and varying species. Good Heavens ! to think of the British

---

* Third edition of 2000 copies, published in April, 1861.

† In the 'Geologist,' 1861, p. 132, by Lieutenant Frederick Wollaston Hutton, now Professor of Biology and Geology at Canterbury College, New Zealand.

‡ "On the Species and Genera of Plants, &c.," 'Natural History Review,' 1861, p. 133.

botanists turning up their noses, and saying that he knows nothing of British plants ! I was also pleased at his remarks on classification, because it showed me that I wrote truly on this subject in the 'Origin.' I saw Bentham at the Linnean Society, and had some talk with him and Lubbock, and Edgeworth, Wallich, and several others. I asked Bentham to give us his ideas of species; whether partially with us or dead against us, he would write *excellent* matter. He made no answer, but his manner made me think he might do so if urged ; so do you attack him. Every one was speaking with affection and anxiety of Henslow.* I dined with Bell at the Linnean Club, and liked my dinner. . . . . Dining out is such a novelty to me that I enjoyed it. Bell has a real good heart. I liked Rolleston's paper, but I never read anything so obscure and not self-evident as his 'Canons.'† . . . . I called on R. Chambers, at his very nice house in St. John's Wood, and had a very pleasant half-hour's talk ; he is really a capital fellow. He made one good remark and chuckled over it, that the laymen universally had treated the controversy on the 'Essays and Reviews' as a merely professional subject, and had not joined in it, but had left it to the clergy. I shall be anxious for your next letter about Henslow.‡ Farewell, with sincere sympathy, my old friend,

C. DARWIN.

P.S.—We are very much obliged for the 'London Review.' We like reading much of it, and the science is incomparably better than in the *Athenæum*. You shall not go on very long sending it, as you will be ruined by pennies and trouble, but I am under a horrid spell to the *Athenæum* and

---

* Prof. Henslow was in his last illness.

† George Rolleston, M. D., F. R. S., b. 1829, d. 1881. Linacre Professor of Anatomy and Physiology at Oxford. A man of much learning, who left but few published works, among which may be mentioned his handbook, 'Forms of Animal Life.' For the 'Canons,' see 'Nat. Hist. Review,' 1861, p. 206.

‡ Sir Joseph Hooker was Prof. Henslow's son-in-law.

the *Gardener's Chronicle,* but I have taken them in for so
many years, that I *cannot* give them up.

[The next letter refers to Lyell's visit to the Biddenham
gravel-pits near Bedford in April 1861. The visit was made
at the invitation of Mr. James Wyatt, who had recently discovered two stone implements " at the depth of thirteen feet
from the surface of the soil," resting "immediately on solid
beds of oolitic-limestone." * Here, says Sir C. Lyell, " I .
. . . for the first time, saw evidence which satisfied me of
the chronological relations of those three phenomena—the
antique tools, the extinct mammalia, and the glacial formation."]

C. Darwin to C. Lyell.

Down, April 12 [1861].

MY DEAR LYELL,—I have been most deeply interested
by your letter. You seem to have done the grandest work,
and made the greatest step, of any one with respect to man.

It is an especial relief to hear that you think the French
superficial deposits are deltoid and semi-marine ; but two
days ago I was saying to a friend, that the unknown manner
of the accumulation of these deposits, seemed the great blot
in all the work done. I could not stomach debacles or lacus-
trine beds. It is grand. I remember Falconer told me that
he thought some of the remains in the Devonshire caverns
were pre-glacial, and this, I presume, is now your conclusion
for the older celts with hyena and hippopotamus. It is grand.
What a fine long pedigree you have given the human race !

I am sure I never thought of parallel roads having been
accumulated during subsidence. I think I see some difficulties on this view, though, at first reading your note, I
jumped at the idea. But I will think over all I saw there. I
am (stomacho volente) coming up to London on Tuesday to
work on cocks and hens, and on Wednesday morning, about
a quarter before ten, I will call on you (unless I hear to the

---

* 'Antiquity of Man,' fourth edition, p. 214.

contrary), for I long to see you.   I congratulate you on your grand work.

Ever yours,
C. DARWIN.

P.S.—Tell Lady Lyell that I was unable to digest the funereal ceremonies of the ants, notwithstanding that Erasmus has often told me that I should find some day that they have their bishops.   After a battle I have always seen the ants carry away the dead for food.   Ants display the utmost economy, and always carry away a dead fellow-creature as food.   But I have just forwarded two most extraordinary letters to Busk, from a backwoodsman in Texas, who has evidently watched ants carefully, and declares most positively that they plant and cultivate a kind of grass for store food, and plant other bushes for shelter !   I do not know what to think, except that the old gentleman is not fibbing intentionally.   I have left the responsibility with Busk whether or no to read the letters.*

C. Darwin to Thomas Davidson.†

Down, April 26, 1861.

MY DEAR SIR,—I hope that you will excuse me for venturing to make a suggestion to you which I am perfectly well aware it is a very remote chance that you would adopt.   I do not know whether you have read my ' Origin of Species '; in that book I have made the remark, which I apprehend will be universally admitted, that *as a whole*, the fauna of any formation is intermediate in character between that of the

---

* *I. e.* to read them before the Linnean Society.

† Thomas Davidson, F.R.S., born in Edinburgh, May 17, 1817 ; died 1885.   His researches were chiefly connected with the sciences of geology and palæontology, and were directed especially to the elucidation of the characters, classification, history, geological and geographical distribution of recent and fossil Brachiopoda.   On this subject he brought out an important work, ' British Fossil Brachiopoda,' 5 vols. 4to. (Cooper, ' Men of the Time,' 1884.)

formations above and below.   But several really good judges
have remarked to me how desirable it would be that this
should be exemplified and worked out in some detail and
with some single group of beings.   Now every one will admit that no one in the world could do this better than you
with Brachiopods.   The result might turn out very unfavourable to the views which I hold; if so, so much the better for
those who are opposed to me.*   But I am inclined to suspect
that on the whole it would be favourable to the notion of
descent with modification ; for about a year ago, Mr. Salter †
in the Musuem in Jermyn Street, glued on a board some
Spirifers, &c., from three palæozoic stages, and arranged them
in single and branching lines, with horizontal lines marking
the formations (like the diagram in my book, if you know
it), and the result seemed to me very striking, though I was
too ignorant fully to appreciate the lines of affinities.   I
longed to have had these shells engraved, as arranged by
Mr. Salter, and connected by dotted lines, and would have
gladly paid the expense : but I could not persuade Mr. Salter
to publish a little paper on the subject.   I can hardly doubt
that many curious points would occur to any one thoroughly
instructed in the subject, who would consider a group of
beings under this point of view of descent with modification.
All those forms which have come down from an ancient
period very slightly modified ought, I think, to be omitted,
and those forms alone considered which have undergone

---

* " Mr. Davidson is not at all a full believer in great changes of species,
which will make his work all the more valuable."—C. Darwin to R. Chambers (April 30, 1861).

† John William Salter ; b. 1820, d. 1869.   He entered the service of
the Geological Survey in 1846, and ultimately became its Palæontologist,
on the retirement of Edward Forbes, and gave up the office in 1863.   He
was associated with several well-known naturalists in their work—with
Sedgwick, Murchison, Lyell, Ramsay, and Huxley.   There are sixty entries under his name in the Royal Society Catalogue.   The above facts
are taken from an obituary notice of Mr. Salter in the ' Geological Magazine,' 1869.

considerable change at each successive epoch. My fear is whether brachiopods have changed enough. The absolute amount of difference of the forms in such groups at the opposite extremes of time ought to be considered, and how far the early forms are intermediate in character between those which appeared much later in time. The antiquity of a group is not really diminished, as some seem vaguely to think, because it has transmitted to the present day closely allied forms. Another point is how far the succession of each genus is unbroken, from the first time it appeared to its extinction, with due allowance made for formations poor in fossils. I cannot but think that an important essay (far more important than a hundred literary reviews) might be written by one like yourself, and without very great labour. I know it is highly probable that you may not have leisure, or not care for, or dislike the subject, but I trust to your kindness to forgive me for making this suggestion. If by any extraordinary good fortune you were inclined to take up this notion, I would ask you to read my Chapter X. on Geological Succession. And I should like in this case to be permitted to send you a copy of the new edition, just published, in which I have added and corrected somewhat in Chapters IX. and X.

Pray excuse this long letter, and believe me,

My dear Sir, yours very faithfully,

C. DARWIN.

P.S.—I write so bad a hand that I have had this note copied.

C. Darwin to Thomas Davidson.

Down, April 30, 1861.

MY DEAR SIR,—I thank you warmly for your letter; I did not in the least know that you had attended to my work. I assure you that the attention which you have paid to it, considering your knowledge and the philosophical tone of your mind (for I well remember one remarkable letter you wrote

to me, and have looked through your various publications),
I consider one of the highest, perhaps the very highest, compliments which I have received. I live so solitary a life that
I do not often hear what goes on, and I should much like to
know in what work you have published some remarks on my
book. I take a deep interest in the subject, and I hope not
simply an egotistical interest ; therefore you may believe how
much your letter has gratified me ; I am perfectly contented
if any one will fairly consider the subject, whether or not he
fully or only very slightly agrees with me. Pray do not
think that I feel the least surprise at your demurring to a
ready acceptance ; in fact, I should not much respect anyone's
judgment who did so : that is, if I may judge others from
the long time which it has taken me to go round. Each
stage of belief cost me years. The difficulties are, as you say,
many and very great ; but the more I reflect, the more they
seem to me to be due to our underestimating our ignorance.
I belong so much to old times that I find that I weigh
the difficulties from the imperfection of the geological
record, heavier than some of the younger men. I find, to
my astonishment and joy, that such good men as Ramsay,
Jukes, Geikie, and one old worker, Lyell, do not think that
I have in the least exaggerated the imperfection of the
record.* If my views ever are proved true, our current geological views will have to be considerably modified. My
greatest trouble is, not being able to weigh the direct effects

---

* Professor Sedgwick treated this part of the ' Origin of Species ' very
differently, as might have been expected from his vehement objection to
Evolution in general. In the article in the *Spectator* of March 24, 1860,
already noticed, Sedgwick wrote : " We know the complicated organic
phenomena of the Mesozoic (or Oolitic) period. It defies the trasmuta-
tionist at every step. Oh ! but the document, says Darwin, is a fragment ;
I will interpolate long periods to account for all the changes. I say, in reply, if you deny my conclusion, grounded on positive evidence, I toss back
your conclusion, derived from negative evidence,—the inflated cushion on
which you try to bolster up the defects of your hypothesis." [The punc-
tuation of the imaginary dialogue is slightly altered from the original,
which is obscure in one place.]

of the long-continued action of changed conditions of life without any selection, with the action of selection on mere accidental (so to speak) variability.   I oscillate much on this head, but generally return to my belief that the direct action of the conditions of life has not been great.   At least this direct action can have played an extremely small part in producing all the numberless and beautiful adaptations in every living creature.   With respect to a person's belief, what does rather surprise me is that any one (like Carpenter) should be willing *to go so very far* as to believe that all birds may have descended from one parent, and not go a little farther and include all the members of the same great division ; for on such a scale of belief, all the facts in Morphology and in Embryology (the most important in my opinion of all subjects) become mere Divine mockeries. . . . . I cannot express how profoundly glad I am that some day you will publish your theoretical view on the modification and endurance of Brachiopodous species ; I am sure it will be a most valuable contribution to knowledge.

Pray forgive this very egotistical letter, but you yourself are partly to blame for having pleased me so much.   I have told Murray to send a copy of my new edition to you, and have written your name.

With cordial thanks, pray believe me, my dear Sir,

Yours very sincerely,

CH. DARWIN.

[In Mr. Davidson's Monograph on British Brachiopoda, published shortly afterwards by the Palæontographical Society, results such as my father anticipated were to some extent obtained.   "No less than fifteen commonly received species are demonstrated by Mr. Davidson by the aid of a long series of transitional forms to appertain to . . . one type."*

In the autumn of 1860, and the early part of 1861, my

---

* Lyell, 'Antiquity of Man,' first edition, p. 428.

father had a good deal of correspondence with Professor
Asa Gray on a subject to which reference has already been
made—the publication in the form of a pamphlet, of Professor Gray's three articles in the July, August, and October
numbers of the 'Atlantic Monthly,' 1860.   The pamphlet was
published by Messrs. Trübner, with reference to whom my
father wrote, "Messrs. Trübner have been most liberal and
kind, and say they shall make no charge for all their trouble.
I have settled about a few advertisements, and they will
gratuitously insert one in their own periodicals."

The reader will find these articles republished in Dr. Gray's
'Darwiniana,' p. 87, under the title " Natural Selection not
inconsistent with Natural Theology."   The pamphlet found
many admirers among those most capable of judging of its
merits, and my father believed that it was of much value in
lessening opposition, and making converts to Evolution. His
high opinion of it is shown not only in his letters, but by the
fact that he inserted a special notice of it in a most prominent
place in the third edition of the 'Origin.'   Lyell, among
others, recognised its value as an antidote to the kind of
criticism from which the cause of Evolution suffered.   Thus
my father wrote to Dr. Gray :—" Just to exemplify the use
of your pamphlet, the Bishop of London was asking Lyell
what he thought of the review in the 'Quarterly,' and Lyell
answered, ' Read Asa Gray in the 'Atlantic.'' "   It comes out
very clearly that in the case of such publications as Dr. Gray's,
my father did not rejoice over the success of his special view
of Evolution, viz. that modification is mainly due to Natural
Selection ; on the contrary, he felt strongly that the really
important point was that the doctrine of Descent should be
accepted.   Thus he wrote to Professor Gray (May 11, 1863),
with reference to Lyell's 'Antiquity of Man' :—

" You speak of Lyell as a judge ; now what I complain of
is that he declines to be a judge. . . . I have sometimes
almost wished that Lyell had pronounced against me. When
I say 'me,' I only mean *change of species by descent.* That
seems to me the turning-point. Personally, of course, I care

much about Natural Selection ; but that seems to me utterly unimportant, compared to the question of Creation *or* Modification."]

C. Darwin to Asa Gray.

Down, April 11 [1861].

MY DEAR GRAY,—I was very glad to get your photograph : I am expecting mine, which I will send off as soon as it comes. It is an ugly affair, and I fear the fault does not lie with the photographer. . . . . Since writing last, I have had several letters full of the highest commendation of your Essay ; all agree that it is by far the best thing written, and I do not doubt it has done the 'Origin' much good. I have not yet heard how it has sold. You will have seen a review in the *Gardeners' Chronicle.* Poor dear Henslow, to whom I owe much, is dying, and Hooker is with him. Many thanks for two sets of sheets of your Proceedings. I cannot understand what Agassiz is driving at. You once spoke, I think, of Professor Bowen as a very clever man. I should have thought him a singularly unobservant man from his writings. He never can have seen much of animals, or he would have seen the difference of old and wise dogs and young ones. His paper about hereditariness beats everything. Tell a breeder that he might pick out his worst *individual* animals and breed from them, and hope to win a prize, and he would think you . . . . . insane.

[Professor Henslow died on May 16, 1861, from a complication of bronchitis, congestion of the lungs, and enlargement of the heart. His strong constitution was slow in giving way, and he lingered for weeks in a painful condition of weakness, knowing that his end was near, and looking at death with fearless eyes. In Mr. Blomefield's (Jenyns) 'Memoir of Henslow' (1862) is a dignified and touching description of Prof. Sedgwick's farewell visit to his old friend. Sedgwick said afterwards that he had never seen "a human being whose soul was nearer heaven."

My father wrote to Sir J. D. Hooker on hearing of Henslow's death, "I fully believe a better man never walked this earth."

He gave his impressions of Henslow's character in Mr. Blomefield's 'Memoir.' In reference to these recollections he wrote to Sir J. D. Hooker (May 30, 1861) :—

"This morning I wrote my recollections and impressions of character of poor dear Henslow about the year 1830. I liked the job, and so have written four or five pages, now being copied. I do not suppose you will use all, of course you can chop and change as much as you like. If more than a sentence is used, I should like to see a proof-page, as I never can write decently till I see it in print. Very likely some of my remarks may appear too trifling, but I thought it best to give my thoughts as they arose, for you or Jenyns to use as you think fit.

"You will see that I have exceeded your request, but, as I said when I began, I took pleasure in writing my impression of his admirable character."]

C. Darwin to Asa Gray.

Down, June 5 [1861].

MY DEAR GRAY,—I have been rather extra busy, so have been slack in answering your note of May 6th. I hope you have received long ago the third edition of the 'Origin." . . . . I have heard nothing from Trübner of the sale of your Essay, hence fear it has not been great ; I wrote to say you could supply more. I sent a copy to Sir J. Herschel, and in his new edition of his 'Physical Geography' he has a note on the 'Origin of Species,' and agrees, to a certain limited extent, but puts in a caution on design—much like yours. . . . . I have been led to think more on this subject of late, and grieve to say that I come to differ more from you. It is not that designed variation makes, as it seems to me, my deity "Natural Selection" superfluous, but rather from studying, lately, domestic variation, and seeing what an enormous field of undesigned variability there is ready for natural selection to appropriate for any purpose useful to each creature.

I thank you much for sending me your review of Phillips.* I remember once telling you a lot of trades which you ought to have followed, but now I am convinced that you are a born reviewer. By Jove, how well and often you hit the nail on the head! You rank Phillips's book higher than I do, or than Lyell does, who thinks it fearfully retrograde. I amused myself by parodying Phillips's argument as applied to domestic variation ; and you might thus prove that the duck or pigeon has not varied because the goose has not, though more anciently domesticated, and no good reason can be assigned why it has not produced many varieties. . . . .

I never knew the newspapers so profoundly interesting. North America does not do England justice; I have not seen or heard of a soul who is not with the North. Some few, and I am one of them, even wish to God, though at the loss of millions of lives, that the North would proclaim a crusade against slavery. In the long-run, a million horrid deaths would be amply repaid in the cause of humanity. What wonderful times we live in! Massachusetts seems to show noble enthusiasm. Great God! how I should like to see the greatest curse on earth—slavery—abolished!

Farewell. Hooker has been absorbed with poor dear revered Henslow's affairs. Farewell.

Ever yours,
C. Darwin.

Hugh Falconer to C. Darwin.

31 Sackville St., W., June 23, 1861.

My dear Darwin.—I have been to Adelsberg cave and brought back with me a live *Proteus anguinus*, designed for you from the moment I got it ; *i.e.* if you have got an aquarium and would care to have it. I only returned last night from the continent, and hearing from your brother that

---

* 'Life on the Earth,' 1860.

you are about to go to Torquay, I lose no time in making you the offer. The poor dear animal is still alive—although it has had no appreciable means of sustenance for a month—and I am most anxious to get rid of the responsibility of starving it longer. In your hands it will thrive and have a fair chance of being developed without delay into some type of the Columbidæ—say a Pouter or a Tumbler.

My dear Darwin, I have been rambling through the north of Italy, and Germany lately. Everywhere have I heard your views and your admirable essay canvassed—the views of course often dissented from, according to the special bias of the speaker—but the work, its honesty of purpose, grandeur of conception, felicity of illustration, and courageous exposition, always referred to in terms of the highest admiration. And among your warmest friends no one rejoiced more heartily in the just appreciation of Charles Darwin than did

Yours very truly,

H. FALCONER.

C. Darwin to Hugh Falconer.

Down [June 24, 1861].

MY DEAR FALCONER.—I have just received your note, and by good luck a day earlier than properly, and I lose not a moment in answering you, and thanking you heartily for your offer of the valuable specimen; but I have no aquarium and shall soon start for Torquay, so that it would be a thousand pities that I should have it. Yet I should certainly much like to see it, but I fear it is impossible. Would not the Zoological Society be the best place? and then the interest which many would take in this extraordinary animal would repay you for your trouble.

Kind as you have been in taking this trouble and offering me this specimen, to tell the truth I value your note more than the specimen. I shall keep your note amongst a very few precious letters. Your kindness has quite touched me.

Yours affectionately and gratefully,

CH. DARWIN.

C. Darwin to J. D. Hooker.

2 Hesketh Crescent, Torquay,
July 13 [1861].

. . . I hope Harvey is better; I got his review * of me a day or two ago, from which I infer he must be convalescent; it's very good and fair; but it is funny to see a man argue on the succession of animals from Noah's Deluge; as God did not then wholly destroy man, probably he did not wholly destroy the races of other animals at each geological period! I never expected to have a helping hand from the Old Testament. . . .

C. Darwin to C. Lyell.

2, Hesketh Crescent, Torquay,
July 20 [1861].

MY DEAR LYELL.—I sent you two or three days ago a duplicate of a good review of the 'Origin' by a Mr. Maw,† evidently a thoughtful man, as I thought you might like to have it, as you have so many. . . .

This is quite a charming place, and I have actually walked, I believe, good two miles out and back, which is a grand feat.

I saw Mr. Pengelly ‡ the other day, and was pleased at his enthusiasm. I do not in the least know whether you are in London. Your illness must have lost you much time, but I hope you have nearly got your great job of the new edition finished. You must be very busy, if in London, so I will be

---

* The 'Dublin Hospital Gazette,' May 15, 1861. The passage referred to is at p. 150.

† Mr. George Maw, of Benthall Hall. The review was published in the 'Zoologist,' July, 1861. On the back of my father's copy is written, "Must be consulted before new edit. of 'Origin'"—words which are wanting on many more pretentious notices, on which frequently occur my father's brief o/-, or "nothing new."

‡ William Pengelly, the geologist, and well-known explorer of the Devonshire caves.

generous, and on honour bright do not expect any answer to this dull little note. . .

C. Darwin to Asa Gray.

Down, September 17 [1861 ?]

MY DEAR GRAY.—I thank you sincerely for your very long and interesting letter, political and scientific, of August 27th and 29th, and Sept 2nd received this morning. I agree with much of what you say, and I hope to God we English are utterly wrong in doubting (1) whether the N. can conquer the S. ; (2) whether the N. has many friends in the South, and (3) whether you noble men of Massachusetts are right in transferring your own good feelings to the men of Washington. Again I say I hope to God we are wrong in doubting on these points. It is number (3) which alone causes England not to be enthusiastic with you. What it may be in Lancashire I know not, but in S. England cotton has nothing whatever to do with our doubts. If abolition does follow with your victory, the whole world will look brighter in my eyes, and in many eyes. It would be a great gain even to stop the spread of slavery into the Territories ; if that be possible without abolition, which I should have doubted. You ought not to wonder so much at England's coldness, when you recollect at the commencement of the war how many propositions were made to get things back to the old state with the old line of latitude, but enough of this, all I can say is that Massachusetts and the adjoining States have the full sympathy of every good man whom I see ; and this sympathy would be extended to the whole Federal States, if we could be persuaded that your feelings were at all common to them. But enough of this. It is out of my line, though I read every word of news, and formerly well studied Olmsted. . . . . .

Your question what would convince me of Design is a poser. If I saw an angel come down to teach us good, and I was convinced from others seeing him that I was not mad, I should believe in design. If I could be convinced thoroughly that life and mind was in an unknown way a function of other imponderable force, I should be convinced. If man was made of brass or iron and no way connected with any other organism which had ever lived, I should perhaps be convinced. But this is childish writing.

I have lately been corresponding with Lyell, who, I think, adopts your idea of the stream of variation having been led or designed. I have asked him (and he says he will hereafter reflect and answer me) whether he believes that the shape of my nose was designed. If he does I have nothing more to say. If not, seeing what Fanciers have done by selecting individual differences in the nasal bones of pigeons, I must think that it is illogical to suppose that the variations, which natural selection preserves for the good of any being have been designed. But I know that I am in the same sort of muddle (as I have said before) as all the world seems to be in with respect to free will, yet with everything supposed to have been foreseen or pre-ordained.

Farewell, my dear Gray, with many thanks for your interesting letter.

Your unmerciful correspondent,

C. DARWIN.

C. Darwin to H. W. Bates.

Down, Dec. 3 [1861].

MY DEAR SIR.—I thank you for your extremely interesting letter, and valuable references, though God knows when I shall come again to this part of my subject. One cannot of course judge of style when one merely hears a paper,* but yours seemed to me very clear and good. Believe me that I estimate its value most highly. Under a general point of view, I am quite convinced (Hooker and Huxley took the same view some months ago) that a philosophic view of nature can

---

* On Mimetic Butterflies, read before the Linnean Soc., Nov. 21, 1861. For my father's opinion of it when published, see p. 18?.

solely be driven into naturalists by treating special subjects as you have done.   Under a special point of view, I think you have solved one of the most perplexing problems which could be given to solve.   I am glad to hear from Hooker that the Linnean Society will give plates if you can get drawings. . . .

Do not complain of want of advice during your travels; I dare say part of your great originality of views may be due to the necessity of self-exertion of thought.   I can understand that your reception at the British Museum would damp you; they are a very good set of men, but not the sort to appreciate your work.   In fact I have long thought that *too much* systematic work [and] description somehow blunts the faculties.   The general public appreciates a good dose of reasoning, or generalisation, with new and curious remarks on habits, final causes, &c. &c., far more than do the regular naturalists.

I am extremely glad to hear that you have begun your travels . . . I am very busy, but I shall be *truly* glad to render any aid which I can by reading your first chapter or two.   I do not think I shall be able to correct style, for this reason, that after repeated trials I find I cannot correct my own style till I see the MS. in type.   Some are born with a power of good writing, like Wallace; others like myself and Lyell have to labour very hard and slowly at every sentence. I find it a very good plan, when I cannot get a difficult discussion to please me, to fancy that some one comes into the room and asks me what I am doing; and then try at once and explain to the imaginary person what it is all about. I have done this for one paragraph to myself several times, and sometimes to Mrs. Darwin, till I see how the subject ought to go.   It is, I think, good to read one's MS. aloud. But style to me is a great difficulty; yet some good judges think I have succeeded, and I say this to encourage you.

What *I think* I can do will be to tell you whether parts had better be shortened.   It is good, I think, to dash " in medias res," and work in later any descriptions of country or any historical details which may be necessary. Murray likes lots of wood-cuts—give some by all means of ants. The public appreciate monkeys—our poor cousins. What sexual differences are there in monkeys? Have you kept them tame? if so, about their expression. I fear that you will hardly read my vile hand-writing, but I cannot without killing trouble write better.

You shall have my candid opinion on your MS., but remember it is hard to judge from MS., one reads slowly, and heavy parts seem much heavier. A first-rate judge thought my Journal very poor; now that it is in print, I happen to know, he likes it. I am sure you will understand why I am so egotistical.

I was a *little* disappointed in Wallace's book * on the Amazon; hardly facts enough. On other hand, in Gosse's book † there is not reasoning enough to my taste. Heaven knows whether you will care to read all this scribbling. . . .

I am glad you had a pleasant day with Hooker, ‡ he is an admirably good man in every sense.

[The following extract from a letter to Mr. Bates on the same subject is interesting as giving an idea of the plan followed by my father in writing his 'Naturalist's Voyage:'

"As an old hackneyed author, let me give you a bit of advice, viz. to strike out every word which is not quite necessary to the current subject, and which could not interest a stranger. I constantly asked myself, Would a stranger care for this? and struck out or left in accordingly. I think too much pains cannot be taken in making the style transparently clear and throwing eloquence to the dogs."

Mr. Bates's book, 'The Naturalist on the Amazons,' was

---

* 'Travels on the Amazon and Rio Negro,' 1853.

† Probably the 'Naturalist's Sojourn in Jamaica,' 1851.

‡ In a letter to Sir J. D. Hooker (Dec. 1861), my father wrote: "I am very glad to hear that you like Bates. I have seldom in my life been more struck with a man's power of mind."

published in 1865, but the following letter may be given here rather than in its due chronological position :]

C. Darwin to H. W. Bates.

Down, April 18, 1863.

DEAR BATES,—I have finished vol. i. My criticisms may be condensed into a single sentence, namely, that it is the best work of Natural History Travels ever published in England. Your style seems to me admirable. Nothing can be better than the discussion on the struggle for existence, and nothing better than the description of the Forest scenery.* It is a grand book, and whether or not it sells quickly, it will last. You have spoken out boldly on Species ; and boldness on the subject seems to get rarer and rarer. How beautifully illustrated it is. The cut on the back is most tasteful. I heartily congratulate you on its publication.

The *Athenæum* † was rather cold, as it always is, and insolent in the highest degree about your leading facts. Have you seen the *Reader ?* I can send it to you if you have not seen it. . . .

C. Darwin to Asa Gray.

Down, Dec. 11 [1861].

MY DEAR GRAY,—Many and cordial thanks for your two last most valuable notes. What a thing it is that when you receive this we may be at war, and we two be bound, as good patriots, to hate each other, though I shall find this hating you very hard work. How curious it is to see two countries, just like two angry and silly men, taking so opposite a view

---

* In a letter to Lyell my father wrote : " He [*i. e.* Mr. Bates] is second only to Humboldt in describing a tropical forest."

† " I have read the first volume of Bates's Book ; it is capital, and I think the best Natural History Travels ever published in England. He is bold about Species, &c., and the *Athenæum* coolly says 'he bends his facts ' for this purpose."—(From a letter to Sir J. D. Hooker.)

of the same transaction ! I fear there is no shadow of doubt
we shall fight if the two Southern rogues are not given up.*
And what a wretched thing it will be if we fight on the side
of slavery. No doubt it will be said that we fight to get
cotton ; but I fully believe that this has not entered into the
motive in the least. Well, thank Heaven, we private individuals have nothing to do with so awful a responsibility.
Again, how curious it is that you seem to think that you can
conquer the South ; and I never meet a soul, even those who
would most wish it, who thinks it possible—that is, to conquer
and retain it. I do not suppose the mass of people in your
country will believe it, but I feel sure if we do go to war it
will be with the utmost reluctance by all classes, Ministers of
Government and all. Time will show, and it is no use writing
or thinking about it. I called the other day on Dr. Boott,
and was pleased to find him pretty well and cheerful. I see,
by the way, he takes quite an English opinion of American
affairs, though an American in heart.† Buckle might write
a chapter on opinion being entirely dependent on longi-
tude !

. . . With respect to Design, I feel more inclined to show
a white flag than to fire my usual long-range shot. I like to
try and ask you a puzzling question, but when you return the
compliment I have great doubts whether it is a fair way of
arguing. If anything is designed, certainly man must be :
one's "inner consciousness" (though a false guide) tells one
so ; yet I cannot admit that man's rudimentary mammæ . . .
were designed. If I was to say I believed this, I should
believe it in the same incredible manner as the orthodox
believe the Trinity in Unity. You say that you are in a
haze ; I am in thick mud ; the orthodox would say in fetid,

---

* The Confederate Commissioners Slidell and Mason were forcibly removed from the *Trent*, a West India mail steamer on Nov. 8, 1861. The
news that the U. S. agreed to release them reached England on Jan. 8,
1862.

† Dr. Boott was born in the U. S.

abominable mud ; yet I cannot keep out of the question.
My dear Gray, I have written a deal of nonsense.

Yours most cordially,

C. DARWIN.

1862.

[Owing to the illness from scarlet fever of one of his boys,
he took a house at Bournemouth in the autumn. He wrote
to Dr. Gray from Southampton (Aug. 21, 1862) :—

"We are a wretched family, and ought to be exterminated.
We slept here to rest our poor boy on his journey to Bournemouth, and my poor dear wife sickened with scarlet fever,
and has had it pretty sharply, but is recovering well. There
is no end of trouble in this weary world. I shall not feel
safe till we are all at home together, and when that will be I
know not. But it is foolish complaining."

Dr. Gray used to send postage stamps to the scarlet fever
patient; with regard to this good-natured deed my father
wrote—

"I must just recur to stamps ; my little man has calculated that he will now have 6 stamps which no other boy in
the school has. Here is a triumph. Your last letter was
plaistered with many coloured stamps, and he long surveyed
the envelope in bed with much quiet satisfaction."

The greater number of the letters of 1862 deal with the
Orchid work, but the wave of conversion to Evolution was
still spreading, and reviews and letters bearing on the subject
still came in numbers. As an example of the odd letters he
received may be mentioned one which arrived in January of
this year "from a German homœopathic doctor, an ardent
admirer of the 'Origin.' Had himself published nearly the
same sort of book, but goes much deeper. Explains the
origin of plants and animals on the principles of homœopa-
thy or by the law of spirality. Book fell dead in Germany.
Therefore would I translate it and publish it in England."]

C. Darwin to T. H. Huxley.

Down, [Jan.?] 14 [1862].

MY DEAR HUXLEY,—I am heartily glad of your success in the North,* and thank you for your note and slip. By Jove you have attacked Bigotry in its stronghold. I thought you would have been mobbed. I am so glad that you will publish your Lectures. You seem to have kept a due medium between extreme boldness and caution. I am heartily glad that all went off so well. I hope Mrs. Huxley is pretty well. . . . . I must say one word on the Hybrid question. No doubt you are right that here is a great hiatus in the argument; yet I think you overrate it—you never allude to the excellent evidence of *varieties* of Verbascum and Nicotiana being partially sterile together. It is curious to me to read (as I have to-day) the greatest crossing *Gardener* utterly pooh-poohing the distinction which *Botanists* make on this head, and insisting how frequently crossed *varieties* produce sterile offspring. Do oblige me by reading the latter half of my Primula paper in the 'Linn. Journal,' for it leads me to suspect that sterility will hereafter have to be largely viewed as an acquired or *selected* character—a view which I wish I had had facts to maintain in the 'Origin.' †

C. Darwin to J. D. Hooker.

Down, Jan. 25 [1862].

MY DEAR HOOKER,—Many thanks for your last Sunday's letter, which was one of the pleasantest I ever received in my life. We are all pretty well redivivus, and I am at work again. I thought it best to make a clean breast to Asa Gray;

---

* This refers to two of Mr. Huxley's lectures, given before the Philosophical Institution of Edinburgh in 1862. The substance of them is given in 'Man's Place in Nature.'

† The view here given will be discussed in the chapter on hetero-styled plants.

and told him that the Boston dinner, &c. &c., had quite turned my stomach, that I almost thought it would be good for the peace of the world if the United States were split up; on the other hand, I said that I groaned to think of the slave-holders being triumphant, and that the difficulties of making a line of separation were fearful. I wonder what he will say. . . . . Your notion of the Aristocrat being kenspeckle, and the best men of a good lot being thus easily selected is new to me, and striking. The 'Origin' having made you in fact a jolly old Tory, made us all laugh heartily. I have sometimes speculated on this subject; primogeniture* is dreadfully opposed to selection; suppose the first-born bull was necessarily made by each farmer the begetter of his stock! On the other hand, as you say, ablest men are continually raised to the peerage, and get crossed with the older Lord-breeds, and the Lords continually select the most beautiful and charming women out of the lower ranks; so that a good deal of indirect selection improves the Lords. Certainly I agree with you the present American row has a very Torifying influence on us all. I am very glad to hear you are beginning to print the 'Genera;' it is a wonderful satisfaction to be thus brought to bed, indeed it is one's chief satisfaction, I think, though one knows that another bantling will soon be developing. . . .

---

* My father had a strong feeling as to the injustice of primogeniture, and in a similar spirit was often indignant over the unfair wills that appear from time to time. He would declare energetically that if he were law-giver no will should be valid that was not published in the testator's lifetime; and this he maintained would prevent much of the monstrous injustice and meanness apparent in so many wills.

C. Darwin to Maxwell Masters.*

Down, Feb. 26 [1862].

MY DEAR SIR,—I am much obliged to you for sending me your article,† which I have just read with much interest. The history, and a good deal besides, was quite new to me. It seems to me capitally done, and so clearly written. You really ought to write your larger work. You speak too generously of my book; but I must confess that you have pleased me not a little; for no one, as far as I know, has ever remarked on what I say on classification—a part, which when I wrote it, pleased me. With many thanks to you for sending me your article, pray believe me,

My dear Sir, yours sincerely,
C. DARWIN.

[In the spring of this year (1862) my father read the second volume of Buckle's 'History of Civilization.' The following strongly expressed opinion about it may be worth quoting :—

" Have you read Buckle's second volume? it has interested me greatly ; I do not care whether his views are right or wrong, but I should think they contained much truth. There is a noble love of advancement and truth throughout; and to my taste he is the very best writer of the English language that ever lived, let the other be who he may."]

C. Darwin to Asa Gray.

Down, March 15 [1862].

MY DEAR GRAY,—Thanks for the newspapers (though they did contain digs at England), and for your note of Feb.

---

* Dr. Masters is a well-known vegetable teratologist, and has been for many years the editor of the *Gardeners' Chronicle*.

† Refers to a paper on "Vegetable Morphology," by Dr. Masters, in the 'British and Foreign Medico-Chirurgical Review' for 1862.

18th.   It is really almost a pleasure to receive stabs from so smooth, polished, and sharp a dagger as your pen.   I heartily wish I could sympathise more fully with you, instead of merely hating the South.   We cannot enter into your feelings; if Scotland were to rebel, I presume we should be very wrath, but I do not think we should care a penny what other nations thought.   The millennium must come before nations love each other ; but try and do not hate me.   Think of me, if you will as a poor blinded fool.   I fear the dreadful state of affairs must dull your interest in Science. . . . .

I believe that your pamphlet has done my book *great* good ; and I thank you from my heart for myself ; and believing that the views are in large part true, I must think that you have done natural science a good turn.   Natural Selection seems to be making a little progress in England and on the Continent; a new German edition is called for, and a French * one has just appeared.   One of the best men, though at present unknown, who has taken up these views, is Mr. Bates ; pray read his 'Travels in Amazonia,' when they appear ; they will be very good, judging from MS. of the first two chapters.

. . . . Again I say, do not hate me.

Ever yours most truly,

C. DARWIN.

---

* In June, 1862, my father wrote to Dr. Gray : "I received, 2 or 3 days ago, a French translation of the 'Origin,' by a Madlle. Royer, who must be one of the cleverest and oddest women in Europe : is an ardent Deist, and hates Christianity, and declares that natural selection and the struggle for life will explain all morality, nature of man, politics, &c. &c. ! She makes some very curious and good hits, and says she shall publish a book on these subjects."   Madlle. Royer added foot-notes to her translation, and in many places where the author expresses great doubt, she explains the difficulty, or points out that no real difficulty exists.

C. Darwin to C. Lyell.

1 Carlton Terrace, Southampton,*
Aug. 22, [1862].

. . . . I heartily hope that you † will be out in October.
. . . . You say that the Bishop and Owen will be down on
you; the latter hardly can, for I was assured that Owen
in his Lectures this spring advanced as a new idea that
wingless birds had lost their wings by disuse, also that
magpies stole spoons, &c., from a *remnant* of some instinct
like that of the Bower-Bird, which ornaments its playing-
passage with pretty feathers. Indeed, I am told that he
hinted plainly that all birds are descended from one . . . .

Your P.S. touches on, as it seems to me, very difficult
points. I am glad to see [that] in the 'Origin,' I only say
that the naturalists generally consider that low organisms
vary more than high; and this I think certainly is the
general opinion. I put the statement this way to show that
I considered it only an opinion probably true. I must own
that I do not at all trust even Hooker's contrary opinion, as
I feel pretty sure that he has not tabulated any result. I
have some materials at home, I think I attempted to make
this point out, but cannot remember the result.

Mere variability, though the necessary foundation of all
modifications, I believe to be almost always present, enough
to allow of any amount of selected change ; so that it does
not seem to me at all incompatible that a group which at any
one period (or during all successive periods) varies less,
should in the long course of time have undergone more modification than a group which is generally more variable.

Placental animals, e. g. might be at each period less variable than Marsupials, and nevertheless have undergone more
differentiation and development than marsupials, owing to
some advantage, probably brain development.

---

* The house of his son William.
† *I. e.* ' The Antiquity of Man.'

I am surprised, but do not pretend to form an opinion at Hooker's statement that higher species, genera, &c., are best limited. It seems to me a bold statement.

Looking to the 'Origin,' I see that I state that the productions of the land seem to change quicker than those of the sea (Chapter X., p. 339, 3d edition), and I add there is some reason to believe that organisms considered high in the scale change quicker than those that are low. I remember writing these sentences after much deliberation. . . . . I remember well feeling much hesitation about putting in even the guarded sentences which I did. My doubts, I remember, related to the rate of change of the Radiata in the Secondary formation, and of the Foraminifera in the oldest Tertiary beds. . . . .   Good night,

C. Darwin.

C. Darwin to C. Lyell.

Down, Oct. 1 [1862].

. . . . I found here * a short and very kind note of Falconer, with some pages of his 'Elephant Memoir,' which will be published, in which he treats admirably on long persistence of type. I thought he was going to make a good and crushing attack on me, but to my great satisfaction, he ends by pointing out a loophole, and adds, † "with him I have no faith that the mammoth and other extinct elephants made their appearance suddenly. . . . . The most rational view seems to be that they are the modified descendants of earlier progenitors, &c." This is capital. There will not be soon one good palæontologist who believes in immutability. Falconer does not allow for the Proboscidean group being a failing one, and therefore not likely to be giving off new races.

---

* On his return from Bournemouth.

† Falconer, "On the American Fossil Elephant," in the 'Nat. Hist. Review,' 1863, p. 81. The words preceding those cited by my father make the meaning of his quotation clearer. The passage begins as follows: "The inferences which I draw from these facts are not opposed to one of the leading propositions of Darwin's theory. With him," &c. &c.

He adds that he does not think Natural Selection suffices. I do not quite see the force of his argument, and he apparently overlooks that I say over and over again that Natural Selection can do nothing without variability, and that variability is subject to the most complex fixed laws. . . . .

[In his letters to Sir J. D. Hooker, about the end of this year, are occasional notes on the progress of the 'Variation of Animals and Plants.' Thus on November 24th he wrote: "I hardly know why I am a little sorry, but my present work is leading me to believe rather more in the direct action of physical conditions. I presume I regret it, because it lessens the glory of natural selection, and is so confoundedly doubtful. Perhaps I shall change again when I get all my facts under one point of view, and a pretty hard job this will be."

Again, on December 22nd, "To-day I have begun to think of arranging my concluding chapters on Inheritance, Reversion, Selection, and such things, and am fairly paralyzed how to begin and how to end, and what to do, with my huge piles of materials."]

C. Darwin to Asa Gray.

Down, Nov. 6 [1862].

MY DEAR GRAY,—When your note of October 4th and 13th (chiefly about Max Müller) arrived, I was nearly at the end of the same book,* and had intended recommending you to read it. I quite agree that it is extremely interesting, but the latter part about the *first* origin of language much the least satisfactory. It is a marvellous problem. . . . . [There are] covert sneers at me, which he seems to get the better of towards the close of the book. I cannot quite see how it will forward "my cause," as you call it; but I can see how any one with literary talent (I do not feel up to it) could

---

* 'Lectures on the Science of Language, 1st edit. 1861.

make great use of the subject in illustration.* What pretty metaphors you would make from it ! I wish some one would keep a lot of the most noisy monkeys, half free, and study their means of communication !

A book has just appeared here which will, I suppose, make a noise, by Bishop Colenso,† who, judging from extracts, smashes most of the Old Testament. Talking of books, I am in the middle of one which pleases me, though it is very innocent food, viz., Miss Cooper's 'Journal of a Naturalist.' Who is she? She seems a very clever woman, and gives a capital account of the battle between *our* and *your* weeds. Does it not hurt your Yankee pride that we thrash you so confoundedly? I am sure Mrs. Gray will stick up for your own weeds. Ask her whether they are not more honest, downright good sort of weeds. The book gives an extremely pretty picture of one of your villages; but I see your autumn, though so much more gorgeous than ours, comes on sooner, and that is one comfort. . . . .

C. Darwin to H. W. Bates.

Down, Nov. 20 [1862].

DEAR BATES,—I have just finished, after several reads, your paper.‡ In my opinion it is one of the most remarkable

---

* Language was treated in the manner here indicated by Sir C. Lyell in the 'Antiquity of Man.' Also by Prof. Schleicher, whose pamphlet was fully noticed in the *Reader*, Feb. 27, 1864 (as I learn from one of Prof. Huxley's 'Lay Sermon's').

† 'The Pentateuch and Book of Joshua critically examined,' six parts, 1862–71.

‡ This refers to Mr. Bates's paper, "Contributions to an Insect Fauna of the Amazons Valley" ('Linn. Soc. Trans.' xxiii., 1862), in which the now familiar subject of mimicry was founded. My father wrote a short review of it in the 'Natural History Review,' 1863, p. 219, parts of which occur in this review almost verbatim in the later editions of the 'Origin of Species.' A striking passage occurs showing the difficulties of the case from a creationist's point of view :—

"By what means, it may be asked, have so many butterflies of the Amazonian region acquired their deceptive dress? Most naturalists will answer

and admirable papers I ever read in my life. The mimetic
cases are truly marvellous, and you connect excellently a
host of analogous facts. The illustrations are beautiful, and
seem very well chosen ; but it would have saved the reader
not a little trouble, if the name of each had been engraved
below each separate figure. No doubt this would have put
the engraver into fits, as it would have destroyed the beauty
of the plate. I am not at all surprised at such a paper having consumed much time. I am rejoiced that I passed over
the whole subject in the ' Origin,' for I should have made
a precious mess of it. You have most clearly stated and
solved a wonderful problem. No doubt with most people
this will be the cream of the paper; but I am not sure that
all your facts and reasonings on variation, and on the segregation of complete and semi-complete species, is not really
more, or at least as valuable, a part. I never conceived the
process nearly so clearly before; one feels present at the
creation of new forms. I wish, however, you had enlarged

that they were thus clothed from the hour of their creation—an answer
which will generally be so far triumphant that it can be met only by long-
drawn arguments ; but it is made at the expense of putting an effectual bar
to all further inquiry. In this particular case, moreover, the creationist will
meet with special difficulties ; for many of the mimicking forms of *Leptalis*
can be shown by a graduated series to be merely varieties of one species ;
other mimickers are undoubtedly distinct species, or even distinct genera.
So again, some of the mimicked forms can be shown to be merely varieties ; but the greater number must be ranked as distinct species. Hence
the creationist will have to admit that some of these forms have become
imitators, by means of the laws of variation, whilst others he must look at
as separately created under their present guise ; he will further have to
admit that some have been created in imitation of forms not themselves
created as we now see them, but due to the laws of variation? Prof.
Agassiz, indeed, would think nothing of this difficulty ; for he believes that
not only each species and each variety, but that groups of individuals,
though identically the same, when inhabiting distinct countries, have been
all separately created in due proportional numbers to the wants of each
land. Not many naturalists will be content thus to believe that varieties
and individuals have been turned out all ready made, almost as a manu-
facturer turns out toys according to the temporary demand of the market."

a little more on the pairing of similar varieties ; a rather more numerous body of facts seems here wanted. Then, again, what a host of curious miscellaneous observations there are—as on related sexual and individual variability : these will some day, if I live, be a treasure to me.

With respect to mimetic resemblance being so common with insects, do you not think it may be connected with their small size; they cannot defend themselves; they cannot escape by flight, at least, from birds, therefore they escape by trickery and deception?

I have one serious criticism to make, and that is about the title of the paper ; I cannot but think that you ought to have called prominent attention in it to the mimetic resemblances. Your paper is too good to be largely appreciated by the mob of naturalists without souls; but, rely on it, that it will have *lasting* value, and I cordially congratulate you on your first great work. You will find, I should think, that Wallace will fully appreciate it. How gets on your book? Keep your spirits up. A book is no light labour. I have been better lately, and working hard, but my health is very indifferent. How is your health ? Believe me, dear Bates,

Yours very sincerely,

C. DARWIN.

CHAPTER IV.

THE SPREAD OF EVOLUTION.

'VARIATION OF ANIMALS AND PLANTS.'

1863–1866.

⌊HIS book on animals and plants under domestication was my father's chief employment in the year 1863. His diary records the length of time spent over the composition of its chapters, and shows the rate at which he arranged and wrote out for printing the observations and deductions of several years.

The three chapters in vol. ii. on inheritance, which occupy 84 pages of print, were begun in January and finished on April 1st; the five on crossing, making 106 pages, were written in eight weeks, while the two chapters on selection, covering 57 pages, were begun on June 16th and finished on July 20th.

The work was more than once interrupted by ill health, and in September, what proved to be the beginning of a six month's illness, forced him to leave home for the water-cure at Malvern. He returned in October and remained ill and depressed, in spite of the hopeful opinion of one of the most cheery and skilful physicians of the day. Thus he wrote to Sir J. D. Hooker in November :—

"Dr. Brinton has been here (recommended by Busk) ; he does not believe my brain or heart are primarily affected, but I have been so steadily going down hill, I cannot help doubting whether I can ever crawl a little uphill again. Unless I can, enough to work a little, I hope my life may be very short, for to lie on a sofa all day and do nothing but give trouble to the best and kindest of wives and good dear children is dreadful."

The minor works in this year were a short paper in the 'Natural History Review' (N.S. vol. iii. p. 115), entitled "On the so-called *Auditory-Sac* of Cirripedes," and one in the 'Geological Society's Journal' (vol. xix), on the "Thickness of the Pampæan Formation near Buenos Ayres." The paper on Cirripedes was called forth by the criticisms of a German naturalist Krohn,* and is of some interest in illustration of my father's readiness to admit an error.

With regard to the spread of a belief in Evolution, it could not yet be said that the battle was won, but the growth of belief was undoubtedly rapid. So that, for instance, Charles Kingsley could write to F. D. Maurice † :

"The state of the scientific mind is most curious; Darwin is conquering everywhere, and rushing in like a flood, by the mere force of truth and fact."

Mr. Huxley was as usual active in guiding and stimulating the growing tendency to tolerate or accept the views set forth in the 'Origin of Species.' He gave a series of lectures to working men at the School of Mines in November, 1862. These were printed in 1863 from the shorthand notes of Mr. May, as six little blue books, price 4*d.* each, under the title, 'Our Knowledge of the Causes of Organic Nature.' When published they were read with interest by my father, who thus refers to them in a letter to Sir J. D. Hooker :—

"I am very glad you like Huxley's lectures. I have been very much struck with them, especially with the 'Philosophy of Induction.' I have quarrelled with him for overdoing sterility and ignoring cases from Gärtner and Kölreuter about

---

* Krohn stated that the structures described by my father as ovaries were in reality salivary glands, also that the oviduct runs down to the orifice described in the 'Monograph of the Cirripedia' as the auditory *meatus.*

† Kingsley's 'Life,' ii, p. 171.

49

sterile varieties.   His Geology is obscure ; and I rather doubt
about man's mind and language.   But it seems to me *admirably* done, and, as you say, " Oh my," about the praise of
the ' Origin.'   I can't help liking it, which makes me rather
ashamed of myself."

My father admired the clearness of exposition shown in
the lectures, and in the following letter urges their author to
make use of his powers for the advantage of students :]

C. Darwin to T. H. Huxley.

Nov. 5 [1864].

I want to make a suggestion to you, but which may probably have occurred to you. —— was reading your Lectures
and ended by saying, " I wish he would write a book."   I
answered, " he has just written a great book on the skull."   " I
don't call that a book," she replied, and added, " I want
something that people can read ; he does write so well."
Now, with your ease in writing, and with knowledge at your
fingers' ends, do you not think you could write a popular
Treatise on Zoology ?   Of course it would be some waste of
time, but I have been asked more than a dozen times to
recommend something for a beginner and could only think of
Carpenter's Zoology.   I am sure that a striking Treatise
would do real service to science by educating naturalists.   If
you were to keep a portfolio open for a couple of years, and
throw in slips of paper as subjects crossed your mind, you
would soon have a skeleton (and that seems to me the difficulty) on which to put the flesh and colours in your inimitable
manner.   I believe such a book might have a brilliant success,
but I did not intend to scribble so much about it.

Give my kindest remembrance to Mrs. Huxley, and tell
her I was looking at ' Enoch Arden,' and as I know how she
admires Tennyson, I must call her attention to two sweetly
pretty lines (p. 105) . . .

. . . and he meant, he said he meant,
Perhaps he meant, or partly meant, you well.

Such a gem as this is enough to make me young again, and like poetry with pristine fervour.

My dear Huxley,

Yours affectionately,

CH. DARWIN.

[In another letter (Jan. 1865) he returns to the above suggestion, though he was in general strongly opposed to men of science giving up to the writing of text-books, or to teaching, the time that might otherwise have been given to original research.

"I knew there was very little chance of your having time to write a popular Treatise on Zoology, but you are about the one man who could do it. At the time I felt it would be almost a sin for you to do it, as it would of course destroy some original work. On the other hand I sometimes think that general and popular treatises are almost as important for the progress of science as original work."

The series of letters will continue the history of the year 1863.]

C. Darwin to J. D. Hooker.

Down, Jan. 3 [1863].

MY DEAR HOOKER.—I am burning with indignation and must exhale. . . . I could not get to sleep till past 3 last night for indignation.* . . . .

Now for pleasanter subjects ; we were all amused at your defence of stamp collecting and collecting generally. . . . But, by Jove, I can hardly stomach a grown man collecting stamps. Who would ever have thought of your collecting Wedgwood-ware ! but that is wholly different, like engravings or pictures. We are degenerate descendants of old Josiah W., for we have not a bit of pretty ware in the house.

---

* It would serve no useful purpose if I were to go into the matter which so strongly roused my father's anger. It was a question of literary dishonesty, in which a friend was the sufferer, but which in no way affected himself.

. . . Notwithstanding the very pleasant reason you give for our not enjoying a holiday, namely, that we have no vices, it is a horrid bore. I have been trying for health's sake to be idle, with no success. What I shall now have to do, will be to erect a tablet in Down Church, "Sacred to the Memory, &c.," and officially die, and then publish books, "by the late Charles Darwin," for I cannot think what has come over me of late ; I always suffered from the excitement of talking, but now it has become ludicrous. I talked lately 1½ hours (broken by tea by myself) with my nephew, and I was [ill] half the night. It is a fearful evil for self and family.

Good-night.   Ever yours.
C. DARWIN.

[The following letter to Sir Julius von Haast,* is an example of the sympathy which he felt with the spread and growth of science in the colonies. It was a feeling not expressed once only, but was frequently present in his mind, and often found utterance. When we, at Cambridge, had the satisfaction of receiving Sir J. von Haast into our body as a Doctor of Science (July 1886), I had the opportunity of hearing from him of the vivid pleasure which this, and other letters from my father, gave him. It was pleasant to see how strong had been the impression made by my father's warm-hearted sympathy—an impression which seemed, after more than twenty years, to be as fresh as when it was first received :]

C. Darwin to Julius von Haast.

Down, Jan. 22 [1863].

DEAR SIR,—I thank you most sincerely for sending me your Address and the Geological Report.† I have seldom in

---

* Sir Julius von Haast was a German by birth, but had long been resident in New Zealand. He was, in 1862, Government Geologist to the Province of Canterbury.

† Address to the 'Philosophical Institute of Canterbury (N. Z.).' The

my life read anything more spirited and interesting than your address. The progress of your colony makes one proud, and it is really admirable to see a scientific institution founded in so young a nation. I thank you for the very honorable notice of my 'Origin of Species.' You will easily believe how much I have been interested by your striking facts on the old glacial period, and I suppose the world might be searched in vain for so grand a display of terraces. You have, indeed, a noble field for scientific research and discovery. I have been extremely much interested by what you say about the tracks of supposed [living] mammalia. Might I ask, if you succeed in discovering what the creatures are, you would have the great kindness to inform me? Perhaps they may turn out something like the Solenhofen bird creature, with its long tail and fingers, with claws to its wings! I may mention that in South America, in completely uninhabited regions, I found spring rat-traps, baited with *cheese*, were very successful in catching the smaller mammals. I would venture to suggest to you to urge on some of the capable members of your institution to observe annually the rate and manner of spreading of European weeds and insects, and especially to observe *what native plants most fail ;* this latter point has never been attended to. Do the introduced hive-bees replace any other insect? &c. All such points are, in my opinion, great desiderata in science. What an interesting discovery that of the remains of prehistoric man!

> Believe me, dear Sir,
> > With the most cordial respect and thanks,
> > > Yours very faithfully,
> > > > CHARLES DARWIN.

"Report" is given in *The New Zealand Government Gazette, Province of Canterbury,* Oct. 1862.

C. Darwin to Camille Dareste.*

Down, Feb. 16 [1863].

DEAR AND RESPECTED SIR.—I thank you sincerely for your letter and your pamphlet. I had heard (I think in one of M. Quatrefage's books) of your work, and was most anxious to read it, but did not know where to find it. You could not have made me a more valuable present. I have only just returned home, and have not yet read your work; when I do if I wish to ask any questions I will venture to trouble you. Your approbation of my book on Species has gratified me extremely. Several naturalists in England, North America, and Germany, have declared that their opinions on the subject have in some degree been modified, but as far as I know, my book has produced no effect whatever in France, and this makes me the more gratified by your very kind expression of approbation. Pray believe me, dear Sir, with much respect,

Yours faithfully and obliged,

CH. DARWIN.

C. Darwin to J. D. Hooker.

Down, Feb. 24 [1863].

MY DEAR HOOKER.—I am astonished at your note, I have not seen the *Athenæum*,† but I have sent for it, and may get it to-morrow; and will then say what I think.

---

* Professor Dareste is a well-known worker in Animal Teratology. He was in 1863 living at Lille, but has since then been called to Paris. My father took a special interest in Dareste's work on the production of monsters, as bearing on the causes of variation.

† In the 'Antiquity of Man,' first edition, p. 480, Lyell criticised somewhat severely Owen's account of the difference between the Human and Simian brains. The number of the *Athenæum* here referred to (1863, p. 262) contains a reply by Professor Owen to Lyell's strictures. The surprise expressed by my father was at the revival of a controversy which every one believed to be closed. Prof. Huxley (*Medical Times*, Oct. 25,

I have read Lyell's book. ['The Antiquity of Man.'] The whole certainty struck me as a compilation, but of the highest class, for when possible the facts have been verified on the spot, making it almost an original work. The Glacial chapters seem to me best, and in parts magnificent. I could hardly judge about Man, as all the gloss of novelty was completely worn off. But certainly the aggregation of the evidence produced a very striking effect on my mind. The chapter comparing language and changes of species, seems most ingenious and interesting. He has shown great skill in picking out salient points in the argument for change of species ; but I am deeply disappointed (I do not mean personally) to find that his timidity prevents him giving any judgment. . . . From all my communications with him I must ever think that he has really entirely lost faith in the immutability of species ; and yet one of his strongest sentences is nearly as follows : "If it should *ever** be rendered highly probable that species change by variation and natural selection," &c., &c. I had hoped he would have guided the public as far as his own belief went. . . . One thing does please me on this subject, that he seems to appreciate your work. No doubt the public or a part may be induced to think that as he gives to us a larger space than to Lamarck, he must think there is something in our views. When reading the brain chapter, it struck me forcibly that if he had said openly that he believed in change of species, and as a consequence that man was derived from some Quadrumanous animal, it would have been very proper to have discussed by compilation the differences in the most important organ, viz. the brain. As it is, the chapter seems to me to come in rather by the head and shoulders. I do not think (but then I am as prejudiced as Falconer and Huxley, or

---

1862, quoted in 'Man's Place in Nature,' p. 117) spoke of the "two years during which this preposterous controversy has dragged its weary length." And this no doubt expressed a very general feeling.

* The italics are not Lyell's.

more so) that it is too severe ; it struck me as given with judicial force.   It might perhaps be said with truth that he had no business to judge on a subject on which he knows nothing ; but compilers must do this to a certain extent. (You know I value and rank high compilers, being one my-self !)   I have taken you at your word, and scribbled at great length.   If I get the *Athenæum* to-morrow, I will add my impression of Owen's letter.

. . . . The Lyells are coming here on Sunday evening to stay till Wednesday.   I dread it, but I must say how much disappointed I am that he has not spoken out on species, still less on man.   And the best of the joke is that he thinks he has acted with the courage of a martyr of old.   I hope I may have taken an exaggerated view of his timidity, and shall *particularly* be glad of your opinion on this head.*   When I got his book I turned over the pages, and saw he had dis-cussed the subject of species, and said that I thought he would do more to convert the public than all of us, and now (which makes the case worse for me) I must, in common honesty, retract.   I wish to Heaven he had said not a word on the subject.

Wednesday morning : I have read the *Athenæum*.   I do not think Lyell will be nearly so much annoyed as you ex-pect.   The concluding sentence is no doubt very stinging. No one but a good anatomist could unravel Owen's letter ; at least it is quite beyond me.

. . . Lyell's memory plays him false when he says all anatomists were astonished at Owen's paper ;† it was often quoted with approbation.   I *well* remember Lyell's admira-tion at this new classification !   (Do not repeat this.)   I re-member it, because, though I knew nothing whatever about

---

* On this subject my father wrote to Sir Joseph Hooker: "Cordial thanks for your deeply interesting letters about Lyell, Owen, and Co.   I cannot say how glad I am to hear that I have not been unjust about the species-question towards Lyell.   I feared I had been unreasonable."

† " On the Characters, &c., of the Class Mammalia." ' Linn. Soc. Jour-nal,' ii, 1858.

the brain, I felt a conviction that a classification thus founded on a single character would break down, and it seemed to me a great error not to separate more completely the Marsupialia. . . .

What an accursed evil it is that there should be all this quarreling within, what ought to be, the peaceful realms of science.

I will go to my own present subject of inheritance and forget it all for a time.   Farewell, my dear old friend,

C. Darwin.

C. Darwin to Asa Gray.

Down, Feb. 23 [1863].

. . . If you have time to read you will be interested by parts of Lyell's book on man ; but I fear that the best part, about the Glacial period, may be too geological for any one except a regular geologist.   He quotes you at the end with gusto.   By the way, he told me the other day how pleased some had been by hearing that they could purchase your pamphlet.   The *Parthenon* also speaks of it as the ablest contribution to the literature of the subject.   It delights me when I see your work appreciated.

The Lyells come here this day week, and I shall grumble at his excessive caution. . . . The public may well say, if such a man dare not or will not speak out his mind, how can we who are ignorant form even a guess on the subject ?   Lyell was pleased when I told him lately that you thought that language might be used as an excellent illustration of derivation of species ; you will see that he has an *admirable* chapter on this. . . .

I read Cairns's excellent Lecture,* which shows so well how your quarrel arose from Slavery.   It made me for a time wish honestly for the North ; but I could never help, though I tried, all the time thinking how we should be bullied and

---

* Prof. J. E. Cairns, ' The Slave Power, &c. : an attempt to explain the real issues involved in the American contest.'   1862.

forced into a war by you, when you were triumphant. But I do most truly think it dreadful that the South, with its accursed slavery, should triumph, and spread the evil. I think if I had power, which thank God, I have not, I would let you conquer the border States, and all west of the Mississippi, and then force you to acknowledge the cotton States. For do you not now begin to doubt whether you can conquer and hold them? I have inflicted a long tirade on you.

The Times is getting more detestable (but that is too weak a word) than ever. My good wife wishes to give it up, but I tell her that is a pitch of heroism to which only a woman is equal. To give up the "Bloody Old *Times*," as Cobbett used to call it, would be to give up meat, drink and air. Farewell, my dear Gray,

Yours most truly,
C. DARWIN.

C. Darwin to C. Lyell.

Down, March 6, [1863].

. . . I have been of course deeply interested by your book.* I have hardly any remarks worth sending, but will scribble a little on what most interested me. But I will first get out what I hate saying, viz., that I have been greatly disappointed that you have not given judgment and spoken fairly out what you think about the derivation of species. I should have been contented if you had boldly said that species have not been separately created, and had thrown as much doubt as you like on how far variation and natural selection suffices. I hope to Heaven I am wrong (and from what you say about Whewell it seems so), but I cannot see how your chapters can do more good than an extraordinary able review. I think the *Parthenon* is right, that you will leave the public in a fog. No doubt they may infer that as you give more space to myself, Wallace, and Hooker, than to Lamarck, you think more of us. But I had always thought that your judgment

---

* ' Antiquity of Man.'

would have been an epoch in the subject. All that is over with me, and I will only think on the admirable skill with which you have selected the striking points, and explained them. No praise can be too strong, in my opinion, for the inimitable chapter on language in comparison with species.

 * p. 505—A sentence at the top of the page makes me groan. . . .

 I know you will forgive me for writing with perfect freedom, for you must know how deeply I respect you as my old honoured guide and master. I heartily hope and expect that your book will have gigantic circulation and may do in many ways as much good as it ought to do. I am tired, so no more. I have written so briefly that you will have to guess my meaning. I fear my remarks are hardly worth sending. Farewell, with kindest remembrance to Lady Lyell.

Ever yours,
C. Darwin.

[Mr. Huxley has quoted (vol. i. p. 546) some passages from Lyell's letters which show his state of mind at this time. The following passage, from a letter of March 11th to my father, is also of much interest :—

 "My feelings, however, more than any thought about policy or expediency, prevent me from dogmatising as to the descent of man from the brutes, which, though I am prepared to accept it, takes away much of the charm from my speculations on the past relating to such matters. . . . But you ought to be satisfied, as I shall bring hundreds towards you who, if I treated the matter more dogmatically, would have rebelled."]

---

 * After speculating on the sudden appearance of individuals far above the average of the human race, Lyell asks if such leaps upwards in the scale of intellect may not "have cleared at one bound the space which separated the higher stage of the unprogressive intelligence of the inferior animals from the first and lowest form of improvable reason manifested by man."

C. Darwin to C. Lyell.

Down, 12 [March, 1863].

My Dear Lyell,—I thank you for your very interesting and kind, I may say, charming letter. I feared you might be huffed for a little time with me. I know some men would have been so. I have hardly any more criticisms, anyhow, worth writing. But I may mention that I felt a little surprise that old B. de Perthes * was not rather more honourably mentioned. I would suggest whether you could not leave out some references to the ' Principles ; ' one for the real student is as good as a hundred, and it is rather irritating, and gives a feeling of incompleteness to the general reader to be often referred to other books. As you say that you have gone as far as you believe on the species question, I have not a word to say ; but I must feel convinced that at times, judging from conversation, expressions, letters, &c., you have as completely given up belief in immutability of specific forms as I have done. I must still think a clear expression from you, *if you could have given it*, would have been potent with the public, and all the more so, as you formerly held opposite opinions. The more I work the more satisfied I become with variation and natural selection, but that part of the case I look at as less important, though more interesting to me personally. As you ask for criticisms on this head (and believe me that I should not have made them unasked), I may specify (pp. 412, 413) that such words as " Mr. D. labours to show," " is believed by the author to throw light," would lead a common reader to think that you yourself do *not* at all agree, but merely think it fair to give my opinion. Lastly, you refer repeatedly to my view as a modification of Lamarck's doctrine of development and progression. If this is your deliberate opinion there is nothing to be said, but it does not seem so to me. Plato, Buffon, my grandfather before

---

* Born 1788, died 1868.   See footnote, p. 200.

Lamarck, and others, propounded the *obvious* views that if species were not created separately they must have descended from other species, and I can see nothing else in common between the 'Origin' and Lamarck. I believe this way of putting the case is very injurious to its acceptance, as it implies necessary progression, and closely connects Wallace's and my views with what I consider, after two deliberate readings, as a wretched book, and one from which (I well remember my surprise) I gained nothing. But I know you rank it higher, which is curious, as it did not in the least shake your belief. But enough, and more than enough. Please remember you have brought it all down on yourself!!

I am very sorry to hear about Falconer's "reclamation." * I hate the very word, and have a sincere affection for him.

Did you ever read anything so wretched as the *Athenæum* reviews of you, and of Huxley † especially. Your *object* to make man old, and Huxley's *object* to degrade him. The wretched writer has not a glimpse what the discovery of scientific truth means. How splendid some pages are in Huxley, but I fear the book will not be popular. . . .

C. Darwin to J. D. Hooker.

Down [March 13, 1863].

I should have thanked you sooner for the *Athenæum* and very pleasant previous note, but I have been busy, and not a little uncomfortable from frequent uneasy feeling of fullness, slight pain and tickling about the heart. But as I have no other symptoms of heart complaint I do not suppose it is affected. . . . I have had a most kind and delightfully candid letter from Lyell, who says he spoke out as far as he be-

---

* "Falconer, whom I referred to oftener than to any other author, says I have not done justice to the part he took in resuscitating the cave question, and says he shall come out with a separate paper to prove it. I offered to alter anything in the new edition, but this he declined."—C. Lyell to C. Darwin, March 11, 1863; Lyell's 'Life,' vol. ii. p. 364.

† 'Man's Place in Nature,' 1863.

lieves. I have no doubt his belief failed him as he wrote, for I feel sure that at times he no more believed in Creation than you or I. I have grumbled a bit in my answer to him at his *always* classing my work as a modification of Lamarck's, which it is no more than any author who did not believe in immutability of species, and did believe in descent. I am very sorry to hear from Lyell that Falconer is going to publish a formal reclamation of his own claims. . . .

It is cruel to think of it, but we must go to Malvern in the middle of April; it is ruin to me.* . . .

C. *Darwin to C. Lyell.*

Down, March 17 [1863].

MY DEAR LYELL,—I have been much interested by your letters and enclosure, and thank you sincerely for giving me so much time when you must be so busy. What a curious letter from B. de P. [Boucher de Perthes]. He seems perfectly satisfied, and must be a very amiable man. I know something about his errors, and looked at his book many years ago, and am ashamed to think that I concluded the whole was rubbish! Yet he has done for man something like what Agassiz did for glaciers.†

I cannot say that I agree with Hooker about the public not liking to be told what to conclude, *if coming from one in your position.* But I am heartily sorry that I was led to make complaints, or something very like complaints, on the manner in which you have treated the subject, and still more so anything about myself. I steadily *endeavour* never to forget my firm belief that no one can at all judge about his own

---

* He went to Hartfield in Sussex, on April 27, and to Malvern in the autumn.

† In his 'Antiquités Celtiques' (1847), Boucher de Perthes described the flint tools found at Abbeville with bones of rhinoceros, hyæna, &c. " But the scientific world had no faith in the statement that works of art, however rude, had been met with in undisturbed beds of such antiquity." (' Antiquity of Man,' first edition, p. 95).

work.   As for Lamarck, as you have such a man as Grove
with you, you are triumphant; not that I can alter my opinion that to me it was an absolutely useless book.   Perhaps
this was owing to my always searching books for facts, perhaps from knowing my grandfather's earlier and identically
the same speculation.   I will only further say that if I can
analyse my own feelings (a very doubtful process), it is nearly as much for your sake as for my own, that I so much wish
that your state of belief could have permitted you to say
boldly and distinctly out that species were not separately
created.   I have generally told you the progress of opinion,
as I have heard it, on the species question.   A first-rate German naturalist * (I now forget the name !), who has lately
published a grand folio, has spoken out to the utmost extent
on the 'Origin.'   De Candolle, in a very good paper on
"Oaks," goes, in Asa Gray's opinion, as far as he himself
does; but De Candolle, in writing to me, says *we*, "we think
this and that; " so that I infer he really goes to the full extent with me, and tells me of a French good botanical palæontologist (name forgotten),† who writes to De Candolle that
he is sure that my views will ultimately prevail.   But I did
not intend to have written all this.   It satisfies me with the
final results, but this result, I begin to see, will take two or
three lifetimes.   The entomologists are enough to keep the
subject back for half a century.   I really pity your having to
balance the claims of so many eager aspirants for notice ; it
is clearly impossible to satisfy all. . . . Certainly I was struck
with the full and due honour you conferred on Falconer.
I have just had a note from Hooker. . . . I am heartily glad
that you have made him so conspicuous; he is so honest, so
candid, and so modest. . . .

I have read ——.   I could find nothing to lay hold of,

. * No doubt Haeckel, whose monograph on the Radiolaria was published in 1862.   In the same year Professor W. Preyer of Jena published
a Dissertation on *Alca impennis*, which was one of the earliest pieces of
special work on the basis of the 'Origin of Species.'

† The Marquis de Saporta.

which in one sense I am very glad of, as I should hate a controversy; but in another sense I am very sorry for, as I long
to be in the same boat with all my friends. . . . I am heartily glad the book is going off so well.

                              Ever yours,
                                   C. DARWIN.

C. Darwin to J. D. Hooker.

                              Down [March 29, 1863].

. . . Many thanks for *Athenæum*, received this morning,
and to be returned to-morrow morning. Who would have
ever thought of the old stupid *Athenæum* taking to Oken-like
transcendental philosophy written in Owenian style ! * . . . .
It will be some time before we see " slime, protoplasm, &c.,"
generating a new animal.† But I have long regretted that I

---

* This refers to a review of Dr. Carpenter's 'Introduction to the study
of Foraminifera,' that appeared in the *Athenæum* of March 28, 1863 (p.
417). The reviewer attacks Dr. Carpenter's views in as much as they support the doctrine of Descent; and he upholds spontaneous generation
(Heterogeny) in place of what Dr. Carpenter, naturally enough, believed
in, viz. the genetic connection of living and extinct Foraminifera. In the
next number is a letter by Dr. Carpenter, which chiefly consists of a protest against the reviewer's somewhat contemptuous classification of Dr.
Carpenter and my father as disciple and master. In the course of the letter Dr. Carpenter says—p. 461 :—

" Under the influence of his foregone conclusion that I have accepted
Mr. Darwin as my master, and his hypothesis as my guide, your reviewer
represents me as blind to the significance of the general fact stated by me,
that ' there has been no advance in the foraminiferous type from the palæozoic period to the present time.' But for such a foregone conclusion he
would have recognised in this statement the expression of my conviction
that the present state of scientific evidence, instead of sanctioning the idea
that the descendants of the primitive type or types of Foraminifera can ever
rise to any higher grade, justifies the *anti-Darwinian* inference, that however widely they diverge from each other and from their originals, *they
still remain Foraminifera.*"

† On the same subject my father wrote in 1871: " It is often said that
all the conditions for the first production of a living organism are now
present, which could ever have been present. But if (and oh ! what a big

truckled to public opinion, and used the Pentateuchal term of creation,* by which I really meant "appeared" by some wholly unknown process. It is mere rubbish, thinking at present of the origin of life ; one might as well think of the origin of matter.

C. Darwin to J. D. Hooker.

Down, Friday night [April 17, 1863].

MY DEAR HOOKER,—I have heard from Oliver that you will be now at Kew, and so I am going to amuse myself by scribbling a bit. I hope you have thoroughly enjoyed your tour. I never in my life saw anything like the spring flowers this year. What a lot of interesting things have been lately published. I liked extremely your review of De Candolle. What an awfully severe article that by Falconer on Lyell ; †　I am very sorry for it ; I think Falconer on his side does not

---

if !) we could conceive in some warm little pond, with all sorts of ammonia and phosphoric salts, light, heat, electricity, &c., present, that a proteine compound was chemically formed ready to undergo still more complex changes, at the present day such matter would be instantly devoured or absorbed, which would not have been the case before living creatures were formed."

* This refers to a passage in which the reviewer of Dr. Carpenter's books speaks of "an operation of force," or "a concurrence of forces which have now no place in nature," as being, "a creative force, in fact, which Darwin could only express in Pentateuchal terms as the primordial form 'into which life was first breathed.'" The conception of expressing a creative force as a primordial form is the Reviewer's.

† *Athenæum*, April 4, 1863, p. 459. The writer asserts that justice has not been done either to himself or Mr. Prestwich—that Lyell has not made it clear that it was their original work which supplied certain material for the 'Antiquity of Man.' Falconer attempts to draw an unjust distinction between a "philosopher" (here used as a polite word for compiler) like Sir Charles Lyell, and original observers, presumably such as himself, and Mr. Prestwich. Lyell's reply was published in the *Athenæum*, April 18, 1863. It ought to be mentioned that a letter from Mr. Prestwich (*Athenæum*, p. 555), which formed part of the controversy, though of the nature of a reclamation, was written in a very different spirit and tone from Dr. Falconer's.

do justice to old Perthes and Schmerling. . . . . I shall be
very curious to see how he [Lyell] answers it to-morrow. (I
have been compelled to take in the *Athenæum* for a while.) I
am very sorry that Falconer should have written so spitefully,
even if there is some truth in his accusations; I was rather
disappointed in Carpenter's letter, no one could have given a
better answer, but the chief object of his letter seems to me
to be to show that though he has touched pitch he is not de-
filed. No one would suppose he went so far as to believe all
birds came from one progenitor. I have written a letter to
the *Athenæum* * (the first and last time I shall take such a step)
to say, under the cloak of attacking Heterogeny, a word in
my own defence. My letter is to appear next week, so the
Editor says; and I mean to quote Lyell's sentence † in his
second edition, on the principle if one puffs oneself, one had
better puff handsomely. . . .

---

* *Athenæum*, 1863, p. 554: " The view given by me on the origin or
derivation of species, whatever its weaknesses may be, connects (as has
been candidly admitted by some of its opponents, such as Pictet, Bronn,
&c.), by an intelligible thread of reasoning, a multitude of facts: such as
the formation of domestic races by man's selection,—the classification and
affinities of all organic beings,—the innumerable gradations in structure
and instincts,—the similarity of pattern in the hand, wing, or paddle of
animals of the same great class,—the existence of organs become rudimentary by disuse,—the similarity of an embryonic reptile, bird, and mammal,
with the retention of traces of an apparatus fitted for aquatic respiration ;
the retention in the young calf of incisor teeth in the upper jaw, &c.—the
distribution of animals and plants, and their mutual affinities within the
same region,—their general geological succession, and the close relationship of the fossils in closely consecutive formations and within the same
country ; extinct marsupials having preceded living marsupials in Australia, and armadillo-like animals having preceded and generated armadil-
loes in South America,—and many other phenomena, such as the gradual
extinction of old forms and their gradual replacement by new forms better
fitted for their new conditions in the struggle for life. When the advocate
of Heterogeny can thus connect large classes of facts, and not until then,
he will have respectful and patient listeners."

† See the next letter.

C. Darwin to C. Lyell.

Down, April 18 [1863].

MY DEAR LYELL,—I was really quite sorry that you had sent me a second copy * of your valuable book. But after a few hours my sorrow vanished for this reason : I have written a letter to the *Athenæum*, in order, under the cloak of attacking the monstrous article on Heterogeny, to say a word for myself in answer to Carpenter, and now I have inserted a few sentences in allusion to your analagous objection † about bats on islands, and then with infinite slyness have quoted your amended sentence, with your parenthesis (" as I fully believe ") ‡ ; I do not think you can be annoyed at my doing this, and you see, that I am determined as far as I can, that the public shall see how far you go. This is the first time I have ever said a word for myself in any journal, and it shall, I think, be the last. My letter is short, and no great things. I was extremely concerned to see Falconer's disrespectful and virulent letter. I like extremely your answer just read ; you take a lofty and dignified position, to which you are so well entitled.§

---

* The second edit. of the ' Antiquity of Man ' was published a few months after the first had appeared.

† Lyell objected that the mammalia (e.g. bats and seals) which alone have been able to reach oceanic islands ought to have become modified into various terrestrial forms fitted to fill various places in their new home. My father pointed out in the *Athænum* that Sir Charles has in some measu answered his own objection, and went on to quote the "amended sentence" (' Antiquity of Man,' 2nd Edit. p. 469) as showing how far Lyell agreed with the general doctrines of the ' Origin of Species ' : "Yet we ought by no means to undervalue the importance of the step which will have been made, should it hereafter become the generally received opinion of men of science (as I fully expect it will) that the past changes of the organic world have been brought about by the subordinate agency of such causes as Variation and Natural Selection." In the first edition the words " as I fully expect it will," do not occur.

‡ My father here quotes Lyell incorrectly ; see the previous footnote.

§ In a letter to Sir J. D. Hooker he wrote : " I much like Lyell's letter.

I suspect that if you had inserted a few more superlatives in speaking of the several authors there would have been none of this horrid noise. No one, I am sure, who knows you could doubt about your hearty sympathy with every one who makes any little advance in science. I still well remember my surprise at the manner in which you listened to me in Hart Street on my return from the *Beagle's* voyage. You did me a world of good. It is horridly vexatious that so frank and apparently amiable a man as Falconer should have behaved so.* Well it will all soon be forgotten. . . .

[In reply to the above-mentioned letter of my father's to the *Athenæum*, an article appeared in that Journal (May 2nd, 1863, p. 586), accusing my father of claiming for his views the exclusive merit of " connecting by an intelligible thread of reasoning " a number of facts in morphology, &c. The writer remarks that, " The different generalizations cited by Mr. Darwin as being connected by an intelligible thread of reasoning exclusively through his attempt to explain specific transmutation are in fact related to it in this wise, that they have prepared the minds of naturalists for a better reception of such attempts to explain the way of the origin of species from species."

To this my father replied in the *Athenæum* of May 9th, 1863 :]

Down, May 5 [1863].

I hope that you will grant me space to own that your reviewer is quiet correct when he states that any theory of descent will connect, " by an intelligible thread of reasoning," the several generalizations before specified. I ought to have made this admission expressly; with the reservation, how-

---

But all this squabbling will greatly sink scientific men. I have seen sneers already in the *Times*."

*It is to this affair that the extract from a letter to Falconer, given vol. i. p. 134, refers.

ever, that, as far as I can judge, no theory so well explains or connects these several generalizations (more especially the formation of domestic races in comparison with natural species, the principles of classification, embryonic resemblance, &c.) as the theory, or hypothesis, or guess, if the reviewer so likes to call it, of Natural Selection.   Nor has any other satisfactory explanation been ever offered of the almost perfect adaptation of all organic beings to each other, and to their physical conditions of life.   Whether the naturalist believes in the views given by Lamarck, by Geoffroy St. Hilaire, by the author of the 'Vestiges,' by Mr. Wallace and myself, or in any other such view, signifies extremely little in comparison with the admission that species have descended from other species, and have not been created immutable : for he who admits this as a great truth has a wide field opened to him for further inquiry.   I believe, however, from what I see of the progress of opinion on the Continent, and in this country, that the theory of Natural Selection will ultimately be adopted, with, no doubt, many subordinate modifications and improvements.

CHARLES DARWIN.

[In the following, he refers to the above letter to the *Athenæum :*]

C. Darwin to J. D. Hooker.

Leith Hill Place,
Saturday [May 11, 1863].

MY DEAR HOOKER,—You give good advice about not writing in newspapers ; I have been gnashing my teeth at my own folly ; and this not caused by ———'s sneers, which were so good that I almost enjoyed them.   I have written once again to own to a certain extent of truth in what he says, and then if I am ever such a fool again, have no mercy on me.   I have read the squib in *Public Opinion ;* * it is capi-

---

* *Public Opinion*, April 23, 1863.   A lively account of a police case, in which the quarrels of scientific men are satirised.   Mr. John Bull gives evidence that—

tal; if there is more, and you have a copy, do lend it. It shows well that a scientific man had better be trampled in dirt than squabble. I have been drawing diagrams, dissecting shoots, and muddling my brains to a hopeless degree about the divergence of leaves, and have of course utterly failed. But I can see that the subject is most curious, and indeed astonishing. . . . .

[The next letter refers to Mr. Bentham's presidential address to the Linnean Society (May 25, 1863). Mr. Bentham does not yield to the new theory of Evolution, " cannot surrender at discretion so long as many important outworks remain contestable." But he shows that the great body of scientific opinion is flowing in the direction of belief.

The mention of Pasteur by Mr. Bentham is in reference to the promulgation " as it were *ex cathedrâ*," of a theory of spontaneous generation by the reviewer of Dr. Carpenter in the *Athenæum* (March 28, 1863). Mr. Bentham points out that in ignoring Pasteur's refutation of the supposed facts of spontaneous generation, the writer fails to act with " that impartiality which every reviewer is supposed to possess."]

" The whole neighbourhood was unsettled by their disputes ; Huxley quarrelled with Owen, Owen with Darwin, Lyell with Owen, Falconer and Prestwich with Lyell, and Gray the menagerie man with everybody. He had pleasure, however, in stating that Darwin was the quietest of the set. They were always picking bones with each other and fighting over their gains. If either of the gravel sifters or stone breakers found anything, he was obliged to conceal it immediately, or one of the old bone collectors would be sure to appropriate it first and deny the theft afterwards, and the consequent wrangling and disputes were as endless as they were wearisome.

" Lord Mayor.—Probably the clergyman of the parish might exert some influence over them ?

" The gentleman smiled, shook his head, and stated that he regretted to say that no class of men paid so little attention to the opinions of the clergy as that to which these unhappy men belonged."

C. Darwin to G. Bentham.

Down, May 22 [1863].

MY DEAR BENTHAM,—I am much obliged for your kind and interesting letter. I have no fear of anything that a man like you will say annoying me in the very least degree. On the other hand, any approval from one whose judgment and knowledge I have for many years so sincerely respected, will gratify me much. The objection which you well put, of certain forms remaining unaltered through long time and space, is no doubt formidable in appearance, and to a certain extent in reality according to my judgment. But does not the difficulty rest much on our silently assuming that we know more than we do? I have literally found nothing so difficult as to try and always remember our ignorance. I am never weary, when walking in any new adjoining district or country, of reflecting how absolutely ignorant we are why certain old plants are not there present, and other new ones are, and others in different proportions. If we once fully feel this, then in judging the theory of Natural Selection, which implies that a form will remain unaltered unless some alteration be to its benefit, is it so very wonderful that some forms should change much slower and much less, and some few should have changed not at all under conditions which to us (who really know nothing what are the important conditions) seem very different. Certainly à priori we might have anticipated that all the plants anciently introduced into Australia would have undergone some modification ; but the fact that they have not been modified does not seem to me a difficulty of weight enough to shake a belief grounded on other arguments. I have expressed myself miserably, but I am far from well to-day.

I am very glad that you are going to allude to Pasteur ; I was struck with infinite admiration at his work. With cordial thanks, believe me, dear Bentham,

Yours very sincerely,

CH. DARWIN.

P.S.—In fact, the belief in Natural Selection must at present be grounded entirely on general considerations. (1) On
its being a *vera causa*, from the struggle for existence; and
the certain geological fact that species do somehow change.
(2) From the analogy of change under domestication by
man's selection. (3) And chiefly from this view connecting
under an intelligible point of view a host of facts. When we
descend to details, we can prove that no one species has
changed [*i. e.* we cannot prove that a single species has
changed]; nor can we prove that the supposed changes are
beneficial, which is the groundwork of the theory. Nor can
we explain why some species have changed and others have
not. The latter case seems to me hardly more difficult to
understand precisely and in detail than the former case of
supposed change. Bronn may ask in vain, the old creationist
school and the new school, why one mouse has longer ears
than another mouse, and one plant more pointed leaves than
another plant.

C. Darwin to G. Bentham.

Down, June 19 [1863].

MY DEAR BENTHAM,—I have been extremely much pleased
and interested by your address, which you kindly sent me.
It seems to be excellently done, with as much judicial calmness and impartiality as the Lord Chancellor could have
shown. But whether the "immutable" gentlemen would
agree with the impartiality may be doubted, there is too much
kindness shown towards me, Hooker, and others, they might
say. Moreover I verily believe that your address, written as
it is, will do more to shake the unshaken and bring on those
leaning to our side, than anything written directly in favor of
transmutation. I can hardly tell why it is, but your address
has pleased me as much as Lyell's book disappointed me,
that is, the part on species, though so cleverly written. I
agree with all your remarks on the reviewers. By the way,
Lecoq * is a believer in the change of species. I, for one, can

---

* Author of 'Géographie Botanique.' 9 vols. 1854-58.

conscientiously declare that I never feel surprised at any one sticking to the belief. of immutability ; though I am often not a little surprised at the arguments advanced on this side. I remember too well my endless oscillations of doubt and difficulty. It is to me really laughable when I think of the years which elapsed before I saw what I believe to be the explanation of some parts of the case ; I believe it was fifteen years after I began before I saw the meaning and cause of the divergence of the descendants of any one pair. You pay me some most elegant and pleasing compliments. There is much in your address which has pleased me much, especially your remarks on various naturalists. I am so glad that you have alluded so honourably to Pasteur. I have just read over this note ; it does not express strongly enough the interest which I have felt in reading your address. You have done, I believe, a real good turn to the *right side*. Believe me, dear Bentham,

> Yours very sincerely,
> CH. DARWIN.

1864.

[In my father's diary for 1864 is the entry, " Ill all January, February, March." About the middle of April (seven months after the beginning of the illness in the previous autumn) his health took a turn for the better. As soon as he was able to do any work, he began to write his papers on Lythrum, and on Climbing Plants, so that the work which now concerns us did not begin until September, when he again set to work on ' Animals and Plants.' A letter to Sir J. D. Hooker gives some account of the re-commencement of the work : " I have begun looking over my old MS., and it is as fresh as if I had never written it ; parts are astonishingly dull, but yet worth printing, I think ; and other parts strike me as very good. I am a complete millionaire in odd and curious little facts, and I have been really astounded at my own industry whilst reading my chapters on Inheritance and Selection. God knows when the book will ever be completed, for I find that I am very weak and on my best days cannot do more than one or one and a half hours' work. It is a good deal harder than writing about my dear climbing plants."

In this year he received the greatest honour which a scientific man can receive in this country—the Copley Medal of the Royal Society. It is presented at the Anniversary Meeting on St. Andrew's Day (Nov. 30), the medalist being usually present to receive it, but this the state of my father's health prevented. He wrote to Mr. Fox on this subject:—

"I was glad to see your hand-writing. The Copley, being open to all sciences and all the world, is reckoned a great honor; but excepting from several kind letters, such things make little difference to me. It shows, however, that Natural Selection is making some progress in this country, and that pleases me. The subject, however, is safe in foreign lands."

To Sir J. D. Hooker, also, he wrote :—

"How kind you have been about this medal; indeed, I am blessed with many good friends, and I have received four or five notes which have warmed my heart. I often wonder that so old a worn-out dog as I am is not quite forgotten. Talking of medals, has Falconer had the Royal? he surely ought to have it, as ought John Lubbock. By the way, the latter tells me that some old members of the Royal are quite shocked at my having the Copley. Do you know who?"

He wrote to Mr. Huxley :—

"I must and will answer you, for it is a real pleasure for me to thank you cordially for your note. Such notes as this of yours, and a few others, are the real medal to me, and not the round bit of gold. These have given me a pleasure which will long endure ; so believe in my cordial thanks for your note."

Sir Charles Lyell, writing to my father in November 1864 ('Life,' vol. ii. p. 384), speaks of the supposed malcontents as being afraid to crown anything so unorthodox as the 'Origin.' But he adds that if such were their feelings "they had the good sense to draw in their horns." It appears, however, from the same letter, that the proposal to give the Copley Medal to my father in the previous year failed owing to a similar want of courage—to Lyell's great indignation.

In the *Reader*, December 3, 1864, General Sabine's presidential address at the Anniversary Meeting is reported at some length. Special weight was laid on my father's work in Geology, Zoology, and Botany, but the 'Origin of Species' is praised chiefly as containing "a mass of observations," &c. It is curious that as in the case of his election to the French Institute, so in this case, he was honored not for the great work of his life, but for his less important work in special lines. The paragraph in General Sabine's address which refers to the 'Origin of Species,' is as follows :—

"In his most recent work 'On the Origin of Species,' although opinions may be divided or undecided with respect to its merits in some respects, all will allow that it contains a mass of observations bearing upon the habits, structure, affinities, and distribution of animals, perhaps unrivalled for interest, minuteness, and patience of observation. Some amongst us may perhaps incline to accept the theory indicated by the title of this work, while others may perhaps incline to refuse, or at least to remit it to a future time, when increased knowledge shall afford stronger grounds for its ultimate acceptance or rejection. Speaking generally and collectively, we have expressly omitted it from the grounds of our award."

I believe I am right in saying that no little dissatisfaction at the President's manner of allusion to the 'Origin' was felt by some Fellows of the Society.

The presentation of the Copley Medal is of interest in another way, inasmuch as it led to Sir C. Lyell making, in his after-dinner speech, a "confession of faith as to the 'Origin.'" He wrote to my father ('Life,' vol. ii. p. 384), "I said I had been forced to give up my old faith without thoroughly seeing my way to a new one. But I think you would have been satisfied with the length I went."]

C. Darwin to T. H. Huxley.

Down, Oct. 3 [1864].

MY DEAR HUXLEY,—If I do not pour out my admiration of your article * on Kölliker, I shall explode. I never read anything better done. I had much wished his article answered, and indeed thought of doing so myself, so that I considered several points. You have hit on all, and on some in addition, and oh! by Jove, how well you have done it. As I read on and came to point after point on which I had thought, I could not help jeering and scoffing at myself, to see how infinitely better you had done it than I could have done. Well, if any one, who does not understand Natural Selection, will read this, he will be a blockhead if it is not as as clear as daylight. Old Flourens † was hardly worth the powder and shot ; but how capitally you bring in about the Academician, and your metaphor of the sea-sand is *inimitable.*

It is a marvel to me how you can resist becoming a regular reviewer. Well, I have exploded now, and it has done me a deal of good. . . .

[In the same article in the 'Natural History Review,' Mr. Huxley speaks of the book above alluded to by Flourens, the Secrétaire Perpétuel of the Académie des Sciences, as one of the two "most elaborate criticisms" of the 'Origin of Species' of the year. He quotes the following passage :—

" M. Darwin continue : 'Aucune distinction absolue n'a été et ne peut être établie entre les espèces et les variétés!'

---

* "Criticisms on the Origin of Species," 'Nat. Hist. Review,' 1864. Republished in 'Lay Sermons,' 1870, p. 328. The work of Professor Kölliker referred to is ' Ueber die Darwin'sche Schöpfungstheorie' (Leipzig, 1864). Toward Professor Kölliker my father felt not only the respect due to so distinguished a naturalist (a sentiment well expressed in Professor Huxley's review), but he had also a personal regard for him, and often alluded with satisfaction to the visit which Professor Kölliker paid at Down.

† 'Examen du livre de M. Darwin sur l'origine des espèces.' Par P. Flourens. 8vo. Paris, 1864.

Je vous ai déjà dit que vous vous trompiez; une distinction absolue sépare les variétés d'avec les espèces." Mr. Huxley remarks on this, "Being devoid of the blessings of an Academy in England, we are unaccustomed to see our ablest men treated in this way even by a Perpetual Secretary." After demonstrating M. Flourens' misapprehension of Natural Selection, Mr. Huxley says, "How one knows it all by heart, and with what relief one reads at p. 65, 'Je laisse M. Darwin.'"

On the same subject my father wrote to Mr. Wallace :—

"A great gun, Flourens, has written a little dull book against me which pleases me much, for it is plain that our good work is spreading in France. He speaks of the "engouement" about this book [the 'Origin'] "so full of empty and presumptuous thoughts." The passage here alluded to is as follows :—

"Enfin l'ouvrage de M. Darwin a paru. On ne peut qu'être frappé du talent de l'auteur. Mais que d'idées obscures, que d'idées fausses ! Quel jargon métaphysique jeté mal à propos dans l'histoire naturelle, qui tombe dans le galimatias dès qu'elle sort des idées claires, des idées justes. Quel langage prétentieux et vide ! Quelles personifications puériles et surannées ! O lucidité ! O solidité de l'esprit français, que devenez-vous ? "]

1865.

[This was again a time of much ill-health, but towards the close of the year he began to recover under the care of the late Dr. Bence-Jones, who dieted him severely, and as he expressed it, "half-starved him to death." He was able to work at 'Animals and Plants' until nearly the end of April, and from that time until December he did practically no work, with the exception of looking over the 'Origin of Species' for a second French edition. He wrote to Sir J. D. Hooker : —"I am, as it were, reading the 'Origin' for the first time, for I am correcting for a second French edition : and upon my life, my dear fellow, it is a very good book, but oh! my gracious, it is tough reading, and I wish it were done." *

The following letter refers to the Duke of Argyll's address to the Royal Society of Edinburgh, December 5th, 1864, in which he criticises the 'Origin of Species.' My father seems to have read the Duke's address as reported in the *Scotsman* of December 6th, 1865. In a letter to my father (Jan. 16, 1865, 'Life,' vol. ii. p. 385), Lyell wrote, "The address is a great step towards your views—far greater, I believe, than it seems when read merely with reference to criticisms and objections."]

C. Darwin to C. Lyell.

Down, January 22, 1865.

MY DEAR LYELL,—I thank you for your very interesting letter. I have the true English instinctive reverence for rank, and therefore liked to hear about the Princess Royal.† You ask what I think of the Duke's address, and I shall be glad to tell you. It seems to me *extremely* clever, like everything I have read of his; but I am not shaken—perhaps you will say that neither gods nor men could shake me. I demur to the Duke reiterating his objection that the brilliant plumage of the male humming-bird could not have been acquired through selection, at the same time entirely ignoring my discussion (p. 93, 3rd edition) on beautiful plumage being acquired

---

* Towards the end of the year my father received the news of a new convert to his views, in the person of the distinguished American naturalist Lesquereux. He wrote to Sir J. D. Hooker: " I have had an enormous letter from Leo Lesquereux (after doubts, I did not think it worth sending you) on Coal Flora. He wrote some excellent articles in 'Silliman' against 'Origin' views; but he says now, after repeated reading of the book, he is a convert ! "

† " I had . . . an animated conversation on Darwinism with the Princess Royal, who is a worthy daughter of her father, in the reading of good books, and thinking of what she reads. She was very much *au fait* at the 'Origin,' and Huxley's book, the 'Antiquity,' &c."—(Lyell's 'Life,' vol. ii. p. 385.)

through *sexual* selection. The duke may think this insufficient, but that is another question. All analogy makes me quite disagree with the Duke that the difference in the beak, wing and tail, are not of importance to the several species. In the only two species which I have watched, the difference in flight and in the use of the tail was conspicuously great.

The Duke, who knows my Orchid book so well, might have learnt a lesson of caution from it, with respect to his doctrine of differences for mere variety or beauty. It may be confidently said that no tribe of plants presents such grotesque and beautiful differences, which no one until lately, conjectured were of any use; but now in almost every case I have been able to show their important service. It should be remembered that with humming-birds or orchids, a modification in one part will cause correlated changes in other parts. I agree with what you say about beauty. I formerly thought a good deal on the subject, and was led quite to repudiate the doctrine of beauty being created for beauty's sake. I demur also to the Duke's expression of "new births." That may be a very good theory, but it is not mine, unless indeed he calls a bird born with a beak $\frac{1}{100}$th of an inch longer than usual "a new birth;" but this is not the sense in which the term would usually be understood. The more I work the more I feel convinced that it is by the accumulation of such extremely slight variations that new species arise. I do not plead guilty to the Duke's charge that I forget that natural selection means only the preservation of variations which independently arise.* I have expressed this in as strong language as I could use, but it would have been infinitely tedious had I on every occasion thus guarded myself. I will cry "peccavi" when I hear of the Duke or you attacking breeders for saying that man has

* "Strickly speaking, therefore, Mr. Darwin's theory is not a theory on the Origin of Species at all, but only a theory on the causes which lead to the relative success and failure of such new forms as may be born into the world."—*Scotsman*, Dec. 6, 1864.

made his improved shorthorns, or pouter pigeons, or bantams. And I could quote still stronger expressions used by agriculturists. Man does make his artificial breeds, for his selective power is of such importance relatively to that of the slight spontaneous variations. But no one will attack breeders for using such expressions, and the rising generation will not blame me.

Many thanks for your offer of sending me the 'Elements.'* I hope to read it all, but unfortunately reading makes my head whiz more than anything else. I am able most days to work for two or three hours, and this makes all the difference in my happiness. I have resolved not to be tempted astray, and to publish nothing till my volume on Variation is completed. You gave me excellent advice about the footnotes in my Dog chapter, but their alteration gave me infinite trouble, and I often wished all the dogs, and I fear sometimes you yourself, in the nether regions.

We (dictator and writer) send our best love to Lady Lyell.

Yours affectionately,

CHARLES DARWIN.

P.S.—If ever you should speak with the Duke on the subject, please say how much interested I was with his address.

[In his autobiographical sketch my father has remarked (p. 36) that owing to certain early memories he felt the honour of being elected to the Royal and Royal Medical Societies of Edinburgh "more than any similar honour." The following extract from a letter to Sir Joseph Hooker refers to his election to the former of these societies. The latter part of the extract refers to the Berlin Academy, to which he was elected in 1878 :—

"Here is a really curious thing, considering that Brewster is President and Balfour Secretary. I have been elected Honorary Member of the Royal Society of Edinburgh. And

---

* Sixth edition in one volume.

this leads me to a third question. Does the Berlin Academy of Sciences send their Proceedings to Honorary Members? I want to know, to ascertain whether I am a member; I suppose not, for I think it would have made some impression on me; yet I distinctly remember receiving some diploma signed by Ehrenberg. I have been so careless; I have lost several diplomas, and now I want to know what Societies I belong to, as I observe every [one] tacks their titles to their names in the catalogue of the Royal Soc."]

C. Darwin to C. Lyell.

Down, Feb. 21 [1865].

My dear Lyell,—I have taken a long time to thank you very much for your present of the ' Elements.'

I am going through it all, reading what is new, and what I have forgotten, and this is a good deal.

I am simply astonished at the amount of labour, knowledge, and clear thought condensed in this work. The whole strikes me as something quite grand. I have been particularly interested by your account of Heer's work and your discussion on the Atlantic Continent. I am particularly delighted at the view which you take on this subject; for I have long thought Forbes did an ill service in so freely making continents.

I have also been very glad to read your argument on the denudation of the Weald, and your excellent *résumé* on the Purbeck Beds; and this is the point at which I have at present arrived in your book. I cannot say that I am quite convinced that there is no connection beyond that pointed out by you, between glacial action and the formation of lake basins; but you will not much value my opinion on this head, as I have already changed my mind some half-dozen times.

I want to make a suggestion to you. I found the weight of your volume intolerable, especially when lying down, so with great boldness cut it into two pieces, and took it out of its cover; now could not Murray without any other change

51

add to his advertisement a line saying, "if bound in two volumes, one shilling or one shilling and sixpence extra." You thus might originate a change which would be a blessing to all weak-handed readers.

Believe me, my dear Lyell,
Yours most sincerely,
CHARLES DARWIN.

Originate a second *real blessing* and have the edges of the sheets cut like a bound book.*

C. Darwin to John Lubbock.

Down, June 11 [1865].

MY DEAR LUBBOCK,—The latter half of your book † has been read aloud to me, and the style is so clear and easy (we both think it perfection) that I am now beginning at the beginning. I cannot resist telling you how excellently well, in my opinion, you have done the very interesting chapter on savage life. Though you have necessarily only compiled the materials the general result is most original. But I ought to keep the term original for your last chapter, which has struck me as an admirable and profound discussion. It has quite delighted me, for now the public will see what kind of man you are, which I am proud to think I discovered a dozen years ago.

I do sincerely wish you all success in your election and in

---

* This was a favourite reform of my father's. He wrote to the *Athenæum* on the subject, Feb. 5, 1867, pointing out how that a book cut, even carefully, with a paper knife collects dust on its edges far more than a machine-cut book. He goes on to quote .the case of a lady of his acquaintance who was in the habit of cutting books with her thumb, and finally appeals to the *Athenæum* to earn the gratitude of children "who have to cut through dry and pictureless books for the benefit of their elders." He tried to introduce the reform in the case of his own books, but found the conservatism of booksellers too strong for him. The presentation copies, however, of all his later books were sent out with the edges cut.

† 'Prehistoric Times,' 1865.

politics; but after reading this last chapter, you must let me say : oh, dear ! oh, dear ! oh dear !

Yours affectionately,

CH. DARWIN.

P.S.—You pay me a superb compliment,* but I fear you will be quizzed for it by some of your friends as too exaggerated.

[The following letter refers to Fritz Müller's book, 'Für Darwin,' which was afterwards translated, at my father's suggestion, by Mr. Dallas. It is of interest as being the first of the long series of letters which my father wrote to this distinguished naturalist. They never met, but the correspondence with Müller, which continued to the close of my father's life, was a source of very great pleasure to him. My impression is that of all his unseen friends Fritz Müller was the one for whom he had the strongest regard. Fritz Müller is the brother of another distinguished man, the late Hermann Müller, the author of ' Die Befruchtung der Blumen,' and of much other valuable work :]

C. Darwin to F. Müller.

Down, August 10 [1865].

MY DEAR SIR,—I have been for a long time so ill that I have only just finished hearing read aloud your work on species. And now you must permit me to thank you cordially for the great interest with which I have read it. You have done admirable service in the cause in which we both believe. Many of your arguments seem to me excellent, and many of your facts wonderful. Of the latter, nothing has surprised me so much as the two forms of males. I have lately investigated the cases of dimorphic plants, and I should much like to send you one or two of my papers if I knew how. I did

---

* ' Prehistoric Times,' p. 487, where the words, "the discoveries of a Newton or a Darwin," occur.

send lately by post a paper on climbing plants, as an experiment to see whether it would reach you.   One of the points which has struck me most in your paper is that on the differences in the air-breathing apparatus of the several forms. This subject appeared to me very important when I formerly considered the electric apparatus of fishes.   Your observations on Classification and Embryology seem to me very good and original.   They show what a wonderful field there is for enquiry on the development of crustacea, and nothing has convinced me so plainly what admirable results we shall arrive at in Natural History in the course of a few years.   What a marvellous range of structure the crustacea present, and how well adapted they are for your enquiry!   Until reading your book I knew nothing of the Rhizocephala; pray look at my account and figures of Anelasma, for it seems to me that this latter cirripede is a beautiful connecting link with the Rhizocephala.

If ever you have any opportunity, as you are so skilful a dissector, I much wish that you would look to the orifice at the base of the first pair of cirrhi in cirripedes, and at the curious organ in it, and discover what its nature is; I suppose I was quite in error, yet I cannot feel fully satisfied at Krohn's * observations.   Also if you ever find any species of Scalpellum, pray look for complemental males; a German author has recently doubted my observations for no reason except that the facts appeared to him so strange.

Permit me again to thank you cordially for the pleasure which I have derived from your work and to express my sincere admiration for your valuable researches.

Believe me, dear Sir, with sincere respect,

Yours very faithfully,

CH. DARWIN.

P.S.—I do not know whether you care at all about plants, but if so, I should much like to send you my little work on

---

* See vol. ii., pp. 138, 187.

the 'Fertilization of Orchids,' and I think I have a German copy.

Could you spare me a photograph of yourself? I should much like to possess one.

C. Darwin to J. D. Hooker.

Down, Thursday, 27th [Sept., 1865].

MY DEAR HOOKER,—I had intended writing this morning to thank Mrs. Hooker most sincerely for her last and several notes about you, and now your own note in your hand has rejoiced me. To walk between five and six miles is splendid, with a little patience you must soon be well. I knew you had been very ill, but I hardly knew how ill, until yesterday, when Bentham (from the Cranworths*) called here, and I was able to see him for ten minutes. He told me also a little about the last days of your father; † I wish I had known your father better, my impression is confined to his remarkably cordial, courteous, and frank bearing. I fully concur and understand what you say about the difference of feeling in the loss of a father and child. I do not think any one could love a father much more than I did mine, and I do not believe three or four days ever pass without my still thinking of him, but his death at eighty-four caused me nothing of that insufferable grief ‡ which the loss of poor dear Annie caused. And this

---

* Robert Rolfe, Lord Cranworth, and Lord Chancellor of England, lived at Holwood, near Down.

† Sir William Hooker; b. 1785, d. 1865. He took charge of the Royal Gardens at Kew, in 1840, when they ceased to be the private gardens of the Royal Family. In doing so, he gave up his professorship at Glasgow—and with it half of his income. He founded the herbarium and library, and within ten years he succeeded in making the gardens the first in the world. It is, thus, not too much to say that the creation of the establishment at Kew is due to the abilities and self-devotion of Sir William Hooker. While, for the subsequent development of the gardens up to their present magnificent condition, the nation must thank Sir Joseph Hooker, in whom the same qualities are so conspicuous.

‡ I may quote here a passage from a letter of November, 1863. It was

seems to me perfectly natural, for one knows that for years previously that one's father's death is drawing slowly nearer and nearer, while the death of one's child is a sudden and dreadful wrench. What a wonderful deal you read; it is a horrid evil for me that I can read hardly anything, for it makes my head almost immediately begin to sing violently. My good womenkind read to me a great deal, but I dare not ask for much science, and am not sure that I could stand it. I enjoyed Tylor * *extremely*, and the first part of Lecky ; † but I think the latter is often vague, and gives a false appearance of throwing light on his subject by such phrases as "spirit of the age," "spread of civilization," &c. I confine my reading to a quarter or half hour per day in skimming through the back volumes of the Annals and Magazine of Natural History, and find much that interests me. I miss my climbing plants very much, as I could observe them when very poorly.

I did not enjoy the ' Mill on the Floss' so much as you, but from what you say we will read it again. Do you know 'Silas Marner'? it is a charming little story; if you run short, and like to have it, we could send it by post. . . . We have almost finished the first volume of Palgrave,‡ and I like it much ; but did you ever see a book so badly arranged? The frequency of the allusions to what will be told in the future are quite laughable. . . . By the way, I was very much pleased with the foot-note # about Wallace in Lubbock's last chapter. I had not heard that Huxley had backed up

---

written to a friend who had lost his child : " How well I remember your feeling, when we lost Annie. It was my greatest comfort that I had never spoken a harsh word to her. Your grief has made me shed a few tears over our poor darling ; but believe me that these tears have lost that un-utterable bitterness of former days."

* ' Researches into the Early History of Mankind,' by E. B. Tylor. 1865.

† ' The Rise of Rationalism in Europe,' by W. E. H. Lecky. 1865.

‡ William Gifford Palgrave's ' Travels in Arabia,' published in 1865.

The passage which seems to be referred to occurs in the text (p. 479) of ' Prehistoric Times.' It expresses admiration of Mr. Wallace's paper in

Lubbock about Parliament. . . . Did you see a sneer some time ago in the *Times* about how incomparably more interesting politics were compared with science even to scientific men? Remember what Trollope says, in 'Can you Forgive her,' about getting into Parliament, as the highest earthly ambition. Jeffrey, in one of his letters, I remember, says that making an effective speech in Parliament is a far grander thing than writing the grandest history. All this seems to me a poor short-sighted view. I cannot tell you how it has rejoiced me once again seeing your handwriting—my best of old friends.

Yours affectionately,

CH. DARWIN.

[In October he wrote Sir J. D. Hooker :—

"Talking of the 'Origin,' a Yankee has called my attention to a paper attached to Dr. Wells's famous 'Essay on Dew,' which was read in 1813 to the Royal Soc., but not [then] printed, in which he applies most distinctly the principle of Natural Selection to the Races of Man. So poor old Patrick Matthew is not the first, and he cannot, or ought not, any longer to put on his title-pages, 'Discoverer of the principle of Natural Selection' ! "]

*C. Darwin to F. W. Farrar.**

Down, Nov. 2 [1865 ?].

DEAR SIR,—As I have never studied the science of language, it may perhaps seem presumptuous, but I cannot resist the pleasure of telling you what interest and pleasure I have derived from hearing read aloud your volume.†

I formerly read Max Müller, and thought his theory (if it deserves to be called so) both obscure and weak ; and now,

---

the 'Anthropological Review' (May, 1864), and speaks of the author's "characteristic unselfishness" in ascribing the theory of Natural Selection "unreservedly to Mr. Darwin."

* Canon of Westminster.

† 'Chapters on Language,' 1865.

after hearing what you say, I feel sure that this is the case, and that your cause will ultimately triumph. My indirect interest in your book has been increased from Mr. Hensleigh Wedgwood, whom you often quote, being my brother-in-law.

No one could dissent from my views on the modification of species with more courtesy than you do. But from the tenor of your mind I feel an entire and comfortable conviction (and which cannot possibly be disturbed) that if your studies led you to attend much to general questions in natural history you would come to the same conclusion that I have done.

Have you ever read Huxley's little book of Lectures? I would gladly send you a copy if you think you would read it.

Considering what Geology teaches us, the argument from the supposed immutability of specific types seems to me much the same as if, in a nation which had no old writings, some wise old savage was to say that his language had never changed; but my metaphor is too long to fill up.

Pray believe me, dear Sir, yours very sincerely obliged,

C. DARWIN.

1866.

[The year 1866 is given in my father's Diary in the following words :—

"Continued correcting chapters of 'Domestic Animals.'

March 1st.—Began on 4th edition of 'Origin' of 1250 copies (received for it £238), making 7500 copies altogether.

May 10th.—Finished 'Origin,' except revises, and began going over Chapter XIII. of 'Domestic Animals.'

Nov. 21st.—Finished 'Pangenesis.'

Dec. 21st.—Finished re-going over all chapters, and sent them to printers.

Dec. 22nd.—Began concluding chapter of book."

He was in London on two occasions for a week at a time, staying with his brother, and for a few days (May 29th–June 2nd) in Surrey ; for the rest of the year he was at Down.

There seems to have been a gradual mending in his

health; thus he wrote to Mr. Wallace (January 1866) :—
"My health is so far improved that I am able to work one or two hours a day."

With respect to the 4th edition he wrote to sir Sir J. D. Hooker :—

"The new edition of the 'Origin' has caused me two great vexations. I forgot Bates's paper on variation,* but I remembered in time his mimetic work, and now, strange to say, I find I have forgotten your Arctic paper! I know how it arose ; I indexed for my bigger work, and never expected that a new edition of the 'Origin' would be wanted.

"I cannot say how all this has vexed me. Everything which I have read during the last four years I find is quite washy in my mind." As far as I know, Mr. Bates's paper was not mentioned in the later editions of the 'Origin,' for what reason I cannot say.

In connection with his work on 'The Variation of Animals and Plants,' I give here extracts from three letters addressed to Mr. Huxley, which are of interest as giving some idea of the development of the theory of 'Pangenesis,' ultimately published in 1868 in the book in question :]

C. Darwin to T. H. Huxley.

Down, May 27, [1865?].

. . . I write now to ask a favour of you, a very great favour from one so hard worked as you are. It is to read thirty pages of MS., excellently copied out and give me, not lengthened criticism, but your opinion whether I may venture to publish it. You may keep the MS. for a month or two. I would not ask this favour, but I *really* know no one else whose judgment on the subject would be final with me.

The case stands thus : in my next book I shall publish long chapters on bud- and seminal-variation, on inheritance,

---

* This appears to refer to "Notes on South American Butterflies," Trans. Entomolog. Soc., vol. v. (N.S.).

reversion, effects of use and disuse, &c. I have also for many years speculated on the different forms of reproduction. Hence it has come to be a passion with me to try to connect all such facts by some sort of hypothesis. The MS. which I wish to send you gives such a hypothesis ; it is a very rash and crude hypothesis, yet it has been a considerable relief to my mind, and I can hang on it a good many groups of facts. I well know that a mere hypothesis, and this is nothing more, is of little value ; but it is very useful to me as serving as a kind of summary for certain chapters. Now I earnestly wish for your verdict given briefly as, " Burn it "—or, which is the most favourable verdict I can hope for, " It does rudely connect together certain facts, and I do not think it will immediately pass out of my mind." If you can say this much, and you do not think it absolutely ridiculous, I shall publish it in my concluding chapter. Now will you grant me this favour ? You must refuse if you are too much overworked.

I must say for myself that I am a hero to expose my hypothesis to the fiery ordeal of your criticism.

July 12, [1865 ?].

MY DEAR HUXLEY,—I thank you most sincerely for having so carefully considered my MS. It has been a real act of kindness. It would have annoyed me extremely to have re-published Buffon's views, which I did not know of, but I will get the book ; and if I have strength I will also read Bonnet. I do not doubt your judgment is perfectly just, and I will try to persuade myself not to publish. The whole affair is much too speculative ; yet I think some such view will have to be adopted, when I call to mind such facts as the inherited effects of use and disuse, &c. But I will try to be cautious. . . .

[1865 ?].

MY DEAR HUXLEY,—Forgive my writing in pencil, as I can do so lying down. I have read Buffon : whole pages are laughably like mine.   It is surprising how candid it makes one to see one's views in another man's words.   I am rather ashamed of the whole affair, but not converted to a no-belief.   What a kindness you have done me with your "vulpine sharpness."   Nevertheless, there is a fundamental distinction between Buffon's views and mine.   He does not suppose that each cell or atom of tissue throws off a little bud ; but he supposes that the sap or blood includes his "organic molecules," *which are ready formed*, fit to nourish each organ, and when this is fully formed, they collect to form buds and the sexual elements.   It is all rubbish to speculate as I have done ; yet, if I ever have strength to publish my next book, I fear I shall not resist "Pangenesis," but I assure you I will put it humbly enough.   The ordinary course of development of beings, such as the Echinodermata, in which new organs are formed at quite remote spots from the analogous previous parts, seem to me extremely difficult to reconcile on any view except the free diffusion in the parent of the germs or gemmules of each separate new organ ; and so in cases of alternate generation.   But I will not scribble any more.   Hearty thanks to you, you best of critics and most learned man. . . . . .

[The letters now take up the history of the year 1866.]

C. Darwin to A. R. Wallace.

Down, July 5 [1866].

My dear Wallace,—I have been much interested by your letter, which is as clear as daylight.   I fully agree with all that you say on the advantages of H. Spencer's excellent expression of "the survival of the fittest." *   This, however,

---

* Extract from a letter of Mr. Wallace's, July 2, 1866 : "The term 'survival of the fittest' is the plain expression of the fact ; 'natural selection' is a metaphorical expression of it, and to a certain degree indirect and incorrect, since . . . Nature . . . does not so much select special varieties as exterminate the most unfavourable ones."

had not occurred to me till reading your letter. It is, however, a great objection to this term that it cannot be used as
a substantive governing a verb; and that this is a real objection I infer from H. Spencer continually using the words,
natural selection. I formerly thought, probably in an exaggerated degree, that it was a great advantage to bring into connection natural and artificial selection; this indeed led me to
use a term in common, and I still think it some advantage.
I wish I had received your letter two months ago, for I would
have worked in "the survival, &c.," often in the new edition
of the 'Origin,' which is now almost printed off, and of which
I will of course send you a copy. I will use the term in
my next book on Domestic Animals, &c., from which, by the
way, I plainly see that you expect *much*, too much. The term
Natural Selection has now been so largely used abroad and
at home, that I doubt whether it could be given up, and with
all its faults I should be sorry to see the attempt made.
Whether it will be rejected must now depend "on the survival of the fittest." As in time the term must grow intelligible the objections to its use will grow weaker and weaker.
I doubt whether the use of any term would have made the
subject intelligible to some minds, clear as it is to others;
for do we not see even to the present day Malthus on Population absurdly misunderstood? This reflection about Malthus has often comforted me when I have been vexed at the
misstatement of my views. As for M. Janet,* he is a meta-
physician, and such gentlemen are so acute that I think they
often misunderstand common folk. Your criticism on the
double sense † in which I have used Natural Selection is new
to me and unanswerable; but my blunder has done no harm,
for I do not believe that any one, excepting you, has ever

---

* This no doubt refers to Janet's 'Matérialisme Contemporain.'

† "I find you use 'Natural Selection' in two senses. 1st, for the simple preservation of favourable and rejection of unfavourable variations, in
which case it is equivalent to the 'survival of the fittest,'—and 2ndly, for
the effect or *change* produced by this preservation." Extract from Mr.
Wallace's letter above quoted.

observed it. Again, I agree that I have said too much about ": favourable variations; " but I am inclined to think that you put the opposite side too strongly; if every part of every being varied, I do not think we should see the same end, or object, gained by such wonderfully diversified means.

I hope you are enjoying the country, and are in good health, and are working hard at your Malay Archipelago book, for I will always put this wish in every note I write to you, like some good people always put in a text. My health keeps much the same, or rather improves, and I am able to work some hours daily. With many thanks for your interesting letter.

Believe me, my dear Wallace, yours sincerely,
CH. DARWIN.

C. Darwin to J. D. Hooker.

Down, Aug. 30 [1866].

MY DEAR HOOKER,—I was very glad to get your note and the Notts. Newspaper. I have seldom been more pleased in my life than at hearing how successfully your lecture * went off. Mrs. H. Wedgwood sent us an account, saying that you read capitally, and were listened too with profound attention and great applause. She says, when your final allegory † began, "for a minute or two we were all mystified, and then came such bursts of applause from the audience. It was thoroughly enjoyed amid roars of laughter and noise, making a most brilliant conclusion."

I am rejoiced that you will publish your lecture, and felt sure that sooner or later it would come to this, indeed it

---

* At the Nottingham meeting of the British Association, Aug. 27, 1866. The subject of the lecture was ' Insular Floras.' See *Gardener's Chronicle*, 1866.

† Sir Joseph Hooker allegorized the Oxford meeting of the British Association as the gathering of a tribe of savages who believed that the new moon was created afresh each month. The anger of the priests and medicine man at a certain heresy, according to which the new moon is but the offspring of the old one, is excellently given.

would have been a sin if you had not done so. I am especially rejoiced as you give the arguments for occasional transport, with such perfect fairness ; these will now receive a fair share of attention, as coming from you a professed botanist. Thanks also for Grove's address ; as a whole it strikes me as very good and original, but I was disappointed in the part about Species ; it dealt in such generalities that it would apply to any view or no view in particular. . . . .

And now farewell. I do most heartily rejoice at your success, and for Grove's sake at the brilliant success of the whole meeting.

Yours affectionately,
CHARLES DARWIN.

[The next letter is of interest, as giving the beginning of the connection which arose between my father and Professor Victor Carus. The translation referred to is the third German edition made from the fourth English one. From this time forward Professor Carus continued to translate my father's books into German. The conscientious care with which this work was done was of material service, and I well remember the admiration (mingled with a tinge of vexation at his own short-comings) with which my father used to receive the lists of oversights, &c., which Professor Carus discovered in the course of translation. The connection was not a mere business one, but was cemented by warm feelings of regard on both sides.]

C. Darwin to Victor Carus.

Down, November 10, 1866.

MY DEAR SIR,—I thank you for your extremely kind letter. I cannot express too strongly my satisfaction that you have undertaken the revision of the new edition, and I feel the honour which you have conferred on me. I fear that you will find the labour considerable, not only on account of the additions, but I suspect that Bronn's translation is very defective, at least I have heard complaints on this head from

quite a large number of persons.   It would be a great gratification to me to know that the translation was a really good
one, such as I have no doubt you will produce.   According
to our English practice, you will be fully justified in entirely
omitting Bronn's Appendix, and I shall be very glad of its
omission.   A new edition may be looked at as a new work.
. . . . You could add anything of your own that you liked,
and I should be much pleased.   Should you make any additions or append notes, it appears to me that Nägeli " Entstehung und Begriff," &c.,* would be worth noticing, as one of
the most able pamphlets on the subject.   I am, however, far
from agreeing with him that the acquisition of certain characters which appear to be of no service to plants, offers any
great difficulty, or affords a proof of some innate tendency
in plants towards perfection.   If you intend to notice this
pamphlet, I should like to write hereafter a little more in
detail on the subject.

. . . . I wish I had known when writing my Historical
Sketch that you had in 1853 published your views on the
genealogical connection of past and present forms.

I suppose you have the sheets of the last English edition
on which I marked with pencil all the chief additions, but
many little corrections of style were not marked.

Pray believe that I feel sincerely grateful for the great
service and honour which you do me by the present translation.

I remain, my dear Sir, yours very sincerely,
CHARLES DARWIN.

P.S.—I should be *very much* pleased to possess your
photograph, and I send mine in case you should like to have
a copy.

---

* 'Entstehung und Begriff der Naturhistorischen Art.'   An Address
given at a public meeting of the ' R. Academy of Sciences' at Munich,
Mar. 28, 1865.

*C. Darwin to C. Nägeli.**

Down, June 12 [1866].

DEAR SIR,—I hope you will excuse the liberty which I take in writing to you. I have just read, though imperfectly, your 'Entstehung und Begriff,' and have been so greatly interested by it, that I have sent it to be translated, as I am a poor German scholar. I have just finished a new [4th] edition of my 'Origin,' which will be translated into German, and my object in writing to you is to say that if you should see this edition you would think that I had borrowed from you, without acknowledgment, two discussions on the beauty of flowers and fruit ; but I assure you every word was printed off before I had opened your pamphlet. Should you like to possess a copy of either the German or English new edition, I should be proud to send one. I may add, with respect to the beauty of flowers, that I have already hinted the same views as you hold in my paper on Lythrum.

Many of your criticisms on my views are the best which I have met with, but I could answer some, at least to my own satisfaction ; and I regret extremely that I had not read your pamphlet before printing my new edition. On one or two points, I think, you have a little misunderstood me, though I dare say I have not been cautious in expressing myself. The remark which has struck me most, is that on the position of the leaves not having been acquired through natural selection, from not being of any special importance to the plant. I well remember being formerly troubled by an analogous difficulty, namely, the position of the ovules, their anatropous condition, &c. It was owing to forgetfulness that I did not notice this difficulty in the 'Origin.' † Although I can offer no explanation of such facts, and only hope to see that they may be explained, yet I hardly see how they support the doctrine of some law of necessary development, for it is not

---

* Professor of Botany at Munich.

† Nägeli's Essay is noticed in the 5th edition.

clear to me that a plant, with its leaves placed at some particular angle, or with its ovules in some particular position, thus stands higher than another plant. But I must apologise for troubling you with these remarks.

As I much wish to possess your photograph, I take the liberty of enclosing my own, and with sincere respect I remain, dear Sir,   Yours faithfully,

                                        CH. DARWIN.

[I give a few extracts from letters of various dates showing my father's interest, alluded to in the last letter, in the problem of the arrangement of the leaves on the stems of plants. It may be added that Professor Schwendener of Berlin has successfully attacked the question in his 'Mechanische Theorie der Blattstellungen,' 1878.

To Dr. Falconer.

August 26 [1863].

"Do you remember telling me that I ought to study Phyllotaxy? well I have often wished you at the bottom of the sea; for I could not resist, and I muddled my brains with diagrams, &c., and specimens, and made out, as might have been expected, nothing. Those angles are a most wonderful problem and I wish I could see some one give a rational explanation of them."

To Dr. Asa Gray.

May 11 [1861].

"If you wish to save me from a miserable death, do tell me why the angles $\frac{1}{2}$, $\frac{1}{3}$, $\frac{2}{5}$, $\frac{3}{8}$, &c., series occur, and no other angles. It is enough to drive the quietest man mad. Did you and some mathematician * publish some paper on, the subject? Hooker says you did; where is it?

---

* Probably my father was thinking of Chauncey Wright's work on Phyllotaxy, in Gould's 'Astronomical Journal,' No. 99, 1856, and in the 'Mathematical Monthly,' 1859. These papers are mentioned in the 'Letters of Chauncey Wright.' Mr. Wright corresponded with my father on the subject.

To Dr. Asa Gray.

[May 31, 1863?].

"I have been looking at Nägeli's work on this subject, and am astonished to see that the angle is not always the same in young shoots when the leaf-buds are first distinguishable, as in full-grown branches. This shows, I think, that there must be some potent cause for those angles which do occur : I dare say there is some explanation as simple as that for the angles of the Bees-cells."

My father also corresponded with Dr. Hubert Airy and was interested in his views on the subject, published in the Royal Soc. Proceedings, 1873, p. 176.

We now return to the year 1866.

In November, when the prosecution of Governor Eyre was dividing England into two bitterly opposed parties, he wrote to Sir J. Hooker :—

"You will shriek at me when you hear that I have just subscribed to the Jamaica Committee." *

On this subject I quote from a letter of my brother's :—

"With respect to Governor Eyre's conduct in Jamaica, he felt strongly that J. S. Mill was right in prosecuting him. I remember one evening, at my Uncle's, we were talking on the subject, and as I happened to think it was too strong a measure to prosecute Governor Eyre for murder, I made some foolish remark about the prosecutors spending the surplus of the fund in a dinner. My father turned on me almost with fury, and told, me if those were my feelings, I had better go back to Southampton ; the inhabitants having given a dinner to Governor Eyre on his landing, but with which I had had nothing to do." The end of the incident, as told by my brother, is so characteristic of my father that I cannot resist giving it, though it has no bearing on the point at issue. "Next morning at 7 o'clock, or so, he came into my bed-

---

* He subscribed £10.

room and sat on my bed, and said that he had not been able to sleep from the thought that he had been so angry with me, and after a few more kind words he left me."

The same restless desire to correct a disagreeable or incorrect impression is well illustrated in an extract which I quote from some notes by Rev. J. Brodie Innes :—

"Allied to the extreme carefulness of observation was his most remarkable truthfulness in all matters. On one occasion, when a parish meeting had been held on some disputed point of no great importance, I was surprised by a visit from Mr. Darwin at night. He came to say that, thinking over the debate, though what he had said was quite accurate, he thought I might have drawn an erroneous conclusion, and he would not sleep till he had explained it. I believe that if on any day some certain fact had come to his knowledge which contradicted his most cherished theories, he would have placed the fact on record for publication before he slept."

This tallies with my father's habits, as described by himself. When a difficulty or an objection occurred to him, he thought it of paramount importance to make a note of it instantly because he found hostile facts to be especially evanescent.

The same point is illustrated by the following incident, for which I am indebted to Mr. Romanes :—

"I have always remembered the following little incident as a good example of Mr. Darwin's extreme solicitude on the score of accuracy. One evening at Down there was a general conversation upon the difficulty of explaining the evolution of some of the distinctively human emotions, especially those appertaining to the recognition of beauty in natural scenery. I suggested a view of my own upon the subject, which, depending upon the principle of association, required the supposition that a long line of ancestors should have inhabited regions, the scenery of which is now regarded as beautiful. Just as I was about to observe that the chief difficulty attaching to my hypothesis arose from feelings of the sublime (seeing that these are associated with awe, and might therefore be expected not to be agreeable), Mr. Darwin anticipated the remark, by asking how the hypothesis was to meet the case of these feelings. In the conversation which followed, he said the occasion in his own life, when he was most affected by the emotions of the sublime was when he stood upon one of the summits of the Cordillera, and surveyed the magnificent prospect all around. It seemed, as he quaintly observed, as if his nerves had become fiddle-strings, and had all taken to rapidly vibrating. This remark was only made incidentally, and the conversation passed into some other branch. About an hour afterwards Mr. Darwin retired to rest, while I sat up in the smoking-room with one of his sons. We continued smoking and talking for several hours, when at about one o'clock in the morning the door gently opened and Mr. Darwin appeared, in his slippers and dressing-gown. As nearly as I can remember, the following are the words he used :—

" 'Since I went to bed I have been thinking over our conversation in the drawing-room, and it has just occurred to me that I was wrong in telling you I felt most of the sublime when on the top of the Cordillera; I am quite sure that I felt it even more when in the forests of Brazil. I thought it best to come and tell you this at once in case I should be putting you wrong. I am sure now that I felt most sublime in the forests.'

" This was all he had come to say, and it was evident that he had come to do so, because he thought that the fact of his feeling 'most sublime in forests' was more in accordance with the hypothesis which we had been discussing, than the fact which he had previously stated. Now, as no one knew better than Mr. Darwin the difference between a speculation and a fact, I thought this little exhibition of scientific conscientiousness very noteworthy, where the only question concerned was of so highly speculative a character. I should not have been so much impressed if he had thought that by his temporary failure of memory he had put me on a wrong scent in any matter of fact, although even in such a case he is the only man I ever knew who would care to get out of bed at such a time at night in order to make the correction immediately, instead of waiting till next morning. But as the correction only had reference to a flimsy hypothesis, I certainly was very much impressed by this display of character."]

C. Darwin to J. D. Hooker.

Down, December 10 [1866].

. . . . I have now read the last No. of H. Spencer.* I do not know whether to think it better than the previous number, but it is wonderfully clever, and I dare say mostly true. I feel rather mean when I read him : I could bear, and rather enjoy feeling that he was twice as ingenious and clever as myself, but when I feel that he is about a dozen times my superior, even in the master art of wriggling, I feel aggrieved. If he had trained himself to observe more, even if at the expense, by the law of balancement, of some loss of thinking power, he would have been a wonderful man.

. . . . I am *heartily* glad you are taking up the Distribution of Plants in New Zealand, and suppose it will make part of your new book. Your view, as I understand it, that New Zealand subsided and formed two or more small islands, and then rose again, seems to me extremely probable. . . . . When I puzzled my brains about New Zealand, I remember I came to the conclusion, as indeed I state in the 'Origin,' that its flora, as well as that of other southern lands, had been tinctured by an Antarctic flora, which must have existed before the Glacial period. I concluded that New Zealand never could have been closely connected with Australia, though I supposed it had received some few Australian forms by occasional means of transport. Is there any reason to suppose that New Zealand could have been more closely connected with South Australia during the glacial period, when the Eucalypti, &c., might have been driven further North? Apparently there remains only the line, which I

---

* ' Principles of Biology.'

think you suggested, of sunken islands from New Caledonia. Please remember that the Edwardsia was certainly drifted there by the sea.

I remember in old days speculating on the amount of life, *i.e.* of organic chemical change, at different periods. There seems to me one very difficult element in the problem, namely, the state of development of the organic beings at each period, for I presume that a Flora and Fauna of cellular cryptogamic plants, of Protozoa and Radiata would lead to much less chemical change than is now going on. But I have scribbled enough.

Yours affectionately,
Ch. Darwin.

[The following letter is in acknowledgment of Mr. Rivers' reply to an earlier letter in which my father had asked for information on bud-variation :

It may find a place here in illustration of the manner of my father's intercourse with those "whose avocations in life had to do with the rearing or use of living things" *—an intercourse which bore such good fruit in the 'Variation of Animals and Plants.' Mr. Dyer has some excellent remarks on the unexpected value thus placed on apparently trivial facts disinterred from weekly journals, or amassed by correspondence. He adds : "Horticulturists who had . . . . moulded plants almost at their will at the impulse of taste or profit were at once amazed and charmed to find that they had been doing scientific work and helping to establish a great theory."]

C. Darwin to T. Rivers.†

Down, December 28 [1866?]

My dear Sir,—Permit me to thank you cordially for your most kind letter. For years I have read with interest

---

* "Mr. Dyer in 'Charles Darwin,'" *Nature Series*, 1882, p. 39.

† The late Mr. Rivers was an eminent horticulturist and writer on horticulture.

every scrap which you have written in periodicals, and abstracted in MS. your book on Roses, and several times I thought I would write to you, but did not know whether you would think me too intrusive. I shall, indeed, be truly obliged for any information you can supply me on bud-variation or sports. When any extra difficult points occur to me in my present subject (which is a mass of difficulties), I will apply to you, but I will not be unreasonable. It is most true what you say that any one to study well the physiology of the life of plants, ought to have under his eye a multitude of plants. I have endeavoured to do what I can by comparing statements by many writers and observing what I could myself. Unfortunately few have observed like you have done. As you are so kind, I will mention one other point on which I am collecting facts ; namely, the effect produced on the stock by the graft ; thus, it is *said*, that the purple-leaved filbert affects the leaves of the common hazel on which it is grafted (I have just procured a plant to try), so variegated jessamine is *said* to affect its stock. I want these facts partly to throw light on the marvellous laburnum Adami, trifacial oranges, &c. That laburnum case seems one of the strangest in physiology. I have now growing splendid, *fertile*, yellow laburnums (with a long raceme like the so-called Waterer's laburnum) from seed of yellow flowers on the *C. Adami*. To a man like myself, who is compelled to live a solitary life, and sees few persons, it is no slight satisfaction to hear that I have been able at all [to] interest by my books observers like yourself.

As I shall publish on my present subject, I presume, within a year, it will be of no use your sending me the shoots of peaches and nectarines which you so kindly offer ; I have recorded your facts.

Permit me again to thank you cordially ; I have not often in my life received a kinder letter.

My dear Sir, yours sincerely,

CH. DARWIN.

CHAPTER V.

JANUARY 1867, TO JUNE 1868.

[AT the beginning of the year 1867 he was at work on the final chapter—"Concluding Remarks" of the 'Variation of Animals and Plants under Domestication,' which was begun after the rest of the MS. had been sent to the printers in the preceding December. With regard to the publication of the book he wrote to Mr. Murray, on January 3 :—

"I cannot tell you how sorry I am to hear of the enormous size of my book.* I fear it can never pay. But I cannot shorten it now; nor, indeed, if I had foreseen its length, do I see which parts ought to have been omitted.

"If you are afraid to publish it, say so at once, I beg you, and I will consider your note as cancelled. If you think fit, get any one whose judgment you rely on, to look over some of the more legible chapters, namely, the Introduction, and on dogs and plants, the latter chapters being in my opinion, the dullest in the book. . . . The list of chapters, and the inspection of a few here and there, would give a good judge

---

* On January 9 he wrote to Sir J. D. Hooker : "I have been these last few days vexed and annoyed to a foolish degree by hearing that my MS. on Dom. An. and Cult. Plants will make 2 vols., both bigger than the 'Origin.' The volumes will have to be full-sized octavo, so I have written to Murray to suggest details to be printed in small type. But I feel that the size is quite ludicrous in relation to the subject. I am ready to swear at myself and at every fool who writes a book."

a fair idea of the whole book. Pray do not publish blindly, as it would vex me all my life if I led you to heavy loss."

Mr. Murray referred the MS. to a literary friend, and, in spite of a somewhat adverse opinion, willingly agreed to publish the book. My father wrote :—

"Your note has been a great relief to me. I am rather alarmed about the verdict of your friend, as he is not a man of science. I think if you had sent the 'Origin' to an unscientific man, he would have utterly condemned it. I am, however, *very glad* that you have consulted any one on whom you can rely.

"I must add, that my 'Journal of Researches' was seen in MS. by an eminent semi-scientific man, and was pronounced unfit for publication."

The proofs were begun in March, and the last revise was finished on November 15th, and during this period the only intervals of rest were two visits of a week each at his brother Erasmus's house in Queen Anne Street. He notes in his Diary :—

"I began this book [in the] beginning of 1860 (and then had some MS.), but owing to interruptions from my illness, and illness of children ; from various editions of the 'Origin,' and Papers, especially Orchis book and Tendrils, I have spent four years and two months over it."

The edition of 'Animals and Plants' was of 1500 copies, and of these 1260 were sold at Mr. Murray's autumnal sale, but it was not published until January 30, 1868. A new edition of 1250 copies was printed in February of the same year.

In 1867 he received the distinction of being made a knight of the Prussian Order "Pour le Mérite." * He seems

---

* The Order "Pour le Mérite" was founded in 1740 by Frederick II. by the re-christening of an "Order of Generosity," founded in 1665. It was at one time strictly military, having been previously both civil and military, and in 1840 the Order was again opened to civilians. The order consists of thirty members of German extraction, but distinguished foreigners are admitted to a kind of extraordinary membership. Faraday, Herschel, and Thomas Moore, have belonged to it in this way. From the

not to have known how great the distinction was, for in June 1868 he wrote to Sir J. D. Hooker :—

"What a man you are for sympathy. I was made "Eques" some months ago, but did not think much about it. Now, by Jove, we all do ; but you, in fact, have knighted me."

The letters may now take up the story.]

C. Darwin to J. D. Hooker.

Down, February 8 [1867].

MY DEAR HOOKER,—I am heartily glad that you have been offered the Presidentship of the British Association, for it is a great honour, and as you have so much work to do, I am equally glad that you have declined it. I feel, however, convinced that you would have succeeded very well; but if I fancy myself in such a position, it actually makes my blood run cold. I look back with amazement at the skill and taste with which the Duke of Argyll made a multitude of little speeches at Glasgow. By the way, I have not seen the Duke's book,* but I formerly thought that some of the articles which appeared in periodicals were very clever, but not very profound. One of these was reviewed in the *Saturday Review* † some years ago, and the fallacy of some main argument was admirably exposed, and I sent the article to you, and you agreed strongly with it. . . . There was the other day a rather good review of the Duke's book in the *Spectator*, and with a new explanation, either by the Duke or the reviewer (I could not make out which), of rudimentary organs, namely, that economy of labour and material was a great

---

thirty members a chancellor is elected by the king (the first officer of this kind was Alexander v. Humboldt) ; and it is the duty of the chancellor to notify a vacancy in the Order to the remainder of the thirty, who then elect by vote the new member—but the king has technically the appointment in his own hands.

* 'The Reign of Law,' 1867.

† *Sat. Review*, Nov. 15, 1862, 'The *Edinburgh Review* on the Supernatural.' Written by my cousin, Mr. Henry Parker.

guiding principle with God (ignoring waste of seed and of young monsters, &c.), and that making a new plan for the structure of animals was thought, and thought was labour, and therefore God kept to a uniform plan, and left rudiments. This is no exaggeration. In short, God is a man, rather cleverer than us. . . . I am very much obliged for the *Nation* (returned by this post) ; it is *admirably* good. You say I always guess wrong, but I do not believe any one, except Asa Gray, could have done the thing so well. I would bet even, or three to two, that it is Asa Gray, though one or two passages staggered me.

I finish my book on ' Domestic Animals,' &c., by a single paragraph, answering, or rather throwing doubt, in so far as so little space permits, on Asa Gray's doctrine that each variation has been specially ordered or led along a beneficial line. It is foolish to touch such subjects, but there have been so many allusions to what I think about the part which God has played in the formation of organic beings,* that I thought it shabby to evade the question. . . . I have even received several letters on the subject. . . . I overlooked your sentence about Providence, and suppose I treated it as Buckland did his own theology, when his Bridgewater Treatise was read aloud to him for correction. . . .

[The following letter, from Mrs. Boole, is one of those referred to in the last letter to Sir J. D. Hooker :]

Dear Sir,—Will you excuse my venturing to ask you a question, to which no one's answer but your own would be quite satisfactory ?

---

* Prof. Judd allows me to quote from some notes which he has kindly given me :—" Lyell once told me that he had frequently been asked if Darwin was not one of the most unhappy of men, it being suggested that his outrage upon public opinion should have filled him with remorse." Sir Charles Lyell must have been able, I think, to give a satisfactory answer on this point. Professor Judd continues :—

" I made a note of this and other conversations of Lyell's at the time.

Do you consider the holding of your theory of Natural Selection, in its fullest and most unreserved sense, to be inconsistent—I do not say with any particular scheme of theological doctrine—but with the following belief, namely :—

That knowledge is given to man by the direct inspiration of the Spirit of God.

That God is a personal and Infinitely good Being.

That the effect of the action of the Spirit of God on the brain of man is especially a moral effect.

And that each individual man has within certain limits a power of choice as to how far he will yield to his hereditary animal impulses, and how far he will rather follow the guidance of the Spirit, who is educating him into a power of resisting those impulses in obedience to moral motives?

The reason why I ask you is this : my own impression has always been, not only that your theory was perfectly *compatible* with the faith to which I have just tried to give expression, but that your books afforded me a clue which would guide me in applying that faith to the solution of certain complicated psychological problems which it was of practical importance to me as a mother to solve. I felt that you had supplied one of the missing links—not to say *the* missing link—between the facts of science and the promises of religion. Every year's experience tends to deepen in me that impression.

But I have lately read remarks on the probable bearing of your theory on religious and moral questions which have perplexed and pained me sorely. I know that the persons who make such remarks must be cleverer and wiser than myself. I cannot feel sure that they are mistaken, unless you will tell me so. And I think—I cannot know for certain —but I *think*—that if I were an author, I would rather that the humblest student of my works should apply to me directly

---

At the present time such statements must appear strange to any one who does not recollect the revolution in opinion which has taken place during the last 23 years [1882]."

in a difficulty, than that she should puzzle too long over adverse and probably mistaken or thoughtless criticisms.

At the same time I feel that you have a perfect right to refuse to answer such questions as I have asked you. Science must take her path, and Theology hers, and they will meet when and where and how God pleases, and you are in no sense responsible for it if the meeting-point should still be very far off. If I receive no answer to this letter I shall infer nothing from your silence, except that you felt I had no right to make such inquiries of a stranger.

[My father replied as follows :]

Down, December 14, [1866].

DEAR MADAM,—It would have gratified me much if I could have sent satisfactory answers to your questions, or, indeed, answers of any kind. But I cannot see how the belief that all organic beings, including man, have been genetically derived from some simple being, instead of having been separately created, bears on your difficulties. These, as it seems to me, can be answered only by widely different evidence from science, or by the so-called "inner consciousness." My opinion is not worth more than that of any other man who has thought on such subjects, and it would be folly in me to give it. I may, however, remark that it has always appeared to me more satisfactory to look at the immense amount of pain and suffering in this world as the inevitable result of the natural sequence of events, *i.e.* general laws, rather than from the direct intervention of God, though I am aware this is not logical with reference to an omniscient Deity. Your last question seems to resolve itself into the problem of free will and necessity, which has been found by most persons insoluble. I sincerely wish that this note had not been as utterly valueless as it is. I would have sent full answers, though I have little time or strength to spare, had it been in my power. I have the honour to remain, dear Madam,

Yours very faithfully,

CHARLES DARWIN.

P.S.—I am grieved that my views should incidentally have caused trouble to your mind, but I thank you for your judgment, and honour you for it, that theology and science should each run its own course, and that in the present case I am not responsible if their meeting-point should still be far off.

[The next letter discusses the ' Reign of Law,' referred to a few pages back :]

C. Darwin to C. Lyell.

Down, June 1 [1867].

. . . I am at present reading the Duke, and am *very much* interested by him ; yet I cannot but think, clever as the whole is, that parts are weak, as when he doubts whether each curvature of the beak of humming-birds is of service to each species.   He admits, perhaps too fully, that I have shown the use of each little ridge and shape of each petal in orchids, and how strange he does not extend the view to humming-birds.   Still odder, it seems to me, all that he says on beauty, which I should have thought a nonentity, except in the mind of some sentient being.   He might have as well said that love existed during the secondary or Palæozoic periods.   I hope you are getting on with your book better than I am with mine, which kills me with the labour of correcting, and is intolerably dull, though I did not think so when I was writing it.   A naturalist's life would be a happy one if he had only to observe, and never to write.

We shall be in London for a week in about a fortnight's time, and I shall enjoy having a breakfast talk with you.

Yours affectionately,

C. DARWIN.

[The following letter refers to the new and improved translation of the ' Origin,' undertaken by Professor Carus :]

C. Darwin to J. Victor Carus.

Down, February 17 [1867].

MY DEAR SIR,—I have read your preface with care. It seems to me that you have treated Bronn with complete respect and great delicacy, and that you have alluded to your own labour with much modesty. I do not think that any of Bronn's friends can complain of what you say and what you have done. For my own sake, I grieve that you have not added notes, as I am sure that I should have profited much by them; but as you have omitted Bronn's objections, I believe that you have acted with excellent judgment and fairness in leaving the text without comment to the independent verdict of the reader. I heartily congratulate you that the main part of your labour is over; it would have been to most men a very troublesome task, but you seem to have indomitable powers of work, judging from those two wonderful and most useful volumes on zoological literature * edited by you, and which I never open without surprise at their accuracy, and gratitude for their usefulness. I cannot sufficiently tell you how much I rejoice that you were persuaded to superintend the translation of the present edition of my book, for I have now the great satisfaction of knowing that the German public can judge fairly of its merits and demerits. . . . .

With my cordial and sincere thanks, believe me,

My dear Sir, yours very faithfully,

CH. DARWIN.

[The earliest letter which I have seen from my father to Professor Haeckel, was written in 1865, and from that time forward they corresponded (though not, I think, with any regularity) up to the end of my father's life. His friendship with Haeckel was not merely growth of correspondence, as was

---

* 'Bibliotheca Zoologica,' 1861.

the case with some others, for instance, Fritz Müller. Haeckel paid more than one visit to Down, and these were thoroughly enjoyed by my father. The following letter will serve to show the strong feeling of regard which he entertained for his correspondent—a feeling which I have often heard him emphatically express, and which was warmly returned. The book referred to is Haeckel's 'Generelle Morphologie,' published in 1866, a copy of which my father received from the author in January 1867.

Dr. E. Krause* has given a good account of Professor Haeckel's services to the cause of Evolution. After speaking of the lukewarm reception which the 'Origin' met with in Germany on its first publication, he goes on to describe the first adherents of the new faith as more or less popular writers, not especially likely to advance its acceptance with the professorial or purely scientific world. And he claims for Haeckel that it was his advocacy of Evolution in his 'Radiolaria' (1862), and at the "Versammlung" of Naturalists at Stettin in 1863, that placed the Darwinian question for the first time publicly before the forum of German science, and his enthusiastic propagandism that chiefly contributed to its success.

Mr. Huxley, writing in 1869, paid a high tribute to Professor Haeckel as the Coryphæus of the Darwinian movement in Germany. Of his 'Generelle Morphologie,' "an attempt to work out the practical application" of the doctrine of Evolution to their final results, he says that it has the "force and suggestiveness, and . . . systematising power of Oken without his extravagance." Professor Huxley also testifies to the value of Haeckel's 'Schöpfungs-Geschichte' as an exposition of the 'Generelle Morphologie' "for an educated public."

Again, in his 'Evolution in Biology,'† Mr. Huxley wrote :

---

* 'Charles Darwin und sein Verhältniss zu Deutschland,' 1885.

† An article in the 'Encyclopædia Britannica,' 9th edit., reprinted in 'Science and Culture,' 1881, p. 298.

"Whatever hesitation may, not unfrequently, be felt by less daring minds, in following Haeckel in many of his speculations, his attempt to systematise the doctrine of Evolution, and to exhibit its influence as the central thought of modern biology, cannot fail to have a far-reaching influence on the progress of science."

In the following letter my father alludes to the somewhat fierce manner in which Professor Haeckel fought the battle of 'Darwinismus,' and on this subject Dr. Krause has some good remarks (p. 162). He asks whether much that happened in the heat of the conflict might not well have been otherwise, and adds that Haeckel himself is the last man to deny this. Nevertheless he thinks that even these things may have worked well for the cause of Evolution, inasmuch as Haeckel "concentrated on himself by his 'Ursprung des Menschen-Geschlechts,' his 'Generelle Morphologie,' and 'Schöpfungs-Geschichte,' all the hatred and bitterness which Evolution excited in certain quarters," so that, "in a surprisingly short time it became the fashion in Germany that Haeckel alone should be abused, while Darwin was held up as the ideal of forethought and moderation."]

C. Darwin to E. Haeckel.

Down, May 21, 1867.

DEAR HAECKEL.—Your letter of the 18th has given me great pleasure, for you have received what I said in the most kind and cordial manner. You have in part taken what I said much stronger than I had intended. It never occurred to me for a moment to doubt that your work, with the whole subject so admirably and clearly arranged, as well as fortified by so many new facts and arguments, would not advance our common object in the highest degree. All that I think is that you will excite anger, and that anger so completely blinds every one, that your arguments would have no chance of influencing those who are already opposed to our views. Moreover, I do not at all like that you, towards whom I feel

53

so much friendship, should unnecessarily make enemies, and there is pain and vexation enough in the world without more being caused. But I repeat that I can feel no doubt that your work will greatly advance our subject, and I heartily wish it could be translated into English, for my own sake and that of others. With respect to what you say about my advancing too strongly objections against my own views, some of my English friends think that I have erred on this side; but truth compelled me to write what I did, and I am inclined to think it was good policy. The belief in the descent theory is slowly spreading in England,* even amongst those who can give no reason for their belief. No body of men were at first so much opposed to my views as the members of the London Entomological Society, but now I am assured that, with the exception of two or three old men, all the members concur with me to a certain extent. It has been a great disappointment to me that I have never received your long letter written to me from the Canary Islands. I am rejoiced to hear that your tour, which seems to have been a most interesting one, has done your health much good. I am working away at my new book, but make very slow progress, and the work tries my health, which is much the same as when you were here.

Victor Carus is going to translate it, but whether it is worth translation, I am rather doubtful. I am very glad to hear that there is some chance of your visiting England this autumn, and all in this house will be delighted to see you here.

Believe me, my dear Haeckel,

Yours very sincerely,

CHARLES DARWIN.

---

* In October 1867 he wrote to Mr. Wallace :—" Mr. Warrington has lately read an excellent and spirited abstract of the 'Origin' before the Victoria Institute, and as this is a most orthodox body, he has gained the name of the Devil's Advocate. The discussion which followed during three consecutive meetings is very rich from the nonsense talked. If you would care to see the number I could send it you."

C. Darwin to F. Müller.

Down, July 31 [1867].

MY DEAR SIR,—I received a week ago your letter of June 2, full as usual of valuable matter and specimens. It arrived at exactly the right time, for I was enabled to give a pretty full abstract of your observations on the plant's own pollen being poisonous. I have inserted this abstract in the proof-sheets in my chapter on sterility, and it forms the most striking part of my whole chapter.* I thank you very sincerely for the most interesting observations, which, however, I regret that you did not publish independently. I have been forced to abbreviate one or two parts more than I wished. . . . Your letters always surprise me, from the number of points to which you attend. I wish I could make my letters of any interest to you, for I hardly ever see a naturalist, and live as retired a life as you in Brazil. With respect to mimetic plants, I remember Hooker many years ago saying he believed that there were many, but I agree with you that it would be most difficult to distinguish between mimetic resemblance and the effects of peculiar conditions. Who can say to which of these causes to attribute the several plants with heath-like foliage at the Cape of Good Hope? Is it not also a difficulty that quadrupeds appear to recognise plants more by their [scent] than their appearance? What I have just said reminds me to ask you a question. Sir J. Lubbock brought me the other day what appears to be a terrestrial Planaria (the first ever found in the northern hemisphere) and which was coloured exactly like our dark-coloured slugs. Now slugs are not devoured by birds, like the shell-bearing species, and this made me remember that I found the Brazilian Planariæ actually together with striped Vaginuli which I believe were similarly coloured. Can you throw any light on this? I wish to know, because I was puzzled some months ago how it would be possible to ac-

* In 'The Variation of Animals and Plants.'

count for the bright colours of the Planariæ in reference to sexual selection.   By the way, I suppose they are hermaphrodites.

Do not forget to aid me, if in your power, with answers to *any* of my questions on expression, for the subject interests me greatly.   With cordial thanks for your never-failing kindness, believe me,

Yours very sincerely,
CHARLES DARWIN.

C. Darwin to C. Lyell.

Down, July 18 [1867].

MY DEAR LYELL,—Many thanks for your long letter.   I am sorry to hear that you are in despair about your book ; * I well know that feeling, but am now getting out of the lower depths.   I shall be very much pleased, if you can make the least use of my present book, and do not care at all whether it is published before yours.   Mine will appear towards the end of November of this year ; you speak of yours as not coming out till November, 1868, which I hope may be an error.   There is nothing about Man in my book which can interfere with you, so I will order all the completed clean sheets to be sent (and others as soon as ready) to you, but please observe you will not care for the first volume, which is a mere record of the amount of variation ; but I hope the second will be somewhat more interesting.   Though I fear the whole must be dull.

I rejoice from my heart that you are going to speak out plainly about species.   My book about Man, if published, will be short, and a large portion will be devoted to sexual selection, to which subject I alluded in the ' Origin ' as bearing on Man. . . .

---

* The 2nd volume of the 10th Edit. of the ' Principles.'

C. Darwin to C. Lyell.

Down, August 22 [1867].

MY DEAR LYELL,—I thank you cordially for your last two letters. The former one did me *real* good, for I had got so wearied with the subject that I could hardly bear to correct the proofs,* and you gave me fresh heart. I remember thinking that when you came to the Pigeon chapter you would pass it over as quite unreadable. Your last letter has interested me in very many ways, and I have been glad to hear about those horrid unbelieving Frenchmen. I have been particularly pleased that you have noticed Pangenesis. I do not know whether you ever had the feeling of having thought so much over a subject that you had lost all power of judging it. This is my case with Pangenesis (which is 26 or 27 years old), but I am inclined to think that if it be admitted as a probable hypothesis it will be a somewhat important step in Biology.

I cannot help still regretting that you have ever looked at the slips, for I hope to improve the whole a good deal. It is surprising to me, and delightful, that you should care in the least about the plants. Altogether you have given me one of the best cordials I ever had in my life, and I heartily thank you. I despatched this morning the French edition.† The introduction was a complete surprise to me, and I dare say has injured the book in France ; nevertheless . . . it shows, I think, that the woman is uncommonly clever. Once again many thanks for the renewed courage with which I shall attack the horrid proof-sheets.

Yours affectionately,

CHARLES DARWIN.

---

* The proofs of 'Animals and Plants,' which Lyell was then reading.

† Of the 'Origin.' It appears that my father was sending a copy of the French edition to Sir Charles. The introduction was by Mdlle. Royer, who translated the book.

P.S.—A Russian who is translating my new book into Russian has been here, and says you are immensely read in Russia, and many editions—how many I forget. Six editions of Buckle and four editions of the 'Origin.'

C. Darwin to Asa Gray.

Down, October 16 [1867].

MY DEAR GRAY,—I send by this post clean sheets of Vol. I. up to p. 336, and there are only 411 pages in this vol. I am *very* glad to hear that you are going to review my book ; but if the *Nation* * is a newspaper I wish it were at the bottom of the sea, for I fear that you will thus be stopped reviewing me in a scientific journal. The first volume is all details, and you will not be able to read it ; and you must remember that the chapters on plants are written for naturalists who are not botanists. The last chapter in Vol. I. is, however, I think, a curious compilation of facts ; it is on bud-variation. In Vol. II. some of the chapters are more interesting; and I shall be very curious to hear your verdict on the chapter on close inter-breeding. The chapter on what I call Pangenesis will be called a mad dream, and I shall be pretty well satisfied if you think it a dream worth publishing; but at the bottom of my own mind I think it contains a great truth. I finish my book with a semi-theological paragraph, in which I quote and differ from you ; what you will think of it, I know not. . . .

C. Darwin to J. D. Hooker.

Down, November 17 [1867].

MY DEAR HOOKER,—Congratulate me, for I have finished the last revise of the last sheet of my book. It has been an awful job : seven and a half months correcting the press : the book, from much small type, does not look big, but is really very big. I have had hard work to keep up to the mark, but

---

* The book was reviewed by Dr. Gray in the *Nation*, Mar. 19, 1868.

during the last week only few revises came, so that I have rested and feel more myself. Hence, after our long mutual silence, I enjoy myself by writing a note to you, for the sake of exhaling, and hearing from you. On account of the index,* I do not suppose that you will receive your copy till the middle of next month. I shall be intensely anxious to hear what you think about Pangenesis; though I can see how fearfully imperfect, even in mere conjectural conclusions, it is; yet it has been an infinite satisfaction to me somehow to connect the various large groups of facts, which I have long considered, by an intelligible thread. I shall not be at all surprised if you attack it and me with unparalleled ferocity. It will be my endeavor to do as little as possible for some time, but [I] shall soon prepare a paper or two for the Linnean Society. In a short time we shall go to London for ten days, but the time is not yet fixed. Now I have told you a deal about myself, and do let me hear a good deal about your own past and future doings. Can you pay us a visit, early in December? . . . . I have seen no one for an age, and heard no news.

. . . About my book I will give you a bit of advice. Skip the *whole* of Vol. I., except the last chapter (and that need only be skimmed) and skip largely in the 2nd volume; and then you will say it is a very good book.

1868.

['The Variation of Animals and Plants' was, as already mentioned, published on January 30, 1868, and on that day he sent a copy to Fritz Müller, and wrote to him :—

"I send by this post, by French packet, my new book, the publication of which has been much delayed. The greater part, as you will see, is not meant to be read; but I should very much like to hear what you think of 'Pangenesis,' though I fear it will appear to *every one* far too speculative."]

---

* The index was made by Mr. W. S. Dallas; I have often heard my father express his admiration of this excellent piece of work.

C. Darwin to J. D. Hooker.

February 3 [1868].

. . . I am very much pleased at what you say about my Introduction; after it was in type I was as near as possible cancelling the whole. I have been for some time in despair about my book, and if I try to read a few pages I feel fairly nauseated, but do not let this make you praise it; for I have made up my mind that it is not worth a fifth part of the enormous labour it has cost me. I assure you that all that is worth your doing (if you have time for so much) is glancing at Chapter VI., and reading parts of the later chapters. The facts on self-impotent plants seem to me curious, and I have worked out to my own satisfaction the good from crossing and evil from interbreeding. I did read Pangenesis the other evening, but even this, my beloved child, as I had fancied, quite disgusted me. The devil take the whole book; and yet now I am at work again as hard as I am able. It is really a great evil that from habit I have pleasure in hardly anything except Natural History, for nothing else makes me forget my ever-recurrent uncomfortable sensations. But I must not howl any more, and the critics may say what they like; I did my best, and man can do no more. What a splendid pursuit Natural History would be if it was all observing and no writing! . . . .

C. Darwin to J. D. Hooker.

Down, February 10 [1868].

MY DEAR HOOKER,—What is the good of having a friend, if one may not boast to him? I heard yesterday that Murray has sold in a week the whole edition of 1500 copies of my book, and the sale so pressing that he has agreed with Clowes to get another edition in fourteen days! This has done me a world of good, for I had got into a sort of dogged hatred of my book. And now there has appeared a review in the *Pall Mall* which has pleased me excessively, more perhaps than is reasonable. I am quite content, and do not care how much I may be pitched into. If by any chance you should hear who wrote the article in the *Pall Mall*, do please tell me ; it is some one who writes capitally, and who knows the subject. I went to luncheon on Sunday, to Lubbock's, partly in hopes of seeing you, and, be hanged to you, you were not there.

Your cock-a-hoop friend,

C. D.

[Independently of the favourable tone of the able series of notices in the *Pall Mall Gazette* (Feb. 10, 15, 17, 1868), my father may well have been gratified by the following passages :—

"We must call attention to the rare and noble calmness with which he expounds his own views, undisturbed by the heats of polemical agitation which those views have excited, and persistently refusing to retort on his antagonists by ridicule, by indignation, or by contempt. Considering the amount of vituperation and insinuation which has come from the other side, this forbearance is supremely dignified."

And again in the third notice, Feb. 17 :—

"Nowhere has the author a word that could wound the most sensitive self-love of an antagonist ; nowhere does he, in text or note, expose the fallacies and mistakes of brother investigators . . . but while abstaining from impertinent censure, he is lavish in acknowledging the smallest debts he may owe ; and his book will make many men happy."

I am indebted to Messrs. Smith & Elder for the information that these articles were written by Mr. G. H. Lewes.]

C. Darwin to J. D. Hooker.

Down, February 23 [1868].

MY DEAR HOOKER,—I have had almost as many letters to write of late as you can have, viz. from 8 to 10 per diem.

chiefly getting up facts on sexual selection, therefore I have felt no inclination to write to you, and now I mean to write solely about my book for my own satisfaction, and not at all for yours. The first edition was 1500 copies, and now the second is printed off ; sharp work. Did you look at the review in the *Athenæum*,* showing profound contempt of me? . . . It is a shame that he should have said that I have taken much from Pouchet, without acknowledgment; for I took literally nothing, there being nothing to take. There is a capital review in the *Gardeners' Chronicle* which will sell the book if anything will. I don't quite see whether I or the writer is in a muddle about man *causing* variability. If a man drops a bit of iron into sulphuric acid he does not cause the affinities to come into play, yet he may be said to make sulphate of iron. I do not know how to avoid ambiguity.

After what the *Pall Mall Gazette* and the *Chronicle* have said I do not care a d——.

I fear Pangenesis is stillborn ; Bates says he has read it twice, and is not sure that he understands it. H. Spencer says the view is quite different from his (and this is a great relief to me, as I feared to be accused of plagiarism, but

---

* *Athenæum*, February 15, 1868. My father quoted Pouchet's assertion that " variation under domestication throws no light on the natural modification of species." The reviewer quotes the end of a passage in which my father declares that he can see no force in Pouchet's arguments, or rather assertions, and then goes on : " We are sadly mistaken if there are not clear proofs in the pages of the book before us that, on the contrary, Mr. Darwin has perceived, felt, and yielded to the force of the arguments or assertions of his French antagonist." The following may serve as samples of the rest of the review :—

" Henceforth the rhetoricians will have a better illustration of anti-climax than the mountain which brought forth a mouse, . . . in the discoverer of the origin of species, who tried to explain the variation of pigeons !

" A few summary words. On the ' Origin of Species ' Mr. Darwin has nothing, and is never likely to have anything, to say ; but on the vastly important subject of inheritance, the transmission of peculiarities once acquired through successive generations, this work is a valuable store-house of facts for curious students and practical breeders."

utterly failed to be sure what he meant, so thought it safest to give my view as almost the same as his), and he says he is not sure he understands it. . . . Am I not a poor devil ? yet I took such pains, I must think that I expressed myself clearly. Old Sir H. Holland says he has read it twice, and thinks it very tough ; but believes that sooner or later " some view akin to it " will be accepted.

You will think me very self-sufficient, when I declare that I feel *sure* if Pangenesis is now stillborn it will, thank God, at some future time reappear, begotten by some other father, and christened by some other name.

Have you ever met with any tangible and clear view of what takes place in generation, whether by seeds or buds, or how a long-lost character can possibly reappear ; or how the male element can possibly affect the mother plant, or the mother animal, so that her future progeny are affected ? Now all these points and many others are connected together, whether truely or falsely is another question, by Pangenesis. You see I die hard, and stick up for my poor child.

This letter is written for my own satisfaction, and not for yours. So bear it.

Yours affectionately,

Ch. Darwin.

*C. Darwin to A. Newton.**

Down, February 9 [1870].

Dear Newton,—I suppose it would be universally held extremely wrong for a defendant to write to a Judge to express his satisfaction at a judgment in his favour ; and yet I am going thus to act. I have just read what you have said in the ' Record ' † about my pigeon chapters, and it has gratified me beyond measure. I have sometimes felt a little disappointed that the labour of so many years seemed to be almost thrown away, for you are the first man capable of

---

* Prof. of Zoology at Cambridge.

† ' Zoological Record.' The volume for 1868, published Dec. 1869.

forming a judgment (excepting partly Quatrefages), who seems to have thought anything of this part of my work. The amount of labour, correspondence, and care, which the subject cost me, is more than you could well suppose. I thought the article in the *Athenæum* was very unjust; but now I feel amply repaid, and I cordially thank you for your sympathy and too warm praise. What labour you have bestowed on your part of the 'Record'! I ought to be ashamed to speak of my amount of work. I thoroughly enjoyed the Sunday, which you and the others spent here, and

I remain, dear Newton, yours very sincerely,

CH. DARWIN.

C. Darwin to A. R. Wallace.

Down, February 27 [1868].

MY DEAR WALLACE,—You cannot well imagine how much I have been pleased by what you say about 'Pangenesis.' None of my friends will speak out. . . . Hooker, as far as I understand him, which I hardly do at present, seems to think that the hypothesis is little more than saying that organisms have such and such potentialities. What you say exactly and fully expresses my feeling, viz. that it is a relief to have some feasible explanation of the various facts, which can be given up as soon as any better hypothesis is found. It has certainly been an immense relief to my mind ; for I have been stumbling over the subject for years, dimly seeing that some relation existed between the various classes of facts. I now hear from H. Spencer that his views quoted in my foot-note refer to something quite distinct, as you seem to have perceived.

I shall be very glad to hear at some future day your criticisms on the " causes of variability." Indeed I feel sure that I am right about sterility and natural selection. . . . I do not quite understand your case, and we think that a word or two is misplaced. I wish sometime you would consider the case under the following point of view :—If sterility is caused or accumulated through natural selection, then as every degree exists up to absolute barrenness, natural selection must have the power of increasing it. Now take two species, A and B, and assume that they are (by any means) half-sterile, *i.e.* produce half the full number of offspring. Now try and make (by natural selection) A and B absolutely sterile when crossed, and you will find how difficult it is. I grant indeed, it is certain, that the degree of sterility of the individuals A and B will vary, but any such extra-sterile individuals of, we will say A, if they should hereafter breed with other individuals of A, will bequeath no advantage to their progeny, by which these families will tend to increase in number over other families of A, which are not more sterile when crossed with B. But I do not know that I have made this any clearer than in the chapter in my book. It is a most difficult bit of reasoning, which I have gone over and over again on paper with diagrams.

. . . Hearty thanks for your letter. You have indeed pleased me, for I had given up the great god Pan as a still-born deity. I wish you could be induced to make it clear with your admirable powers of elucidation in one of the scientific journals. . . .

C. Darwin to J. D. Hooker.

Down, February 28 [1868].

MY DEAR HOOKER,—I have been deeply interested by your letter, and we had a good laugh over Huxley's remark, which was so deuced clever that you could not recollect it. I cannot quite follow your train of thought, for in the last page you admit all that I wish, having apparently denied all, or thought all mere words in the previous pages of your note; but it may be my muddle. I see clearly that any satisfaction which Pan may give will depend on the constitution of each man's mind. If you have arrived already at any similar conclusion, the whole will of course appear stale to you. I heard yesterday from Wallace, who says (excuse horrid vanity), " I can hardly tell you how much I admire the chapter on 'Pangenesis.' It is a *positive comfort* to me to have any feasible explanation of a difficulty that has always been haunting me, and I shall never be able to give it up till a better one supplies its place, and that I think hardly possible, &c." Now his foregoing [italicised] words express my sentiments exactly and fully : though perhaps I feel the relief extra strongly from having during many years vainly attempted to form some hypothesis. When you or Huxley say that a single cell of a plant, or the stump of an amputated limb, have the " potentiality " of reproducing the whole —or " diffuse an influence," these words give me no positive idea ;—but when it is said that the cells of a plant, or stump, include atoms derived from every other cell of the whole organism and capable of development, I gain a distinct idea. But this idea would not be worth a rush, if it applied to one case alone ; but it seems to me to apply to all the forms of reproduction—inheritance—metamorphosis—to the abnormal transposition of organs—to the direct action of the male element on the mother plant, &c. Therefore I fully believe that each cell does *actually* throw off an atom or gemmule of its contents ;—but whether or not, this hypothesis serves as a useful connecting link for various grand classes of physiological facts, which at present stand absolutely isolated.

I have touched on the doubtful point (alluded to by Huxley) how far atoms derived from the same cell may become developed into different structure accordingly as they are differently nourished ; I advanced as illustrations galls and polypoid excrescences. . . .

It is a real pleasure to me to write to you on this subject, and I should be delighted if we can understand each other; but you must not let your good nature lead you on. Remember, we always fight tooth and nail. We go to London on Tuesday, first for a week to Queen Anne Street, and afterwards to Miss Wedgwood's, in Regent's Park, and stay the whole month, which, as my gardener truly says, is a " terrible thing " for my experiments.

C. Darwin to W. Ogle.*

Down, March 6 [1868].

DEAR SIR,—I thank you most sincerely for your letter, which is very interesting to me. I wish I had known of these views of Hippocrates before I had published, for they seem almost identical with mine—merely a change of terms—and an application of them to classes of facts necessarily unknown to the old philosopher. The whole case is a good illustration of how rarely anything is new.

Hippocrates has taken the wind out of my sails, but I care very little about being forestalled. I advance the views merely as a provisional hypothesis, but with the secret expectation that sooner or later some such view will have to be admitted.

. . . I do not expect the reviewers will be so learned as you : otherwise, no doubt, I shall be accused of wilfully stealing Pangenesis from Hippocrates,—for this is the spirit some reviewers delight to show.

C. Darwin to Victor Carus.

Down, March 21 [1868].

. . . I am very much obliged to you for sending me so frankly your opinion on Pangenesis, and I am sorry it is un-favourable, but I cannot quite understand your remark on pangenesis, selection, and the struggle for life not being more methodical. I am not at all surprised at your unfavourable verdict ; I know many, probably most, will come to the same conclusion. One English Review says it is much too com-plicated. . . . Some of my friends are enthusiastic on the hypothesis. . . . Sir C. Lyell says to every one, " You may not believe in ' Pangenesis,' but if you once understand it, you will never get it out of your mind." And with this criticism

---

* Dr. William Ogle, now the Superintendent of Statistics to the Registrar-General.

I am perfectly content.   All cases of inheritance and re-version and development now appear to me under a new light. . . .

[An extract from a letter to Fritz Müller, though of later date (June), may be given here :—

"Your letter of April 22 has much interested me.   I am delighted that you approve of my book, for I value your opinion more than that of almost any one.   I have yet hopes that you will think well of Pangenesis.   I feel sure that our minds are somewhat alike, and I find it a great relief to have some definite, though hypothetical view, when I reflect on the wonderful transformations of animals, — the re-growth of parts, — and especially the direct action of pollen on the mother-form, &c.   It often appears to me almost certain that the characters of the parents are "photographed" on the child, only by means of material atoms derived from each cell in both parents, and developed in the child."]

C. Darwin to Asa Gray.

Down, May 8 [1868].

MY DEAR GRAY,—I have been a most ungrateful and un-gracious man not to have written to you an immense time ago to thank you heartily for the *Nation*, and for all your most kind aid in regard to the American edition [of 'Animals and Plants']. But I have been of late overwhelmed with letters, which I was forced to answer, and so put off writing to you. This morning I received the American edition (which looks capital), with your nice preface, for which hearty thanks. I hope to heaven that the book will succeed well enough to prevent you repenting of your aid. This arrival has put the finishing stroke to my conscience, which will endure its wrongs no longer.

. . . Your article in the *Nation* [Mar. 19] seems to me very good, and you give an excellent idea of Pangenesis—an infant cherished by few as yet, except his tender parent, but which will live a long life. There is parental presumption for you !

You give a good slap at my concluding metaphor : * un-doubtedly I ought to have brought in and contrasted natural and artificial selection ; but it seemed so obvious to me that natural selection depended on contingencies even more com-plex than those which must have determined the shape of each fragment at the base of my precipice. What I wanted to show was that in reference to pre-ordainment whatever holds good in the formation of a pouter pigeon holds good in the formation of a natural species of pigeon. I cannot see that this is false. If the right variations occurred, and no others, natural selection would be superfluous. A reviewer in an Edinburgh paper, who treats me with profound contempt, says on this subject that Professor Asa Gray could with the greatest ease smash me into little pieces.†

Believe me, my dear Gray,

Your ungrateful but sincere friend,

CHARLES DARWIN.

C. Darwin to G. Bentham.

Down, June 23, 1868.

MY DEAR MR. BENTHAM,—As your address ‡ is somewhat of the nature of a verdict from a judge, I do not know whether

---

* A short abstract of the precipice metaphor is given at p. 307, vol. i. Dr. Gray's criticism on this point is as follows : " But in Mr. Darwin's parallel, to meet the case of nature according to his own view of it, not only the fragments of rock (answering to variation) should fall, but the edi-fice (answering to natural selection) should rise, irrespective of will or choice !" But my father's parallel demands that natural selection shall be the architect, not the edifice—the question of design only comes in with regard to the form of the building materials.

† The *Daily Review*, April 27, 1868. My father has given rather a highly coloured version of the reviewer's remarks : " We doubt not that Professor Asa Gray . . . could show that natural selection . . . is simply an instrument in the hands of an omnipotent and omniscient creator." The reviewer goes on to say that the passage in question is a " very melan-choly one," and that the theory is the " apotheosis of materialism."

‡ Presidential Address to the Linnean Society.

it is proper for me to do so, but I must and will thank you for the pleasure which you have given me. I am delighted at what you say about my book. I got so tired of it, that for months together I thought myself a perfect fool for having given up so much time in collecting and observing little facts, but now I do not care if a score of common critics speak as contemptuously of the book as did the *Athenæum*. I feel justified in this, for I have so complete a reliance on your judgment that I feel certain that I should have bowed to your judgment had it been as unfavourable as it is the contrary. What you say about Pangenesis quite satisfies me, and is as much perhaps as any one is justified in saying. I have read your whole Address with the greatest interest. It must have cost you a vast amount of trouble. With cordial thanks, pray believe me,

Yours very sincerely,
CH. DARWIN.

P.S.—I fear that it is not likely that you have a superfluous copy of your Address; if you have, I should much like to send one to Fritz Müller in the interior of Brazil. By the way let me add that I discussed bud-variation chiefly from a belief which is common to several persons. that all variability is related to sexual generation; I wished to show clearly that this was an error.

[The above series of letters may serve to show to some extent the reception which the new book received. Before passing on (in the next chapter) to the 'Descent of Man,' I give a letter referring to the translation of Fritz Müller's book, 'Für Darwin.' It was originally published in 1864, but the English translation, by Mr. Dallas, which bore the title suggested by Sir C. Lyell, of 'Facts and Arguments for Darwin,' did not appear until 1869 :]

C. Darwin to F. Müller.

Down, March 16 [1868].

My DEAR SIR,—Your brother, as you will have heard from him, felt so convinced that you would not object to a translation of 'Für Darwin,' * that I have ventured to arrange for a translation. Engelmann has very liberally offered me clichés of the woodcuts for 22 thalers; Mr. Murray has agreed to bring out a translation (and he is our best publisher) on commission, for he would not undertake the work on his own risk; and I have agreed with Mr. W. S. Dallas (who has translated Von Siebold on Parthenogenesis, and many German works, and who writes very good English) to translate the book. He thinks (and he is a good judge) that it is important to have some few corrections or additions, in order to account for a translation appearing so lately [*i.e.* at such a long interval of time] after the original; so that I hope you will be able to send some. . . . .

[Two letters may be placed here as bearing on the spread of Evolutionary ideas in France and Germany :]

C. Darwin to A. Gaudry.

Down, January 21 [1868].

DEAR SIR,—I thank you for your interesting essay on the influence of the Geological features of the country on the mind and habits of the Ancient Athenians,† and for your very obliging letter. I am delighted to hear that you intend to consider the relations of fossil animals in connection with their genealogy; it will afford you a fine field for the exercise of your extensive knowledge and powers of reasoning. Your

---

* In a letter to Fritz Müller, my father wrote:—"I am vexed to see that on the title my name is more conspicuous than yours, which I especially objected to, and I cautioned the printers after seeing one proof."

† This appears to refer to M. Gaudry's paper translated in the 'Geol. Mag.,' 1868, p. 372.

belief will I suppose, at present, lower you in the estimation of your countrymen : but judging from the rapid spread in all parts of Europe, excepting France, of the belief in the common descent of allied species, I must think that this belief will before long become universal.   How strange it is that the country which gave birth to Buffon, the elder Geoffroy, and especially to Lamarck, should now cling so pertinaciously to the belief that species are immutable creations.

My work on Variation, &c., under domestication, will appear in a French translation in a few months' time, and I will do myself the pleasure and honour of directing the publisher to send a copy to you to the same address as this letter.

With sincere respect, I remain, dear sir,

Yours very faithfully,

CHARLES DARWIN.

[The next letter is of especial interest, as showing how high a value my father placed on the support of the younger German naturalists :]

*C. Darwin to W. Preyer.**

March 31, 1868.

. . . . I am delighted to hear that you uphold the doctrine of the Modification of Species, and defend my views.   The support which I receive from Germany is my chief ground for hoping that our views will ultimately prevail.   To the present day I am continually abused or treated with contempt by writers of my own country ; but the younger naturalists are almost all on my side, and sooner or later the public must follow those who make the subject their special study. The abuse and contempt of ignorant writers hurts me very little. . . .

---

* Now Professor of Physiology at Jena.

CHAPTER VI.

Work on 'Man.'

1864–1870.

[IN the autobiographical chapter (vol. i. p. 76), my father gives the circumstances which led to his writing the ' Descent of Man.' He states that his collection of facts, begun in 1837 or 1838, was continued for many years without any definite idea of publishing on the subject. The following letter to Mr. Wallace shows that in the period of ill-health and depression about 1864 he despaired of ever being able to do so :]

C. Darwin to A. R. Wallace.

Down, [May?] 28 [1864].

DEAR WALLACE,—I am so much better that I have just finished a paper for Linnean Society ; * but I am not yet at all strong, I felt much disinclination to write, and therefore you must forgive me for not having sooner thanked you for your paper on ' Man,' † received on the 11th. But first let me say that I have hardly ever in my life been more struck by any paper than that on ' Variation,' &c. &c., in the *Reader.*‡ I feel sure that such papers will do more for the spreading of our views on the modification of species than any separate Treatises on the simple subject itself. It is really admirable; but you ought not in the Man paper to speak of the theory

---

* On the three forms, &c., of Lythrum.

† ' Anthropological Review,' March 1864.

‡ *Reader*, Ap. 16, 1864. "On the Phenomena of Variation," &c. Abstract of a paper read before the Linnean Society, March 17, 1864.

as mine; it is just as much yours as mine.   One correspondent has already noticed to me your "high-minded" conduct
on this head.   But now for your Man paper, about which I
should like to write more than I can.   The great leading
idea is quite new to me, viz. that during late ages, the mind
will have been modified more than the body ; yet I had got
as far as to see with you that the struggle between the races
of man depended entirely on intellectual and *moral* qualities.
The latter part of the paper I can designate only as grand
and most eloquently done.   I have shown your paper to two
or three persons who have been here, and they have been
equally struck with it.   I am not sure that I go with you on
all minor points : when reading Sir G. Grey's account of the
constant battles of Australian savages, I remember thinking
that natural selection would come in, and likewise with the
Esquimaux, with whom the art of fishing and managing ca-
noes is said to be hereditary.   I rather differ on the rank,
under a classificatory point of view, which you assign to man ;
I do not think any character simply in excess ought ever to
be used for the higher divisions.   Ants would not be separated from other hymenopterous insects, however high the
instinct of the one, and however low the instincts of the other.
With respect to the differences of race, a conjecture has occurred to me that much may be due to the correlation of
complexion (and consequently hair) with constitution.   Assume that a dusky individual best escaped miasma, and you
will readily see what I mean.   I persuaded the Director-
General of the Medical Department of the Army to send
printed forms to the surgeons of all regiments in tropical
countries to ascertain this point, but I dare say I shall never
get any returns.   Secondly, I suspect that a sort of sexual
selection has been the most powerful means of changing the
races of man.   I can show that the different races have a
widely different standard of beauty.   Among savages the
most powerful men will have the pick of the women, and they
will generally leave the most descendants.   I have collected
a few notes on man, but I do not suppose that I shall ever

use them. Do you intend to follow out your views, and if so, would you like at some future time to have my few references and notes? I am sure I hardly know whether they are of any value, and they are at present in a state of chaos.

There is much more that I should like to write, but I have not strength.

Believe me, dear Wallace, yours very sincerely,

CH. DARWIN.

P.S. —Our aristocracy is handsomer (more hideous according to a Chinese or Negro) than the middle classes, from (having the) pick of the women; but oh, what a scheme is primogeniture for destroying natural selection! I fear my letter will be barely intelligible to you.

[In February 1867, when the manuscript of 'Animals and Plants' had been sent to Messrs. Clowes to be printed, and before the proofs began to come in, he had an interval of spare time, and began a "chapter on Man," but he soon found it growing under his hands, and determined to publish it separately as a "very small volume."

The work was interrupted by the necessity of correcting the proofs of 'Animals and Plants,' and by some botanical work, but was resumed in the following year, 1868, the moment he could give himself up to it.

He recognized with regret the gradual change in his mind that rendered continuous work more and more necessary to him as he grew older. This is expressed in a letter to Sir J. D. Hooker, June 17, 1868, which repeats to some extent what is expressed in the Autobiography :—

"I am glad you were at the 'Messiah,' it is the one thing that I should like to hear again, but I dare say I should find my soul too dried up to appreciate it as in old days; and then I should feel very flat, for it is a horrid bore to feel as I constantly do, that I am a withered leaf for every subject except Science. It sometimes makes me hate Science, though God knows I ought to be thankful for such a perennial interest, which makes me forget for some hours every day my accursed stomach."

The work on Man was interrupted by illness in the early summer of 1868, and he left home on July 16th for Freshwater, in the Isle of Wight, where he remained with his family until August 21st. Here he made the acquaintance of Mrs. Cameron. She received the whole family with openhearted kindness and hospitality, and my father always retained a warm feeling of friendship for her. She made an excellent photograph of him, which was published with the inscription written by him : " I like this photograph very much better than any other which has been taken of me." Further interruption occurred in the autumn so that continuous work on the 'Descent of Man ' did not begin until 1869. The following letters give some idea of the earlier work in 1867 :]

C. Darwin to A. R. Wallace.

Down, February 22, [1867?]

MY DEAR WALLACE,—I am hard at work on sexual selection, and am driven half mad by the number of collateral points which require investigation, such as the relative number of the two sexes, and especially on polygamy. Can you aid me with respect to birds which have strongly marked secondary sexual characters, such as birds of paradise, hummingbirds, the Rupicola, or any other such cases ? Many gallinaceous birds certainly are polygamous. I suppose that birds may be known not to be polygamous if they are seen during the whole breeding season to associate in pairs, or if the male incubates or aids in feeding the young. Will you have the kindness to turn this in your mind ? But it is a shame to trouble you now that, as I am *heartily* glad to hear, you are at work on your Malayan travels. I am fearfully puzzled how far to extend your protective views with respect to the females in various classes. The more I work the more important sexual selection apparently comes out.

Can butterflies be polygamous ! *i. e.* will one male impregnate more than one female ?　Forgive me troubling you, and I dare say I shall have to ask forgiveness again. . . .

C. Darwin to A. R. Wallace.

Down, February 23 [1867].

DEAR WALLACE,—I much regretted that I was unable to call on you, but after Monday I was unable even to leave the house.　On Monday evening I called on Bates, and put a difficulty before him, which he could not answer, and, as on some former similar occasion, his first suggestion was, "You had better ask Wallace."　My difficulty is, why are caterpillars sometimes so beautifully and artistically coloured ?　Seeing that many are coloured to escape danger, I can hardly attribute their bright color in other cases to mere physical conditions.　Bates says the most gaudy caterpillar he ever saw in Amazonia (of a sphinx) was conspicuous at the distance of yards, from its black and red colours, whilst feeding on large green leaves.　If any one objected to male butterflies having been made beautiful by sexual selection, and asked why should they not have been made beautiful as well as their caterpillars, what would you answer ?　I could not answer, but should maintain my ground.　Will you think over this, and some time, either by letter or when we meet, tell me what you think ?　Also I want to know whether your *female* mimetic butterfly is more beautiful and brighter than the male.　When next in London I must get you to show me your kingfishers.　My health is a dreadful evil ; I failed in half my engagements during this last visit to London.

Believe me, yours very sincerely,

C. DARWIN.

C. Darwin to A. R. Wallace.

Down, February 26 [1867].

MY DEAR WALLACE,—Bates was quite right; you are the man to apply to in a difficulty. I never heard anything more ingenious than your suggestion,* and I hope you may be able to prove it true. That is a splendid fact about the white moths; it warms one's very blood to see a theory thus almost proved to be true.† With respect to the beauty of male butterflies, I must as yet think that it is due to sexual selection. There is some evidence that dragon-flies are attracted by bright colours; but what leads me to the above belief is, so many male Orthoptera and Cicadas having musical instruments. This being the case, the analogy of birds makes me believe in sexual selection with respect to colour in insects. I wish I had strength and time to make some of the experiments suggested by you, but I thought butterflies would not pair in confinement. I am sure I have heard of some such difficulty. Many years ago I had a dragon-fly painted with gorgeous colours, but I never had an opportunity of fairly trying it.

The reason of my being so much interested just at present about sexual selection is, that I have almost resolved to publish a little essay on the origin of Mankind, and I still strongly think (though I failed to convince you, and this, to me, is the heaviest blow possible) that sexual selection has been the main agent in forming the races of man.

By the way, there is another subject which I shall introduce in my essay, namely, expression of countenance. Now,

---

* The suggestion that conspicuous caterpillars or perfect insects (e. g. white butterflies), which are distasteful to birds, are protected by being easily recognised and avoided. See Mr. Wallace's 'Natural Selection,' 2nd edit., p. 117.

† Mr. Jenner Weir's observations published in the Transactions of the Entomolog. Soc. (1869 and 1870) give strong support to the theory in question.

do you happen to know by any odd chance a very good-natured and acute observer in the Malay Archipelago, who you think would make a few easy observations for me on the expression of the Malays when excited by various emotions? For in this case I would send to such person a list of queries. I thank you for your most interesting letter, and remain,

Yours very sincerely,

CH. DARWIN.

C. Darwin to A. R. Wallace.

Down, March [1867].

MY DEAR WALLACE,—I thank you much for your two notes. The case of Julia Pastrana* is a splendid addition to my other cases of correlated teeth and hair, and I will add it in correcting the press of my present volume. Pray let me hear in the course of the summer if you get any evidence about the gaudy caterpillars. I should much like to give (or quote if published) this idea of yours, if in any way supported, as suggested by you. It will, however, be a long time hence, for I can see that sexual selection is growing into quite a large subject, which I shall introduce into my essay on Man, supposing that I ever publish it. I had intended giving a chapter on man, inasmuch as many call him (not *quite* truly) an eminently domesticated animal, but I found the subject too large for a chapter. Nor shall I be capable of treating the subject well, and my sole reason for taking it up is, that I am pretty well convinced that sexual selection has played an important part in the formation of races, and sexual selection has always been a subject which has interested me much. I have been very glad to see your impression from memory on the expression of Malays. I fully agree with you that the subject is in no way an important one; it is simply a "hobby-horse" with me, about twenty-seven years old; and *after* thinking that I would write

---

* A bearded woman having an irregular double set of teeth. 'Animals and Plants,' vol. ii. p. 328.

an essay on man, it flashed on me that I could work in some "supplemental remarks on expression." After the horrid, tedious, dull work of my present huge, and I fear unreadable, book ['The Variation of Animals and Plants'], I thought I would amuse myself with my hobby-horse. The subject is, I think, more curious and more amenable to scientific treatment than you seem willing to allow. I want, anyhow, to upset Sir C. Bell's view, given in his most interesting work, 'The Anatomy of Expression,' that certain muscles have been given to man solely that he may reveal to other men his feelings. I want to try and show how expressions have arisen. That is a good suggestion about newspapers, but my experience tells me that private applications are generally most fruitful. I will, however, see if I can get the queries inserted in some Indian paper. I do not know the names or addresses of any other papers.

. . . My two female amanuenses are busy with friends, and I fear this scrawl will give you much trouble to read. With many thanks,

Yours very sincerely,
CH. DARWIN.

[The following letter may be worth giving, as an example of his sources of information, and as showing what were the thoughts at this time occupying him :]

C. Darwin to F. Müller.

Down, February 22 [1867].

. . . Many thanks for all the curious facts about the unequal number of the sexes in Crustacea, but the more I investigate this subject the deeper I sink in doubt and difficulty. Thanks also for the confirmation of the rivalry of Cicadæ. I have often reflected with surprise on the diversity of the means for producing music with insects, and still more with birds. We thus get a high idea of the importance of song in the animal kingdom. Please to tell me where I can find any account of the auditory organs in the Orthoptera. Your facts are quite new to me. Scudder has described an insect in the Devonian strata, furnished with a stridulating apparatus. I believe he is to be trusted, and, if so, the apparatus is of astonishing antiquity. After reading Landois's paper I have been working at the stridulating organ in the Lamellicorn beetles, in expectation of finding it sexual ; but I have only found it as yet in two cases, and in these it was equally developed in both sexes. I wish you would look at any of your common lamellicorns, and take hold of both males and females, and observe whether they make the squeaking or grating noise equally. If they do not, you could, perhaps, send me a male and female in a light little box. How curious it is that there should be a special organ for an object apparently so unimportant as squeaking. Here is another point ; have you any toucans ? if so, ask any trustworthy hunter whether the beaks of the males, or of both sexes, are more brightly coloured during the breeding season than at other times of the year. . . . Heaven knows whether I shall ever live to make use of half the valuable facts which you have communicated to me ! Your paper on *Balanus armatus*, translated by Mr. Dallas, has just appeared in our 'Annals and Magazine of Natural History,' and I have read it with the greatest interest. I never thought that I should live to hear of a hybrid Balanus ! I am very glad that you have seen the cement tubes ; they appear to me extremely curious, and, as far as I know, you are the first man who has verified my observations on this point.

With most cordial thanks for all your kindness, my dear Sir,

Yours very sincerely,
C. Darwin.

C. Darwin to A. De Candolle.

Down, July 6, 1868.

My dear Sir,—I return you my *sincere* thanks for your long letter, which I consider a great compliment, and which is quite full of most interesting facts and views. Your references and remarks will be of great use should a new adition of my book * be demanded, but this is hardly probable, for the whole edition was sold within the first week, and another large edition immediately reprinted, which I should think would supply the demand for ever. You ask me when I shall publish on the 'Variation of Species in a State of Nature.' I have had the MS. for another volume almost ready during several years, but I was so much fatigued by my last book that I determined to amuse myself by publishing a short essay on the 'Descent of Man.' I was partly led to do this by having been taunted that I concealed my views, but chiefly from the interest which I had long taken in the subject. Now this essay has branched out into some collateral subjects, and I suppose will take me more than a year to complete. I shall then begin on 'Species,' but my health makes me a very slow workman. I hope that you will excuse these details, which I have given to show that you will have plenty of time to publish your views first, which will be a great advantage to me. Of all the curious facts which you mention in your letter, I think that of the strong inheritance of the scalp-muscles has interested me most. I presume that you would not object to my giving this very curious case on your authority. As I believe all anatomists look at the scalp-muscles as a remnant of the *Panniculus carnosus* which is common to all the lower quadrupeds, I should look at the unusual development and inheritance of these muscles as probably a case of reversion. Your observation on so many remarkable men in noble families having been illegitimate is extremely curious; and should I ever meet any one capable of writing an essay on this subject, I will mention your remarks as a good suggestion. Dr. Hooker has several times remarked to me that morals and politics would be very interesting if discussed like any branch of natural history, and this is nearly to the same effect with your remarks. . . .

---

* 'Variation of Animals and Plants.'

C. *Darwin to L. Agassiz.*

Down, August 19, 1868.

DEAR SIR,—I thank you cordially for your very kind letter. I certainly thought that you had formed so low an opinion of my scientific work that it might have appeared indelicate in me to have asked for information from you, but it never occurred to me that my letter would have been shown to you. I have never for a moment doubted your kindness and generosity, and I hope you will not think it presumption in me to say, that when we met, many years ago, at the British Association at Southampton, I felt for you the warmest admiration.

Your information on the Amazonian fishes has interested me *extremely*, and tells me exactly what I wanted to know. I was aware, through notes given me by Dr. Günther, that many fishes differed sexually in colour and other characters, but I was particularly anxious to learn how far this was the case with those fishes in which the male, differently from what occurs with most birds, takes the largest share in the care of the ova and young. Your letter has not only interested me much, but has greatly gratified me in other respects, and I return you my sincere thanks for your kindness. Pray believe me, my dear Sir,

Yours very faithfully,

CHARLES DARWIN.

C. *Darwin to J. D. Hooker.*

Down, Sunday, August 23 [1868].

MY DEAR OLD FRIEND,—I have received your note. I can hardly say how pleased I have been at the success of your address,* and of the whole meeting. I have seen the *Times, Telegraph, Spectator,* and *Athenæum,* and have heard

---

* Sir Joseph Hooker was President of the British Association at the Norwich Meeting in 1868.

of other favourable newspapers, and have ordered a bundle. There is a " chorus of praise." The *Times* reported miserably, *i.e.* as far as errata was concerned; but I was very glad at the leader, for I thought the way you brought in the megalithic monuments most happy.* I particularly admired Tyndall's little speech.† . . . The *Spectator* pitches a little into you about Theology, in accordance with its usual spirit. . . .

Your great success has rejoiced my heart. I have just carefully read the whole address in the *Athenæum ;* and though, as you know, I liked it very much when you read it to me, yet, as I was trying all the time to find fault, I missed to a certain extent the effect as a whole ; and this now appears to me most striking and excellent. How you must rejoice at all your bothering labour and anxiety having had so grand an end. I must say a word about myself ; never has such a eulogium been passed on me, and it makes me very proud. I cannot get over my *amazement* at what you say about my botanical work. By Jove, as far as my memory goes, you have strengthened instead of weakened some of the expressions. What is far more important than anything personal, is the conviction which I feel that you will have immensely advanced the belief in the evolution of species. This will follow from the publicity of the occasion, your position, so responsible, as President, and your own high reputation. It will make a great step in public opinion, I feel sure, and I had not thought of this before. The *Athenæum* takes your snubbing ‡ with the utmost mildness. I certainly do rejoice over the snubbing, and hope [the reviewer] will feel it a little. Whenever you have *spare* time to write again, tell me whether any astronomers § took your remarks in ill

---

* The British Association was desirous of interesting the Government in certain modern cromlech builders, the Khasia race of East Bengal, in order that their megalithic monuments might be efficiently described.

† Professor Tyndall was President of Section A.

‡ Sir Joseph Hooker made some reference to the review of ' Animals and Plants ' in the *Athenæum* of Feb. 15, 1868.

§ In discussing the astronomer's objection to Evolution, namely that part ; as they now stand they do not seem at all too harsh and presumptuous. Many of your sentences strike me as extremely felicitous and eloquent. That of Lyell's "under-pinning," * is capital. Tell me, was Lyell pleased? I am so glad that you remembered my old dedication.† Was Wallace pleased?

How about photographs? Can you spare time for a line to our dear Mrs. Cameron?‡ She came to see us off, and loaded us with presents of photographs, and Erasmus called after her, " Mrs. Cameron, there are six people in this house all in love with you." When I paid her, she cried out, " Oh what a lot of money ! " and ran to boast to her husband.

I must not write any more, though I am in tremendous spirits at your brilliant success.

Yours ever affectionately,
C. DARWIN.

[In the *Athenæum* of November 29, 1868, appeared an article which was in fact a reply to Sir Joseph Hooker's remarks at Norwich. He seems to have consulted my father as to the wisdom of answering the article. My father wrote on September 1 :

" In my opinion Dr. Joseph Dalton Hooker need take no notice of the attack in the *Athenæum* in reference to Mr. Charles Darwin. What an ass the man is to think he cuts one to the quick by giving one's Christian name in full. How transparently false is the statement that my sole groundwork

---

our globe has not existed for a long enough period to give time for the assumed transmutation of living beings, Hooker challenged Whewell's dictum that, astronomy is the queen of sciences—the only perfect science.

* After a eulogium on Sir Charles Lyell's heroic renunciation of his old views in accepting Evolution, Sir J. D. Hooker continued, " Well may he be proud of a superstructure, raised on the foundations of an insecure doctrine, when he finds that he can underpin it and substitute a new foundation ; and after all is finished, survey his edifice, not only more secure but more harmonious in its proportion than it was before."

† The ' Naturalist's Voyage ' was dedicated to Lyell.

‡ See p. 274.

is from pigeons, because I state I have worked them out more fully than other beings ! He muddles together two books of Flourens."

The following letter refers to a paper* by Judge Caton, of which my father often spoke with admiration :]

C. Darwin to John D. Caton.

Down, September 18, 1868.

DEAR SIR,—I beg leave to thank you very sincerely for your kindness in sending me, through Mr. Walsh, your admirable paper on American Deer.

It is quite full of most interesting observations, stated with the greatest clearness. I have seldom read a paper with more interest, for it abounds with facts of direct use for my work. Many of them consist of little points which hardly any one besides yourself has observed, or perceived the importance of recording. I would instance the age at which the horns are developed (a point on which I have lately been in vain searching for information), the rudiment of horns in the female elk, and especially the different nature of the plants devoured by the deer and elk, and several other points. With cordial thanks for the pleasure and instruction which you have afforded me, and with high respect for your power of observation, I beg leave to remain, dear Sir,

Yours faithfully and obliged,

CHARLES DARWIN.

[The following extract from a letter (Sept. 24, 1868) to the Marquis de Saporta, the eminent palæo-botanist, refers to the growth of evolutionary views in France :—†

"As I have formerly read with great interest many of your papers on fossil plants, you may believe with what high

---

* 'Transactions of the Ottawa Academy of Natural Sciences,' 1868. By John D. Caton, late Chief Justice of Illinois.

† In 1868 he was pleased at being asked to authorise a French translation of his ' Naturalist's Voyage.'

satisfaction I hear that you are a believer in the gradual evolution of species. I had supposed that my book on the 'Origin of Species' had made very little impression in France, and therefore it delights me to hear a different statement from you. All the great authorities of the Institute seem firmly resolved to believe in the immutability of species, and this has always astonished me. . . . Almost the one exception, as far as I know, is M. Gaudry, and I think he will be soon one of the chief leaders in Zoological Palæontology in Europe ; and now I am delighted to hear that in the sister department of Botany you take nearly the same view."]

C. Darwin to E. Haeckel.

Down, Nov. 19 [1868].

My dear Haeckel,—I must write to you again, for two reasons. Firstly, to thank you for your letter about your baby, which has quite charmed both me and my wife ; I heartily congratulate you on its birth. I remember being surprised in my own case how soon the paternal instincts became developed, and in you they seem to be unusually strong, . . . I hope the large blue eyes and the principles of inheritance will make your child as good a naturalist as you are ; but, judging from my own experience, you will be astonished to find how the whole mental disposition of your children changes with advancing years. A young child, and the same when nearly grown, sometimes differ almost as much as do a caterpillar and butterfly.

The second point is to congratulate you on the projected translation of your great work,* about which I heard from Huxley last Sunday. I am heartily glad of it, but how it has been brought about, I know not, for a friend who supported the supposed translation at Norwich, told me he thought there would be no chance of it. Huxley tells me that you

---

* 'Generelle Morphologie,' 1866. No English translation of this book has appeared.

consent to omit and shorten some parts, and I am confident
that this is very wise.   As I know your object is to instruct
the public, you will assuredly thus get many more readers in
England.   Indeed, I believe that almost every book would
be improved by condensation.   I have been reading a good
deal of your last book,* and the style is beautifully clear and
easy to me ; but why it should differ so much in this respect
from your great work I cannot imagine.   I have not yet read
the first part, but began with the chapter on Lyell and myself,
which you will easily believe pleased me *very much*.   I think
Lyell, who was apparently much pleased by your sending
him a copy, is also much gratified by this chapter.†   Your
chapters on the affinities and genealogy of the animal kingdom strike me as admirable and full of original thought.
Your boldness, however, sometimes makes me tremble, but
as Huxley remarked, some one must be bold enough to make
a beginning in drawing up tables of descent.   Although you
fully admit the imperfection of the geological record, yet
Huxley agreed with me in thinking that you are sometimes
rather rash in venturing to say at what periods the several
groups first appeared.   I have this advantage over you, that
I remember how wonderfully different any statement on this
subject made 20 years ago, would have been to what would
now be the case, and I expect the next 20 years will make
quite as great a difference.   Reflect on the monocotyle-
donous plant just discovered in the *primordial* formation in
Sweden.

I repeat how glad I am at the prospect of the translation,
for I fully believe that this work and all your works will have
a great influence in the advancement of Science.

Believe me, my dear Häckel, your sincere friend,

CHARLES DARWIN.

---

* 'Die Natürliche Schöpfungs-Geschichte,' 1868.   It was translated
and published in 1876, under the title, 'The History of Creation.'

† See Lyell's interesting letter to Haeckel.   'Life of Sir C. Lyell,' ii
p. 435.

[It was in November of this year that he sat for the bust by Mr. Woolner: he wrote :—

"I should have written long ago, but I have been pestered with stupid letters, and am undergoing the purgatory of sitting for hours to Woolner, who, however, is wonderfully pleasant, and lightens as much as man can, the penance; as far as I can judge, it will make a fine bust."

If I may criticise the work of so eminent a sculptor as Mr. Woolner, I should say that the point in which the bust fails somewhat as a portrait, is that it has a certain air, almost of pomposity, which seems to me foreign to my father's expression.]

1869.

[At the beginning of the year he was at work in preparing the fifth edition of the 'Origin.' This work was begun on the day after Christmas, 1868, and was continued for "forty-six days," as he notes in his diary, *i.e.* until February 10th, 1869. He then, February 11th, returned to Sexual Selection, and continued at this subject (excepting for ten days given up to Orchids, and a week in London), until June 10th, when he went with his family to North Wales, where he remained about seven weeks, returning to Down on July 31st.

Caerdeon, the house where he stayed, is built on the north shore of the beautiful Barmouth estuary, and is pleasantly placed, in being close to wild hill country behind, as well as to the picturesque wooded "hummocks," between the steeper hills and the river. My father was ill and somewhat depressed throughout this visit, and I think felt saddened at being imprisoned by his want of strength, and unable even to reach the hills over which he had once wandered for days together.

He wrote from Caerdeon to Sir J. D. Hooker (June 22nd) :—

"We have been here for ten days, how I wish it was possible for you to pay us a visit here ; we have a beautiful house with a terraced garden, and a really magnificent view of Cader, right opposite.   Old Cader is a grand fellow, and shows himself off superbly with every changing light.   We remain here till the end of July, when the H. Wedgwoods have the house.   I have been as yet in a very poor way; it seems as soon as the stimulus of mental work stops, my whole strength gives way.   As yet I have hardly crawled half a mile from the house, and then have been fearfully fatigued. It is enough to make one wish oneself quiet in a comfortable tomb."

With regard to the fifth edition of the 'Origin,' he wrote to Mr. Wallace (January 22, 1869):—

"I have been interrupted in my regular work in preparing a new edition of the 'Origin,' which has cost me much labour, and which I hope I have considerably improved in two or three important points.   I always thought individual differences more important than single variations, but now I have come to the conclusion that they are of paramount importance, and in this I believe I agree with you.   Fleeming Jenkin's arguments have convinced me."

This somewhat obscure sentence was explained, February 2, in another letter to Mr. Wallace:—

"I must have expressed myself atrociously; I meant to say exactly the reverse of what you have understood.   F. Jenkin argued in the 'North British Review' against single variations ever being perpetuated, and has convinced me, though not in quite so broad a manner as here put.   I always thought individual differences more important; but I was blind and thought that single variations might be preserved much oftener than I now see is possible or probable.   I mentioned this in my former note merely because I believed that you had come to a similar conclusion, and I like much to be in accord with you.   I believe I was mainly deceived by single variations offering such simple illustrations, as when man selects."

The late Mr. Fleeming Jenkin's review, on the 'Origin of Species,' was published in the 'North British Review' for June 1867.   It is not a little remarkable that the criticisms, which my father, as I believe, felt to be the most valuable ever made on his views should have come, not from a professed naturalist but from a Professor of Engineering.

It is impossible to give in a short compass an account of Fleeming Jenkin's argument. My father's copy of the paper (ripped out of the volume as usual, and tied with a bit of string) is annotated in pencil in many places. I may quote one passage opposite which my father has written "good sneers"—but it should be remembered that he used the word "sneer" in rather a special sense, not as necessarily implying a feeling of bitterness in the critic, but rather in the sense of "banter." Speaking of the 'true believer,' Fleeming Jenkin says, p. 293 :—

"He can invent trains of ancestors of whose existence there is no evidence ; he can marshal hosts of equally imaginary foes; he can call up continents, floods, and peculiar atmospheres ; he can dry up oceans, split islands, and parcel out eternity at will; surely with these advantages he must be a dull fellow if he cannot scheme some series of animals and circumstances explaining our assumed difficulty quite naturally. Feeling the difficulty of dealing with adversaries who command so huge a domain of fancy, we will abandon these arguments, and trust to those which at least cannot be assailed by mere efforts of imagination."

In the fifth edition of the 'Origin,' my father altered a passage in the Historical Sketch (fourth edition p. xviii.). He thus practically gave up the difficult task of understanding whether or no Sir R. Owen claims to have discovered the principle of Natural Selection. Adding, "As far as the mere enunciation of the principle of Natural Selection is concerned, it is quite immaterial whether or not Professor Owen preceded me, for both of us. . . . were long ago preceded by Dr. Wells and Mr. Matthew."

A somewhat severe critique on the fifth edition, by Mr. John Robertson, appeared in the *Athenæum*, August 14, 1869. The writer comments with some little bitterness on the success of the 'Origin :' "Attention is not acceptance. Many

editions do not mean real success. The book has sold ; the
guess has been talked over ; and the circulation and discussion sum up the significance of the editions." Mr. Robertson makes the true, but misleading statement : "Mr. Darwin
prefaces his fifth English edition with an Essay, which he
calls 'An Historical Sketch,' &c." As a matter of fact the
Sketch appeared in the third edition in 1861.

Mr. Robertson goes on to say that the Sketch ought to
be called a collection of extracts anticipatory or corroborative
of the hypothesis of Natural Selection. "For no account is
given of any hostile opinions. The fact is very significant.
This historical sketch thus resembles the histories of the
reign of Louis XVIII., published after the Restoration, from
which the Republic and the Empire, Robespierre and Buo-
naparte were omitted."

The following letter to Prof. Victor Carus gives an idea
of the character of the new edition of the ' Origin :']

C. Darwin to Victor Carus.

Down, May 4, 1869.

. . . I have gone very carefully through the whole, trying
to make some parts clearer, and adding a few discussions and
facts of some importance. The new edition is only two
pages at the end longer than the old ; though in one part
nine pages in advance, for I have condensed several parts
and omitted some passages. The translation I fear will cause
you a great deal of trouble ; the alterations took me six weeks,
besides correcting the press ; you ought to make a special
agreement with M. Koch [the publisher]. Many of the corrections are only a few words, but they have been made from
the evidence on various points appearing to have become a
little stronger or weaker.

Thus I have been led to place somewhat more value on
the definite and direct action of external conditions ; to think
the lapse of time, as measured by years, not quite so great as
most geologists have thought ; and to infer that single varia-

tions are of even less importance, in comparison with individual differences, than I formerly thought. I mention these points because I have been thus led to alter in many places *a few words ;* and unless you go through the whole new edition, one part will not agree with another, which would be a great blemish. . . .

[The desire that his views might spread in France was always strong with my father, and he was therefore justly annoyed to find that in 1869 the Editor of the first French edition had brought out a third edition without consulting the author. He was accordingly glad to enter into an arrangement for a French translation of the fifth edition ; this was undertaken by M. Reinwald, with whom he continued to have pleasant relations as the publisher of many of his books into French.

He wrote to Sir J. D. Hooker :—

" I must enjoy myself and tell you about Mdlle. C. Royer, who translated the ' Origin ' into French, and for whose second edition I took infinite trouble. She has now just brought out a third edition without informing me, so that all the corrections, &c., in the fourth and fifth English editions are lost. Besides her enormously long preface to the first edition, she has added a second preface abusing me like a pickpocket for Pangenesis, which of course has no relation to the ' Origin.' So I wrote to Paris ; and Reinwald agrees to bring out at once a new translation from the fifth English edition, in competition with her third edition. . . . This fact shows that " evolution of species " must at last be spreading in France."

With reference to the spread of Evolution among the orthodox, the following letter is of some interest. In March he received, from the author, a copy of a lecture by Rev. T. R. R. Stebbing, given before the Torquay Natural History Society, February 1, 1869, bearing the title " Darwinism." My father wrote to Mr. Stebbing :]

Down, March 3, 1869.

DEAR SIR,—I am very much obliged to you for your kindness in sending me your spirited and interesting lecture; if a layman had delivered the same address, he would have done good service in spreading what, as I hope and believe, is to a large extent the truth ; but a clergyman in delivering such an address does, as it appears to me, much more good by his power to shake ignorant prejudices, and by setting, if I may be permitted to say so, an admirable example of liberality.

　　　With sincere respect, I beg leave to remain,
　　　　　Dear Sir, yours faithfully and obliged,
　　　　　　　　CHARLES DARWIN.

[The references to the subject of expression in the following letter are explained by the fact that my father's original intention was to give his essay on this subject as a chapter in the 'Descent of Man,' which in its turn grew, as we have seen, out of a proposed chapter in 'Animals and Plants :']

C. Darwin to F. Müller.

Down, February 22 [1869 ?]

. . . Although you have aided me to so great an extent in many ways, I am going to beg for any information on two other subjects. I am preparing a discussion on "Sexual Selection," and I want much to know how low down in the animal scale sexual selection of a particular kind extends. Do you know of any lowly organised animals, in which the sexes are separated, and in which the male differs from the female in arms of offence, like the horns and tusks of male mammals, or in gaudy plumage and ornaments, as with birds and butterflies? I do not refer to secondary sexual characters, by which the male is able to discover the female, like the plumed antennæ of moths, or by which the male is enabled to seize the female, like the curious pincers described by you in some of the lower Crustaceans. But what I want to know is, how low in the scale sexual differences occur which require some degree of self-consciousness in the males, as weapons by which they fight for the female, or ornaments which attract the opposite sex. Any differences between males and females which follow different habits of life would have to be excluded. I think you will easily see what I wish to learn. *A priori*, it would never have been anticipated that insects would have been attracted by the beautiful colouring of the opposite sex, or by the sounds emitted by the various musical instruments of the male Orthoptera. I know no one so likely to answer this question as yourself, and should be grateful for any information, however small.

My second subject refers to expression of countenance, to which I have long attended, and on which I feel a keen interest; but to which, unfortunately, I did not attend when I had the opportunity of observing various races of man. It has occurred to me that you might, without much trouble, make a *few* observations for me, in the course of some months, on Negroes, or possibly on native South Americans, though I care most about Negroes; accordingly I enclose some questions as a guide, and if you could answer me even one or two I should feel truly obliged. I am thinking of writing a little essay on the Origin of Mankind, as I have been taunted with concealing my opinions, and I should do this immediately after the completion of my present book. In this case I should add a chapter on the cause or meaning of expression. . . .

[The remaining letters of this year deal chiefly with the books, reviews, &c., which interested him.]

C. Darwin to H. Thiel.

Down, February 25 1869.

DEAR SIR,—On my return home after a short absence, I found your very courteous note, and the pamphlet,* and I

---

* 'Ueber einige Formen der Landwirthschaftlichen Genossenschaften.' By Dr. H. Thiel, then of the Agricultural Station at Poppelsdorf.

hasten to thank you for both, and for the very honourable mention which you make of my name. You will readily believe how much interested I am in observing that you apply to moral and social questions analogous views to those which I have used in regard to the modification of species. It did not occur to me formerly that my views could be extended to such widely different, and most important, subjects. With much respect, I beg leave to remain, dear Sir,

Yours faithfully and obliged,

CHARLES DARWIN.

C. Darwin to T. H. Huxley.

Down, March 19 [1869].

MY DEAR HUXLEY,—Thanks for your ' Address.' * People complain of the unequal distribution of wealth, but it is a much greater shame and injustice that any one man should have the power to write so many brilliant essays as you have lately done. There is no one who writes likes you. . . . If I were in your shoes, I should tremble for my life. I agree with all you say, except that I must think that you draw too great a distinction between the evolutionists and the uniformitarians.

I find that the few sentences which I have sent to press in the ' Origin ' about the age of the world will do fairly well . . .

Ever yours,

C. DARWIN.

C. Darwin to A. R. Wallace.

Down, March 22 [1869].

MY DEAR WALLACE,—I have finished your book;† it seems to me excellent, and at the same time most pleasant to read. That you ever returned alive is wonderful after all

---

* In his ' Anniversary Address ' to the Geological Society, 1869, Mr. Huxley criticised Sir William Thomson's paper (' Trans. Geol. Soc., Glasgow,' vol. iii.) " On Geological Time."

† ' The Malay Archipelago,' &c., 1869.

your risks from illness and sea voyages, especially that most interesting one to Waigiou and back.   Of all the impressions which I have received from your book, the strongest is that your perseverance in the cause of science was heroic.   Your descriptions of catching the splendid butterflies have made me quite envious, and at the same time have made me feel almost young again, so vividly have they brought before my mind old days when I collected, though I never made such captures as yours.   Certainly collecting is the best sport in the world.   I shall be astonished if your book has not a great success ; and your splendid generalizations on Geographical Distribution, with which I am familiar from your papers, will be new to most of your readers.   I think I enjoyed most the Timor case, as it is best demonstrated ; but perhaps Celebes is really the most valuable.   I should prefer looking at the whole Asiatic continent as having formerly been more African in its fauna, than admitting the former existence of a continent across the Indian Ocean. . . .

[The following letter refers to Mr. Wallace's article in the April number of the 'Quarterly Review,' * 1869, which to a large extent deals with the tenth edition of Sir Charles Lyell's 'Principles,' published in 1867 and 1868.   The review contains a striking passage on Sir Charles Lyell's confession of evolutionary faith in the tenth edition of his 'Principles,' which is worth quoting : " The history of science hardly presents so striking an instance of youthfulness of mind in advanced life as is shown by this abandonment of opinions so long held and so powerfully advocated; and if we bear in mind the extreme caution, combined with the ardent love of truth which characterise every work which our author has produced, we shall be convinced that so great a change was not decided on without long and anxious deliberation, and

---

* My father wrote to Mr. Murray : " The article by Wallace is inimitably good, and it is a great triumph that such an article should appear in the ' Quarterly,' and will make the Bishop of Oxford and —— gnash their teeth."

that the views now adopted must indeed be supported by arguments of overwhelming force. If for no other reason than that Sir Charles Lyell in his tenth edition has adopted it, the theory of Mr. Darwin deserves an attentive and respectful consideration from every earnest seeker after truth."]

C. Darwin to A. R. Wallace.

Down, April 14, 1869.

My dear Wallace,—I have been wonderfully interested by your article, and I should think Lyell will be much gratified by it. I declare if I had been editor, and had the power of directing you, I should have selected for discussion the very points which you have chosen. I have often said to younger geologists (for I began in the year 1830) that they did not know what a revolution Lyell had effected; nevertheless, your extracts from Cuvier have quite astonished me. Though not able really to judge, I am inclined to put more confidence in Croll than you seem to do; but I have been much struck by many of your remarks on degradation. Thomson's views of the recent age of the world have been for some time one of my sorest troubles, and so I have been glad to read what you say. Your exposition of Natural Selection seems to me inimitably good; there never lived a better expounder than you. I was also much pleased at your discussing the difference between our views and Lamarck's. One sometimes sees the odious expression, "Justice to myself compels me to say," &c., but you are the only man I ever heard of who persistently does himself an injustice, and never demands justice. Indeed, you ought in the review to have alluded to your paper in the 'Linnean Journal,' and I feel sure all our friends will agree in this. But you cannot "Burke" yourself, however much you may try, as may be seen in half the articles which appear. I was asked but the other day by a German professor for your paper, which I sent him. Altogether I look at your article as appearing in the 'Quarterly' as an immense triumph for our cause. I presume that your remarks on Man are those to which you alluded in your note. If you had not told me I should have thought that they had been added by some one else. As you expected, I differ grievously from you, and I am very sorry for it. I can see no necessity for calling in an additional and proximate cause in regard to man.* But the subject is too long for a letter. I have been particularly glad to read your discussion because I am now writing and thinking much about man.

I hope that your Malay book sells well ; I was extremely pleased with the article in the ' Quarterly Journal of Science,' inasmuch as it is thoroughly appreciative of your work : alas ! you will probably agree with what the writer says about the uses of the bamboo.

I hear that there is also a good article in the *Saturday Review*, but have heard nothing more about it. Believe me my dear Wallace,

Yours ever sincerely,

CH. DARWIN.

C. Darwin to C. Lyell.

Down, May 4 [1869].

MY DEAR LYELL,—I have been applied to for some photographs (carte de visite) to be copied to ornament the diplomas of honorary members of a new Society in Servia! Will you give me one for this purpose ? I possess only a full-length one of you in my own album, and the face is too small, I think, to be copied.

I hope that you get on well with your work, and have satisfied yourself on the difficult point of glacier lakes. Thank

---

* Mr. Wallace points out that any one acquainted merely with the " unaided productions of nature," might reasonably doubt whether a dray-horse, for example, could have been developed by the power of man directing the " action of the laws of variation, multiplication, and survival, for his own purpose. We know, however, that this has been done, and we must therefore admit the possibility that in the development of the human race, a higher intelligence has guided the same laws for nobler ends."

heaven, I have finished correcting the new edition of the 'Origin,' and am at my old work of Sexual Selection.

Wallace's article struck me as *admirable ;* how well he brought out the revolution which you effected some 30 years ago. I thought I had fully appreciated the revolution, but I was astounded at the extracts from Cuvier. What a good sketch of natural selection ! but I was dreadfully disappointed about Man, it seems to me incredibly strange . . ..; and had I not known to the contrary, would have sworn it had been inserted by some other hand. But I believe that you will not agree quite in all this.

My dear Lyell, ever yours sincerely,
C. DARWIN.

C. Darwin to J. L. A. de Quatrefages.

Down, May 28 [1869 or 1870].

DEAR SIR,—I have received and read your volume,* and am much obliged for your present. The whole strikes me as a wonderfully clear and able discussion, and I was much interested by it to the last page. It is impossible that any account of my views could be fairer, or, as far as space permitted, fuller, than that which you have given. The way in which you repeatedly mention my name is most gratifying to me. When I had finished the second part, I thought that you had stated the case so favourably that you would make more converts on my side than on your own side. On reading the subsequent parts I had to change my sanguine view. In these latter parts many of your strictures are severe enough, but all are given with perfect courtesy and fairness. I can truly say I would rather be criticised by you in this manner than praised by many others. I agree with some of your criticisms, but differ entirely from the remainder ; but I will not trouble you with any remarks. I may, however, say, that you must have been deceived by the French translation,

---

* Essays reprinted from the 'Revue des Deux Mondes,' under the title 'Histoire Naturelle Générale,' &c., 1869.

as you infer that I believe that the Parus and the Nuthatch (or Sitta) are related by direct filiation. I wished only to show by an imaginary illustration, how either instincts or structures might first change. If you had seen *Canis Magellanicus* alive you would have perceived how foxlike its appearance is, or if you had heard its voice, I think that you would never have hazarded the idea that it was a domestic dog run wild ; but this does not much concern me. It is curious how nationality influences opinion ; a week hardly passes without my hearing of some naturalist in Germany who supports my views, and often puts an exagg rated value on my works ; whilst in France I have not heard of a single zoologist, except M. Gaudry (and he only partially), who supports my views. But I must have a good many readers as my books are translated, and I must hope, notwithstanding your strictures, that I may influence some embryo naturalists in France.

You frequently speak of my good faith, and no compliment can be more delightful to me, but I may return you the compliment with interest, for every word which you write bears the stamp of your cordial love for the truth. Believe me, dear Sir, with sincere respect,

Yours very faithfully,
CHARLES DARWIN.

C. Darwin to T. H. Huxley.

Down, October 14 [1869].

MY DEAR HUXLEY,—I have been delighted to see your review of Häckel,[*] and as usual you pile honours high on my head. But I write now (*requiring no answer*) to groan a little over what you have said about rudimentary organs.[†] Many heretics will take advantage of what you have said. I cannot

---

[*] A review of Haeckel's ' Schöpfungs-Geschichte.' The *Academy*, 1869. Reprinted in ' Critiques and Addresses,' p. 303.

[†] In discussing Teleology and Haeckel's " Dysteleology," Prof. Huxley says :—" Such cases as the existence of lateral rudiments of toes, in the foot of a horse, place us in a dilemma. For either these rudiments are of no use to the animals, in which case . . . they surely ought to have dis-

but think that the explanation given at p. 541 of the last edition of the 'Origin' of the long retention of rudimentary organs and of their greater relative size during early life, is satisfactory. Their final and complete abortion seems to me a much greater difficulty. Do look in my 'Variations under Domestication,' vol. ii. p. 397, at what Pangenesis suggests on this head, though I did not dare to put in the 'Origin.' The passage bears also a little on the struggle between the molecules or gemmules.* There is likewise a word or two indirectly bearing on this subject at pp. 394-395. It won't take you five minutes, so do look at these passages. I am very glad that you have been bold enough to give your idea about Natural Selection amongst the molecules, though I can not quite follow you.

1870 AND BEGINNING OF 1871.

[My father wrote in his Diary :—" The whole of this year [1870] at work on the 'Descent of Man.' . . . Went to Press August 30, 1870."

The letters are again of miscellaneous interest, dealing, not only with his work, but also serving to indicate the course of his reading.]

C. Darwin to E. Ray Lankester.

Down, March 15 [1870].

MY DEAR SIR,—I do not know whether you will consider me a very troublesome man, but I have just finished your

---

appeared ; or they are of some use to the animal, in which case they are of no use as arguments against Teleology."—(' Critiques and Addresses,' p. 308.)

* " It is a probable hypothesis, that what the world is to organisms in general, each organism is to the molecules of which it is composed. Multitudes of these having diverse tendencies, are competing with one another for opportunity to exist and multiply ; and the organism, as a whole, is as much the product of the molecules which are victorious as the Fauna, or Flora, of a country is the product of the victorious organic beings in it."— (' Critiques and Addresses,' p. 309.)

book,* and can not resist telling you how the whole has much
interested me.   No doubt, as you say, there must be much
speculation on such a subject, and certain results can not be
reached ; but all your views are highly suggestive, and to my
mind that is high praise.   I have been all the more interested
as I am now writing on closely allied though not quite identical points.   I was pleased to see you refer to my much
despised child, ' Pangenesis,' who I think will some day, under
some better nurse, turn out a fine stripling.   It has also
pleased me to see how thoroughly you appreciate (and I do
not think that this is general with the men of science)
H. Spencer; I suspect that hereafter he will be looked at as
by far the greatest living philosopher in England ; perhaps
equal to any that have lived.   But I have no business to
trouble you with my notions.   With sincere thanks for the
interest which your work has given me,

I remain, yours very faithfully,

CH. DARWIN.

[The next letter refers to Mr. Wallace's 'Natural Selection' (1870), a collection of essays reprinted with certain alterations of which a list is given in the volume :]

C. Darwin to A. R. Wallace.

Down, April 20 [1870].

MY DEAR WALLACE,—I have just received your book,
and read the preface.   There never has been passed on me,
or indeed on any one, a higher eulogium than yours.   I wish
that I fully deserved it.   Your modesty and candour are very
far from new to me.   I hope it is a satisfaction to you to
reflect—and very few things in my life have been more satisfactory to me—that we have never felt any jealousy towards
each other, though in one sense rivals.   I believe that I can
say this of myself with truth, and I am absolutely sure that
it is true of you.

---

* ' Comparative Longevity.'

You have been a good Christian to give a list of your additions, for I want much to read them, and I should hardly have had time just at present to have gone through all your articles. Of course I shall immediately read those that are new or greatly altered, and I will endeavour to be as honest as can reasonably be expected. Your book looks remarkably well got up.

Believe me, my dear Wallace, to remain,
Yours very cordially,
CH. DARWIN.

[Here follow one or two letters indicating the progress of the 'Descent of Man;' the woodcuts referred to were being prepared for that work :]

*C. Darwin to A. Günther.**

March 23, [1870?]

DEAR GÜNTHER,—As I do not know Mr. Ford's address, will you hand him this note, which is written solely to express my unbounded admiration of the woodcuts. I fairly gloat over them. The only evil is that they will make all the other woodcuts look very poor! They are all excellent, and for the feathers I declare I think it the most wonderful woodcut I ever saw ; I can not help touching it to make sure that it is smooth. How I wish to see the two other, and even more important, ones of the feathers, and the four [of] reptiles, &c. Once again accept my very sincere thanks for all your kindness. I am greatly indebted to Mr. Ford. Engravings have always hitherto been my greatest misery, and now they are a real pleasure to me.

Yours very sincerely,
CH. DARWIN.

P. S.—I thought I should have been in press by this time, but my subject has branched off into sub-branches, which

---

* Dr. Günther, Keeper of Zoology in the British Museum.

have cost me infinite time, and heaven knows when I shall have all my MS ready ; but I am never idle.

C. Darwin to A. Günther.

May 15 [1870].

MY DEAR DR. GÜNTHER,—Sincere thanks. Your answers are wonderfully clear and complete. I have some analogous questions on reptiles, &c., which I will send in a few days, and then I think I shall cause no more trouble. I will get the books you refer me to. The case of the Solenostoma * is magnificent, so exactly analogous to that of those birds in which the female is the more gay, but ten times better for me, as she is the incubator. As I crawl on with the successive classes I am astonished to find how similar the rules are about the nuptial or " wedding dress " of all animals. The subject has begun to interest me in an extraordinary degree; but I must try not to fall into my common error of being too speculative. But a drunkard might as well say he would drink a little and not too much ! My essay, as far as fishes, batrachians and reptiles are concerned, will be in fact yours, only written by me. With hearty thanks.

Yours very sincerely,
CH. DARWIN.

[The following letter is of interest, as showing the excessive care and pains which my father took in forming his opinion on a difficult point :]

C. Darwin to A. R. Wallace.

Down, September 23 [undated].

MY DEAR WALLACE,—I am very much obliged for all your trouble in writing me your long letter, which I will keep by

---

* In most of the Lophobranchii the male has a marsupial sack in which the eggs are hatched, and in these species the male is slightly brighter coloured than the female. But in Solenostoma the female is the hatcher, and is also the more brightly coloured.—' Descent of Man,' ii. 21.

me and ponder over. To answer it would require at least
200 folio pages! If you could see how often I have re-written
some pages you would know how anxious I am to arrive as
near as I can to the truth. I lay great stress on what I know
takes place under domestication; I think we start with
different fundamental notions on inheritance. I find it is
most difficult, but not I think impossible, to see how, for instance, a few red feathers appearing on the head of a male
bird, and which *are at first transmitted to both sexes*, could
come to be transmitted to males alone. It is not enough that
females should be produced from the males with red feathers,
which should be destitute of red feathers; but these females
must have a *latent tendency* to produce such feathers, otherwise they would cause deterioration in the red head-feathers
of their male offspring. Such latent tendency would be
shown by their producing the red feathers when old, or dis-
eased in their ovaria. But I have no difficulty in making the
whole head red if the few red feathers in the male from the
first tended to be sexually transmitted. I am quite willing
to admit that the female may have been modified, either at
the same time or subsequently, for protection by the accumulation of variations limited in their transmission to the female
sex. I owe to your writings the consideration of this latter
point. But I cannot yet persuade myself that females *alone*
have often been modified for protection. Should you grudge
the trouble briefly to tell me whether you believe that the
plainer head and less bright colours of ♀ chaffinch,* the less
red on the head and less clean colours of ♀ goldfinch, the
much less red on the breast of ♀ bull-finch, the paler crest of
golden-crested wren, &c., have been acquired by them for
protection. I cannot think so any more than I can that the
considerable differences between ♀ and ♂ house sparrow, or
much greater brightness of ♂ *Parus cœruleus* (both of which
build under cover) than of ♀ *Parus*, are related to protection.
I even mis-doubt much whether the less blackness of ♀ black-
bird is for protection.

---

* The symbols ♂ ♀ stand for male and female.

Again, can you give me reasons for believing that the moderate differences between the female pheasant, the female *Gallus bankiva*, the female black grouse, the pea-hen, the female partridge, [and their respective males,] have all special references to protection under slightly different conditions? I, of course, admit that they are all protected by dull colours, derived, as I think, from some dull-ground progenitor; and I account partly for their difference by partial transference of colour from the male and by other means too long to specify; but I earnestly wish to see reason to believe that each is specially adapted for concealment to its environment.

I grieve to differ from you, and it actually terrifies me and makes me constantly distrust myself. I fear we shall never quite understand each other. I value the cases of bright-coloured, incubating male fishes, and brilliant female butterflies, solely as showing that one sex may be made brilliant without any necessary transference of beauty to the other sex; for in these cases I cannot suppose that beauty in the other sex was checked by selection.

I fear this letter will trouble you to read it. A very short answer about your belief in regard to the ♀ finches and gallinaceæ would suffice.

Believe me, my dear Wallace,

Yours very sincerely,

CH. DARWIN.

C. Darwin to J. D. Hooker.

Down, May 25 [1870].

. . . . Last Friday we all went to the Bull Hotel at Cambridge to see the boys, and for a little rest and enjoyment. The backs of the Colleges are simply paradisaical. On Monday I saw Sedgwick, who was most cordial and kind; in the morning I thought his brain was enfeebled; in the evening he was brilliant and quite himself. His affection and kindness charmed us all. My visit to him was in one way unfortunate; for after a long sit he proposed to take me to the museum, and I could not refuse, and in consequence he utterly prostrated me; so that we left Cambridge next morning, and I have not recovered the exhaustion yet. Is it not humiliating to be thus killed by a man of eighty-six, who evidently never dreamed that he was killing me? As he said to me, "Oh, 1 consider you as a mere baby to me!" I saw Newton several times, and several nice friends of F.'s. But Cambridge without dear Henslow was not itself; I tried to get to the two old houses, but it was too far for me. . . .

C. Darwin to B. J. Sulivan.*

Down, June 30 [1870].

MY DEAR SULIVAN,—It was very good of you to write to me so long a letter, telling me much about yourself and your children, which I was extremely glad to hear. Think what a benighted wretch I am, seeing no one and reading but little in the newspapers, for I did not know (until seeing the paper of your Natural History Society) that you were a K.C.B. Most heartily glad I am that the Government have at last appreciated your most just claim for this high distinction. On the other hand, I am sorry to hear so poor an account of your health; but you were surely very rash to do all that you did and then pass through so exciting a scene as a ball at the Palace. It was enough to have tired a man in robust health. Complete rest will, however, I hope, quite set you up again. As for myself, I have been rather better of late, and if nothing disturbs me I can do some hours' work every day. I shall this autumn publish another book partly on man, which I dare say many will decry as very wicked. I could have travelled to Oxford, but could no more have withstood the excitement of a commemoration † than I could a ball at

---

* Admiral Sir James Sulivan was a lieutenant on board the *Beagle*.

† This refers to an invitation to receive the honorary degree of D.C.L. He was one of those nominated for the degree by Lord Salisbury on assuming the office of Chancellor of the University of Oxford. The fact that the honour was declined on the score of ill-health was published in the *Oxford University Gazette*, June 17, 1870.

Buckingham Palace. Many thanks for your kind remarks about my boys. Thank God, all give me complete satisfaction; my fourth stands second at Woolwich, and will be an Engineer Officer at Christmas. My wife desires to be very kindly remembered to Lady Sulivan, in which I very sincerely join, and in congratulation about your daughter's marriage. We are at present solitary, for all our younger children are gone a tour in Switzerland. I had never heard a word about the success of the T. del Fuego mission. It is most wonderful, and shames me, as I always prophesied utter failure. It is a grand success. I shall feel proud if your Committee think fit to elect me an honorary member of your society. With all good wishes and affectionate remembrances of ancient days,

Believe me, my dear Sulivan,

Your sincere friend,

CH. DARWIN.

[My father's connection with the South American Mission, which is referred to in the above letter, has given rise to some public comment, and has been to some extent misunderstood. The Archbishop of Canterbury, speaking at the annual meeting of the South American Missionary Society, April 21st, 1885,* said that the Society "drew the attention of Charles Darwin, and made him, in his pursuit of the wonders of the kindom of nature, realise that there was another kingdom just as wonderful and more lasting." Some discussion on the subject appeared in the *Daily News* of April 23rd, 24th, 29th, 1885, and finally Admiral Sir James Sulivan, on April 24th, wrote to the same journal, giving a clear account of my father's connection with the Society :—

"Your article in the *Daily News* of yesterday induces me to give you a correct statement of the connection between the South American Missionary Society and Mr. Charles Darwin, my old friend and shipmate for five years. I have been

---

* I quote a 'Leaflet,' published by the Society.

closely connected with the Society from the time of Captain Allen Gardiner's death, and Mr. Darwin has often expressed to me his conviction that it was utterly useless to send Missionaries to such a set of savages as the Fuegians, probably the very lowest of the human race. I had always replied that I did not believe any human beings existed too low to comprehend the simple message of the Gospel of Christ. After many years, I think about 1869,* but I cannot find the letter, he wrote to me that the recent accounts of the Mission proved to him that he had been wrong and I right in our estimates of the native character, and the possibility of doing them good through Missionaries; and he requested me to forward to the Society an enclosed cheque for £5, as a testimony of the interest he took in their good work. On June 6th, 1874, he wrote : 'I am very glad to hear so good an account of the Fuegians, and it is wonderful.' On June 10th, 1879 : 'The progress of the Fuegians is wonderful, and had it not occurred would have been to me quite incredible.' On January 3rd, 1880 : 'Your extracts' [from a journal] 'about the Fuegians are extremely curious, and have interested me much. I have often said that the progress of Japan was the greatest wonder in the world, but I declare that the progress of Fuegia is almost equally wonderful. On March 20th, 1881 : 'The account of the Fuegians interested not only me, but all my family. It is truly wonderful what you have heard from Mr. Bridges about their honesty and their language. I certainly should have predicted that not all the Missionaries in the world could have done what has been done.' On December 1st, 1881, sending me his annual subscription to the Orphanage at the Mission Station, he wrote : 'Judging from the *Missionary Journal*, the Mission in Tierra del Fuego seems going on quite wonderfully well.' "]

---

* It seems to have been in 1867.

C. Darwin to John Lubbock.

Down, July 17, 1870.

MY DEAR LUBBOCK,—As I hear that the Census will be brought before the House to-morrow, I write to say how much I hope that you will express your opinion on the desirability of queries in relation to consanguineous marriages being inserted. As you are aware, I have made experiments on the subject during several years ; *and it is my clear conviction that there is now ample evidence of the existence of a great physiological law, rendering an enquiry with reference to mankind of much importance. In England and many parts of Europe the marriages of cousins are objected to from their supposed injurious consequences ; but this belief rests on no direct evidence. It is therefore manifestly desirable that the belief should either be proved false, or should be confirmed,* so that in this latter case the marriages of cousins might be discouraged. If the proper queries are inserted, the returns would show whether married cousins have in their households on the night of the census as many children as have parents who are not related ; and should the number prove fewer, we might safely infer either lessened fertility in the parents, or which is more probable, lessened vitality in the offspring.

It is, moreover, much to be wished that the truth of the often repeated assertion that consanguineous marriages lead to deafness, and dumbness, blindness, &c., should be ascertained ; and all such assertions could be easily tested by the returns from a single census.

Believe me,

Yours very sincerely,

CHARLES DARWIN.

[When the Census Act was passing through the House of Commons, Sir John Lubbock and Dr. Playfair attempted to carry out this suggestion. The question came to a division, which was lost, but not by many votes.

The subject of cousin marriages was afterwards investigated by my brother.* The results of this laborious piece of work were negative; the author sums up in the sentence :—

"My paper is far from giving any thing like a satisfactory solution of the question as to the effects of consanguineous marriages, but it does, I think, show that the assertion that this question has already been set at rest, cannot be substantiated."]

---

* "Marriages between First Cousins in England, and their Effects." By George Darwin. 'Journal of the Statistical Society,' June, 1875.

CHAPTER VII.

PUBLICATION OF THE 'DESCENT OF MAN.'

WORK ON 'EXPRESSION.'

1871–1873.

[THE last revise of the 'Descent of Man' was corrected on January 15th, 1871, so that the book occupied him for about three years. He wrote to Sir J. Hooker: "I finished the last proofs of my book a few days ago, the work half-killed me, and I have not the most remote idea whether the book is worth publishing."

He also wrote to Dr. Gray:—

"I have finished my book on the 'Descent of Man,' &c., and its publication is delayed only by the Index: when published, I will send you a copy, but I do not know that you will care about it. Parts, as on the moral sense, will, I dare say, aggravate you, and if I hear from you, I shall probably receive a few stabs from your polished stiletto of a pen."

The book was published on February 24, 1871. 2500 copies were printed at first, and 5000 more before the end of the year. My father notes that he received for this edition £1470. The letters given in the present chapter deal with its reception, and also with the progress of the work on Expression. The letters are given, approximately, in chronological order, an arrangement which necessarily separates letters of kindred subject-matter, but gives perhaps a truer picture of the mingled interests and labours of my father's life.

Nothing can give a better idea (in small compass) of the

growth of Evolutionism and its position at this time, than a quotation from Mr. Huxley* :—

"The gradual lapse of time has now separated us by more than a decade from the date of the publication of the 'Origin of Species;' and whatever may be thought or said about Mr. Darwin's doctrines, or the manner in which he has propounded them, this much is certain, that in a dozen years the 'Origin of Species' has worked as complete a revolution in Biological Science as the 'Principia' did in Astronomy;" and it has done so, "because, in the words of Helmholtz, it contains 'an essentially new creative thought.' And, as time has slipped by, a happy change has come over Mr. Darwin's critics. The mixture of ignorance and insolence which at first characterised a large proportion of the attacks with which he was assailed, is no longer the sad distinction of anti-Darwinian criticism."

A passage in the Introduction to the 'Descent of Man' shows that the author recognised clearly this improvement in the position of Evolution. "When a naturalist like Carl Vogt ventures to say in his address, as President of the National Institution of Geneva (1869), 'personne, en Europe au moins, n'ose plus soutenir la création indépendante et de toutes pièces, des espèces,' it is manifest that at least a large number of naturalists must admit that species are the modified descendants of other species; and this especially holds good with the younger and rising naturalists. . . . Of the older and honoured chiefs in natural science, many, unfortunately, are still opposed to Evolution in every form."

In Mr. James Hague's pleasantly written article, "A Reminiscence of Mr. Darwin" ('Harper's Magazine,' October 1884), he describes a visit to my father "early in 1871,"† shortly after the publication of the 'Descent of Man.' Mr. Hague represents my father as "much impressed by the gen-

---

* 'Contemporary Review,' 1871.

† It must have been at the end of February, within a week after the publication of the book.

eral assent with which his views had been received," and as remarking that "everybody is talking about it without being shocked."

Later in the year the reception of the book is described in different language in the 'Edinburgh Review' : *   "On every side it is raising a storm of mingled wrath, wonder, and admiration."

With regard to the subsequent reception of the 'Descent of Man,' my father wrote to Dr. Dohrn, February 3, 1872 :—

"I did not know until reading your article, † that my 'Descent of Man' had excited so much *furore* in Germany. It has had an immense circulation in this country and in America, but has met the approval of hardly any naturalists as far as I know.   Therefore I suppose it was a mistake on my part to publish it ; but, anyhow, it will pave the way for some better work."

The book on the 'Expression of the Emotions ' was begun on January 17th, 1871, the last proof of the 'Descent of Man ' having been finished on January 15th.   The rough copy was finished by April 27th, and shortly after this (in June) the work was interrupted by the preparation of a sixth edition of the 'Origin.'   In November and December the proofs of the 'Expression' book were taken in hand, and occupied him until the following year, when the book was published.

Some references to the work on Expression have occurred in letters already given, showing that the foundation of the book was, to some extent, laid down for some years before he began to write it.   Thus he wrote to Dr. Asa Gray, April 15, 1867 :—

"I have been lately getting up and looking over my old notes on Expression, and fear that I shall not make so much of my hobby-horse as I thought I could ; nevertheless, it

---

* July 1871. An adverse criticism. The reviewer sums up by saying that : "Never perhaps in the history of philosophy have such wide gen-eralisations been derived from such a small basis of fact."

† In ' Das Ausland.'

seems to me a curious subject which has been strangely neglected."

It should, however, be remembered that the subject had been before his mind, more or less, from 1837 or 1838, as I judge from entries in his early note-books. It was in December, 1839, that he began to make observations on children.

The work required much correspondence, not only with missionaries and others living among savages, to whom he sent his printed queries, but among physiologists and physicians. He obtained much information from Professor Donders, Sir W. Bowman, Sir James Paget, Dr. W. Ogle, Dr. Crichton Browne, as well as from other observers.

The first letter refers to the ' Descent of Man.']

C. Darwin to A. R. Wallace.

Down, January 30 [1871].

MY DEAR WALLACE,—Your note * has given me very great pleasure, chiefly because I was so anxious not to treat you with the least disrespect, and it is so difficult to speak fairly when differing from any one. If I had offended you, it would have grieved me more than you will readily believe. Secondly, I am greatly pleased to hear that Vol. I. interests

---

* In the note referred to, dated January 27, Mr. Wallace wrote :— " Many thanks for your first volume which I have just finished reading through with the greatest pleasure and interest ; and I have also to thank you for the great tenderness with which you have treated me and my heresies."

The heresy is the limitation of natural selection as applied to man. My father wrote ('Descent of Man,' i. p. 137) :—" I cannot therefore understand how it is that Mr. Wallace maintains that 'natural selection could only have endowed the savage with a brain a little superior to that of an ape.' " In the above quoted letter Mr. Wallace wrote :—" Your chapters on ' Man ' are of intense interest, but as touching my special heresy not as yet altogether convincing, though of course I fully agree with every word and every argument which goes to prove the evolution or development of man out of a lower form."

you ; I have got so sick of the whole subject that I felt in utter doubt about the value of any part. I intended, when speaking of females not having been specially modified for protection, to include the prevention of characters acquired by the ♂ being transmitted to ♀ ; but I now see it would have been better to have said " specially acted on," or some such term. Possibly my intention may be clearer in Vol. II. Let me say that my conclusions are chiefly founded on the consideration of all animals taken in a body, bearing in mind how common the rules of sexual differences appear to be in all classes. The first copy of the chapter on Lepidoptera agreed pretty closely with you. I then worked on, came back to Lepidoptera, and thought myself compelled to alter it— finished Sexual Selection and for the last time went over Lepidoptera, and again I felt forced to alter it. I hope to God there will be nothing disagreeable to you in Vol. II., and that I have spoken fairly of your views ; I am fearful on this head, because I have just read (but not with sufficient care) Mivart's book,* and I feel *absolutely certain* that he meant to be fair (but he was stimulated by theological fervour) ; yet I do not think he has been quite fair. . . . The part which, I think, will have most influence is where he gives the whole series of cases like that of the whalebone, in which we cannot explain the gradational steps ; but such cases have no weight on my mind—if a few fish were extinct, who on earth would have ventured even to conjecture that lungs had originated in a swim-bladder ? In such a case as the Thylacine, I think he was bound to say that the resemblance of the jaw to that of the dog is superficial ; the number and correspondence and development of teeth being widely different. I think again when speaking of the necessity of altering a number of characters together, he ought to have thought of man having power by selection to modify simultaneously or almost simultaneously many points, as in making a greyhound or racehorse—as enlarged upon in my ' Domes-

---

* ' The Genesis of Species,' by St. G. Mivart, 1871.

tic Animals.' Mivart is savage or contemptuous about my "moral sense," and so probably will you be. I am extremely pleased that he agrees with my position, *as far as animal nature is concerned*, of man in the series ; or if anything, thinks I have erred in making him too distinct.

Forgive me for scribbling at such length. You have put me quite in good spirits ; I did so dread having been unintentionally unfair towards your views. I hope earnestly the second volume will escape as well. I care now very little what others say. As for our not quite agreeing, really in such complex subjects, it is almost impossible for two men who arrive independently at their conclusions to agree fully, it would be unnatural for them to do so.

Yours ever, very sincerely,
CH. DARWIN.

[Professor Haeckel seems to have been one of the first to write to my father about the 'Descent of Man.' I quote from his reply :—

" I must send you a few words to thank you for your interesting, and I may truly say, charming letter. I am delighted that you approve of my book, as far as you have read it. I felt very great difficulty and doubt how often I ought to allude to what you have published ; strictly speaking every idea, although occurring independently to me, if published by you previously ought to have appeared as if taken from your works, but this would have made my book very dull reading ; and I hoped that a full acknowledgment at the beginning would suffice.* I cannot tell you how glad I am to find that I have expressed my high admiration of your labours with

---

* In the introduction to the 'Descent of Man' the author wrote :— " This last naturalist [Haeckel] . . . has recently . . . published his 'Natürliche Schöpfungs-geschichte,' in which he fully discusses the genealogy of man. If this work had appeared before my essay had been written, I should probably never have completed it. Almost all the conclusions at which I have arrived, I find confirmed by this naturalist, whose knowledge on many points is much fuller than mine."

sufficient clearness; I am sure that I have not expressed it too strongly."]

C. Darwin to A. R. Wallace.

Down, March 16, 1871.

My dear Wallace,—I have just read your grand review.* It is in every way as kindly expressed towards myself as it is excellent in matter. The Lyells have been here, and Sir C. remarked that no one wrote such good scientific reviews as you, and as Miss Buckley added, you delight in picking out all that is good, though very far from blind to the bad. In all this I most entirely agree. I shall always consider your review as a great honour; and however much my book may hereafter be abused, as no doubt it will be, your review will console me, notwithstanding that we differ so greatly. I will keep your objections to my views in my mind, but I fear that the latter are almost stereotyped in my mind. I thought for long weeks about the inheritance and selection difficulty, and covered quires of paper with notes in trying to get out of it, but could not, though clearly seeing that it would be a great relief if I could. I will confine myself to two or three remarks. I have been much impressed with what you urge against colour† in the case of insects, having been acquired through sexual selection. I always saw that the evidence was very weak; but I still think, if it be admitted that the musical instruments of insects have been gained through sexual selection, that there is not the least improbability in colour having been thus gained. Your argument with respect to the denudation of mankind and also to insects, that taste on the part of one sex would have to re-

---

* *Academy*, March 15, 1871.

† Mr. Wallace says that the pairing of butterflies is probably determined by the fact that one male is stronger-winged, or more pertinacious than the rest, rather than by the choice of the females. He quotes the case of caterpillars which are brightly coloured and yet sexless. Mr. Wallace also makes the good criticism that the 'Descent of Man' consists of two books mixed together.

main nearly the same during many generations, in order that sexual selection should produce any effect, I agree to ; and I think this argument would be sound if used by one who denied that, for instance, the plumes of birds of Paradise had been so gained. I believe you admit this, and if so I do not see how your argument applies in other cases. I have recognized for some short time that I have made a great omission in not having discussed, as far as I could, the acquisition of taste, its inherited nature, and its permanence within pretty close limits for long periods.

[With regard to the success of the 'Descent of Man,' I quote from a letter to Professor Ray Lankester (March 22, 1871):—

"I think you will be glad to hear, as a proof of the increasing liberality of England, that my book has sold wonderfully . . . . and as yet no abuse (though some, no doubt, will come, strong enough), and only contempt even in the poor old *Athenæum*."

As to reviews that struck him he wrote to Mr. Wallace (March 24, 1871) :—

"There is a very striking second article on my book in the *Pall Mall*. The articles in the *Spectator** have also interested me much."

On March 20 he wrote to Mr. Murray :—

"Many thanks for the *Nonconformist* [March 8, 1871]. I like to see all that is written, and it is of some real use. If you hear of reviewers in out-of-the-way papers, especially the religious, as *Record*, *Guardian*, *Tablet*, kindly inform me. It is wonderful that there has been no abuse† as yet, but I

---

* *Spectator*, March 11 and 18, 1871. With regard to the evolution of conscience the reviewer thinks that my father comes much nearer to the "kernel of the psychological problem" than many of his predecessors. The second article contains a good discussion of the bearing of the book on the question of design, and concludes by finding in it a vindication of Theism more wonderful than that in Paley's 'Natural Theology.'

† "I feel a full conviction that my chapter on man will excite attention

suppose I shall not escape. On the whole, the reviews have been highly favourable."

The following extract from a letter to Mr. Murray (April 13, 1871) refers to a review in the *Times*.†

"I have no idea who wrote the *Times* review. He has no knowledge of science, and seems to me a wind-bag full of metaphysics and classics, so that I do not much regard his adverse judgment, though I suppose it will injure the sale."

A review of the 'Descent of Man,' which my father spoke of as "capital," appeared in the *Saturday Review* (Mar. 4 and 11, 1871). A passage from the first notice (Mar. 4) may be quoted in illustration of the broad basis as regards general acceptance, on which the doctrine of Evolution now stood : " He claims to have brought man himself, his origin and constitution, within that unity which he had previously sought to trace through all lower animal forms. The growth of opinion in the interval, due in chief measure to his own intermediate works, has placed the discussion of this problem in a position very much in advance of that held by it fifteen years ago. The problem of Evolution is hardly any longer to be treated as one of first principles ; nor has Mr. Darwin to do battle for a first hearing of his central hypothesis, upborne as it is by a phalanx of names full of distinction and promise, in either hemisphere."

The infolded point of the human ear, discovered by Mr. Woolner, and described in the 'Descent of Man,' seems especially to have struck the popular imagination ; my father wrote to Mr. Woolner :—

---

and plenty of abuse, and I suppose abuse is as good as praise for selling a book."—(From a letter to Mr. Murray, Jan. 31, 1867.)

† *Times*, April 7 and 8, 1871. The review is not only unfavourable as regards the book under discussion, but also as regards Evolution in general, as the following citation will show : " Even had it been rendered highly probable, which we doubt, that the animal creation has been developed into its numerous and widely different varieties by mere evolution, it would still require an independent investigation of overwhelming force and completeness to justify the presumption that man is but a term in this self-evolving series."

" The tips to the ears have become quite celebrated. One reviewer (' Nature ') says they ought to be called, as I suggested in joke, *Angulus Woolnerianus.** A German is very proud to find that he has the tips well developed, and I believe will send me a photograph of his ears."]

C. Darwin to John Brodie Innes.†

Down, May 29 [1871].

MY DEAR INNES,—I have been very glad to receive your pleasant letter, for to tell you the truth, I have sometimes wondered whether you would not think me an outcast and a reprobate after the publication of my last book [' Descent '].‡ I do not wonder at all at your not agreeing with me, for a good many professed naturalists do not. Yet when I see in how extraordinary a manner the judgment of naturalists has changed since I published the ' Origin,' I feel convinced that there will be in ten years quite as much unanimity about man, as far as his corporeal frame is concerned. . . .

[The following letters addressed to Dr. Ogle deal with the progress of the work on expression.]

Down, March 12 [1871].

MY DEAR DR. OGLE,—I have received both your letters, and they tell me all that I wanted to know in the clearest possible way, as, indeed, all your letters have ever done. I thank you cordially. I will give the case of the murderer # in my hobby-horse essay on expression. I fear that the Eustachian tube question must have cost you a deal of labour ;

---

* ' Nature' Ap. 6, 1871.   The term suggested is *Angulus Woolnerii.*

† Rev. J. Brodie Innes, of Milton Brodie, formerly Vicar of Down.

‡ In a former letter of my father's to Mr. Innes :—" We often differed, but you are one of those rare mortals from whom one can differ and yet feel no shade of animosity, and that is a thing which I should feel very proud of, if any one could say it of me."

' Expression of the Emotions,' p. 294.   The arrest of a murderer, as witnessed by Dr. Ogle in a hospital.

it is quite a complete little essay. It is pretty clear that the mouth is not opened under surprise merely to improve the hearing. Yet why do deaf men generally keep their mouths open? The other day a man here was mimicking a deaf friend, leaning his head forward and sideways to the speaker, with his mouth well open; it was a lifelike representation of a deaf man. Shakespeare somewhere says : "Hold your breath, listen" or "hark," I forget which. Surprise hurries the breath, and it seems to me one can breathe, at least hurriedly, much quieter through the open mouth than through the nose. I saw the other day you doubted this. As objection is your province at present, I think breathing through the nose ought to come within it likewise, so do pray consider this point, and let me hear your judgment. Consider the nose to be a flower to be fertilised, and then you will make out all about it.* I have had to allude to your paper on 'Sense of Smell;'† is the paging right, namely, 1, 2, 3? If not, I protest by all the gods against the plan followed by some, of having presentation copies falsely paged; and so does Rolleston, as he wrote to me the other day. In haste.

Yours very sincerely,

C. DARWIN.

C. Darwin to W. Ogle.

Down, March 25 [1871].

MY DEAR DR. OGLE,—You will think me a horrid bore, but I beg you, *in relation to a new point for observation*, to imagine as well as you can that you suddenly come across some dreadful object, and act with a sudden little start, a *shudder of horror;* please do this once or twice, and observe yourself as well as you can, and *afterwards* read the rest of this note, which I have consequently pinned down. I find, to my surprise, whenever I act thus my platysma contracts.

---

* Dr. Ogle had corresponded with my father on his own observations on the fertilisation of flowers.

† Medico-chirurg. Trans. liii.

Does yours? (N.B.—See what a man will do for science; I began this note with a horrid fib, namely, that I want you to attend to a new point.*) I will try and get some persons thus to act who are so lucky as not to know that they even possess this muscle, so troublesome for any one making out about expression. Is a shudder akin to the rigor or shivering before fever? If so, perhaps the platysma could be observed in such cases. Paget told me that he had attended much to shivering, and had written in MS. on the subject, and been much perplexed about it. He mentioned that passing a catheter often causes shivering. Perhaps I will write to him about the platysma. He is always most kind in aiding me in all ways, but he is so overworked that it hurts my conscience to trouble him, for I have a conscience, little as you have reason to think so. Help me if you can, and forgive me. Your murderer case has come in splendidly as the acme of prostration from fear.

Yours very sincerely,

CH. DARWIN.

C. Darwin to Dr. Ogle.

Down, April 29 [1871].

MY DEAR DR. OGLE,—I am truly obliged for all the great trouble which you have so kindly taken. I am sure you have no cause to say that you are sorry you can give me no definite information, for you have given me far more than I ever expected to get. The action of the platysma is not very important for me, but I believe that you will fully understand (for I have always fancied that our minds were very similar) the intolerable desire I had not to be utterly baffled. Now I know that it sometimes contracts from fear and from shuddering, but not apparently from a prolonged state of fear such as the insane suffer. . . . .

---

* The point was doubtless described as a new one, to avoid the possibility of Dr. Ogle's attention being directed to the platysma, a muscle which had been the subject of discussion in other letters.

[Mr. Mivart's 'Genesis of Species,'—a contribution to the literature of Evolution, which excited much attention—was published in 1871, before the appearance of the 'Descent of Man.' To this book the following letter (June 21, 1871) from the late Chauncey Wright * to my father refers] :

"I send . . . revised proofs of an article which will be published in the July number of the 'North American Review,' sending it in the hope that it will interest or even be of greater value to you. Mr. Mivart's book ['Genesis of Species'] of which this article is substantially a review, seems to me a very good background from which to present the considerations which I have endeavoured to set forth in the article, in defence and illustration of the theory of Natural Selection. My special purpose has been to contribute to the theory by placing it in its proper relations to philosophical inquiries in general." †

With regard to the proofs received from Mr. Wright, my father wrote to Mr. Wallace :]

Down, July 9 [1871].

MY DEAR WALLACE,—I send by this post a review by Chauncey Wright, as I much want your opinion of it as soon as you can send it. I consider you an incomparably better critic than I am. The article, though not very clearly written, and poor in parts from want of knowledge, seems to me admirable. Mivart's book is producing a great effect

---

* Chauncey Wright was born at Northampton, Massachusetts, Sept. 20, 1830, and came of a family settled in that town since 1654. He became in 1852 a computer in the Nautical Almanac office at Cambridge, Mass., and lived a quiet uneventful life, supported by the small stipend of his office, and by what he earned from his occasional articles, as well as by a little teaching. He thought and read much on metaphysical subjects, but on the whole with an outcome (as far as the world was concerned) not commensurate to the power of his mind. He seems to have been a man of strong individuality, and to have made a lasting impression on his friends. He died in Sept., 1875.

† 'Letters of Chauncey Wright,' by J. B. Thayer. Privately printed, 1878, p. 230.

against Natural Selection, and more especially against me. Therefore if you think the article even somewhat good I will write and get permission to publish it as a shilling pamphlet, together with the MS. additions (enclosed), for which there was not room at the end of the review. . . .

I am now at work at a new and cheap edition of the 'Origin,' and shall answer several points in Mivart's book, and introduce a new chapter for this purpose; but I treat the subject so much more concretely, and I dare say less philosophically, than Wright, that we shall not interfere with each other. You will think me a bigot when I say, after studying Mivart, I was never before in my life so convinced of the *general* (*i. e.* not in detail) truth of the views in the 'Origin.' I grieve to see the omission of the words by Mivart, detected by Wright.* I complained to Mivart that in two cases he quotes only the commencement of sentences by me, and thus modifies my meaning; but I never supposed he would have omitted words. There are other cases of what I consider unfair treatment. I conclude with sorrow that though he means to be honourable he is so bigoted that he cannot act fairly. . . .

C. Darwin to Chauncey Wright.

Down, July 14, 1871.

MY DEAR SIR,—I have hardly ever in my life read an article which has given me so much satisfaction as the review which you have been so kind as to send me. I agree to almost everything which you say. Your memory must be wonderfully accurate, for you know my works as well as I do myself, and your power of grasping other men's thoughts is something quite surprising; and this, as far as my experience

---

* 'North American Review,' vol. 113, pp. 83, 84. Chauncey Wright points out that the words omitted are "essential to the point on which he [Mr. Mivart] cites Mr. Darwin's authority." It should be mentioned that the passage from which words are omitted is not given within inverted commas by Mr. Mivart.

goes, is a very rare quality. As I read on I perceived how you have acquired this power, viz. by thoroughly analyzing each word.

. . . Now I am going to beg a favour. Will you provisionally give me permission to reprint your article as a shilling pamphlet? I ask only provisionally, as I have not yet had time to reflect on the subject. It would cost me, I fancy, with advertisements, some £20 or £30; but the worst is that, as I hear, pamphlets never will sell. And this makes me doubtful. Should you think it too much trouble to send me a title *for the chance*? The title ought, I think, to have Mr. Mivart's name on it.

. . . If you grant permission and send a title, you will kindly understand that I will first make further enquiries whether there is any chance of a pamphlet being read.

Pray believe me yours very sincerely obliged,

CH. DARWIN.

[The pamphlet was published in the autumn, and on October 23 my father wrote to Mr. Wright :—

"It pleases me much that you are satisfied with the appearance of your pamphlet.. I am sure it will do our cause good service; and this same opinion Huxley has expressed to me. ('Letters of Chauncey Wright,' p. 235)"]

C. Darwin to A. R. Wallace.

Down, July 12 [1871].

. . . . I feel very doubtful how far I shall succeed in answering Mivart, it is so difficult to answer objections to doubtful points, and make the discussion readable. I shall make only a selection. The worst of it is, that I cannot possibly hunt through all my references for isolated points, it would take me three weeks of intolerably hard work. I wish I had your power of arguing clearly. At present I feel sick of everything, and if I could occupy my time and forget my daily discomforts, or rather miseries, I would never publish another word.   But I shall cheer up, I dare say, soon, having only just got over a bad attack.   Farewell ; God knows why I bother you about myself.   I can say nothing more about missing-links than what I have said.   I should rely much on pre-silurian times; but then comes Sir W. Thomson like an odious spectre.   Farewell.

. . . There is a most cutting review of me in the ' Quarterly ' ; * I have only read a few pages.   The skill and style make me think of Mivart.   I shall soon be viewed as the most despicable of men.   This ' Quarterly Review ' tempts me to republish Ch. Wright, even if not read by any one, just to show some one will say a word against Mivart, and that his (*i.e.* Mivart's) remarks ought not to be swallowed without some reflection. . . . God knows whether my strength and spirit will last out to write a chapter versus Mivart and others ; I do so hate controversy and feel I shall do it so badly.

[The above-mentioned ' Quarterly ' review was the subject of an article by Mr. Huxley in the November number of the ' Contemporary Review.'   Here, also, are discussed Mr. Wallace's ' Contribution to the Theory of Natural Selection,' and the second edition of Mr. Mivart's ' Genesis of Species.' What follows is taken from Mr. Huxley's article.   The ' Quarterly ' reviewer, though being to some extent an evolutionist, believes that Man " differs more from an elephant or a gorilla, than do these from the dust of the earth on which they tread."   The reviewer also declares that my father has " with needless opposition, set at naught the first principles of both philosophy and religion."   Mr. Huxley passes from the ' Quarterly ' reviewer's further statement, that there is no necessary opposition between evolution and religion, to the more definite position taken by Mr. Mivart, that the orthodox authorities of the Roman Catholic Church agree in distinctly asserting derivative creation, so that " their teachings harmonize with all that modern science can possibly require." Here Mr. Huxley felt the want of that " study of Christian

---

* July 1871.

philosophy " (at any rate, in its Jesuitic garb), which Mr. Mivart speaks of, and it was a want he at once set to work to fill up. He was then staying at St. Andrews, whence he wrote to my father :—

"By great good luck there is an excellent library here, with a good copy of Suarez,* in a dozen big folios. Among these I dived, to the great astonishment of the librarian, and looking into them 'as the careful robin eyes the delver's toil' (*vide* 'Idylls'), l carried off the two venerable clasped volumes which were most promising." Even those who know Mr. Huxley's unrivalled power of tearing the heart out of a book must marvel at the skill with which he has made Suarez speak on his side. "So I have come out," he wrote, "in the new character of a defender of Catholic orthodoxy, and upset Mivart out of the mouth of his own prophet."

The remainder of Mr. Huxley's critique is largely occupied with a dissection of the 'Quarterly' reviewer's psychology, and his ethical views. He deals, too, with Mr. Wallace's objections to the doctrine of Evolution by natural causes when applied to the mental faculties of Man. Finally, he devotes a couples of pages to justifying his description of the 'Quarterly' reviewer's "treatment of Mr. Darwin as alike unjust and unbecoming."

It will be seen that the two following letters were written before the publication of Mr. Huxley's article.]

C. Darwin to T. H. Huxley.

Down, September 21 [1871].

MY DEAR HUXLEY,—Your letter has pleased me in many ways, to a wonderful degree. . . . What a wonderful man you are to grapple with those old metaphisico-divinity books. It quite delights me that you are going to some extent to answer and attack Mivart. His book, as you say, has produced a great effect ; yesterday I perceived the reverberations from it, even from Italy. It was this that made me ask Chauncey

---

* The learned Jesuit on whom Mr. Mivart mainly relies.

Wright to publish at my expense his article, which seems to me very clever, though ill-written. He has not knowledge enough to grapple with Mivart in detail. I think there can be no shadow of doubt that he is the author of the article in the 'Quarterly Review' . . . I am preparing a new edition of the 'Origin,' and shall introduce a new chapter in answer to miscellaneous objections, and shall give up the greater part to answer Mivart's cases of difficulty of incipient structures being of no use : and I find it can be done easily. He never states his case fairly, and makes wonderful blunders. . . . The pendulum is now swinging against our side, but I feel positive it will soon swing the other way ; and no mortal man will do half as much as you in giving it a start in the right direction, as you did at the first commencement. God forgive me for writing so long and egotistical a letter ; but it is your fault, for you have so delighted me ; I never dreamed that you would have time to say a word in defence of the cause which you have so often defended. It will be a long battle, after we are dead and gone. . . . Great is the power of misrepresentation. . . .

C. Darwin to T. H. Huxley.

Down, September 30 [1871].

MY DEAR HUXLEY,—It was very good of you to send the proof-sheets, for I was *very* anxious to read your article. I have been delighted with it. How you do smash Mivart's theology : it is almost equal to your article versus Comte,—* that never can be transcended. . . . But I have been pre-eminently glad to read your discussion on [the 'Quarterly' reviewer's] metaphysics, especially about reason and his definition of it. I felt sure he was wrong, but having only

---

* 'Fortnightly Review,' 1869. With regard to the relations of Positivism to Science my father wrote to Mr. Spencer in 1875 : "How curious and amusing it is to see to what an extent the Positivists hate all men of science ; I fancy they are dimly conscious what laughable and gigantic blunders their prophet made in predicting the course of science."

common observation and sense to trust to, I did not know what to say in my second edition of my 'Descent.' Now a footnote and reference to you will do the work. . . . For me, this is one of the most *important* parts of the review. But for *pleasure*, I have been particularly glad that my few words * on the distinction, if it can be so called, between Mivart's two forms of morality, caught your attention. I am so pleased that you take the same view, and give authorities for it ; but I searched Mill in vain on this head. How well you argue the whole case. I am mounting climax on climax ; for after all there is nothing, I think, better in your whole review than your arguments *v.* Wallace on the intellect of savages. I must tell you what Hooker said to me a few years ago. "When I read Huxley, I feel quite infantile in intellect." By Jove I have felt the truth of this throughout your review. What a man you are. There are scores of splendid passages, and vivid flashes of wit. I have been a good deal more than merely pleased by the concluding part of your review ; and all the more, as I own I felt mortified by the accusation of bigotry, arrogance, &c., in the 'Quarterly Review.' But I assure you, he may write his worst, and he will never mortify me again.

My dear Huxley, yours gratefully,

CHARLES DARWIN.

C. Darwin to F. Müller.

Haredene, Albury, August 2 [1871].

MY DEAR SIR,—Your last letter has interested me greatly ; it is wonderfully rich in facts and original thoughts. First, let me say that I have been much pleased by what you say about my book. It has had a *very large* sale ; but I have been much abused for it, especially for the chapter on the moral sense ; and most of my reviewers consider the book as a poor affair. God knows what its merits may really be ; all

---

* 'Descent of Man,' vol. i. p. 87. A discussion on the question whether an act done impulsively or instinctively can be called moral.

that I know is that I did my best.   With familiarity I think naturalists will accept sexual selection to a greater extent than they now seem inclined to do.   I should very much like to publish your letter, but I do not see how it could be made intelligible, without numerous coloured illustrations, but I will consult Mr. Wallace on this head.   I earnestly hope that you keep notes of all your letters, and that some day you will publish a book : ' Notes of a Naturalist in S Brazil,' or some such title.   Wallace will hardly admit the possibility of sexual selection with Lepidoptera, and no doubt it is very improbable.   Therefore, I am very glad to hear of your cases (which I will quote in the next edition) of the two sets of Hesperiadæ, which display their wings differently, according to which surface is coloured.   I cannot believe that such display is accidental and purposeless. . . .

No fact of your letter has interested me more than that about mimicry.   It is a capital fact about the males pursuing the wrong females.   You put the difficulty of the first steps in imitation in a most striking and *convincing* manner.   Your idea of sexual selection having aided protective imitation interests me greatly, for the same idea had occurred to me in quite different cases, viz. the dulness of all animals in the Galapagos Islands, Patagonia, &c., and in some other cases ; but I was afraid even to hint at such an idea.   Would you object to my giving some such sentence as follows : " F. Müller suspects that sexual selection may have come into play, in aid of protective imitation, in a very peculiar manner, which will appear extremely improbable to those who do not fully believe in sexual selection.   It is that the appreciation of certain colour is developed in those species which frequently behold other species thus ornamented."   Again let me thank you cordially for your most interesting letter. . . .

C. Darwin to E. B. Tylor.*

Down [Sept. 24, 1871].

My dear Sir,—I hope that you will allow me to have the pleasure of telling you how greatly I have been interested by your 'Primitive Culture,' now that I have finished it. It seems to me a most profound work, which will be certain to have permanent value, and to be referred to for years to come. It is wonderful how you trace animism from the lower races up to the religious belief of the highest races. It will make me for the future look at religion—a belief in the soul, &c.— from a new point of view. How curious, also, are the survivals or rudiments of old customs. . . . You will perhaps be surprised at my writing at so late a period, but I have had the book read aloud to me, and from much ill-health of late could only stand occasional short reads. The undertaking must have cost you gigantic labour. Nevertheless, I earnestly hope that you may be induced to treat morals in the same enlarged yet careful manner, as you have animism. I fancy from the last chapter that you have thought of this. No man could do the work so well as you, and the subject assuredly is a most important and interesting one. You must now possess references which would guide you to a sound estimation of the morals of savages ; and how writers like Wallace, Lubbock, &c., &c., do differ on this head. Forgive me for troubling you, and believe me, with much respect,

Yours very sincerely,

Ch. Darwin.

1872.

[At the beginning of the year the sixth edition of the 'Origin,' which had been begun in June, 1871, was nearly completed. The last sheet was revised on January 10, 1872, and the book was published in the course of the month. This volume differs from the previous ones in appearance

---

* Keeper of the Museum, and Reader in Anthropology at Oxford.

58

and size—it consists of 458 pp. instead of 596 pp. and is a few ounces lighter ; it is printed on bad paper, in small type, and with the lines unpleasantly close together. It had, however, one advantage over previous editions, namely that it was issued at a lower price. It is to be regretted that this the final edition of the 'Origin' should have appeared in so unattractive a form ; a form which has doubtless kept off many readers from the book.

The discussion suggested by the 'Genesis of Species' was perhaps the most important addition to the book. The objection that incipient structures cannot be of use was dealt with in some detail, because it seemed to the author that this was the point in Mr. Mivart's book which has struck most readers in England.

It is a striking proof of how wide and general had become the acceptance of his views that my father found it necessary to insert (sixth edition, p. 424), the sentence : " As a record of a former state of things, I have retained in the foregoing paragraphs and also elsewhere, several sentences which imply that naturalists believe in the separate creation of each species ; and I have been much censured for having thus expressed myself. But undoubtedly this was the general belief when the first edition of the present work appeared. . . Now things are wholly changed, and almost every naturalist admits the great principle of evolution."

A small correction introduced into this sixth edition is connected with one of his minor papers : " Note on the habits of the Pampas Woodpecker." * In the fifth edition of the 'Origin,' p. 220, he wrote :—

" Yet as I can assert not only from my own observation, but from that of the accurate Azara, it [the ground woodpecker] never climbs a tree." The paper in question was a reply to Mr. Hudson's remarks on the woodpecker in a previous number of the same journal. The last sentence of my father's paper is worth quoting for its temperate tone :

* Zoolog. Soc. Proc. 1870.

"Finally, I trust that Mr. Hudson is mistaken when he says that any one acquainted with the habits of this bird might be induced to believe that I 'had purposely wrested the truth' in order to prove my theory. He exonerates me from this charge; but I should be loath to think that there are many naturalists who, without any evidence, would accuse a fellow-worker of telling a deliberate falsehood to prove his theory." In the sixth edition, p. 142, the passage runs "in certain large districts it does not climb trees." And he goes on to give Mr. Hudson's statement that in other regions it does frequent trees.

One of the additions in the sixth edition (p. 149), was a reference to Mr. A. Hyatt's and Professor Cope's theory of "acceleration." With regard to this he wrote (October 10, 1872) in characteristic words to Mr. Hyatt:—

"Permit me to take this opportunity to express my sincere regret at having committed two grave errors in the last edition of my 'Origin of Species,' in my allusion to yours and Professor Cope's views on acceleration and retardation of development. I had thought that Professor Cope had preceded you; but I now well remember having formerly read with lively interest, and marked, a paper by you somewhere in my library, on fossil Cephalopods with remarks on the subject. It seems also that I have quite misrepresented your joint view. This has vexed me much. I confess that I have never been able to grasp fully what you wish to show, and I presume that this must be owing to some dulness on my part."

Lastly, it may be mentioned that this cheap edition being to some extent intended as a popular one, was made to include a glossary of technical terms, "given because several readers have complained. . . . that some of the terms used were unintelligible to them." The glossary was compiled by Mr. Dallas, and being an excellent collection of clear and sufficient definitions, must have proved useful to many readers.]

C. Darwin to J. L. A. de Quatrefages.

Down, January 15, 1872.

MY DEAR SIR,—I am much obliged for your very kind letter and exertions in my favour. I had thought that the publication of my last book ['Descent of Man'] would have destroyed all your sympathy with me, but though I estimated very highly your great liberality of mind, it seems that I underrated it.

I am gratified to hear that M. Lacaze-Duthiers will vote[*] for me, for I have long honoured his name. I cannot help regretting that you should expend your valuable time in trying to obtain for me the honour of election, for I fear, judging from the last time, that all your labour will be in vain. Whatever the result may be, I shall always retain the most lively recollection of your sympathy and kindness, and this will quite console me for my rejection.

With much respect and esteem, I remain, dear Sir,

Yours truly obliged,

CHARLES DARWIN.

P.S.—With respect to the great stress which you lay on man walking on two legs, whilst the quadrumana go on all fours, permit me to remind you that no one much values the great difference in the mode of locomotion, and consequently in structure, between seals and the terrestrial carnivora, or between the almost biped kangaroos and other marsupials.

C. Darwin to August Weismann.[†]

Down, April 5, 1872.

MY DEAR SIR,—I have now read your essay[‡] with very great interest. Your view of the 'Origin' of local races

---

[*] He was not elected as a corresponding member of the French Academy until 1878.

[†] Professor of Zoology in Freiburg.

[‡] 'Ueber den Einfluss der Isolirung auf die Artbildung.' Leipzig, 1872.

through "Amixie," is altogether new to me, and seems to throw an important light on an obscure problem. There is, however, something strange about the periods or endurance of variability. I formerly endeavoured to investigate the subject, not by looking to past time, but to species of the same genus widely distributed; and I found in many cases that all the species, with perhaps one or two exceptions, were variable. It would be a very interesting subject for a conchologist to investigate, viz., whether the species of the same genus were variable during many successive geological formations. I began to make inquiries on this head, but failed in this, as in so many other things, from the want of time and strength. In your remarks on crossing, you do not, as it seems to me, lay nearly stress enough on the increased vigour of the offspring derived from parents which have been exposed to different conditions. I have during the last five years been making experiments on this subject with plants, and have been astonished at the results, which have not yet been published.

In the first part of your essay, I thought that you wasted (to use an English expression) too much powder and shot on M. Wagner;* but I changed my opinion when I saw how admirably you treated the whole case, and how well you used the facts about the Planorbis. I wish I had studied this latter case more carefully. The manner in which, as you show, the different varieties blend together and make a constant whole, agrees perfectly with my hypothetical illustrations.

Many years ago the late E. Forbes described three closely consecutive beds in a secondary formation, each with representative forms of the same fresh-water shells: the case is evidently analogous with that of Hilgendorf,† but the inter-

---

* Prof. Wagner has written two essays on the same subject. 'Die Darwin'sche Theorie und das Migrationsgesetz, in 1868, and 'Ueber den Einfluss der Geographischen Isolirung, &c.,' an address to the Bavarian Academy of Sciences at Munich, 1870.

† "Ueber *Planorbis multiformis* im Steinheimer Süsswasser-kalk." Monatsbericht of the Berlin Academy, 1866.

esting connecting varieties or links were here absent. I rejoice to think that I formerly said as emphatically as I could,
that neither isolation nor time by themselves do anything for
the modification of species.   Hardly anything in your essay
has pleased me so much personally, as to find that you believe
to a certain extent in sexual selection. As far as I can judge,
very few naturalists believe in this. I may have erred on
many points, and extended the doctrine too far, but I feel
a strong conviction that sexual selection will hereafter be
admitted to be a powerful agency. I cannot agree with what
you say about the taste for beauty in animals not easily varying. It may be suspected that even the habit of viewing
differently coloured surrounding objects would influence their
taste, and Fritz Müller even goes so far as to believe that the
sight of gaudy butterflies might influence the taste of distinct
species. There are many remarks and statements in your
essay which have interested me greatly, and I thank you for
the pleasure which I have received from reading it.

> With sincere respect, I remain,
> My dear Sir, yours very faithfully,
> CHARLES DARWIN.

P.S.—If you should ever be induced to consider the whole
doctrine of sexual selection, I think that you will be led to
the conclusion, that characters thus gained by one sex are
very commonly transferred in a greater or less degree to the
other sex.

[With regard to Moritz Wagner's first Essay, my father
wrote to that naturalist, apparently in 1868 :]

DEAR AND RESPECTED SIR,—I thank you sincerely for
sending me your ' Migrationsgesetz, &c.,' and for the very
kind and most honourable notice which you have taken of my
works. That a naturalist who has travelled into so many and
such distant regions, and who has studied animals of so many
classes, should, to a considerable extent, agree with me, is, I

can assure you, the highest gratification of which I am capable. . . . Although I saw the effects of isolation in the case of islands and mountain-ranges, and knew of a few instances of rivers, yet the greater number of your facts were quite unknown to me. I now see that from the want of knowledge I did not make nearly sufficient use of the views which you advocate; and I almost wish I could believe in its importance to the same extent with you ; for you well show, in a manner which never occurred to me, that it removes many difficulties and objections. But I must still believe that in many large areas all the individuals of the same species have been slowly modified, in the same manner, for instance, as the English race-horse has been improved, that is by the continued selection of the fleetest individuals, without any separation. But I admit that by this process two or more new species could hardly be found within the same limited area ; some degree of separation, if not indispensable, would be highly advantageous; and here your facts and views will be of great value. . . .

[The following letter bears on the same subject. It refers to Professor M. Wagner's Essay, published in *Das Ausland*, May 31, 1875 :]

C. Darwin to Moritz Wagner.

Down, October 13, 1876.

DEAR SIR, — I have now finished reading your essays, which have interested me in a very high degree, notwithstanding that I differ much from you on various points. For instance, several considerations make me doubt whether species are much more variable at one period than at another, except through the agency of changed conditions. I wish, however, that I could believe in this doctrine, as it removes many difficulties. But my strongest objection to your theory is that it does not explain the manifold adaptations in structure in every organic being — for instance in a Picus for climbing trees and catching insects—or in a Strix for catching animals at night, and so on *ad infinitum*. No theory is in the least satisfactory to me unless it clearly explains such adaptations. I think that you misunderstand my views on isolation. I believe that all the individuals of a species can be slowly modified within the same district, in nearly the same manner as man effects by what I have called the process of unconscious selection. . . . I do not believe that one species will give birth to two or more new species as long as they are mingled together within the same district. Nevertheless I cannot doubt that many new species have been simultaneously developed within the same large continental area ; and in my 'Origin of Species' I endeavoured to explain how two new species might be developed, although they met and intermingled on the *borders* of their range. It would have been a strange fact if I had overlooked the importance of isolation, seeing that it was such cases as that of the Galapagos Archipelago, which chiefly led me to study the origin of species. In my opinion the greatest error which I have committed, has been not allowing sufficient weight to the direct action of the environment, *i.e.* food, climate, &c., independently of natural selection. Modifications thus caused, which are neither of advantage nor disadvantage to the modified organism, would be especially favoured, as I can now see chiefly through your observations, by isolation in a small area, where only a few individuals lived under nearly uniform conditions.

When I wrote the 'Origin,' and for some years afterwards, I could find little good evidence of the direct action of the environment ; now there is a large body of evidence, and your case of the Saturnia is one of the most remarkable of which I have heard. Although we differ so greatly, I hope that you will permit me to express my respect for your long-continued and successful labours in the good cause of natural science.

I remain, dear Sir, yours very faithfully,
CHARLES DARWIN.

[The two following letters are also of interest as bearing

on my father's views on the action of isolation as regards the origin of new species :]

C. Darwin to K. Semper.

Down, November 26, 1878.

My dear Professor Semper,—When I published the sixth edition of the 'Origin,' I thought a good deal on the subject to which you refer, and the opinion therein expressed was my deliberate conviction. I went as far as I could, perhaps too far in agreement with Wagner ; since that time I have seen no reason to change my mind, but then I must add that my attention has been absorbed on other subjects. There are two different classes of cases, as it appears to me, viz. those in which a species becomes slowly modified in the same country (of which I cannot doubt there are innumerable instances) and those cases in which a species splits into two or three or more new species, and in the latter case, I should think nearly perfect separation would greatly aid in their " specification," to coin a new word.

I am very glad that you are taking up this subject, for you will be sure to throw much light on it. I remember well, long ago, oscillating much ; when I thought of the Fauna and Flora of the Galapagos Islands I was all for isolation, when I thought of S. America I doubted much. Pray believe me,

Yours very sincerely,

CH. DARWIN.

P.S.—I hope that this letter will not be quite illegible, but I have no amanuensis at present.

C. Darwin to K. Semper.

Down, November 30, 1878.

Dear Professor Semper,—Since writing I have recalled some of the thoughts and conclusions which have passed through my mind of late years. In North America, in going from north to south or from east to west, it is clear that the changed conditions of life have modified the organisms in the different regions, so that they now form distinct races or even species. It is further clear that in isolated districts, however small, the inhabitants almost always get slightly modified, and how far this is due to the nature of the slightly different conditions to which they are exposed, and how far to mere interbreeding, in the manner explained by Weismann, I can form no opinion. The same difficulty occurred to me (as shown in my 'Variation of Animals and Plants under Domestication') with respect to the aboriginal breeds of cattle, sheep, &c., in the separated districts of Great Britain, and indeed throughout Europe. As our knowledge advances, very slight differences, considered by systematists as of no importance in structure, are continually found to be functionally important; and I have been especially struck with this fact in the case of plants to which my observations have of late years been confined. Therefore it seems to me rather rash to consider the slight differences between representative species, for instance those inhabiting the different islands of the same archipelago, as of no functional importance, and as not in any way due to natural selection. With respect to all adapted structures, and these are innumerable, I cannot see how M. Wagner's view throws any light, nor indeed do I see at all more clearly than I did before, from the numerous cases which he has brought forward, how and why it is that a long isolated form should almost always become slightly modified. I do not know whether you will care about hearing my further opinion on the point in question, for as before remarked I have not attended much of late years to such questions, thinking it prudent, now that I am growing old, to work at easier subjects.

Believe me, yours very sincerely,

CH. DARWIN.

I hope and trust that you will throw light on these points.

P.S.—I will add another remark which I remember occurred to me when I first read M. Wagner. When a species first arrives on a small island, it will probably increase rapidly, and unless all the individuals change instantaneously (which is improbable in the highest degree), the slowly, more or less, modifying offspring must intercross one with another, and with their unmodified parents, and any offspring not as yet modified. The case will then be like that of domesticated animals which have slowly become modified, either by the action of the external conditions or by the process which I have called the *unconscious selection* by man—*i.e.*, in contrast with methodical selection.

[The letters continue the history of the year 1872, which has been interrupted by a digression on Isolation.]

C. Darwin to the Marquis de Saporta.

Down, April 8, 1872.

Dear Sir,—I thank you very sincerely and feel much honoured by the trouble which you have taken in giving me your reflections on the origin of Man. It gratifies me extremely that some parts of my work have interested you, and that we agree on the main conclusion of the derivation of man from some lower form.

I will reflect on what you have said, but I cannot at present give up my belief in the close relationship of Man to the higher Simiæ. I do not put much trust in any single character, even that of dentition ; but I put the greatest faith in resemblances in many parts of the whole organisation, for I cannot believe that such resemblances can be due to any cause except close blood relationship. That man is closely allied to the higher Simiæ is shown by the classification of Linnæus, who was so good a judge of affinity. The man who in England knows most about the structure of the Simiæ, namely, Mr. Mivart, and who is bitterly opposed to my doctrines about the derivation of the mental powers, yet has publicly admitted that I have not put man too close to the higher Simiæ, as far as bodily structure is concerned. I do not think the absence of reversions of structure in man is of much weight; C. Vogt, indeed, argues that [the existence of] Micro-cephalous idiots is a case of reversion. No one who believes in Evolution will doubt that the Phocæ are descended from some terrestrial Carnivore. Yet no one would expect to meet with any such reversion in them. The lesser divergence of character in the races of man in comparison with the species of Simiadæ may perhaps be accounted for by man having spread over the world at a much later period than did the Simiadæ. I am fully prepared to admit the high antiquity of man; but then we have evidence, in the Dryopithecus, of the high antiquity of the Anthropomorphous Simiæ.

I am glad to hear that you are at work on your fossil plants, which of late years have afforded so rich a field for discovery. With my best thanks for your great kindness, and with much respect, I remain,

Dear Sir, yours very faithfully,

CHARLES DARWIN.

[In April, 1872, he was elected to the Royal Society of Holland, and wrote to Professor Donders:—

"Very many thanks for your letter. The honour of being elected a foreign member of your Royal Society has pleased me much. The sympathy of his fellow workers has always appeared to me by far the highest reward to which any scientific man can look. My gratification has been not a little increased by first hearing of the honour from you."]

C. Darwin to Chauncey Wright.

Down, June 3, 1872.

MY DEAR SIR,—Many thanks for your article * in the 'North American Review,' which I have read with great

---

* The proof-sheets of an article which appeared in the July number of the 'North American Review.' It was a rejoinder to Mr. Mivart's reply ('N. Am. Review,' April 1872) to Mr. Chauncey Wright's pamphlet. Chauncey Wright says of it ('Letters,' p. 238):—"It is not properly a rejoinder but a new article, repeating and expounding some of the points of my pamphlet, and answering some of Mr. Mivart's replies incidentally."

interest.   Nothing can be clearer than the way in which you
discuss the permanence or fixity of species.   It never occurred to me to suppose that any one looked at the case as
it seems Mr. Mivart does.   Had I read his answer to you,
perhaps I should have perceived this ; but I have resolved
to waste no more time in reading reviews of my works or on
Evolution, excepting when I hear that they are good and
contain new matter. . . . It is pretty clear that Mr. Mivart
has come to the end of his tether on this subject.

As your mind is so clear, and as you consider so carefully
the meaning of words, I wish you would take some incidental
occasion to consider when a thing may properly be said to be
effected by the will of man.   I have been led to the wish by
reading an article by your Professor Whitney *versus* Schleicher.
He argues, because each step of change in language is made
by the will of man, the whole language so changes ; but I do
not think that this is so, as man has no intention or wish to
change the language.   It is a parallel case with what I have
called "unconscious selection," which depends on men consciously preserving the best individuals, and thus unconsciously altering the breed.

My dear Sir, yours sincerely,

CHARLES DARWIN.

[Not long afterwards (September) Mr. Chauncey Wright
paid a visit to Down,* which he described in a letter † to Miss

---

* Mr. and Mrs. C. L. Brace, who had given much of their lives to
philanthropic work in New York, also paid a visit at Down in this summer.   Some of their work is recorded in Mr. Brace's ' The Dangerous
Classes of New York,' and of this book my father wrote to the author :—

" Since you were here my wife has read aloud to me more than half of
your work, and it has interested us both in the highest degree, and we
shall read every word of the remainder.   The facts seem to me very well
told, and the inferences very striking.   But after all this is but a weak
part of the impression left on our minds by what we have read ; for we are
both filled with earnest admiration at the heroic labours of yourself and
others."

† ' Letters,' p. 246–248.

S. Sedgwick (now Mrs. William Darwin) : " If you can imagine me enthusiastic—absolutely and unqualifiedly so, without a *but* or criticism, then think of my last evening's and this morning's talks with Mr. Darwin. . . . I was never so worked up in my life, and did not sleep many hours under the hospitable roof. . . . It would be quite impossible to give by way of report any idea of these talks before and at and after dinner, at breakfast, and at leave-taking ; and yet I dislike the egotism of 'testifying' like other religious enthusiasts, without any verification, or hint of similar experience."]

C. Darwin to Herbert Spencer.

Bassett, Southampton, June 10 [1872].

DEAR SPENCER,—I dare say you will think me a foolish fellow, but I cannot resist the wish to express my unbounded admiration of your article * in answer to Mr. Martineau. It is, indeed, admirable, and hardly less so your second article on Sociology (which, however, I have not yet finished) : I never believed in the reigning influence of great men on the world's progress ; but if asked why I did not believe, I should have been sorely perplexed to have given a good answer. Every one with eyes to see and ears to hear (the number, I fear, are not many) ought to bow their knee to you, and I for one do.

Believe me, yours most sincerely,

C. DARWIN.

C. Darwin to J. D. Hooker.

Down, July 12 [1872].

MY DEAR HOOKER,—I must exhale and express my joy at the way in which the newspapers have taken up your case. I have seen the *Times*, the *Daily News*, and the *Pall Mall*, and hear that others have taken up the case.

The Memorial has done great good this way, whatever

---

* 'Mr. Martineau on Evolution,' by Herbert Spencer, 'Contemporary Review,' July 1872.

may be the result in the action of our wretched Government. On my soul, it is enough to make one turn into an old honest Tory. . . .

If you answer this, I shall be sorry that I have relieved my feelings by writing.

Yours affectionately,

C. DARWIN.

[The memorial here referred to was addressed to Mr. Gladstone, and was signed by a number of distinguished men, including Sir Charles Lyell, Mr. Bentham, Mr. Huxley, and Sir James Paget. It gives a complete account of the arbitrary and unjust treatment received by Sir J. D. Hooker at the hands of his official chief, the First Commissioner of Works. The document is published in full in ' Nature' (July 11, 1872), and is well worth studying as an example of the treatment which it is possible for science to receive from officialism. As 'Nature' observes, it is a paper which must be read with the greatest indignation by scientific men in every part of the world, and with shame by all Englishmen. The signatories of the memorial conclude by protesting against the expected consequences of Sir Joseph Hooker's persecution—namely his resignation, and the loss of "a man honoured for his integrity, beloved for his courtesy and kindliness of heart; and who has spent in the public service not only a stainless but an illustrious life."

Happily this misfortune was averted, and Sir Joseph was freed from further molestation.]

C. Darwin to A. R. Wallace.

Down, August 3 [1872].

MY DEAR WALLACE,—I hate controversy, chiefly perhaps because I do it badly; but as Dr. Bree accuses you* of "blundering," I have thought myself bound to send the en-

---

* Mr. Wallace had reviewed Dr. Bree's book, 'An Exposition of Fallacies in the Hypothesis of Mr. Darwin,' in ' Nature,' July 25, 1872.

closed letter * to 'Nature,' that is if you in the least desire it. In this case please post it. If you do not *at all* wish it, I should rather prefer not sending it, and in this case please to tear it up. And I beg you to do the same, if you intend answering Dr. Bree yourself, as you will do it incomparably better than I should. Also please tear it up if you don't like the letter.

My dear Wallace, yours very sincerely,

CH. DARWIN.

C. Darwin to A. R. Wallace.

Down, August 28, 1872.

MY DEAR WALLACE,—I have at last finished the gigantic job of reading Dr. Bastian's book,† and have been deeply, interested by it. You wished to hear my impression, but it is not worth sending.

He seems to me an extremely able man, as, indeed, I thought when I read his first essay. His general argument in favour of Archebiosis ‡ is wonderfully strong, though I cannot think much of some few of his arguments. The result is that I am bewildered and astonished by his statements, but am not convinced, though, on the whole, it seems to me probable that Archebiosis is true. I am not convinced, part-

---

* The letter is as follows :—"Bree on Darwinism." 'Nature,' Aug. 8, 1872. Permit me to state—though the statement is almost superfluous— that Mr. Wallace, in his review of Dr. Bree's work, gives with perfect correctness what I intended to express, and what I believe was expressed clearly, with respect to the probable position of man in the early part of his pedigree. As I have not seen Dr. Bree's recent work, and as his letter is unintelligible to me, I cannot even conjecture how he has so completely mistaken my meaning : but, perhaps, no one who has read Mr. Wallace's article, or who has read a work formerly published by Dr. Bree on the same subject as his recent one, will be surprised at any amount of misunderstanding on his part.—CHARLES DARWIN.

Aug. 3.

† 'The Beginnings of Life.' H. C. Bastian, 1872.

‡ That is to say, Spontaneous Generation. For the distinction between Archebiosis and Heterogenesis, see Bastian, chapter vi.

ly I think owing to the deductive cast of much of his reasoning; and I know not why, but I never feel convinced by deduction, even in the case of H. Spencer's writings. If Dr. Bastian's book had been turned upside down, and he had begun with the various cases of Heterogenesis, and then gone on to organic, and afterwards to saline solutions, and had then given his general arguments, I should have been, I believe, much more influenced. I suspect, however, that my chief difficulty is the effect of old convictions being stereotyped on my brain. I must have more evidence that germs, or the minutest fragments of the lowest forms, are always killed by 212° of Fahr. Perhaps the mere reiteration of the statements given by Dr. Bastian [by] other men, whose judgment I respect, and who have worked long on the lower organisms, would suffice to convince me. Here is a fine confession of intellectual weakness; but what an inexplicable frame of mind is that of belief!

As for Rotifers and Tardigrades being spontaneously generated, my mind can no more digest such statements, whether true or false, than my stomach can digest a lump of lead. Dr. Bastian is always comparing Archebiosis, as well as growth, to crystallisation; but, on this view, a Rotifer or Tardigrade is adapted to its humble conditions of life by a happy accident, and this I cannot believe. . . . He must have worked with very impure materials in some cases, as plenty of organisms appeared in a saline solution not containing an atom of nitrogen.

I wholly disagree with Dr. Bastian about many points in his latter chapters. Thus the frequency of generalised forms in the older strata seems to me clearly to indicate the common descent with divergence of more recent forms. Notwithstanding all his sneers, I do not strike my colours as yet about Pangenesis. I should like to live to see Archebiosis proved true, for it would be a discovery of transcendent importance; or, if false, I should like to see it disproved, and the facts otherwise explained; but I shall not live to see all this. If ever proved, Dr. Bastian will have taken a prominent part in the work. How grand is the onward rush of science ; it is enough to console us for the many errors which we have committed, and for our efforts being overlaid and forgotten in the mass of new facts and new views which are daily turning up.

This is all I have to say about Dr. Bastian's book, and it certainly has not been worth saying. . . .

C. Darwin to A. De Candolle.

Down, December 11, 1872.

MY DEAR SIR—I began reading your new book * sooner than I intended, and when I once began, I could not stop ; and now you must allow me to thank you for the very great pleasure which it has given me. I have hardly ever read anything more original and interesting than your treatment of the causes which favour the development of scientific men. The whole was quite new to me, and most curious. When I began your essay I was afraid that you were going to attack the principle of inheritance in relation to mind, but I soon found myself fully content to follow you and accept your limitations. I have felt, of course, special interest in the latter part of your work, but there was here less novelty to me. In many parts you do me much honour, and everywhere more than justice. Authors generally like to hear what points most strike different readers, so I will mention that of your shorter essays, that on the future prevalence of languages, and on vaccination interested me the most, as, indeed, did that on statistics, and free will. Great liability to certain diseases, being probably liable to atavism, is quite a new idea to me. At p. 322 you suggest that a young swallow ought to be separated, and then let loose in order to test the power of instinct ; but nature annually performs this experiment, as old cockoos migrate in England some weeks before the young birds of the same year. By the way, I have just used the forbidden word " nature," which, after reading

---

* ' Histoire des Sciences et des Savants,' 1873.

your essay, I almost determined never to use again. There are very few remarks in your book to which I demur, but when you back up Asa Gray in saying that all instincts are congenital habits, I must protest.

Finally, will you permit me to ask you a question : have you yourself, or some one who can be quite trusted, observed (p. 322) that the butterflies on the Alps are tamer than those on the lowlands ? Do they belong to the same species ? Has this fact been observed with more than one species ? Are they brightly coloured kinds ? I am especially curious about their alighting on the brightly coloured parts of ladies' dresses, more especially because I have been more than once assured that butterflies like bright colours, for instance, in India the scarlet leaves of Pointsettia.

Once again allow me to thank you for having sent me your work, and for the very unusual amount of pleasure which I have received in reading it.

With much respect, I remain, my dear Sir,

Yours very sincerely,

CHARLES DARWIN.

[The last revise of the 'Expression of the Emotions' was finished on August 22nd, 1872, and he wrote in his Diary :— " Has taken me about twelve months." As usual he had no belief in the possibility of the book being generally success- ful. The following passage in a letter to Haeckel gives the impression that he had felt the writing of this book as a some- what severe strain :—

" I have finished my little book on ' Expression,' and when it is published in November I will of course send you a copy, in case you would like to read it for amusement. I have re- sumed some old botanical work, and perhaps I shall never again attempt to discuss theoretical views.

" I am growing old and weak, and no man can tell when his intellectual powers begin to fail. Long life and happiness to you for your own sake and for that of science."

It was published in the autumn. The edition consisted of 7000, and of these 5267 copies were sold at Mr. Murray's sale in November. Two thousand were printed at the end of the year, and this proved a misfortune, as they did not afterwards sell so rapidly, and thus a mass of notes collected by the author was never employed for a second edition during his lifetime.

Among the reviews of the 'Expression of the Emotions' may be mentioned the unfavourable notices in the *Athenæum*, Nov. 9, 1872, and the *Times*, Dec. 13, 1872. A good review by Mr. Wallace appeared in the 'Quarterly Journal of Science,' Jan. 1873. Mr. Wallace truly remarks that the book exhibits certain "characteristics of the author's mind in an eminent degree," namely, "the insatiable longing to discover the causes of the varied and complex phenomena presented by living things." He adds that in the case of the author "the restless curiosity of the child to know the 'what for?' the 'why?' and the 'how?' of everything" seems "never to have abated its force."

A writer in one of the theological reviews describes the book as the most "powerful and insidious" of all the author's works.

Professor Alexander Bain criticised the book in a postscript to the 'Senses and the Intellect;' to this essay the following letter refers :]

C. Darwin to Alexander Bain.

Down, October 9, 1873.

MY DEAR SIR,—I am particularly obliged to you for having sent me your essay. Your criticisms are all written in a quite fair spirit, and indeed no one who knows you or your works would expect anything else. What you say about the vagueness of what I have called the direct action of the nervous system, is perfectly just. I felt it so at the time, and even more of late. I confess that I have never been able fully to grasp your principle of spontaneity,* as well as some other of your points, so as to apply them to special cases. But as we look at everything from different points of view, it is not likely that we should agree closely.

I have been greatly pleased by what you say about the crying expression and about blushing. Did you read a review in a late 'Edinburgh?'† It was magnificently contemptuous towards myself and many others.

I retain a very pleasant recollection of our sojourn together at that delightful place, Moor Park.

With my renewed thanks, I remain, my dear Sir,

Yours sincerely,

CH. DARWIN.

---

* Professor Bain expounded his theory of Spontaneity in the essay here alluded to. It would be impossible to do justice to it within the limits of a foot-note. The following quotations may give some notion of it :—

" By Spontaneity I understand the readiness to pass into movement in the absence of all stimulation whatever ; the essential requisite being that the nerve-centres and muscles shall be fresh and vigorous. . . . . The gesticulations and the carols of young and active animals are mere overflow of nervous energy ; and although they are very apt to concur with pleasing emotion, they have an independent source. . . . . They are not properly movements of expression ; they express nothing at all except an abundant stock of physical power."

† The review on the 'Expression of the Emotions' appeared in the April number of the 'Edinburgh Review,' 1873. The opening sentence is a fair sample of the general tone of the article : " Mr. Darwin has added another volume of amusing stories and grotesque illustrations to the remarkable series of works already devoted to the exposition and defence of the evolutionary hypothesis." A few other quotations may be worth giving. " His one-sided devotion to an *à priori* scheme of interpretation seems thus steadily tending to impair the author's hitherto unrivalled powers as an observer. However this may be, most impartial critics will, we think, admit that there is a marked falling off both in philosophical tone and scientific interest in the works produced since Mr. Darwin committed himself to the crude metaphysical conception so largely associated with his name." The article is directed against Evolution as a whole, almost as much as against the doctrines of the book under discussion. We find throughout plenty of that effective style of criticism which consists in the

C. Darwin to Mrs. Haliburton.[*]

Down, November 1 [1872].

MY DEAR MRS. HALIBURTON,—I dare say you will be surprised to hear from me. My object in writing now is to say that I have just published a book on the 'Expression of the Emotions in Man and Animals;' and it has occurred to me that you might possibly like to read some parts of it; and I can hardly think that this would have been the case with any of the books which I have already published. So I send by this post my present book. Although I have had no communication with you or the other members of your family for so long a time, no scenes in my whole life pass so frequently or so vividly before my mind as those which relate to happy old days spent at Woodhouse. I should very much like to hear a little news about yourself and the other members of your family, if you will take the trouble to write to me. Formerly I used to glean some news about you from my sisters.

I have had many years of bad health and have not been able to visit anywhere; and now I feel very old. As long as I pass a perfectly uniform life, I am able to do some daily work in Natural History, which is still my passion, as it was in old days, when you used to laugh at me for collecting beetles with such zeal at Woodhouse. Excepting from my continued ill-health, which has excluded me from society, my life has been a very happy one; the greatest drawback being

---

use of such expressions as "dogmatism," "intolerance," "presumptuous," "arrogant." Together with accusations of such various faults a "virtual abandonment of the inductive method," and the use of slang and vulgarisms.

The part of the article which seems to have interested my father is the discussion on the use which he ought to have made of painting and sculpture.

[*] Mrs. Haliburton was a daughter of my father's old friend, Mr. Owen of Woodhouse. Her husband, Judge Haliburton, was the well-known author of 'Sam Slick.'

that several of my children have inherited from me feeble health.   I hope with all my heart that you retain, at least to a large extent, the famous "Owen constitution."   With sincere feelings of gratitude and affection for all bearing the name of Owen, I venture to sign myself,

Yours affectionately,
CHARLES DARWIN.

C. Darwin to Mrs. Haliburton.

Down, November 6 [1872].

MY DEAR SARAH,—I have been very much pleased by your letter, which I must call charming.   I hardly ventured to think that you would have retained a friendly recollection of me for so many years.   Yet I ought to have felt assured that you would remain as warm-hearted and as true-hearted as you have ever been from my earliest recollection.   I know well how many grievous sorrows you have gone through ; but I am very sorry to hear that your health is not good.   In the spring or summer, when the weather is better, if you can summon up courage to pay us a visit here, both my wife, as she desires me to say, and myself, would be truly glad to see you, and I know that you would not care about being rather dull here.   It would be a real pleasure to me to see you. —Thank you much for telling about your family,—much of which was new to me.   How kind you all were to me as a boy, and you especially, and how much happiness I owe to you.   Believe me your affectionate and obliged friend,

CHARLES DARWIN.

P.S.—Perhaps you would like to see a photograph of me now that I am old.

1873.

[The only work (other than botanical) of this year was the preparation of a second edition of the 'Descent of Man,' the publication of which is referred to in the following chapter. This work was undertaken much against the grain, as he was at the time deeply immersed in the manuscript of 'Insect-ivorous Plants.' Thus he wrote to Mr. Wallace (November 19), " I never in my lifetime regretted an interruption so much as this new edition of the 'Descent.'" And later (in December) he wrote to Mr. Huxley : " The new edition of the 'Descent' has turned out an awful job. It took me ten days merely to glance over letters and reviews with criticisms and new facts. It is a devil of a job."

The work was continued until April 1, 1874, when he was able to return to his much loved Drosera. He wrote to Mr. Murray :—

" I have at last finished, after above three months as hard work as I have ever had in my life, a corrected edition of the 'Descent,' and I much wish to have it printed off as soon as possible. As it is to be stereotyped I shall never touch it again."

The first of the miscellaneous letters of 1873 refers to a pleasant visit received from Colonel Higginson of Newport, U.S.]

C. Darwin to Thos. Wentworth Higginson.

Down, February 27th [1873].

MY DEAR SIR,—My wife has just finished reading aloud your 'Life with a Black Regiment,' and you must allow me to thank you heartily for the very great pleasure which it has in many ways given us. I always thought well of the negroes, from the little which I have seen of them ; and I have been delighted to have my vague impressions confirmed, and their character and mental powers so ably discussed. When you were here I did not know of the noble position which you had filled. I had formerly read about the black regiments, but failed to connect your name with your admirable undertaking. Although we enjoyed greatly your visit to Down, my wife and myself have over and over again regretted that we did not know about the black regiment, as we should have greatly liked to have heard a little about the South from your own lips.

Your descriptions have vividly recalled walks taken forty

years ago in Brazil. We have your collected Essays, which were kindly sent us by Mr. [Moncure] Conway, but have not yet had time to read them. I occasionally glean a little news of you in the 'Index'; and within the last hour have read an interesting article of yours on the progress of Free Thought.

Believe me, my dear Sir, with sincere admiration,

Yours very faithfully,

CH. DARWIN.

[On May 28th he sent the following answers to the questions that Mr. Galton was at that time addressing to various scientific men, in the course of the inquiry which is given in his 'English Men of Science, their Nature and Nurture,' 1874. With regard to the questions, my father wrote, "I have filled up the answers as well as I could, but it is simply impossible for me to estimate the degrees." For the sake of convenience, the questions and answers relating to *Nurture* are made to precede those on *Nature:*

Education? { How taught?	I consider that all I have learnt of any value has been self-taught.
Conducive to or restrictive of habits of observation?	Restrictive of observation, being almost entirely classical.
Conducive to health or otherwise?	Yes.
Peculiar merits?	None whatever.
Chief omissions?	No mathematics or modern languages, nor any habits of observation or reasoning.
Has the religious creed taught in your youth had any deterrent effect on the freedom of your researches?	No.
Do your scientific tastes appear to have been innate?	Certainly innate.
Were they determined by any and what events?	My innate taste for natural history strongly confirmed and directed by the voyage in the *Beagle*.

Question.	Yourself.	Your Father.
Specify any interests that have been very actively pursued.	Science, and field sports to a passionate degree during youth.	
Religion?	Nominally to Church of England.	Nominally to Church of England.
Politics?	Liberal or Radical.	Liberal.
Health?	Good when young—bad for last 33 years.	Good throughout life, except from gout.
Height, &c. ?	**Height?** 6 ft. — **Figure, &c.?** Spare, whilst young rather stout. — **Measurement round inside of hat.** 22¼ in. **Colour of Hair?** Brown. — **Complexion?** Rather sallow.	**Height?** 6 ft. 2 in. — **Figure, &c.?** Very broad and corpulent. **Colour of Hair?** Brown. — **Complexion?** Ruddy.
Temperament?	Somewhat nervous.	Sanguine.
Energy of body, &c. ?	Energy shown by much activity, and whilst I had health, power of resisting fatigue. I and one other man were alone able to fetch water for a large party of officers and sailors utterly prostrated. Some of my expeditions in S. America were adventurous. An early riser in the morning.	Great power of endurance although feeling much fatigue, as after consultations after long journeys; very active—not restless—very early riser, no travels. My father said his father suffered much from sense of fatigue, that he worked very hard.

Energy of mind, &c.?	Shown by rigorous and long-continued work on same subject, as 20 years on the 'Origin of Species,' and 9 years on 'Cirripedia.'	Habitually very active mind—shown in conversation with a succession of people during the whole day.
Memory?	Memory very bad for dates, and for learning by rote; but good in retaining a general or vague recollection of many facts.	Wonderful memory for dates. In old age he told a person, reading aloud to him a book only read in youth, the passages which were coming—knew the birthdays and death, &c., of all friends and acquaintances.
Studiousness?	Very studious, but not large acquirements.	Not very studious or mentally receptive, except for facts in conversation—great collector of anecdotes.
Independence of Judgment?	I think fairly independent; but I can give no instances. I gave up common religious belief almost independently from my own reflections.	Free thinker in religious matters. Liberal, with rather a tendency to Toryism.
Originality or Eccentricity?	—— thinks this applies to me; I do not think so—i. e., as far as eccentricity. I suppose that I have shown originality in science, as I have made discoveries with regard to common objects.	Original character, had great personal influence and power of producing fear of himself in others. He kept his accounts with great care in a peculiar way, in a number of separate little books, without any general ledger.
Special talents?	None, except for business as evinced by keeping accounts, replies to correspondence, and investing money very well. Very methodical in all my habits.	Practical business—made a large fortune and incurred no losses.
Strongly marked mental peculiarities, bearing on scientific success, and not specified above?	Steadiness—great curiosity about facts and their meaning. Some love of the new and marvellous. N. B.—I find it quite impossible to estimate my character by your degrees.	Strong social affection and great sympathy in the pleasures of others. Sceptical as to new things. Curious as to facts. Great foresight. Not much public spirit—great generosity in giving money and assistance.

The following letter refers *inter alia* to a letter which appeared in 'Nature' (Sept. 25, 1873), "On the Males and Complemental Males of certain Cirripedes, and on Rudimentary Organs :"]

C. Darwin to E. Haeckel.

Down, September 25, 1873.

MY DEAR HÄCKEL,—I thank you for the present of your book,* and I am heartily glad to see its great success. You will do a wonderful amount of good in spreading the doctrine of Evolution, supporting it as you do by so many original observations. I have read the new preface with very great interest. The delay in the appearance of the English translation vexes and surprises me, for I have never been able to read it thoroughly in German, and I shall assuredly do so when it appears in English. Has the problem of the later stages of reduction of useless structures ever perplexed you? This problem has of late caused me much perplexity. I have just written a letter to 'Nature' with a hypothetical explanation of this difficulty, and I will send you the paper with the passage marked. I will at the same time send a paper which has interested me ; it need not be returned. It contains a singular statement bearing on so-called Spontaneous Generation. I much wish that this latter question could be settled, but I see no prospect of it. If it could be proved true this would be most important to us. . . .

Wishing you every success in your admirable labours,

I remain, my dear Häckel, yours very sincerely,

CHARLES DARWIN.

---

* 'Schöpfungs-geschichte,' 4th ed. The translation (' The History of Creation ') was not published until 1876.

CHAPTER VIII.

Miscellanea, including Second Editions of 'Coral Reefs,' the 'Descent of Man,' and the 'Variations of Animals and Plants.'

1874 and 1875.

[The year 1874 was given up to 'Insectivorous Plants,' with the exception of the months (see vol. ii, p. 353) devoted to the second edition of the 'Descent of Man,' and with the further exception of the time given to a second edition of his 'Coral Reefs' (1874). The Preface to the latter states that new facts have been added, the whole book revised, and "the latter chapters almost rewritten." In the Appendix some account is given of Professor Semper's objections, and this was the occasion of correspondence between that naturalist and my father. In Professor Semper's volume, 'Animal Life' (one of the International Series), the author calls attention to the subject in the following passage which I give in German, the published English translation being, as it seems to me, incorrect : "Es scheint mir als ob er in der zweiten Ausgabe seines allgemein bekannten Werks über Korallenriffe einem Irrthume über meine Beobachtungen zum Opfer gefallen ist, indem er die Angaben, die ich allerdings bisher immer nur sehr kurz gehalten hatte, vollständig falsch wiedergegeben hat."

The proof-sheets containing this passage were sent by Professor Semper to my father before 'Animal Life' was published, and this was the occasion for the following letter, which was afterwards published in Professor Semper's book.]

C. Darwin to K. Semper.

Down, October 2, 1879.

MY DEAR PROFESSOR SEMPER,—I thank you for your extremely kind letter of the 19th, and for the proof-sheets. I believe that I understand all, excepting one or two sentences, where my imperfect knowledge of German has interfered. This is my sole and poor excuse for the mistake which I made in the second edition of my ' Coral ' book. Your account of the Pellew Islands is a fine addition to our knowledge on coral reefs. I have very little to say on the subject, even if I had formerly read your account and seen your maps, but had known nothing of the proofs of recent elevation, and of your belief that the islands have not since subsided. I have no doubt that I should have considered them as formed during subsidence. But I should have been much troubled in my mind by the sea not being so deep as it usually is round atolls, and by the reef on one side sloping so gradually beneath the sea ; for this latter fact, as far as my memory serves me, is a very unusual and almost unparalleled case. I always foresaw that a bank at the proper depth beneath the surface would give rise to a reef which could not be distinguished from an atoll, formed during subsidence. I must still adhere to my opinion that the atolls and barrier reefs in the middle of the Pacific and Indian Oceans indicate subsidence ; but I fully agree with you that such cases as that of the Pellew Islands, if of at all frequent occurrence, would make my general conclusions of very little value. Future observers must decide between us. It will be a strange fact if there has not been subsidence of the beds of the great oceans, and if this has not affected the forms of the coral reefs.

In the last three pages of the last sheet sent I am extremely glad to see that you are going to treat of the dispersion of animals. Your preliminary remarks seem to me quite excellent. There is nothing about M. Wagner, as I expected to find. I suppose that you have seen Moseley's last book, which contains some good observations on dispersion.

I am glad that your book will appear in English, for then I can read it with ease. Pray believe me,

Yours very sincerely,

CHARLES DARWIN.

[The most recent criticism on the Coral-reef theory is by Mr. Murray, one of the staff of the *Challenger*, who read a paper before the Royal Society of Edinburgh, April 5, 1880.* The chief point brought forward is the possibility of the building up of submarine mountains, which may serve as foundations for coral reefs. Mr. Murray also seeks to prove that "the chief features of coral reefs and islands can be accounted for without calling in the aid of great and general subsidence." The following letter refers to this subject :]

C. Darwin to A. Agassiz.

Down, May 5, 1881.

. . . You will have seen Mr. Murray's views on the formation of atolls and barrier reefs. Before publishing my book, I thought long over the same view, but only as far as ordinary marine organisms are concerned, for at that time little was known of the multitude of minute oceanic organisms. I rejected this view, as from the few dredgings made in the *Beagle*, in the south temperate regions, I concluded that shells, the smaller corals, &c., decayed, and were dissolved, when not protected by the deposition of sediment, and sediment could not accumulate in the open ocean. Certainly, shells, &c., were in several cases completely rotten, and crumbled into mud between my fingers; but you will know well whether this is in any degree common. I have expressly said that a bank at the proper depth would give rise to an atoll, which could not be distinguished from one formed during subsidence. I can,

---

* An abstract is published in vol. x. of the 'Proceedings,' p. 505, and in 'Nature,' August 12, 1880.

however, hardly believe in the former presence of as many banks (there having been no subsidence) as there are atolls in the great oceans, within a reasonable depth, on which minute oceanic organisms could have accumulated to the thickness of many hundred feet. . . . Pray forgive me for troubling you at such length, but it has occurred [to me] that you might be disposed to give, after your wide experience, your judgment. If I am wrong, the sooner I am knocked on the head and annihilated so much the better. It still seems to me a marvellous thing that there should not have been much, and long continued, subsidence in the beds of the great oceans. I wish that some doubly rich millionaire would take it into his head to have borings made in some of the Pacific and Indian atolls, and bring home cores for slicing from a depth of 500 or 600 feet. . . .

[The second edition of the 'Descent of Man' was published in the autumn of 1874. Some severe remarks on the " monistic hypothesis " appeared in the July * number of the 'Quarterly Review' (p. 45). The Reviewer expresses his astonishment at the ignorance of certain elementary distinctions and principles (e. g. with regard to the *verbum mentale*) exhibited, among others, by Mr. Darwin, who does not exhibit the faintest indication of having grasped them, yet a clear perception of them, and a direct and detailed examination of his facts with regard to them, " was a *sine quâ non* for attempting, with a chance of success, the solution of the mystery as to the descent of man."

Some further criticisms of a later date may be here alluded to. In the 'Academy,' 1876 (pp. 562, 587), appeared a review of Mr. Mivart's 'Lessons from Nature,' by Mr. Wallace. When considering the part of Mr. Mivart's book relating to Natural and Sexual Selection, Mr. Wallace says : " In his violent attack on Mr. Darwin's theories our author uses unusually strong language. Not content with mere argument, he

---

* The review necessarily deals with the first edition of the ' Descent of Man.'

expresses 'reprobation of Mr. Darwin's views'; and asserts that though he (Mr. Darwin) has been obliged, virtually, to give up his theory, it is still maintained by Darwinians with 'unscrupulous audacity,' and the actual repudiation of it concealed by the 'conspiracy of silence.'" Mr. Wallace goes on to show that these charges are without foundation, and points out that, "If there is one thing more than another for which Mr. Darwin is pre-eminent among modern literary and scientific men, it is for his perfect literary honesty, his self-abnegation in confessing himself wrong, and the eager haste with which he proclaims and even magnifies small errors in his works, for the most part discovered by himself."

The following extract from a letter to Mr. Wallace (June 17th) refers to Mr. Mivart's statement ('Lessons from Nature,' p. 144) that Mr. Darwin at first studiously disguised his views as to the "bestiality of man" :—

"I have only just heard of and procured your two articles in the Academy. I thank you most cordially for your generous defence of me against Mr. Mivart. In the 'Origin' I did not discuss the derivation of any one species; but that I might not be accused of concealing my opinion, I went out of my way, and inserted a sentence which seemed to me (and still so seems) to disclose plainly my belief. This was quoted in my 'Descent of Man.' Therefore it is very unjust, ... of Mr. Mivart to accuse me of base fraudulent concealment."

The letter which here follows is of interest in connection with the discussion, in the 'Descent of Man,' on the origin of the musical sense in man :]

C. Darwin to E. Gurney.*

Down, July 8, 1876.

MY DEAR MR. GURNEY,—I have read your article† with much interest, except the latter part, which soared above my

---

* Author of 'The Power of Sound.'

† "Some disputed Points in Music."—'Fortnightly Review,' July, 1876.

ken. I am greatly pleased that you uphold my views to a
certain extent. Your criticism of the rasping noise made by
insects being necessarily rhythmical is very good; but though
not made intentionally, it may be pleasing to the females
from the nerve cells being nearly similar in function throughout the animal kingdom. With respect to your letter, I believe that I understand your meaning, and agree with you. I
never supposed that the different degrees and kinds of pleasure derived from different music could be explained by the
musical powers of our semi-human progenitors. Does not
the fact that different people belonging to the same civilized
nation are very differently affected by the same music, almost
show that these diversities of taste and pleasure have been
acquired during their individual lives? Your simile of archi-
tecture seems to me particularly good ; for in this case the
appreciation almost must be individual, though possibly the
sense of sublimity excited by a grand cathedral, may have
some connection with the vague feelings of terror and super-
stition in our savage ancestors, when they entered a great
cavern or gloomy forest. I wish some one could analyse the
feeling of sublimity. It amuses me to think how horrified
some high flying æsthetic men will be at your encouraging
such low degraded views as mine.

> Believe me, yours very sincerely,
> CHARLES DARWIN.

[The letters which follow are of a miscellaneous interest. The first extract (from a letter, Jan. 18, 1874) refers
to a spiritualistic séance, held at Erasmus Darwin's house, 6
Queen Anne Street, under the auspices of a well-known
medium :]

" . . . We had grand fun, one afternoon, for George hired a
medium, who made the chairs, a flute, a bell, and candle-
stick, and fiery points jump about in my brother's dining-
room, in a manner that astounded every one, and took away
all their breaths. It was in the dark, but George and Hens-

leigh Wedgwood held the medium's hands and feet on both sides all the time. I found it so hot and tiring that I went away before all these astounding miracles, or jugglery, took place. How the man could possibly do what was done passes my understanding. I came downstairs, and saw all the chairs, &c., on the table, which had been lifted over the heads of those sitting round it.

The Lord have mercy on us all, if we have to believe in such rubbish. F. Galton was there, and says it was a good séance. . . ."

The séance in question led to a smaller and more carefully organised one being undertaken, at which Mr. Huxley was present, and on which he reported to my father :]

C. Darwin to Professor T. H. Huxley.

Down, January 29 [1874].

MY DEAR HUXLEY,—It was very good of you to write so long an account. Though the séance did tire you so much it was, I think, really worth the exertion, as the same sort of things are done at all the séances, even at ——'s ; and now to my mind an enormous weight of evidence would be requisite to make one believe in anything beyond mere trickery. . . . I am pleased to think that I declared to all my family, the day before yesterday, that the more I thought of all that I had heard happened at Queen Anne St., the more convinced I was it was all imposture . . . . my theory was that [the medium] managed to get the two men on each side of him to hold each other's hands, instead of his, and that he was thus free to perform his antics. I am very glad that I issued my ukase to you to attend.

Yours affectionately,
CH. DARWIN.

[In the spring of this year (1874) he read a book which gave him great pleasure and of which he often spoke with admiration :—The ' Naturalist in Nicaragua,' by the late Thomas

Belt. Mr. Belt, whose untimely death may well be deplored by naturalists, was by profession an Engineer, so that all his admirable observations in Natural History in Nicaragua and elsewhere were the fruit of his leisure. The book is direct and vivid in style and is full of description and suggestive discussions. With reference to it my father wrote to Sir J. D. Hooker :—

" Belt I have read, and I am delighted that you like it so much, it appears to me the best of all natural history journals which have ever been published."]

C. Darwin to the Marquis de Saporta.

Down, May 30, 1874.

DEAR SIR,—I have been very neglectful in not having sooner thanked you for your kindness in having sent me your ' Études sur la Végétation,' &c., and other memoirs. I have read several of them with very great interest, and nothing can be more important, in my opinion, than your evidence of the extremely slow and gradual manner in which specific forms change. I observe that M. A. De Candolle has lately quoted you on this head *versus* Heer. I hope that you may be able to throw light on the question whether such protean, or polymorphic forms, as those of Rubus, Hieracium, &c., at the present day, are those which generate new species ; as for myself, I have always felt some doubt on this head. I trust that you may soon bring many of your countrymen to believe in Evolution, and my name will then perhaps cease to be scorned. With the most sincere respect, I remain, Dear Sir,

Yours faithfully,

CH. DARWIN.

C. Darwin to Asa Gray.

Down, June 5 [1874].

MY DEAR GRAY,—I have now read your article* in 'Nature,' and the last two paragraphs were not included in the slip sent before. I wrote yesterday and cannot remember exactly what I said, and now cannot be easy without again telling you how profoundly I have been gratified. Every one, I suppose, occasionally thinks that he has worked in vain, and when one of these fits overtakes me, I will think of your article, and if that does not dispel the evil spirit, I shall know that I am at the time a little bit insane, as we all are occasionally.

What you say about Teleology † pleases me especially, and I do not think any one else has ever noticed the point.‡ I have always said you were the man to hit the nail on the head.

Yours gratefully and affectionately,

CH. DARWIN.

[As a contribution to the history of the reception of the 'Origin of Species,' the meeting of the British Association in 1874, at Belfast, should be mentioned. It is memorable for Professor Tyndall's brilliant presidential address, in which a sketch of the history of Evolution is given culminating in an eloquent analysis of the 'Origin of Species,' and of the nature of its great success. With regard to Prof. Tyndall's address, Lyell wrote ('Life,' ii. p. 455) congratulating my father on the

---

* The article, "Charles Darwin," in the series of *Scientific Worthies* ('Nature,' June 4, 1874). This admirable estimate of my father's work in science is given in the form of a comparison and contrast between Robert Brown and Charles Darwin.

† "Let us recognise Darwin's great service to Natural Science in bringing back to it Teleology: so that instead of Morphology *versus* Teleology, we shall have Morphology wedded to Teleology."

‡ See, however, Mr. Huxley's chapter on the 'Reception of the Origin of Species' in vol. i.; p. 554.

meeting, "on which occasion you and your theory of Evolution may be fairly said to have had an ovation." In the same letter Sir Charles speaks of a paper * of Professor Judd's, and it is to this that the following letter refers :]

C. Darwin to C. Lyell.

Down, September 23, 1874.

MY DEAR LYELL,—I suppose that you have returned, or will soon return, to London ; † and, I hope, reinvigorated by your outing. In your last letter you spoke of Mr. Judd's paper on the Volcanoes of the Hebrides. I have just finished it, and to ease my mind must express my extreme admiration.

It is years since I have read a purely geological paper which has interested me so greatly. I was all the more interested, as in the Cordillera I often speculated on the sources of the deluges of submarine porphyritic lavas, of which they are built ; and, as I have stated, I saw to a certain extent the causes of the obliteration of the points of eruption. I was also not a little pleased to see my volcanic book quoted, for I thought it was completely dead and forgotten. What fine work will Mr. Judd assuredly do ! . . . Now I have eased my mind ; and so farewell, with both E. D.'s and C. D.'s very kind remembrances to Miss Lyell.

Yours affectionately,

CHARLES DARWIN.

[Sir Charles Lyell's reply to the above letter must have been one of the latest that my father received from his old friend, and it is with this letter that the volumes of his published correspondence closes.]

---

* On the Ancient Volcanoes of the Highlands, 'Journal of Geolog. Soc.,' 1874.

† Sir Charles Lyell returned from Scotland towards the end of September.

C. Darwin to Aug. Forel.

Down, October 15, 1874.

MY DEAR SIR,—I have now read the whole of your admirable work * and seldom in my life have I been more interested by any book. There are so many interesting facts and discussions, that I hardly know which to specify; but I think, firstly, the newest points to me have been about the size of the brain in the three sexes, together with your suggestion that increase of mind power may have led to the sterility of the workers. Secondly about the battles of the ants, and your curious account of the enraged ants being held by their comrades until they calmed down. Thirdly, the evidence of ants of the same community being the offspring of brothers and sisters. You admit, I think, that new communities will often be the product of a cross between not-related ants. Fritz Müller has made some interesting observations on this head with respect to Termites. The case of *Anergates* is most perplexing in many ways, but I have such faith in the law of occasional crossing that I believe an explanation will hereafter be found, such as the dimorphism of either sex and the occasional production of winged males. I see that you are puzzled how ants of the same community recognize each other; I once placed two (*F. rufa*) in a pill-box smelling strongly of asafœtida and after a day returned them to their homes; they were threatened, but at last recognized. I made the trial thinking that they might know each other by their odour; but this cannot have been the case, and I have often fancied that they must have some common signal. Your last chapter is one great mass of wonderful facts and suggestions, and the whole profoundly interesting. I have seldom been more gratified than by [your] honourable mention of my work.

I should like to tell you one little observation which 1 made with care many years ago; I saw ants (*Formica rufa*)

---

* ' Les Fourmis de la Suisse,' 4to, 1874. ·

carrying cocoons from a nest which was the largest I ever saw and which was well known to all the country people near, and an old man, apparently about eighty years of age, told me that he had known it ever since he was a boy. The ants carrying the cocoons did not appear to be emigrating; following the line, I saw many ascending a tall fir tree still carrying their cocoons. But when I looked closely I found that all the cocoons were empty cases. This astonished me, and next day I got a man to observe with me, and we again saw ants bringing empty cocoons out of the nest; each of us fixed on one ant and slowly followed it, and repeated the observation on many others. We thus found that some ants soon dropped their empty cocoons; others carried them for many yards, as much as thirty paces, and others carried them high up the fir tree out of sight. Now here I think we have one instinct in contest with another and mistaken one. The first instinct being to carry the empty cocoons out of the nest, and it would have been sufficient to have laid them on the heap of rubbish, as the first breath of wind would have blown them away. And then came in the contest with the other very powerful instinct of preserving and carrying their cocoons as long as possible; and this they could not help doing although the cocoons were empty. According as the one or other instinct was the stronger in each individual ant, so did it carry the empty cocoon to a greater or less distance. If this little observation should ever prove of any use to you, you are quite at liberty to use it. Again thanking you cordially for the great pleasure which your work has given me, I remain with much respect,

Yours sincerely,

CH. DARWIN.

P.S.—If you read English easily I should like to send you Mr. Belt's book, as I think you would like it as much as did Fritz Müller.

C. Darwin to J. Fiske.

Down, December 8, 1874.

MY DEAR SIR,—You must allow me to thank you for the very great interest with which I have at last slowly read the whole of your work.* I have long wished to know something about the views of the many great men whose doctrines you give. With the exception of special points I did not even understand H. Spencer's general doctrine ; for his style is too hard work for me. I never in my life read so lucid an expositor (and therefore thinker) as you are ; and I think that I understand nearly the whole—perhaps less clearly about Cosmic Theism and Causation than other parts. It is hopeless to attempt out of so much to specify what has interested me most, and probably you would not care to hear. I wish some chemist would attempt to ascertain the result of the cooling of heated gases of the proper kinds, in relation to your hypothesis of the origin of living matter. It pleased me to find that here and there I had arrived from my own crude thoughts at some of the same conclusions with you ; though I could seldom or never have given my reasons for such conclusions. I find that my mind is so fixed by the inductive method, that I cannot appreciate deductive reasoning : I must begin with a good body of facts and not from a principle (in which I always suspect some fallacy) and then as much deduction as you please. This may be very narrow-minded ; but the result is that such parts of H. Spencer, as I have read with care impress my mind with the idea of his inexhaustible wealth of suggestion, but never convince me ; and so I find it with some others. I believe the cause to lie in the frequency with which I have found first-formed theories [to be] erroneous. I thank you for the honourable mention which you make of my works. Parts of the 'Descent of Man' must have appeared laughably weak to you : nevertheless, I have sent you a new edition just published. Thank-

---

* 'Outlines of Cosmic Philosophy,' 2 vols. 8vo. 1874.

ing you for the profound interest and profit with which I have read your work. I remain,

My dear Sir, yours very faithfully,

CH. DARWIN.

1875.

[The only work, not purely botanical, which occupied my father in the present year was the correction of the second edition of 'The Variation of Animals and Plants,' and on this he was engaged from the beginning of July till October 3rd. The rest of the year was taken up with his work on insectivorous plants, and on cross-fertilisation, as will be shown in a later chapter. The chief alterations in the second edition of 'Animals and Plants' are in the eleventh chapter on " Bud-variation and on certain anomalous modes of reproduction ;" the chapter on Pangenesis " was also largely altered and remodelled." He mentions briefly some of the authors who have noticed the doctrine. Professor Delpino's ' Sulla Darwiniana Teoria della Pangenesi ' (1869), an adverse but fair criticism, seems to have impressed him as valuable. Of another critique my father characteristically says,* " Dr. Lionel Beale ('Nature,' May 11, 1871, p. 26) sneers at the whole doctrine with much acerbity and some justice." He also points out that, in Mantegazza's 'Elementi di Igiene,' the theory of Pangenesis was clearly foreseen.

In connection with this subject, a letter of my father's to ' Nature' (April 27, 1871) should be mentioned. A paper by Mr. Galton had been read before the Royal Society (March 30, 1871) in which were described experiments, on intertransfusion of blood, designed to test the truth of the hypothesis of pangenesis. My father, while giving all due credit to Mr. Galton for his ingenious experiments, does not allow that pangenesis has " as yet received its death-blow, though from presenting so many vulnerable points its life is always in jeopardy."

---

* 'Animals and Plants,' 2nd edit. vol. ii. p. 350.

He seems to have found the work of correcting very wearisome, for he wrote :—

"I have no news about myself, as I am merely slaving over the sickening work of preparing new editions. I wish I could get a touch of poor Lyell's feelings, that it was delightful to improve a sentence, like a painter improving a picture."

The feeling of effort or strain over this piece of work, is shown in a letter to Professor Haeckel :—

"What I shall do in future if I live, Heaven only knows; I ought perhaps to avoid general and large subjects, as too difficult for me with my advancing years, and I suppose enfeebled brain."

At the end of March, in this year, the portrait for which he was sitting to Mr. Ouless was finished. He felt the sittings a great fatigue, in spite of Mr. Ouless's considerate desire to spare him as far as was possible. In a letter to Sir J. D. Hooker he wrote. "I look a very venerable, acute, melancholy old dog; whether I really look so I do not know." The picture is in the possession of the family, and is known to many through M. Rajon's etching. Mr. Ouless's portrait is, in my opinion, the finest representation of my father that has been produced.

The following letter refers to the death of Sir Charles Lyell, which took place on February 22nd, 1875, in his seventy-eighth year.]

*C. Darwin to Miss Buckley (now Mrs. Fisher).**

Down, February 23, 1875.

MY DEAR MISS BUCKLEY,—I am grieved to hear of the death of my old and kind friend, though I knew that it could not be long delayed, and that it was a happy thing that his life should not have been prolonged, as I suppose that his mind would inevitably have suffered. I am glad that Lady

---

* Mrs. Fisher acted as Secretary to Sir Charles Lyell.

Lyell * has been saved this terrible blow.   His death makes me think of the time when I first saw him, and how full of sympathy and interest he was about what I could tell him of coral reefs and South America.   I think that this sympathy with the work of every other naturalist was one of the finest features of his character.   How completely he revolutionised Geology: for I can remember something of pre-Lyellian days.

I never forget that almost everything which I have done in science I owe to the study of his great works.   Well, he has had a grand and happy career, and no one ever worked with a truer zeal in a noble cause.   It seems strange to me that I shall never again sit with him and Lady Lyell at their breakfast.   I am very much obliged to you for having so kindly written to me.

Pray give our kindest remembrances to Miss Lyell, and I hope that she has not suffered much in health, from fatigue and anxiety.

Believe me, my dear Miss Buckley,

Yours very sincerely,

CHARLES DARWIN.

C. Darwin to J. D. Hooker.

Down, February 25 [1875].

MY DEAR HOOKER,—Your letter so full of feeling has interested me greatly.   I cannot say that I felt his [Lyell's] death much, for I fully expected it, and have looked for some little time at his career as finished.

I dreaded nothing so much as his surviving with impaired mental powers.   He was, indeed, a noble man in very many ways; perhaps in none more than in his warm sympathy with the work of others.   How vividly I can recall my first conversation with him, and how he astonished me by his interest in what I told him.   How grand also was his candour and

---

* Lady Lyell died in 1873.

pure love of truth. Well, he is gone, and I feel as if we were all soon to go. . . . I am deeply rejoiced about Westminster Abbey,* the possibility of which had not occurred to me when I wrote before. I did think that his works were the most enduring of all testimonials (as you say) to him ; but then I did not like the idea of his passing away with no outward sign of what scientific men thought of his merits. Now all this is changed, and nothing can be better than Westminster Abbey. Mrs. Lyell has asked me to be one of the pall-bearers, but I have written to say that I dared not, as I should so likely fail in the midst of the ceremony, and have my head whirling off my shoulders. All this affair must have cost you much fatigue and worry, and how I do wish you were out of England. . . .

[In 1881 he wrote to Mrs. Fisher in reference to her article on Sir Charles Lyell in the ' Encyclopædia Britannica ' :—

" For such a publication I suppose you do not want to say much about his private character, otherwise his strong sense of humour and love of society might have been added. Also his extreme interest in the progress of the world, and in the happiness of mankind. Also his freedom from all religious bigotry, though these perhaps would be a superfluity."

The following refers to the Zoological station at Naples, a subject on which my father felt an enthusiastic interest :]

C. Darwin to Anton Dohrn.

Down [1875 ?].

MY DEAR DR. DOHRN,—Many thanks for your most kind letter, I most heartily rejoice at your improved health and at the success of your grand undertaking, which will have so much influence on the progress of Zoology throughout Europe.

If we look to England alone, what capital work has already been done at the Station by Balfour and Ray Lankester. . . .

---

* Sir C. Lyell was buried in Westminster Abbey.

When you come to England, I suppose that you will bring Mrs. Dohrn, and we shall be delighted to see you both here. I have often boasted that I have had a live Uhlan in my house! It will be very interesting to me to read your new views on the ancestry of the Vertebrates. I shall be sorry to give up the Ascidians, to whom I feel profound gratitude; but the great thing, as it appears to me, is that any link whatever should be found between the main divisions of the Animal Kingdom. . . .

C. Darwin to August Weismann.

Down, December 6, 1875.

MY DEAR SIR,—I have been profoundly interested by your essay on Amblystoma,* and think that you have removed a great stumbling-block in the way of Evolution. I once thought of reversion in this case; but in a crude and imperfect manner. I write now to call your attention to the sterility of moths when hatched out of their proper season; I give references in chapter 18 of my 'Variation under Domestication' (vol. ii. p. 157, of English edition), and these cases illustrate, I think, the sterility of Amblystoma. Would it not be worth while to examine the reproductive organs of those individuals of *wingless* Hemiptera which occasionally have wings, as in the case of the bed-bug. I think I have heard that the females of Mutilla sometimes have wings. These cases must be due to reversion. I dare say many anomalous cases will be hereafter explained on the same principle.

I hinted at this explanation in the extraordinary case of the black-shouldered peacock, the so-called *Pavo nigripennis* given in my 'Var. under Domest.;' and I might have been bolder, as the variety is in many respects intermediate between the two known species.

With much respect,
Yours sincerely,
CH. DARWIN.

---

* 'Umwandlung des Axolotl.'

THE VIVISECTION QUESTION.

[It was in November 1875 that my father gave his evidence before the Royal Commission on Vivisection.* I have, therefore, placed together here the matter relating to this subject, irrespective of date. Something has already been said of my father's strong feeling with regard to suffering both in man and beast. It was indeed one of the strongest feelings in his nature, and was exemplified in matters small and great, in his sympathy with the educational miseries of dancing dogs, or in his horror at the sufferings of slaves.†

The remembrance of screams, or other sounds heard in Brazil, when he was powerless to interfere with what he believed to be the torture of a slave, haunted him for years, especially at night. In smaller matters, where he could interfere, he did so vigorously. He returned one day from his walk pale and faint from having seen a horse ill-used, and from the agitation of violently remonstrating with the man. On another occasion he saw a horse-breaker teaching his son to ride, the little boy was frightened and the man was rough ; my father stopped, and jumping out of the carriage reproved the man in no measured terms.

One other little incident may be mentioned, showing that his humanity to animals was well known in his own neighbourhood. A visitor, driving from Orpington to Down, told

---

* See vol. i. p. 118.

† He once made an attempt to free a patient in a mad-house, who (as he wrongly supposed) was sane. He had some correspondence with the gardener at the asylum, and on one occasion he found a letter from a patient enclosed with one from the gardener. The letter was rational in tone and declared that the writer was sane and wrongfully confined.

My father wrote to the Lunacy Commissioners (without explaining the source of his information) and in due time heard that the man had been visited by the Commissioners, and that he was certainly insane. Some time afterwards the patient was discharged, and wrote to thank my father for his interference, adding that he had undoubtedly been insane, when he wrote his former letter.

the man to go faster, "Why," said the driver, "If I had whipped the horse *this* much, driving Mr. Darwin, he would have got out of the carriage and abused me well."

With respect to the special point under consideration,— the sufferings of animals subjected to experiment,—nothing could show a stronger feeling than the following extract from a letter to Professor Ray Lankester (March 22, 1871) :—

"You ask about my opinion on vivisection. I quite agree that it is justifiable for real investigations on physiology ; but not for mere damnable and detestable curiosity. It is a subject which makes me sick with horror, so I will not say another word about it, else I shall not sleep to-night."

An extract from Sir Thomas Farrer's notes shows how strongly he expressed himself in a similar manner in conversation :—

" The last time I had any conversation with him was at my house in Bryanston Square, just before one of his last seizures. He was then deeply interested in the vivisection question ; and what he said made a deep impression on me. He was a man eminently fond of animals and tender to them ; he would not knowingly have inflicted pain on a living creature ; but he entertained the strongest opinion that to prohibit experiments on living animals, would be to put a stop to the knowledge of and the remedies for pain and disease."

The Anti-Vivisection agitation, to which the following letters refer, seems to have become specially active in 1874, as may be seen, e.g. by the index to ' Nature ' for that year, in which the word " Vivisection," suddenly comes into prominence. But before that date the subject had received the earnest attention of biologists. Thus at the Liverpool Meeting of the British Association in 1870, a Committee was appointed, which reported, defining the circumstances and conditions under which, in the opinion of the signatories, experiments on living animals were justifiable. In the spring of 1875, Lord Hartismere introduced a Bill into the Upper House to regulate the course of physiological research. Shortly afterwards a Bill more just towards science in its provisions was introduced to the House of Commons by Messrs. Lyon Playfair, Walpole, and Ashley. It was however, withdrawn on the appointment of a Royal Commission to inquire into the whole question. The Commissioners were Lords Cardwell and Winmarleigh, Mr. W. E. Forster, Sir J. B. Karslake, Mr. Huxley, Professor Erichssen, and Mr. R. H. Hutton : they commenced their inquiry in July, 1875, and the Report was published early in the following year.

In the early summer of 1876, Lord Carnarvon's Bill, entitled, "An Act to amend the Law relating to Cruelty to Animals," was introduced It cannot be denied that the framers of this Bill, yielding to the unreasonable clamour of the public, went far beyond the recommendations of the Royal Commission. As a correspondent in 'Nature' put it (1876, p. 248), "the evidence on the strength of which legislation was recommended went beyond the facts, the Report went beyond the evidence, the Recommendations beyond the Report ; and the Bill can hardly be said to have gone beyond the Recommendations ; but rather to have contradicted them."

The legislation which my father worked for, as described in the following letters, was practically what was introduced as Dr. Lyon Playfair's Bill.]

C. Darwin to Mrs. Litchfield.*

January 4, 1875.

My dear H.—Your letter has led me to think over vivisection (I wish some new word like anæs-section could be invented †) for some hours, and I will jot down my conclusions, which will appear very unsatisfactory to you. I have long thought physiology one of the greatest of sciences, sure sooner,

---

* His daughter.

† He communicated to 'Nature' (Sep. 30, 1880) an article by Dr. Wilder, of Cornell University, an abstract of which was published (p. 517). Dr. Wilder advocated the use of the word ' Callisection ' for painless operations on animals.

or more probably later, greatly to benefit mankind ; but, judging from all other sciences, the benefits will accrue only indirectly in the search for abstract truth. It is certain that physiology can progress only by experiments on living animals. Therefore the proposal to limit research to points of which we can now see the bearings in regard to health, &c., I look at as puerile. I thought at first it would be good to limit vivisection to public laboratories ; but I have heard only of those in London and Cambridge, and I think Oxford ; but probably there may be a few others. Therefore only men living in a few great towns would carry on investigation, and this I should consider a great evil. If private men were permitted to work in their own houses, and required a licence, I do not see who is to determine whether any particular man should receive one. It is young unknown men who are the most likely to do good work. I would gladly punish severely any one who operated on an animal not rendered insensible, if the experiment made this possible ; but here again I do not see that a magistrate or jury could possibly determine such a point. Therefore I conclude, if (as is likely) some experiments have been tried too often, or anæsthetics have not been used when they could have been, the cure must be in the improvement of humanitarian feelings. Under this point of view I have rejoiced at the present agitation. If stringent laws are passed, and this is likely, seeing how unscientific the House of Commons is, and that the gentlemen of England are humane, as long as their sports are not considered, which entailed a hundred or thousand-fold more suffering than the experiments of physiologists—if such laws are passed, the result will assuredly be that physiology, which has been until within the last few years at a standstill in England, will languish or quite cease. It will then be carried on solely on the Continent; and there will be so many the fewer workers on this grand subject, and this I should greatly regret. By the way, F. Balfour, who has worked for two or three years in the laboratory at Cambridge, declares to George that he has never seen an experiment, except with animals rendered insensible.

No doubt the names of Doctors will have great weight with the House of Commons ; but very many practitioners neither know nor care anything about the progress of knowledge. I cannot at present see my way to sign any petition, without hearing what physiologists thought would be its effect, and then judging for myself. I certainly could not sign the paper sent me by Miss Cobbe, with its monstrous (as it seems to me) attack on Virchow for experimenting on the Trichinæ. I am tired and so no more.

Yours affectionately,
CHARLES DARWIN.

C. Darwin to J. D. Hooker.

Down, April 14 [1875].

MY DEAR HOOKER,—I worked all the time in London on the vivisection question ; and we now think it advisable to go further than a mere petition. Litchfield * drew up a sketch of a Bill, the essential features of which have been approved by Sanderson, Simon and Huxley, and from conversation, will, I believe, be approved by Paget, and almost certainly, I think, by Michael Foster. Sanderson, Simon and Paget wish me to see Lord Derby, and endeavour to gain his advocacy with the Home Secretary. Now, if this is carried into effect, it will be of great importance to me to be able to say that the Bill in its essential features has the approval of some half-dozen eminent scientific men. I have therefore asked Litchfield to enclose a copy to you in its first rough form ; and if it is not essentially modified may I say that it meets with your approval as President of the Royal Society ? The object is to protect animals, and at the same time not to injure Physiology, and Huxley and Sanderson's approval almost suffices on this head. Pray let me have a line from you soon.

Yours affectionately,
CHARLES DARWIN.

---

* Mr. R. B. Litchfield, his son-in-law.

[The Physiological Society, which was founded in 1876, was in some measure the outcome of the anti-vivisection movement, since it was this agitation which impressed on Physiologists the need of a centre for those engaged in this particular branch of science. With respect to the Society, my father wrote to Mr. Romanes (May 29, 1876) :—

"I was very much gratified by the wholly unexpected honour of being elected one of the Honorary Members. This mark of sympathy has pleased me to a very high degree."

The following letter appeared in the *Times*, April 18th, 1881 :]

*C. Darwin to Frithiof Holmgren.**

Down, April 14, 1881.

DEAR SIR,—In answer to your courteous letter of April 7, I have no objection to express my opinion with respect to the right of experimenting on living animals. I use this latter expression as more correct and comprehensive than that of vivisection. You are at liberty to make any use of this letter which you may think fit, but if published I should wish the whole to appear. I have all my life been a strong advocate for humanity to animals, and have done what I could in my writings to enforce this duty. Several years ago, when the agitation against physiologists commenced in England, it was asserted that inhumanity was here practised, and useless suffering caused to animals; and I was led to think that it might be advisable to have an Act of Parliament on the subject. I then took an active part in trying to get a Bill passed, such as would have removed all just cause of complaint, and at the same time have left physiologists free to pursue their researches,—a Bill very different from the Act which has since been passed. It is right to add that the investigation of the matter by a Royal Commission proved that the accusations made against our English physiologists

---

* Professor of Physiology at Upsala.

were false. From all that I have heard, however, I fear that in some parts of Europe little regard is paid to the sufferings of animals, and if this be the case, I should be glad to hear of legislation against inhumanity in any such country. On the other hand, I know that physiology cannot possibly progress except by means of experiments on living animals, and I feel the deepest conviction that he who retards the progress of physiology commits a crime against mankind. Any one who remembers, as I can, the state of this science half a century ago, must admit that it has made immense progress, and it is now progressing at an ever-increasing rate. What improvements in medical practice may be directly attributed to physiological research is a question which can be properly discussed only by those physiologists and medical practitioners who have studied the history of their subjects; but, as far as I can learn, the benefits are already great. However this may be, no one, unless he is grossly ignorant of what science has done for mankind, can entertain any doubt of the incalculable benefits which will hereafter be derived from physiology, not only by man, but by the lower animals. Look for instance at Pasteur's results in modifying the germs of the most malignant diseases, from which, as it so happens, animals will in the first place receive more relief than man. Let it be remembered how many lives and what a fearful amount of suffering have been saved by the knowledge gained of parasitic worms through the experiments of Virchow and others on living animals. In the future every one will be astonished at the ingratitude shown, at least in England, to these benefactors of mankind. As for myself, permit me to assure you that I honour, and shall always honour, every one who advances the noble science of physiology.

Dear Sir, yours faithfully,
CHARLES DARWIN.

[In the *Times* of the following day appeared a letter headed "Mr. Darwin and Vivisection," signed by Miss Frances Power Cobbe. To this my father replied in the

Times of April 22, 1881. On the same day he wrote to Mr. Romanes :—

"As I have a fair opportunity, I sent a letter to the *Times* on Vivisection, which is printed to-day. I thought it fair to bear my share of the abuse poured in so atrocious a manner on all physiologists."]

C. Darwin to the Editor of the Times.

Sir,—I do not wish to discuss the views expressed by Miss Cobbe in the letter which appeared in the *Times* of the 19th inst. ; but as she asserts that I have "misinformed" my correspondent in Sweden in saying that "the investigation of the matter by a Royal Commission proved that the accusations made against our English physiologists were false," I will merely ask leave to refer to some other sentences from the Report of the Commission.

(1.) The sentence—"It is not to be doubted that inhumanity may be found in persons of very high position as physiologists," which Miss Cobbe quotes from page 17 of the report, and which, in her opinion, "can necessarily concern English physiologists alone and not foreigners," is immediately followed by the words "We have seen that it was so in Magendie." Magendie was a French physiologist who became notorious some half century ago for his cruel experiments on living animals.

(2). The Commissioners, after speaking of the "general sentiment of humanity" prevailing in this country, say (p. 10) :—

"This principle is accepted generally by the very highly educated men whose lives are devoted either to scientific investigation and education or to the mitigation or the removal of the sufferings of their fellow-creatures ; though differences of degree in regard to its practical application will be easily discernible by those who study the evidence as it has been laid before us."

Again, according to the Commissioners (p. 10) :—

"The secretary of the Royal Society for the Prevention of Cruelty to Animals, when asked whether the general tendency of the scientific world in this country is at variance with humanity, says he believes it to be very different, indeed, from that of foreign physiologists; and while giving it as the opinion of the society that experiments are performed which are in their nature beyond any legitimate province of science, and that the pain which they inflict is pain which it is not justifiable to inflict even for the scientific object in view, he readily acknowledges that he does not know a single case of wanton cruelty, and that in general the English physiologists have used anæsthetics where they think they can do so with safety to the experiment."

I am, Sir, your obedient servant,
CHARLES DARWIN.
April 21.

[In the *Times* of Saturday, April 23, 1881, appeared a letter from Miss Cobbe in reply:]

C. Darwin to G. J. Romanes.

Down, April 25, 1881.

MY DEAR ROMANES,—I was very glad to read your last note with much news interesting to me. But I write now to say how I, and indeed all of us in the house have admired your letter in the *Times*.* It was so simple and direct. I was particularly glad about Burton Sanderson, of whom I have been for several years a great admirer. I was also especially glad to read the last sentences. I have been bothered with several letters, but none abusive. Under a *selfish* point of view I am very glad of the publication of your letter, as I was at first inclined to think that I had done mischief by stirring up the mud. Now I feel sure that I have done good. Mr. Jesse has written to me very politely, he says his Society has had nothing to do with placards and diagrams against

---

* April 25, 1881.—Mr. Romanes defended Dr. Sanderson against the accusations made by Miss Cobbe.

physiology, and I suppose, therefore, that these all originate with Miss Cobbe. . . . . Mr. Jesse complains bitterly that the *Times* will "burke" all his letters to this newspaper, nor am I surprised, judging from the laughable tirades advertised in *Nature*. Ever yours, very sincerely,

CH. DARWIN.

[The next letter refers to a projected conjoint article on vivisection, to which Mr. Romanes wished my father to contribute :]

C. Darwin to G. J. Romanes.

Down, September 2, 1881.

MY DEAR ROMANES,—Your letter has perplexed me beyond all measure. I fully recognise the duty of every one whose opinion is worth anything, expressing his opinion publicly on vivisection; and this made me send my letter to the *Times*. I have been thinking at intervals all morning what I could say, and it is the simple truth that I have nothing worth saying. You and men like you, whose ideas flow freely, and who can express them easily, cannot understand the state of mental paralysis in which I find myself. What is most wanted is a careful and accurate attempt to show what physiology has already done for man, and even still more strongly what there is every reason to believe it will hereafter do. Now I am absolutely incapable of doing this, or of discussing the other points suggested by you.

If you wish for my name (and I should be glad that it should appear with that of others in the same cause), could you not quote some sentence from my letter in the *Times* which I enclose, but please return it. If you thought fit you might say you quoted it with my approval, and that after still further reflection I still abide most strongly in my expressed conviction.

For Heaven's sake, do think of this. I do not grudge the labour and thought; but I could write nothing worth any one reading.

Allow me to demur to your calling your conjoint article a
"symposium" strictly a "drinking party." This seems to me
very bad taste, and I do hope every one of you will avoid any
semblance of a joke on the subject I *know* that words, like
a joke, on this subject have quite disgusted some persons not
at all inimical to physiology. One person lamented to me
that Mr. Simon, in his truly admirable Address at the Medical Congress (by far the best thing which I have read), spoke
of the fantastic *sensuality** (or some such term) of the many
mistaken, but honest men and women who are half mad on
the subject. . . .

[To Dr. Lauder Brunton my father wrote in February
1882 :—

"Have you read Mr. [Edmund] Gurney's articles in the
'Fortnightly'† and 'Cornhill?'‡   They seem to me very
clever, though obscurely written, and I agree with almost
everything he says, except with some passages which appear
to imply that no experiments should be tried unless some immediate good can be predicted, and this is a gigantic mistake
contradicted by the whole history of science."]

---

* 'Transactions of the International Medical Congress,' 1881, vol. iv.
p. 413. The expression "lackadaisical" (not fantastic), and "feeble sensuality," are used with regard to the feelings of the anti-vivisectionists.

† "A chapter in the Ethics of Pain," 'Fortnightly Review,' 1881, vol.
xxx. p. 778.

‡ "An Epilogue on Vivisection," 'Cornhill Magazine,' 1882, vol. xlv.
p. 191.

CHAPTER IX.

MISCELLANEA (*continued*)—A REVIVAL OF GEOLOGICAL WORK
—THE BOOK ON EARTHWORMS—LIFE OF ERASMUS DAR-
WIN—MISCELLANEOUS LETTERS.

1876–1882.

[WE have now to consider the work (other than botanical) which occupied the concluding six years of my father's life. A letter to his old friend Rev. L. Blomefield (Jenyns), written in March, 1877, shows what was my father's estimate of his own powers of work at this time :—

"MY DEAR JENYNS (I see I have forgotten your proper names).—Your extremely kind letter has given me warm pleasure. As one gets old, one's thoughts turn back to the past rather than to the future, and I often think of the pleasant, and to me valuable, hours which I spent with you on the borders of the Fens.

"You ask about my future work; I doubt whether I shall be able to do much more that is new, and I always keep before my mind the example of poor old ——, who in his old age had a cacoethes for writing. But I cannot endure doing nothing, so I suppose that I shall go on as long as I can without obviously making a fool of myself. I have a great mass of matter with respect to variation under nature ; but so much has been published since the appearance of the 'Origin of Species,' that I very much doubt whether I retain power of mind and strength to reduce the mass into a digested whole. I have sometimes thought that I would try, but dread the attempt. . . ."

His prophecy proved to be a true one with regard to any continuation of any general work in the direction of Evolution, but his estimate of powers which could afterwards prove capable of grappling with the 'Power of Movement in Plants,' and with the work on 'Earthworms,' was certainly a low one.

The year 1876, with which the present chapter begins, brought with it a revival of geological work. He had been astonished, as I hear from Professor Judd, and as appears in his letters, to learn that his books on 'Volcanic Islands,' 1844, and on 'South America,' 1846, were still consulted by geologists, and it was a surprise to him that new editions should be required. Both these works were originally published by Messrs. Smith and Elder, and the new edition of 1876 was also brought out by them. This appeared in one volume with the title 'Geological Observations on the Volcanic Islands, and Parts of South America visited during the Voyage of H.M.S. *Beagle.*' He has explained in the preface his reasons for leaving untouched the text of the original editions : " They relate to parts of the world which have been so rarely visited by men of science, that I am not aware that much could be corrected or added from observations subsequently made. Owing to the great progress which Geology has made within recent times, my views on some few points may be somewhat antiquated ; but I have thought it best to leave them as they originally appeared."

It may have been the revival of geological speculation, due to the revision of his early books, that led to his recording the observations of which some account is given in the following letter. Part of it has been published in Professor James Geikie's 'Prehistoric Europe,' chaps. vii. and ix.,* a few verbal alterations having been made at my father's request in the passages quoted. Mr. Geikie lately wrote to me : " The views suggested in his letter as to the origin of the

---

* My father's suggestion is also noticed in Prof. Geikie's address on the 'Ice Age in Europe and North America,' given at Edinburgh, Nov. 20, 1884.

angular gravels, &c., in the South of England will, I believe, come to be accepted as the truth. This question has a much wider bearing than might at first appear. In point of fact it solves one of the most difficult problems in Quaternary Geology—and has already attracted the attention of German geologists."]

C. Darwin to James Geikie.

Down, November 16, 1876.

My dear Sir,—I hope that you will forgive me for troubling you with a very long letter. But first allow me to tell you with what extreme pleasure and admiration I have just finished reading your 'Great Ice Age.' It seems to me admirably done, and most clear. Interesting as many chapters are in the history of the world, I do not think that any one comes [up] nearly to the glacial period or periods. Though I have steadily read much on the subject, your book makes the whole appear almost new to me.

I am now going to mention a small observation, made by me two or three years ago, near Southampton, but not followed out, as I have no strength for excursions. I need say nothing about the character of the drift there (which includes palæolithic celts), for you have described its essential features in a few words at p. 506. It covers the whole country [in an] even plain-like surface, almost irrespective of the present outline of the land.

The coarse stratification has sometimes been disturbed. I find that you allude "to the larger stones often standing on end;" and this is the point which struck me so much. Not only moderately sized angular stones, but small oval pebbles often stand vertically up, in a manner which I have never seen in ordinary gravel beds. This fact reminded me of what occurs near my home, in the stiff red clay, full of unworn flints-over the chalk, which is no doubt the residue left undissolved by rain water. In this clay, flints as long and thin as my arm often stand perpendicularly up; and I have been told by the tank-diggers that it is their "natural position!"

I presume that this position may safely be attributed to the differential movement of parts of the red clay as it subsided very slowly from the dissolution of the underlying chalk; so that the flints arrange themselves in the lines of least resistance. The similar but less strongly marked arrangement of the stones in the drift near Southampton makes me suspect that it also must have slowly subsided: and the notion has crossed my mind that during the commencement and height of the glacial period great beds of frozen snow accumulated over the south of England, and that, during the summer, gravel and stones were washed from the higher land over its surface, and in superficial channels. The larger streams may have cut right through the frozen snow, and deposited gravel in lines at the bottom. But on each succeeding autumn, when the running water failed, I imagine that the lines of drainage would have been filled up by blown snow afterwards congealed, and that, owing to great surface accumulations of snow, it would be a mere chance whether the drainage, together with gravel and sand, would follow the same lines during the next summer. Thus, as I apprehend, alternate layers of frozen snow and drift, in sheets and lines, would ultimately have covered the country to a great thickness, with lines of drift probably deposited in various directions at the bottom by the larger streams. As the climate became warmer, the lower beds of frozen snow would have melted with extreme slowness, and the many irregular beds of interstratified drift would have sunk down with equal slowness; and during this movement the elongated pebbles would have arranged themselves more or less vertically. The drift would also have been deposited almost irrespective of the outline of the underlying land. When I viewed the country I could not persuade myself that any flood, however great, could have deposited such coarse gravel over the almost level platforms between the valleys. My view differs from that of Holst, p. 415 ['Great Ice Age'], of which I had never heard, as his relates to channels cut through glaciers, and mine to beds of drift interstratified with frozen snow where no glaciers existed. The upshot of this long letter is to ask you to keep my notion in your head, and look out for upright pebbles in any lowland country which you may examine, where glaciers have not existed. Or if you think the notion deserves any further thought, but not otherwise, to tell any one of it, for instance Mr. Skertchly, who is examining such districts. Pray forgive me for writing so long a letter, and again thanking you for the great pleasure derived from your book,

            I remain yours very faithfully,

                       CH. DARWIN.

P.S. . . . I am glad that you have read Blytt; * his paper seemed to me a most important contribution to Botanical Geography. How curious that the same conclusions should have been arrived at by Mr. Skertchly, who seems to be a first-rate observer ; and this implies, as I always think, a sound theoriser.

I have told my publisher to send you in two or three days a copy (second edition) of my geological work during the voyage of the *Beagle.* The sole point which would perhaps interest you is about the steppe-like plains of Patagonia.

For many years past I have had fearful misgivings that it must have been the level of the sea, and not that of the land which has changed.

I read a few months ago your [brother's] very interesting life of Murchison.† Though I have always thought that he ranked next to W. Smith in the classification of formations, and though I knew how kind-hearted [he was], yet the book has raised him greatly in my respect, notwithstanding his foibles and want of broad philosophical views.

[The only other geological work of his later years was embodied in his book on earthworms (1881), which may

---

* Axel Blytt.—' Essay on the Immigration of the Norwegian Flora during alternate rainy and dry Seasons.' Christiania, 1876.

† By Mr. Archibald Geikie.

therefore be conveniently considered in this place. This subject was one which had interested him many years before this date, and in 1838 a paper on the formation of mould was published in the Proceedings of the Geological Society (see vol. i. p. 255).

Here he showed that "fragments of burnt marl, cinders, &c., which had been thickly strewed over the surface of several meadows were found after a few years lying at a depth of some inches beneath the turf, but still forming a layer." For the explanation of this fact, which forms the central idea of the geological part of the book, he was indebted to his uncle Josiah Wedgwood, who suggested that worms, by bringing earth to the surface in their castings, must undermine any objects lying on the surface and cause an apparent sinking.

In the book of 1881 he extended his observations on this burying action, and devised a number of different ways of checking his estimates as to the amount of work done.* He also added a mass of observations on the habits, natural history and intelligence of worms, a part of the work which added greatly to its popularity.

In 1877 Sir Thomas Farrer had discovered close to his garden the remains of a building of Roman-British times, and thus gave my father the opportunity of seeing for himself the effects produced by earthworms' work on the old concrete-floors, walls, &c. On his return he wrote to Sir Thomas Farrer :—

"I cannot remember a more delightful week than the last. I know very well that E. will not believe me, but the worms were by no means the sole charm."

---

* He received much valuable help from Dr. King, of the Botanical Gardens, Calcutta. The following passage is from a letter to Dr. King, dated January 18, 1873 :—

"I really do not know how to thank you enough for the immense trouble which you have taken. You have attended *exactly* and *fully* to the points about which I was most anxious. If I had been each evening by your side, I could not have suggested anything else."

In the autumn of 1880, when the 'Power of Movement in Plants' was nearly finished, he began once more on the subject. He wrote to Professor Carus (September 21) :—

"In the intervals of correcting the press, I am writing a very little book, and have done nearly half of it. Its title will be (as at present designed) 'The Formation of Vegetable Mould through the Action of Worms.'* As far as I can judge it will be a curious little book."

The manuscript was sent to the printers in April, 1881, and when the proof-sheets were coming in he wrote to Professor Carus : "The subject has been to me a hobby-horse, and I have perhaps treated it in foolish detail."

It was published on October 10, and 2000 copies were sold at once. He wrote to Sir J. D. Hooker, "I am glad that you approve of the 'Worms.' When in old days I used to tell you whatever I was doing, if you were at all interested, I always felt as most men do when their work is finally published."

To Mr. Mellard Reade he wrote (November 8) : "It has been a complete surprise to me how many persons have cared for the subject." And to Mr. Dyer (in November) : "My book has been received with almost laughable enthusiasm, and 3500 copies have been sold ! ! !" Again, to his friend Mr. Anthony Rich, he wrote on February 4, 1882, "I have been plagued with an endless stream of letters on the subject; most of them very foolish and enthusiastic; but some containing good facts which I have used in correcting yesterday the 'Sixth Thousand.'" The popularity of the book may be roughly estimated by the fact that, in the three years following its publication, 8500 copies were sold—a sale relatively greater than that of the 'Origin of Species.'

It is not difficult to account for its success with the non-scientific public. Conclusions so wide and so novel, and so easily understood, drawn from the study of creatures so fa-

---

* The full title is 'The Formation of Vegetable Mould through the Action of Worms with Observations on their Habits,' 1881.

miliar, and treated with unabated vigor and freshness, may
well have attracted many readers. A reviewer remarks : " In
the eyes of most men . . . the earthworm is a mere blind,
dumb, senseless, and unpleasantly slimy annelid. Mr. Darwin
undertakes to rehabilitate his character, and the earthworm
steps forth at once as an intelligent and beneficent person-
age, a worker of vast geological changes, a planer down of
mountain sides. . . . a friend of man. . . and an ally of the
Society for the preservation of ancient monuments." The *St.
James's Gazette*, October 17, 1881, pointed out that the teaching of the cumulative importance of the infinitely little is the
point of contact between this book and the author's previous
work.

One more book remains to be noticed, the ' Life of Erasmus Darwin.'

In February 1879 an essay by Dr. Ernst Krause, on the
scientific work of Erasmus Darwin, appeared in the evolutionary journal, ' Kosmos.' The number of ' Kosmos ' in
question was a " Gratulationsheft," * or special congratulatory
issue in honour of my father's birthday, so that Dr. Krause's
essay, glorifying the older evolutionist, was quite in its place.
He wrote to Dr. Krause, thanking him cordially for the honour paid to Erasmus, and asking his permission to publish †
an English translation of the Essay.

His chief reason for writing a notice of his grandfather's
life was " to contradict flatly some calumnies by Miss Sew-
ard." This appears from a letter of March 27, 1879, to his
cousin Reginald Darwin, in which he asks for any documents
and letters which might throw light on the character of Erasmus. This led to Mr. Reginald Darwin placing in my father's
hands a quantity of valuable material, including a curious

---

* The same number contains a good biographical sketch of my father,
of which the material was to a large extent supplied by him to the writer,
Professor Preyer of Jena. The article contains an excellent list of my
father's publications.

† The wish to do so was shared by his brother, Erasmus Darwin the
younger, who continued to be associated with the project.

folio common-place book, of which he wrote : " I have been deeply interested by the great book, ... reading and looking at it is like having communion with the dead . . . . [it] has taught me a good deal about the occupations and tastes of our grandfather." A subsequent letter (April 8) to the same correspondent describes the source of a further supply of material :—

"Since my last letter I have made a strange discovery ; for an old box from my father marked " Old Deeds," and which consequently I had never opened, I found full of letters—hundreds from Dr. Erasmus—and others from old members of the Family : some few very curious. Also a drawing of Elston before it was altered, about 1750, of which I think I will give a copy."

Dr. Krause's contribution formed the second part of the ' Life of Erasmus Darwin,' my father supplying a "preliminary notice." This expression on the title-page is somewhat misleading ; my father's contribution is more than half the book, and should have been described as a biography. Work of this kind was new to him, and he wrote doubtfully to Mr. Thiselton Dyer, June 18th : " God only knows what I shall make of his life, it is such a new kind of work to me." The strong interest he felt about his forebears helped to give zest to the work, which became a decided enjoyment to him. With the general public the book was not markedly successful, but many of his friends recognised its merits. Sir J. D. Hooker was one of these, and to him my father wrote, " Your praise of the Life of Dr. D. has pleased me exceedingly, for I despised my work, and thought myself a perfect fool to have undertaken such a job."

To Mr. Galton, too, he wrote, November 14 :—

" I am *extremely* glad that you approve of the little ' Life ' of our grandfather, for I have been repenting that I ever undertook it, as the work was quite beyond my tether."

The publication of the ' Life of Erasmus Darwin ' led to an attack by Mr. Samuel Butler, which amounted to a charge of falsehood against my father. After consulting his friends, he came to the determination to leave the charge unanswered, as unworthy of his notice.*   Those who wish to know more of the matter, may gather the facts of the case from Ernst Krause's 'Charles Darwin,' and they will find Mr. Butler's statement of his grievance in the *Athenæum*, January 31, 1880, and in the *St. James's Gazette*, December 8, 1880.   The affair gave my father much pain, but the warm sympathy of those whose opinion he respected soon helped him to let it pass into a well-merited oblivion.

The following letter refers to M. J. H. Fabre's 'Souvenirs Entomologiques.'   It may find a place here, as it contains a defence of Erasmus Darwin on a small point.   The postscript is interesting, as an example of one of my father's bold ideas both as to experiment and theory :]

C. Darwin to J. H. Fabre.

Down, January 31, 1880.

MY DEAR SIR,—I hope that you will permit me to have the satisfaction of thanking you cordially for the lively pleasure which I have derived from reading your book.   Never have the wonderful habits of insects been more vividly described, and it is almost as good to read about them as to see them.   I feel sure that you would not be unjust to even an insect, much less to a man.   Now, you have been misled by some translator, for my grandfather, Erasmus Darwin, states ('Zoonomia,' vol. i. p. 183, 1794) that it was a wasp (guêpe) which he saw cutting off the wings of a large fly.   I have no doubt that you are right in saying that the wings are generally cut off instinctively ; but in the case described by my grandfather, the wasp, after cutting off the two ends of the body, rose in the air, and was turned round by the wind ; he then alighted and cut off the wings.   I must believe, with Pierre Huber, that insects have " une petite dose de raison."

---

* He had, in a letter to Mr. Butler, expressed his regret at the over-sight which caused so much offence.

In the next edition of your book, I hope that you will alter *part* of what you say about my grandfather.

I am sorry that you are so strongly opposed to the Descent theory ; I have found the searching for the history of each structure or instinct an excellent aid to observation ; and wonderful observer as you are, it would suggest new points to you. If I were to write on the evolution of instincts. I could make good use of some of the facts which you give. Permit me to add, that when I read the last sentence in your book, I sympathised deeply with you.*

With the most sincere respect,
I remain, dear Sir, yours faithfully,
CHARLES DARWIN.

P.S.—Allow me to make a suggestion in relation to your wonderful account of insects finding their way home. I formerly wished to try it with pigeons : namely, to carry the insects in their paper " cornets," about a hundred paces in the opposite direction to that which you ultimately intended to carry them ; but before turning round to return, to put the insect in a circular box, with an axle which could be made to revolve very rapidly, first in one direction, and then in another, so as to destroy for a time all sense of direction in the insects. I have sometimes *imagined* that animals may feel in which direction they were at the first start carried.†
If this plan failed, I had intended placing the pigeons within

---

* The book is intended as a memorial of the early death of M. Fabre's son, who had been his father's assistant in his observations on insect life.

† This idea was a favourite one with him, and he has described in ' Nature' (vol. vii. 1873, p. 360) the behaviour of his cob Tommy, in whom he fancied he detected a sense of direction. The horse had been taken by rail from Kent to the Isle of Wight ; when there he exhibited a marked desire to go eastward, even when his stable lay in the opposite direction. In the same volume of ' Nature,' p. 417, is a letter on the ' Origin of Certain Instincts,' which contains a short discussion on the sense of direction.

an induction coil, so as to disturb any magnetic or dia-magnetic sensibility, which it seems just possible that they may possess.   C. D.

[During the latter years of my father's life there was a growing tendency in the public to do him honour. In 1877 he received the honorary degree of LL.D. from the University of Cambridge. The degree was conferred on November 17, and with the customary Latin speech from the Public Orator, concluding with the words : " Tu vero, qui leges naturæ tam docte illustraveris, legum doctor nobis esto."

The honorary degree led to a movement being set on foot in the University to obtain some permanent memorial of my father. A sum of about £400 was subscribed, and after the rejection of the idea that a bust would be the best memorial, a picture was determined on. In June 1879 he sat to Mr. W. Richmond for the portrait in the possession of the University, now placed in the Library of the philosophical Society at Cambridge. He is represented seated in his Doctor's gown, the head turned towards the spectator : the picture has many admirers, but, according to my own view, neither the attitude nor the expression are characteristic of my father.

A similar wish on the part of the Linnean Society—with which my father was so closely associated—led to his sitting in August, 1881, to Mr. John Collier, for the portrait now in the possession of the Society. Of the artist, he wrote, " Collier was the most considerate, kind and pleasant painter a sitter could desire." The portrait represents him standing facing the observer in the loose cloak so familiar to those who knew him, and with his slouch hat in his hand. Many of those who knew his face most intimately, think that Mr. Collier's picture is the best of the portraits, and in this judgment the sitter himself was inclined to agree. According to my feeling it is not so simple or strong a representation of him as that given by Mr. Ouless. There is a certain expression in Mr. Collier's portrait which I am inclined to consider an exaggeration of the almost painful expression which

Professor Cohn has described in my father's face, and which
he had previously noticed in Humboldt. Professor Cohn's
remarks occur in a pleasantly written account of a visit to
Down* in 1876, published in the *Breslauer Zeitung*, April 23,
1882.

Besides the Cambridge degree, he received about the same
time honours of an academic kind from some foreign societies.

On August 5, 1878, he was elected a Corresponding Member of the French Institute † in the Botanical Section, ‡ and
wrote to Dr. Asa Gray :—

"I see that we are both elected Corresponding Members

---

* In this connection may be mentioned a visit (1881) from another distinguished German, Hans Richter. The occurrence is otherwise worthy
of mention, inasmuch as it led to the publication, after my father's death,
of Herr Richter's recollections of the visit. The sketch is simply and sym-
pathetically written, and the author has succeeded in giving a true picture
of my father as he lived at Down. It appeared in the *Neue Tagblatt* of
Vienna, and was republished by Dr. O. Zacharias in his 'Charles R. Darwin,' Berlin, 1882.

† "Lyell always spoke of it as a great scandal that Darwin was so long
kept out of the French Institute. As he said, even if the development
hypothesis were objected to, Darwin's original works on Coral Reefs, the
Cirripedia, and other subjects, constituted a more than sufficient claim."—
From Professor Judd's notes.

‡ The statement has been more than once published that he was
elected to the Zoological Section, but this was not the case.
He received twenty-six votes out of a possible 39, five blank papers
were sent in, and eight votes were recorded for the other candidates.
In 1872 an attempt had been made to elect him to the Section of Zoology, when, however, he only received 15 out of 48 votes, and Lovén was
chosen for the vacant place. It appears ('Nature,' August 1, 1872) that
an eminent member of the Academy wrote to *Les Mondes* to the following effect :—

"What has closed the doors of the Academy to Mr. Darwin is that the
science of those of his books which have made his chief title to fame—the
'Origin of Species,' and still more the 'Descent of Man,' is not science,
but a mass of assertions and absolutely gratuitous hypotheses, often evidently fallacious. This kind of publication and these theories are a bad
example, which a body that respects itself cannot encourage."

of the Institute. It is rather a good joke that I should be elected in the Botanical Section, as the extent of my knowledge is little more than that a daisy is a Compositous plant and a pea a Leguminous one."

In the early part of the same year he was elected a Corresponding Member of the Berlin Academy of Sciences, and he wrote (March 12) to Professor Du Bois Reymond, who had proposed him for election :—

"I thank you sincerely for your most kind letter, in which you announce the great honour conferred on me. The knowledge of the names of the illustrious men, who seconded the proposal is even a greater pleasure to me than the honour itself."

The seconders were Helmholtz, Peters, Ewald, Pringsheim and Virchow.

In 1879 he received the Baly Medal of the Royal College of Physicians.*

Again in 1879 he received from the Royal Academy of Turin the *Bressa* Prize for the years 1875–78, amounting to the sum of 12,000 francs. In the following year he received on his birthday, as on previous occasions, a kind letter of congratulation from Dr. Dohrn of Naples. In writing (February 15th) to thank him and the other naturalists at the Zoological Station, my father added :—

"Perhaps you saw in the papers that the Turin Society honoured me to an extraordinary degree by awarding me the *Bressa* Prize. Now it occurred to me that if your station

---

* The visit to London, necessitated by the presentation of the Baly Medal, was combined with a visit to Miss Forster's house at Abinger, in Surrey, and this was the occasion of the following characteristic letter:— "I must write a few words to thank you cordially for lending us your house. It was a most kind thought, and has pleased me greatly; but I know well that I do not deserve such kindness from any one. On the other hand, no one can be too kind to my dear wife, who is worth her weight in gold many times over, and she was anxious that I should get some complete rest, and here I cannot rest. Your house will be a delightful haven, and again I thank you truly."

wanted some pieces of apparatus, of about the value of £100, I should very much like to be allowed to pay for it. Will you be so kind as to keep this in mind, and if any want should occur to you, I would send you a cheque at any time."

I find from my father's accounts that £100 was presented to the Naples Station.

He received also several tokens of respect and sympathy of a more private character from various sources. With regard to such incidents and to the estimation of the public generally, his attitude may be illustrated by a passage from a letter to Mr. Romanes :—*

"You have indeed passed a most magnificent eulogium upon me, and I wonder that you were not afraid of hearing 'oh! oh!' or some other sign of disapprobation. Many persons think that what I have done in science has been much overrated, and I very often think so myself; but my comfort is that I have never consciously done anything to gain applause. Enough and too much about my dear self."

Among such expressions of regard he valued very highly the two photographic albums received from Germany and Holland on his birthday, 1877. Herr Emil Rade of Münster, originated the idea of the German birthday gift, and undertook the necessary arrangements. To him my father wrote (February 16, 1877) :—

"I hope that you will inform the one hundred and fifty-four men of science, including some of the most highly honoured names in the world, how grateful I am for their kindness and generous sympathy in having sent me their photographs on my birthday."

To Professor Haeckel he wrote (February 16, 1877) :—

"The album has just arrived quite safe. It is most superb.† It is by far the greatest honour which I have ever re-

---

* The lecture referred to was given at the Dublin meeting of the British Association.

† The album is magnificently bound and decorated with a beautifully illuminated title page, the work of an artist, Herr A. Fitger of Bremen, who also contributed the dedicatory poem.

ceived, and my satisfaction has been greatly enhanced by your most kind letter of February 9. . . . I thank you all from my heart. I have written by this post to Herr Rade, and I hope he will somehow manage to thank all my generous friends."

To Professor A. van Bemmelen he wrote, on receiving a similar present from a number of distinguished men and lovers of Natural History in the Netherlands :—

"SIR,—I received yesterday the magnificent present of the album, together with your letter. I hope that you will endeavour to find some means to express to the two hundred and seventeen distinguished observers and lovers of natural science, who have sent me their photographs, my gratitude for their extreme kindness. I feel deeply gratified by this gift, and I do not think that any testimonial more honourable to me could have been imagined. I am well aware that my books could never have been written, and would not have made any impression on the public mind, had not an immense amount of material been collected by a long series of admirable observers ; and it is to them that honour is chiefly due. I suppose that every worker at science occasionally feels depressed, and doubts whether what he has published has been worth the labour which it has cost him, but for the few remaining years of my life, whenever I want cheering, I will look at the portraits of my distinguished co-workers in the field of science, and remember their generous sympathy. When I die, the album will be a most precious bequest to my children. I must further express my obligation for the very interesting history contained in your letter of the progress of opinion in the Netherlands, with respect to Evolution, the whole of which is quite new to me. I must again thank all my kind friends, from my heart, for their ever-memorable testimonial, and I remain, Sir,

Your obliged and grateful servant,

CHARLES R. DARWIN."

[In the June of the following year (1878) he was gratified

by learning that the Emperor of Brazil had expressed a wish to meet him. Owing to absence from home my father was unable to comply with this wish; he wrote to Sir J. D. Hooker :—

"The Emperor has done so much for science, that every scientific man is bound to show him the utmost respect, and I hope that you will express in the strongest language, and which you can do with entire truth, how greatly I feel honoured by his wish to see me; and how much I regret my absence from home."

Finally it should be mentioned that in 1880 he received an address personally presented by members of the Council of the Birmingham Philosophical Society, as well as a memorial from the Yorkshire Naturalist Union presented by some of the members, headed by Dr. Sorby. He also received in the same year a visit from some of the members of the Lewisham and Blackheath Scientific Association,—a visit which was, I think, enjoyed by both guests and host.]

MISCELLANEOUS LETTERS—1876–1882.

[The chief incident of a personal kind (not already dealt with) in the years which we are now considering was the death of his brother Erasmus, who died at his house in Queen Anne Street, on August 26th, 1881. My father wrote to Sir J. D. Hooker (Aug. 30) :—

"The death of Erasmus is a very heavy loss to all of us, for he had a most affectionate disposition. He always appeared to me the most pleasant and clearest headed man, whom I have ever known. London will seem a strange place to me without his presence; I am deeply glad that he died without any great suffering. after a very short illness from mere weakness and not from any definite disease.*

"I cannot quite agree with you about the death of the old

---

* "He was not, I think, a happy man, and for many years did not value life, though never complaining."—From a letter to Sir Thomas Farrer.

and young.   Death in the latter case, when there is a bright future ahead, causes grief never to be wholly obliterated."

An incident of a happy character may also be selected for especial notice, since it was one which strongly moved my father's sympathy. A letter (Dec. 17, 1879) to Sir Joseph Hooker shows that the possibility of a Government Pension being conferred on Mr. Wallace first occurred to my father at this time.   The idea was taken up by others, and my father's letters show that he felt the most lively interest in the success of the plan.   He wrote, for instance, to Mrs. Fisher, " I hardly ever wished for anything more than I do for the success of our plan."   He was deeply pleased when this thoroughly deserved honour was bestowed on his friend, and wrote to the same correspondent (January 7, 1881), on receiving a letter from Mr. Gladstone announcing the fact : " How extraordinarily kind of Mr. Gladstone to find time to write under the present circumstances.*   Good heavens ! how pleased I am ! ' '

The letters which follow are of a miscellaneous character and refer principally to the books he read, and to his minor writings.]

C. Darwin to Miss Buckley (Mrs. Fisher).

Down, February 11 [1876].

MY DEAR MISS BUCKLEY,—You must let me have the pleasure of saying that I have just finished reading with very great interest your new book.†   The idea seems to me a capital one, and as far as I can judge very well carried out. There is much fascination in taking a bird's eye view of all the grand leading steps in the progress of science.   At first I regretted that you had not kept each science more separate ; but I dare say you found it impossible.   I have hardly any

---

* Mr. Gladstone was then in office, and the letter must have been written when he was overwhelmed with business connected with the opening of Parliament (Jan. 6).

† ' A Short History of Natural Science.'

criticisms, except that I think you ought to have introduced Murchison as a great classifier of formations, second only to W. Smith. You have done full justice, and not more than justice, to our dear old master, Lyell. Perhaps a little more ought to have been said about botany, and if you should ever add this, you would find Sachs' 'History,' lately published, very good for your purpose.

You have crowned Wallace and myself with much honour and glory. I heartily congratulate you on having produced so novel and interesting a work, and remain,

My dear Miss Buckley, yours very faithfully,

CH. DARWIN.

C. Darwin to A. R. Wallace.

[Hopedene]*, June 5, 1876.

MY DEAR WALLACE,—I must have the pleasure of expressing to you my unbounded admiration of your book,† tho' I have read only to page 184—my object having been to do as little as possible while resting   I feel sure that you have laid a broad and safe foundation for all future work on Distribution. How interesting it will be to see hereafter plants treated in strict relation to your views ; and then all insects, pulmonate molluscs and fresh-water fishes, in greater detail than I suppose you have given to these lower animals. The point which has interested me most, but I do not say the most valuable point, is your protest against sinking imaginary continents in a quite reckless manner, as was stated by Forbes, followed, alas, by Hooker, and caricatured by Wollaston and [Andrew] Murray ! By the way, the main impression that the latter author has left on my mind is his utter want of all scientific judgment. I have lifted up my voice against the above view with no avail, but I have no doubt that you will succeed, owing to your new arguments and the coloured chart. Of a special value, as it seems to me, is the conclusion

---

* Mr. Hensleigh Wedgwood's house in Surrey.

† 'Geographical Distribution,' 1876.

that we must determine the areas, chiefly by the nature of the mammals. When I worked many years ago on this subject, I doubted much whether the now called Palæarctic and Nearctic regions ought to be separated; and I determined if I made another region that it should be Madagascar. I have, therefore, been able to appreciate your evidence on these points. What progress Palæontology has made during the last 20 years; but if it advances at the same rate in the future, our views on the migration and birth-place of the various groups will, I fear, be greatly altered. I cannot feel quite easy about the Glacial period, and the extinction of large mammals, but I must hope that you are right. I think you will have to modify your belief about the difficulty of dispersal of land molluscs; I was interrupted when beginning to experimentize on the just hatched young adhering to the feet of ground-roosting birds. I differ on one other point, viz. in the belief that there must have existed a Tertiary Antarctic continent, from which various forms radiated to the southern extremities of our present continents. But I could go on scribbling for ever. You have written, as I believe, a grand and memorable work which will last for years as the foundation for all future treatises on Geographical Distribution. My dear Wallace, yours very sincerely,

CHARLES DARWIN.

P.S.—You have paid me the highest conceivable compliment, by what you say of your work in relation to my chapters on distribution in the 'Origin,' and I heartily thank you for it.

[The following letters illustrate my father's power of taking a vivid interest in work bearing on Evolution, but unconnected with his own special researches at the time. The books referred to in the first letter are Professor Weismann's 'Studien zur Descendenzlehre,' * being part of the series of

---

* My father contributed a prefatory note to Mr. Meldola's translation of Prof. Weismann's 'Studein,' 1880–81.

essays by which the author has done such admirable service
to the cause of evolution :]

C. Darwin to Aug. Weismann.

January 12, 1877.

. . . I read German so slowly, and have had lately to read
several other papers, so that I have as yet finished only half
of your first essay and two-thirds of your second. They
have excited my interest and admiration in the highest degree, and whichever I think of last, seems to me the most
valuable. I never expected to see the coloured marks on
caterpillars so well explained ; and the case of the ocelli delights me especially. . . .

. . . There is one other subject which has always seemed
to me more difficult to explain than even the colours of caterpillars, and that is the colour of birds' eggs, and I wish you
would take this up.

C. Darwin to Melchior Neumayr,* Vienna.

Down, Beckenham, Kent, March 9, 1877.

DEAR SIR,—From having been obliged to read other
books, I finished only yesterday your essay on ' Die Congerien,' &c.†

I hope that you will allow me to express my gratitude for
the pleasure and instruction which I have derived from reading it. It seems to me to be an admirable work ; and is by
far the best case which I have ever met with, showing the
direct influence of the conditions of life on the organization.

Mr. Hyatt, who has been studying the Hilgendorf case,
writes to me with respect to the conclusions at which he has
arrived, and these are nearly the same as yours. He insists
that closely similar forms may be derived from distinct lines
of descent ; and this is what I formerly called analogical
variation. There can now be no doubt that species may become greatly modified through the direct action of the envi-

---

* Professor of Palæontology at Vienna.

† ' Die Congerien und Paludinenschichten Slavoniens,' 4to, 1875.

ronment. I have some excuse for not having formerly insisted more strongly on this head in my 'Origin of Species,' as most of the best facts have been observed since its publication.

With my renewed thanks for your most interesting essay, and with the highest respect, I remain, dear Sir,

Yours very faithfully,

CHARLES DARWIN.

C. Darwin to E. S. Morse.

Down, April 23, 1877.

MY DEAR SIR,—You must allow me just to tell you how very much I have been interested with the excellent Address * which you have been so kind as to send me, and which I had much wished to read. I believe that I had read all, or very nearly all, the papers by your countrymen to which you refer, but I have been fairly astonished at their number and importance when seeing them thus put together. I quite agree about the high value of Mr. Allen's works,† as showing how much change may be expected apparently through the direct action of the conditions of life. As for the fossil remains in the West, no words will express how wonderful they are. There is one point which I regret that you did not make clear in your Address, namely what is the meaning and importance of Professors Cope and Hyatt's views on acceleration and retardation. I have endeavoured, and given up in despair, the attempt to grasp their meaning.

Permit me to thank you cordially for the kind feeling shown towards me through your Address, and I remain, my dear Sir,

Yours faithfully,

CH. DARWIN.

---

* "What American Zoologists have done for Evolution," an Address to the American Association for the Advancement of Science, August, 1876. Vol. xxv. of the Proceedings of the Association.

† Mr. J. A. Allen shows the existence of geographical races of birds and mammals. Proc. Boston Soc. Nat. Hist. vol. xv.

[The next letter refers to his 'Biographical Sketch of an Infant,' written from notes made 37 years previously, and published in 'Mind,' July, 1877. The article attracted a good deal of attention, and was translated at the time in 'Kosmos,' and the 'Revue Scientifique,' and has been recently published in Dr. Krause's 'Gesammelte kleinere Schriften von Charles Darwin,' 1887 :]

*C. Darwin to G. Croom Robertson.**

Down, April 27, 1877.

DEAR SIR,—I hope that you will be so good as to take the trouble to read the enclosed MS., and if you think it fit for publication in your admirable journal of 'Mind,' I shall be gratified. If you do not think it fit, as is very likely, will you please to return it to me. I hope that you will read it in an extra critical spirit, as I cannot judge whether it is worth publishing from having been so much interested in watching the dawn of the several faculties in my own infant. I may add that I should never have thought of sending you the MS., had not M. Taine's article appeared in your Journal.† If my MS. is printed, I think that I had better see a proof. I remain, dear Sir,

Yours faithfully,
CH. DARWIN.

[The two following extracts show the lively interest he preserved in diverse fields of inquiry. Professor Cohn, of Breslau had mentioned, in a letter, Koch's researches on Splenic Fever, my father replied, January 3 :—

"I well remember saying to myself, between twenty and thirty years ago, that if ever the origin of any infectious disease could be proved, it would be the greatest triumph to science ; and now I rejoice to have seen the triumph."

---

* The editor of 'Mind.'

† 1877, p. 252. The original appeared in the 'Revue Philosophique' 1876.

In the spring he received a copy of Dr. E. von Mojsisovics' 'Dolomit Riffe,' his letter to the author (June 1, 1878) is interesting as bearing on the influence of his own work on the methods of geology.

"I have at last found time to read the first chapter of your 'Dolomit Riffe,' and have been *exceedingly* interested by it. What a wonderful change in the future of Geological chronology you indicate, by assuming the descent theory to be established, and then taking the graduated changes of the same group of organisms as the true standard! I never hoped to live to see such a step even proposed by any one."

Another geological research which roused my father's admiration was Mr. D. Mackintosh's work on erratic blocks. Apart from its intrinsic merit the work keenly excited his sympathy from the conditions under which it was executed, Mr. Mackintosh being compelled to give nearly his whole time to tuition. The following passage is from a letter to Mr. Mackintosh of October 9, 1879, and refers to his paper in the Journal of the Geological Society, 1878 :—

"I hope that you will allow me to have the pleasure of thanking you for the very great pleasure which I have derived from just reading your paper on erratic blocks. The map is wonderful, and what labour each of those lines show! I have thought for some years that the agency of floating ice, which nearly half a century ago was overrated, has of late been underrated. You are the sole man who has ever noticed the distinction suggested by me * between flat or planed scored rocks, and mammillated scored rocks."]

C. Darwin to C. Ridley.

Down, November 28, 1878.

DEAR SIR,—I just skimmed through Dr. Pusey's sermon, as published in the *Guardian*, but it did [not] seem to me

---

* In his paper on the 'Ancient Glaciers of Carnarvonshire,' Phil. Mag xxi. 1842. See p. 187.

worthy of any attention. As I have never answered criticisms excepting those made by scientific men, I am not willing that this letter should be published; but I have no objection to your saying that you sent me the three questions, and that I answered that Dr. Pusey was mistaken in imagining that I wrote the 'Origin' with any relation whatever to Theology. I should have thought that this would have been evident to any one who had taken the trouble to read the book, more especially as in the opening lines of the introduction I specify how the subject arose in my mind. This answer disposes of your two other questions; but I may add that many years ago, when I was collecting facts for the 'Origin,' my belief in what is called a personal God was as firm as that of Dr. Pusey himself, and as to the eternity of matter I have never troubled myself about such insoluble questions. Dr. Pusey's attack will be as powerless to retard by a day the belief in Evolution, as were the virulent attacks made by divines fifty years ago against Geology, and the still older ones of the Catholic Church against Galileo, for the public is wise enough always to follow Scientific men when they agree on any subject; and now there is almost complete unanimity amongst Biologists about Evolution, though there is still considerable difference as to the means, such as how far natural selection has acted, and how far external conditions, or whether there exists some mysterious innate tendency to perfectability. I remain, dear Sir,

Yours faithfully,
CH. DARWIN.

[Theologians were not the only adversaries of freedom in science. On Sept. 22, 1877, Prof. Virchow delivered an address at the Munich meeting of German Naturalists and Physicians, which had the effect of connecting Socialism with the Descent theory. This point of view was taken up by anti-evolutionists to such an extent that, according to Haeckel, the *Kreuz Zeitung* threw "all the blame of" the "treasonable attempts of the democrats Hödel and Nobiling . . .

directly on the theory of Descent." Prof. Haeckel replied
with vigour and ability in his 'Freedom in Science and
Teaching' (Eng. Transl. 1879), an essay which must have
the sympathy of all lovers of freedom.

The following passage from a letter (December 26, 1879)
to Dr. Scherzer, the author of the 'Voyage of the *Novara*,'
gives a hint of my father's views on this once burning question : —

"What a foolish idea seems to prevail in Germany on the
connection between Socialism and Evolution through Natural Selection."]

*C. Darwin to H. N. Moseley.**

Down, January 20, 1879.

DEAR MOSELEY,—I have just received your book, and I
declare that never in my life have I seen a dedication which
I admired so much.† Of course I am not a fair judge, but I
hope that I speak dispassionately, though you have touched
me in my very tenderest point, by saying that my old Journal
mainly gave you the wish to travel as a Naturalist. I shall
begin to read your book this very evening, and am sure that
I shall enjoy it much.

Yours very sincerely,

CH. DARWIN.

C. Darwin to H. N. Moseley.

Down, February 4, 1879.

DEAR MOSELEY,—I have at last read every word of your
book, and it has excited in me greater interest than any other

---

* Professor of Zoology at Oxford. The book alluded to is Prof. Moseley's 'Notes by a Naturalist on the *Challenger*.'

† "To Charles Darwin, Esquire, LL. D., F. R. S., &c., from the study
of whose 'Journal of Researches' I mainly derived my desire to travel
round the world ; to the development of whose theory I owe the principal pleasures and interests of my life, and who has personally given me
much kindly encouragement in the prosecution of my studies, this book is,
by permission, gratefully dedicated."

scientific book which I have read for a long time. You will perhaps be surprised how slow I have been, but my head prevents me reading except at intervals. If I were asked which parts have interested me most, I should be somewhat puzzled to answer. I fancy that the general reader would prefer your account of Japan. For myself I hesitate between your discussions and description of the Southern ice, which seems to me admirable, and the last chapter which contained many facts and views new to me, though I had read your papers on the stony Hydroid Corals, yet your *résumé* made me realise better than I had done before, what a most curious case it is.

You have also collected a surprising number of valuable facts bearing on the dispersal of plants, far more than in any other book known to me. In fact your volume is a mass of interesting facts and discussions, with hardly a superfluous word ; and I heartily congratulate you on its publication.

Your dedication makes me prouder than ever.

Believe me, yours sincerely,
CH. DARWIN.

[In November, 1879, he answered for Mr. Galton a series of questions utilised in his 'Inquiries into Human Faculty,' 1883. He wrote to Mr. Galton :—

"I have answered the questions as well as I could, but they are miserably answered, for I have never tried looking into my own mind. Unless others answer very much better than I can do, you will get no good from your queries. Do you not think you ought to have the age of the answerer ? I think so, because I can call up faces of many schoolboys, not seen for sixty years, with *much distinctness*, but nowadays I may talk with a man for an hour, and see him several times consecutively, and, after a month, I am utterly unable to recollect what he is at all like. The picture is quite washed out. The greater number of the answers are given in the annexed table."]

Questions on the Faculty of Visualising.

	QUESTIONS.	REPLIES.
1	*Illumination?*	Moderate, but my solitary breakfast was early, and the morning dark.
2	*Definition?*	Some objects quite defined, a slice of cold beef, some grapes and a pear, the state of my plate when I had finished, and a few other objects, are as distinct as if I had photo's before me.
3	*Completeness?*	Very moderately so.
4	*Colouring?*	The objects above named perfectly colored.
5	*Extent of Field of View?*	Rather small.
	DIFFERENT KINDS OF IMAGERY.	
6	*Printed pages.*	I cannot remember a single sentence, but I remember the place of the sentence and the kind of type.
7	*Furniture?*	I have never attended to it.
8	*Persons?*	I remember the faces of persons formerly well-known vividly, and can make them do anything I like.
9	*Scenery?*	Remembrance vivid and distinct, and gives me pleasure.
10	*Geography?*	No.
11	*Military movements?*	No.
12	*Mechanism?*	Never tried.
13	*Geometry?*	I do not think I have any power of the kind.
14	*Numerals?*	When I think of any number, printed figures arise before my mind. I can't remember for an hour four consecutive figures.
15	*Card playing?*	Have not played for many years, but I am sure should not remember.
16	*Chess?*	Never played.

[In 1880 he published a short paper in 'Nature' (vol. xxi. p. 207) on the " Fertility of Hybrids from the common and Chinese goose." He received the hybrids from the Rev. Dr. Goodacre, and was glad of the opportunity of testing the accuracy of the statement that these species are fertile *inter se*. This fact, which was given in the 'Origin' on the authority of Mr. Eyton, he considered the most remarkable as yet recorded with respect to the fertility of hybrids. The fact (as confirmed by himself and Dr. Goodacre) is of interest as giving another proof that sterility is no criterion of specific difference, since the two species of goose now shown to be fertile *inter se* are so distinct that they have been placed by some authorities in distinct genera or subgenera.

The following letter refers to Mr. Huxley's lecture : " The Coming of Age of the Origin of Species," * given at the Royal Institution, April 9, 1880, published in ' Nature,' and in ' Science and Culture,' p. 310 :]

C. Darwin to T. H. Huxley.

Abinger Hall, Dorking, Sunday, April 11, 1880.

MY DEAR HUXLEY,—I wished much to attend your Lecture, but I have had a bad cough, and we have come here to see whether a change would do me good, as it has done. What a magnificent success your lecture seems to have been, as I judge from the reports in the *Standard* and *Daily News*, and more especially from the accounts given me by three of my children. I suppose that you have not written out your lecture, so I fear there is no chance of its being printed *in extenso*. You appear to have piled, as on so many other occasions, honours high and thick on my old head. But I well know how great a part you have played in establishing

---

* This same " Coming of Age " was the subject of an address from the Council of the Otago Institute. It is given in ' Nature,' February 24, 1881.

and spreading the belief in the descent-theory, ever since that grand review in the *Times* and the battle royal at Oxford up to the present day.

Ever my dear Huxley,

Yours sincerely and gratefully,

CHARLES DARWIN.

P.S.—It was absurdly stupid in me, but I had read the announcement of your Lecture, and thought that you meant the maturity of the subject, until my wife one day remarked, "it is almost twenty-one years since the 'Origin' appeared," and then for the first time the meaning of your words flashed on me!

[In the above-mentioned lecture Mr. Huxley made a strong point of the accumulation of palæontological evidence which the years between 1859 and 1880 have given us in favour of Evolution. On this subject my father wrote (August 31, 1880):]

MY DEAR PROFESSOR MARSH,—I received some time ago your very kind note of July 28th, and yesterday the magnificent volume.* I have looked with renewed admiration at the plates, and will soon read the text. Your work on these old birds, and on the many fossil animals of North America has afforded the best support to the theory of Evolution, which has appeared within the last twenty years.† The general appearance of the copy which you have sent me is

---

* Odontornithes. A monograph on the extinct Toothed Birds of N. America. 1880. By O. C. Marsh.

† Mr. Huxley has well pointed out ('Science and Culture,' p. 317) that: "In 1875, the discovery of the toothed birds of the cretaceous formation in N. America, by Prof. Marsh, completed the series of transitional forms between birds and reptiles, and removed Mr. Darwin's proposition that, 'many animal forms of life have been utterly lost, through which the early progenitors of birds were formerly connected with the early progenitors of the other vertebrate classes,' from the region of hypothesis to that of demonstrable fact."

worthy of its contents, and I can say nothing stronger than this.

With cordial thanks, believe me,

Yours very sincerely,

CHARLES DARWIN.

[In November, 1880, he received an account of a flood in Brazil, from which his friend Fritz Müller had barely escaped with his life. My father immediately wrote to Hermann Müller anxiously enquiring whether his brother had lost books, instruments, &c., by this accident, and begging in that case "for the sake of science, so that science should not suffer," to be allowed to help in making good the loss. Fortunately, however, the injury to Fritz Müller's possessions was not so great as was expected, and the incident remains only as a memento, which I trust cannot be otherwise than pleasing to the survivor, of the friendship of the two naturalists.

In 'Nature' (November 11, 1880) appeared a letter from my father, which is, I believe, the only instance in which he wrote publicly with anything like severity. The late Sir Wyville Thomson wrote, in the Introduction to the 'Voyage of the *Challenger*' : "The character of the abyssal fauna refuses to give the least support to the theory which refers the evolution of species to extreme variation guided only by natural selection." My father, after characterising these remarks as a "standard of criticism, not uncommonly reached by theologians and metaphysicians," goes on to take exception to the term "extreme variation," and challenges Sir Wyville to name any one who has "said that the evolution of species depends only on natural selection." The letter closes with an imaginary scene between Sir Wyville and a breeder, in which Sir Wyville criticises artificial selection in a somewhat similar manner. The breeder is silent, but on the departure of his critic he is supposed to make use of "emphatic but irreverent language about naturalists." The letter, as originally written, ended with a quotation from Sedgwick on the invulnerability of those who write on what

they do not understand, but this was omitted on the advice
of a friend, and curiously enough a friend whose combativeness in the good cause my father had occasionally curbed.]

C. Darwin to G. J. Romanes.

Down, April 16, 1881.

MY DEAR ROMANES,—My MS. on 'Worms' has been sent
to the printers, so I am going to amuse myself by scribbling
to you on a few points; but you must not waste your time in
answering at any length this scribble.

Firstly, your letter on intelligence was very useful to me
and I tore up and re-wrote what I sent to you. I have not
attempted to define intelligence; but have quoted your
remarks on experience, and have shown how far they apply
to worms. It seems to me that they must be said to work
with some intelligence, anyhow they are not guided by a
blind instinct.

Secondly, I was greatly interested by the abstract in
'Nature' of your work on Echinoderms,* the complexity with
simplicity, and with such curious co-ordination of the nervous
system is marvellous; and you showed me before what splendid gymnastic feats they can perform.

Thirdly, Dr. Roux has sent me a book just published by
him: 'Der Kampf der Theile,' &c., 1881 (240 pages in
length).

He is manifestly a well-read physiologist and pathologist,
and from his position a good anatomist. It is full of reasoning, and this in German is very difficult to me, so that I have
only skimmed through each page; here and there reading
with a little more care. As far as I can imperfectly judge, it
is the most important book on Evolution, which has appeared
for some time. I believe that G. H. Lewes hinted at the
same fundamental idea, viz. that there is a struggle going on
within every organism between the organic molecules, the

---

* "On the locomotor system of Echinoderms," by G. J. Romanes and
J. Cossar Ewart. 'Philosophical Transactions,' 1881, p. 829.

cells and the organs. I think that his basis is, that every cell which best performs its function is, in consequence, at the same time best nourished and best propagates its kind. The book does not touch on mental phenomena, but there is much discussion on rudimentary or atrophied parts, to which subject you formerly attended. Now if you would like to read this book, I would send it. . . . If you read it, and are struck with it (but I may be *wholly* mistaken about its value), you would do a public service by analysing and criticising it in ' Nature.'

Dr. Roux makes, I think, a gigantic oversight in never considering plants ; these would simplify the problem for him.

Fourthly, I do not know whether you will discuss in your book on the mind of animals any of the more complex and wonderful instincts. It is unsatisfactory work, as there can be no fossilised instincts, and the sole guide is their state in other members of the same order, and mere *probability*.

But if you do discuss any (and it will perhaps be expected of you), I should think that you could not select a better case than that of the sand wasps, which paralyse their prey, as formerly described by Fabre, in his wonderful paper in the ' Annales des Sciences,' and since amplified in his admirable ' Souvenirs.'

Whilst reading this latter book, I speculated a little on the subject. Astonishing nonsense is often spoken of the sand wasp's knowledge of anatomy. Now will any one say that the Gauchos on the plains of La Plata have such knowledge, yet I have often seen them pith a struggling and lassoed cow on the ground with unerring skill, which no mere anatomist could imitate. The pointed knife was infallibly driven in between the vertebræ by a single slight thrust. I presume that the art was first discovered by chance, and that each young Gaucho sees exactly how the others do it, and then with a very little practice learns the art. Now I suppose that the sand wasps originally merely killed their prey by stinging them in many places (see p. 129 of Fabre's ' Souvenirs,' and

p. 241) on the lower and softest side of the body—and that to sting a certain segment was found by far the most successful method ; and was inherited like the tendency of a bulldog to pin the nose of a bull, or of a ferret to bite the cerebellum. It would not be a very great step in advance to prick the ganglion of its prey only slightly, and thus to give its larvæ fresh meat instead of old dried meat. Though Fabre insists so strongly on the unvarying character of instinct, yet it is shown that there is some variability, as at p. 176, 177.

I fear that I shall have utterly wearied you with my scribbling and bad handwriting.

My dear Romanes, yours, very sincerely,
CH. DARWIN.

Postscript of a Letter to Professor A. Agassiz, May 5th, 1881 :—

I read with much interest your address before the American Association. However true your remarks on the genealogies of the several groups may be, I hope and believe that you have over-estimated the difficulties to be encountered in the future :—A few days after reading your address, I interpreted to myself your remarks on one point (I hope in some degree correctly) in the following fashion :—

Any character of an ancient, generalised, or intermediate form may, and often does, re-appear in its descendants, after countless generations, and this explains the extraordinarily complicated affinities of existing groups. This idea seems to me to throw a flood of light on the lines, sometimes used to represent affinities, which radiate in all directions, often to very distant sub-groups,—a difficulty which has haunted me for half a century. A strong case could be made out in favour of believing in such reversion after immense intervals of time. I wish the idea had been put into my head in old days, for I shall never again write on difficult subjects, as I have seen too many cases of old men becoming feeble in their minds, without being in the least conscious of it.   If I have interpreted your ideas at all correctly, I hope that you will re-urge, on any fitting occasion, your view.   I have mentioned it to a few persons capable of judging, and it seemed quite new to them.   I beg you to forgive the proverbial garrulity of old age.

C. D.

[The following letter refers to Sir J. D. Hooker's Geographical address at the York Meeting (1881) of the British Association :]

C. Darwin to J. D. Hooker.

Down, August 6, 1881.

MY DEAR HOOKER,—For Heaven's sake never speak of boring me, as it would be the greatest pleasure to aid you in the slightest degree and your letter has interested me exceedingly.   I will go through your points seriatim, but I have never attended much to the history of any subject, and my memory has become atrociously bad.   It will therefore be a mere chance whether any of my remarks are of any use.

Your idea, to show what travellers have done, seems to me a brilliant and just one, especially considering your audience.

1. I know nothing about Tournefort's works.

2. I believe that you are fully right in calling Humboldt the greatest scientific traveller who ever lived, I have lately read two or three volumes again.   His Geology is funny stuff; but that merely means that he was not in advance of his age.   I should say he was wonderful, more for his near approach to omniscience than for originality.   Whether or not his position as a scientific man is as eminent as we think, you might truly call him the parent of a grand progeny of scientific travellers, who, taken together, have done much for science.

3. It seems to me quite just to give Lyell (and secondarily E. Forbes) a very prominent place.

4. Dana was, I believe, the first man who maintained the

permanence of continents and the great oceans. . . . When I read the '*Challenger's*' conclusion that sediment from the land is not deposited at greater distances than 200 to 300 miles from the land, I was much strengthened in my old belief. Wallace seems to me to have argued the case excellently. Nevertheless, I would speak, if I were in your place, rather cautiously; for T. Mellard Reade has argued lately with some force against the view; but I cannot call to mind his arguments. If forced to express a judgment, I should abide by the view of approximate permanence since Cambrian days.

5. The extreme importance of the Arctic fossil-plants, is self-evident. Take the opportunity of groaning over [our] ignorance of the Lignite Plants of Kerguelen Land, or any Antarctic land. It might do good.

6. I cannot avoid feeling sceptical about the travelling of plants from the North *except during the Tertiary period.* It may of course have been so and probably was so from one of the two poles at the earliest period, during Pre-Cambrian ages; but such speculations seem to me hardly scientific seeing how little we know of the old Floras.

I will now jot down without any order a few miscellaneous remarks.

I think you ought to allude to Alph. De Candolle's great book, for though it (like almost everything else) is washed out of my mind, yet I remember most distinctly thinking it a very valuable work. Anyhow, you might allude to his excellent account of the history of all cultivated plants.

How shall you manage to allude to your New Zealand and Tierra del Fuego work? if you do not allude to them you will be scandalously unjust.

The many Angiosperm plants in the Cretacean beds of the United States (and as far as I can judge the age of these beds has been fairly well made out) seems to me a fact of very great importance, so is their relation to the existing flora of the United States under an Evolutionary point of view.

Have not some Australian extinct forms been lately found in Australia? or have I dreamed it?

Again, the recent discovery of plants rather low down in our Silurian beds is very important.

Nothing is more extraordinary in the history of the Vegetable Kingdom, as it seems to me, than the *apparently* very sudden or abrupt development of the higher plants. I have sometimes speculated whether there did not exist somewhere during long ages an extremely isolated continent, perhaps near the South Pole.

Hence I was greatly interested by a view which Saporta propounded to me, a few years ago, at great length in MS. and which I fancy he has since published, as I urged him to do—viz., that as soon as flower-frequenting insects were developed, during the latter part of the secondary period, an enormous impulse was given to the development of the higher plants by cross-fertilization being thus suddenly formed.

A few years ago I was much struck with Axel Blytt's* Essay showing from observation, on the peat beds in Scandinavia, that there had apparently been long periods with more rain and other with less rain (perhaps connected with Croll's recurrent astronomical periods), and that these periods had largely determined the present distribution of the plants of Norway and Sweden. This seemed to me, a very important essay.

I have just read over my remarks and I fear that they will not be of the slightest use to you.

I cannot but think that you have got through the hardest, or at least the most difficult, part of your work in having made so good and striking a sketch of what you intend to say; but I can quite understand how you must groan over the great necessary labour.

I most heartily sympathise with you on the successes of B. and R. : as years advance what happens to oneself becomes of very little consequence, in comparison with the careers of our children.

---

* See footnote, p. 392.

Keep your spirits up, for I am convinced that you will make an excellent address.

Ever yours, affectionately,
CHARLES DARWIN.

[In September he wrote :—

" I have this minute finished reading your splendid but too short address. I cannot doubt that it will have been fully appreciated by the Geographers of York ; if not, they are asses and fools."]

C. Darwin to John Lubbock.

Sunday evening [1881].

MY DEAR L.,—Your address * has made me think over what have been the great steps in Geology during the last fifty years, and there can be no harm in telling you my impression. But it is very odd that I cannot remember what you have said on Geology. I suppose that the classification of the Silurian and Cambrian formations must be considered the greatest or most important step ; for I well remember when all these older rocks were called grau-wacke, and nobody dreamed of classing them ; and now we have three azoic formations pretty well made out beneath the Cambrian ! But the most striking step has been the discovery of the Glacial period : you are too young to remember the prodigious effect this produced about the year 1840 (?) on all our minds. Elie de Beaumont never believed in it to the day of his death ! the study of the glacial deposits led to the study of the superficial drift, which was formerly *never studied* and called Diluvium, as I well remember. The study under the microscope of rock-sections is another not inconsiderable step. So again the making out of cleavage and the foliation of the metamorphic rocks. But I will not run on, having now eased my mind. Pray do not waste even one minute in acknowledging my horrid scrawls. Ever yours,

CH. DARWIN.

---

* Presidential Address at the York meeting of the British Association.

[The following extracts referring to the late Francis Mait-
land Balfour,* show my father's estimate of his work and
intellectual qualities, but they give merely an indication of
his strong appreciation of Balfour's most lovable personal
character :—

From a letter to Fritz Müller, January 5, 1882 :—

"Your appreciation of Balfour's book ['Comparative Embryology'] has pleased me excessively, for though I could not
properly judge of it, yet it seemed to me one of the most
remarkable books which have been published for some considerable time. He is quite a young man, and if he keeps
his health, will do splendid work. . . . He has a fair fortune
of his own, so that he can give up his whole time to Biology.
He is very modest, and very pleasant, and often visits here
and we like him very much."

From a letter to Dr. Dohrn, February 13, 1882 :—

"I have got one very bad piece of news to tell you, that
F. Balfour is very ill at Cambridge with typhoid fever. . . . .
I hope that he is not in a very dangerous state; but the
fever is severe. Good Heavens, what a loss he would be to
Science, and to his many loving friends !"]

C. Darwin to T. H. Huxley.

Down, January 12, 1882.

MY DEAR HUXLEY,—Very many thanks for 'Science and
Culture,' and I am sure that I shall read most of the essays
with much interest. With respect to Automatism,† I wish
that you could review yourself in the old, and of course forgotten, trenchant style, and then you would here answer
yourself with equal incisiveness; and thus, by Jove, you

---

* Professor of Animal Morphology at Cambridge. He was born in
1851, and was killed, with his guide, on the Aiguille Blanche, near Cour-
mayeur, in July, 1882.

† "On the hypothesis that animals are automata and its history," an
Address given at the Belfast meeting of the British Association, 1874, and
published in the 'Fortnightly Review,' 1874, and in 'Science and Culture.'

might go on *ad infinitum*, to the joy and instruction of the world.   Ever yours very sincerely,

CHARLES DARWIN.

[The following letter refers to Dr. Ogle's translation of Aristotle, 'On the Parts of Animals' (1882):]

C. Darwin to W. Ogle.

Down, February 22, 1882.

MY DEAR DR. OGLE,—You must let me thank you for the pleasure which the introduction to the Aristotle book has given me.   I have rarely read anything which has interested me more, though I have not read as yet more than a quarter of the book proper.

From quotations which I had seen, I had a high notion of Aristotle's merits, but I had not the most remote notion what a wonderful man he was.   Linnæus and Cuvier have been my two gods, though in very different ways, but they were mere schoolboys to old Aristotle.   How very curious, also, his ignorance on some points, as on muscles as the means of movement.   I am glad that you have explained in so probable a manner some of the grossest mistakes attributed to him.   I never realized, before reading your book, to what an enormous summation of labour we owe even our common knowledge. I wish old Aristotle could know what a grand Defender of the Faith he had found in you.   Believe me, my dear Dr. Ogle,

Yours very sincerely,

CH. DARWIN.

[In February, he received a letter and a specimen from a Mr. W. D. Crick, which illustrated a curious mode of dispersal of bivalve shells, namely, by closure of their valves so as to hold on to the leg of a water-beetle.   This class of fact had a special charm for him, and he wrote to 'Nature,' describing the case.*

---

* 'Nature,' April 6, 1882.

In April he received a letter from Dr. W. Van Dyck, Lecturer in Zoology at the Protestant College of Beyrout. The letter showed that the street dogs of Beyrout had been rapidly mongrelised by introduced European dogs, and the facts have an interesting bearing on my father's theory of Sexual Selection.]

C. Darwin to W. T. Van Dyck.

Down, April 3, 1882.

DEAR SIR,—After much deliberation, I have thought it best to send your very interesting paper to the Zoological Society, in hopes that it will be published in their Journal. This journal goes to every scientific institution in the world, and the contents are abstracted in all year-books on Zoology. Therefore I have preferred it to 'Nature,' though the latter has a wider circulation, but is ephemeral.

I have prefaced your essay by a few general remarks, to which I hope that you will not object.

Of course I do not know that the Zoological Society, which is much addicted to mere systematic work, will publish your essay. If it does, I will send you copies of your essay, but these will not be ready for some months. If not published by the Zoological Society, I will endeavour to get 'Nature' to publish it. I am very anxious that it should be published and preserved. Dear Sir,

Yours faithfully,

CH. DARWIN.

[The paper was read at a meeting of the Zoological Society on April 18th—the day before my father's death.

The preliminary remarks with which Dr. Van Dyck's paper is prefaced are thus the latest of my father's writings.]

We must now return to an early period of his life, and give a connected account of his botanical work, which has hitherto been omitted.

CHAPTER X.

FERTILISATION OF FLOWERS.

[IN the letters already given we have had occasion to notice the general bearing of a number of botanical problems on the wider question of Evolution. The detailed work in botany which my father accomplished by the guidance of the light cast on the study of natural history by his own work on Evolution remains to be noticed. In a letter to Mr. Murray, September 24th, 1861, speaking of his book on the 'Fertilisation of Orchids,' he says : " It will perhaps serve to illustrate how Natural History may be worked under the belief of the modification of species." This remark gives a suggestion as to the value and interest of his botanical work, and it might be expressed in far more emphatic language without danger of exaggeration.

In the same letter to Mr. Murray, he says : " I think this little volume will do good to the 'Origin,' as it will show that I have worked hard at details." It is true that his botanical work added a mass of corroborative detail to the case for Evolution, but the chief support to his doctrines given by these researches was of another kind. . They supplied an argument against those critics who have so freely dogmatised as to the uselessness of particular structures, and as to the consequent impossibility of their having been developed by means of natural selection. His observations on Orchids enabled him to say : " I can show the meaning of some of the apparently meaningless ridges, horns, who will now venture to say that this or that structure is useless ? " A kindred point is expressed in a letter to Sir J. D. Hooker (May 14th, 1862) :—

"When many parts of structure, as in the woodpecker, show distinct adaptation to external bodies, it is preposterous to attribute them to the effects of climate, &c., but when a single point alone, as a hooked seed, it is conceivable it may thus have arisen. I have found the study of Orchids eminently useful in showing me how nearly all parts of the flower are co-adapted for fertilization by insects, and therefore the results of natural selection—even the most trifling details of structure."

One of the greatest services rendered by my father to the study of Natural History is the revival of Teleology. The evolutionist studies the purpose or meaning of organs with the zeal of the older Teleology, but with far wider and more coherent purpose. He has the invigorating knowledge that he is gaining not isolated conceptions of the economy of the present, but a coherent view of both past and present. And even where he fails to discover the use of any part, he may, by a knowledge of its structure, unravel the history of the past vicissitudes in the life of the species. In this way a vigour and unity is given to the study of the forms of organised beings, which before it lacked. This point has already been discussed in Mr. Huxley's chapter on the 'Reception of the Origin of Species,' and need not be here considered. It does, however, concern us to recognize that this "great service to natural science," as Dr. Gray describes it, was effected almost as much by his special botanical work as by the 'Origin of Species.'

For a statement of the scope and influence of my father's botanical work, I may refer to Mr. Thiselton Dyer's article in 'Charles Darwin,' one of the *Nature Series.* Mr. Dyer's wide knowledge, his friendship with my father, and especially his power of sympathising with the work of others, combine to give this essay a permanent value. The following passage (p. 43) gives a true picture :—

"Notwithstanding the extent and variety of his botanical work, Mr. Darwin always disclaimed any right to be regarded as a professed botanist. He turned his attention to plants,

doubtless because they were convenient objects for studying
organic phenomena in their least complicated forms ; and
this point of view, which, if one may use the expression
without disrespect, had something of the amateur about it,
was in itself of the greatest importance. For, from not being,
till he took up any point, familiar with the literature bearing
on it, his mind was absolutely free from any prepossession.
He was never afraid of his facts, or of framing any hypothesis, however startling, which seemed to explain them. . . .
In any one else such an attitude would have produced much
work that was crude and rash. But Mr. Darwin—if one may
venture on language which will strike no one who had con-
versed with him as over-strained—seemed by gentle persua-
sion to have penetrated that reserve of nature which baffles
smaller men. In other words, his long experience had given
him a kind of instinctive insight into the method of attack of
any biological problem, however unfamiliar to him, while he
rigidly controlled the fertility of his mind in hypothetical
explanations by the no less fertility of ingeniously devised
experiment."

To form any just idea of the greatness of the revolution
worked by my father's researches in the study of the fertilisation of flowers, it is necessary to know from what a condition
this branch of knowledge has emerged. It should be remembered that it was only during the early years of the present
century that the idea of sex, as applied to plants, became at
all firmly established. Sachs, in his 'History of Botany'
(1875), has given some striking illustrations of the remarkable slowness with which its acceptance gained ground. He
remarks that when we consider the experimental proofs given
by Camerarius (1694), and by Kölreuter (1761–66), it appears
incredible that doubts should afterwards have been raised as
to the sexuality of plants. Yet he shows that such doubts
did actually repeatedly crop up. These adverse criticisms
rested for the most part on careless experiments, but in many
cases on *à priori* arguments. Even as late as 1820, a book of
this kind, which would now rank with circle squaring, or

flat-earth philosophy, was seriously noticed in a botanical journal.

A distinct conception of sex as applied to plants, had not long emerged from the mists of profitless discussion and feeble experiment, at the time when my father began botany by attending Henslow's lectures at Cambridge.

When the belief in the sexuality of plants had become established as an incontrovertible piece of knowledge, a weight of misconception remained, weighing down any rational view of the subject. Camerarius * believed (naturally enough in his day) that hermaphrodite flowers are necessarily self-fertilised. He had the wit to be astonished at this, a degree of intelligence which, as Sachs points out, the majority of his successors did not attain to.

The following extracts from a note-book show that this point occurred to my father as early as 1837 :—

"Do not plants which have male and female organs together [i.e. in the same flower] yet receive influence from other plants? Does not Lyell give some argument about varieties being difficult to keep [true] on account of pollen from other plants? Because this may be applied to show all plants do receive intermixture."

Sprengel,† indeed, understood that the hermaphrodite structure of flowers by no means necessarily leads to self-fertilisation. But although he discovered that in many cases pollen is of necessity carried to the stigma of another *flower*, he did not understand that in the advantage gained by the intercrossing of distinct *plants* lies the key to the whole question. Hermann Müller has well remarked that this "omission was for several generations fatal to Sprengel's work. . . . . For both at the time and subsequently, botanists felt above all the weakness of his theory, and they set aside, along with his defective ideas, his rich store of patient and acute observations and his comprehensive and accurate interpreta-

---

* Sachs, ' Geschichte,' p. 419.
† Christian Conrad Sprengel, born 1750, died 1816.

tions." It remained for my father to convince the world
that the meaning hidden in the structure of flowers was to
be found by seeking light in the same direction in which
Sprengel, seventy years before, had laboured. Robert
Brown was the connecting link between them, for it was
at his recommendation that my father in 1841 read Sprengel's now celebrated 'Secret of Nature Displayed.' * The
book impressed him as being "full of truth," although
"with some little nonsense." It not only encouraged him
in kindred speculation, but guided him in his work, for in
1844 he speaks of verifying Sprengel's observations. It
may be doubted whether Robert Brown ever planted a
more beautiful seed than in putting such a book into such
hands.

A passage in the 'Autobiography' (vol. i. p. 73) shows
how it was that my father was attracted to the subject of
fertilisation : "During the summer of 1839, and I believe
during the previous summer, I was led to attend to the cross-
fertilisation of flowers by the aid of insects, from having come
to the conclusion in my speculations on the origin of species,
that crossing played an important part in keeping specific
forms constant."

The original connection between the study of flowers
and the problem of evolution is curious, and could hardly
have been predicted. Moreover, it was not a permanent
bond. As soon as the idea arose that the offspring of
cross-fertilisation is, in the struggle for life, likely to conquer the seedlings of self-fertilised parentage, a far more
vigorous belief in the potency of natural selection in mould-
ing the structure of flowers is attained. A central idea is
gained towards which experiment and observation may be
directed.

Dr. Gray has well remarked with regard to this central

---

* 'Das entdeckte Geheimniss der Natur im Baue und in der Befruchtung der Blumen.' Berlin, 1793.

idea ('Nature,' June 4, 1874):—"The aphorism, 'Nature abhors a vacuum,' is a characteristic specimen of the science of the middle ages. The aphorism, 'Nature abhors close fertilisation,' and the demonstration of the principle, belong to our age and to Mr. Darwin. To have originated this, and also the principle of Natural Selection . . . . and to have applied these principles to the system of nature, in such a manner as to make, within a dozen years, a deeper impression upon natural history than has been made since Linnæus, is ample title for one man's fame."

The flowers of the Papilionaceæ attracted his attention early, and were the subject of his first paper on fertilisation.* The following extract from an undated letter to Dr. Asa Gray seems to have been written before the publication of this paper, probably in 1856 or 1857 :—

" . . . . What you say on Papilionaceous flowers is very true; and I have no facts to show that varieties are crossed ; but yet (and the same remark is applicable in a beautiful way to Fumaria and Dielytra, as I noticed many years ago), I must believe that the flowers are constructed partly in direct relation to the visits of insects; and how insects can avoid bringing pollen from other individuals I cannot understand. It is really pretty to watch the action of a Humble-bee on the scarlet kidney bean, and in this genus (and in *Lathyrus grandiflorus*) the honey is so placed that the bee invariably alights on that *one* side of the flower towards which the spiral pistil is protruded (bringing out with it pollen), and by the depression of the wing-petal is forced against the bee's side all dusted with pollen.† In the broom the pistil is rubbed on the centre of the back of the bee. I suspect there is some-

---

* *Gardeners' Chronicle*, 1857, p. 725. It appears that this paper was a piece of "over-time" work. He wrote to a friend, "that confounded leguminous paper was done in the afternoon, and the consequence was I had to go to Moor Park for a week."

† If you will look at a bed of scarlet kidney beans you will find that the wing-petals on the *left* side alone are all scratched by the tarsi of the bees. [Note in the original letter by C. Darwin.]

thing to be made out about the Leguminosæ, which will bring the case within *our* theory ; though I have failed to do so.   Our theory will explain why in the vegetable and animal kingdom the act of fertilisation even in hermaphrodites usu - ally takes place *sub-jove*, though thus exposed to *great* injury from damp and rain.   In animals which cannot be [fertilised] by insects or wind, there is *no case* of *land*-animals being hermaphrodite without the concourse of two individuals."

A letter to Dr. Asa Gray (Sept. 5th, 1857) gives the substance of the paper in the *Gardeners' Chronicle* :—

"Lately I was led to examine buds of kidney bean with the pollen shed ; but I was led to believe that the pollen could *hardly* get on the stigma by wind or otherwise, except by bees visiting [the flower] and moving the wing petals : hence I included a small bunch of flowers in two bottles in every way treated the same : the flowers in one I daily just momentarily moved, as if by a bee ; these set three fine pods, the other *not one*.   Of course this little experiment must be tried again, and this year in England it is too late, as the flowers seem now seldom to set.   If bees are necessary to this flower's self-fertilisation, bees must almost cross them, as their dusted right-side of head and right legs constantly touch the stigma.

"I have, also, lately been re-observing daily *Lobelia fulgens*—this in my garden is never visited by insects, and never sets seeds, without pollen be put on the stigma (whereas the small blue Lobelia is visited by bees and does set seed) ; I mention this because there are such beautiful contrivances to prevent the stigma ever getting its own pollen ; which seems only explicable on the doctrine of the advantage of crosses."

The paper was supplemented by a second in 1858.*   The chief object of these publications seems to have been to obtain

---

* *Gardeners' Chronicle*, 1858, p. 828.   In 1861 another paper on Fertilisation appeared in the *Gardeners' Chronicle*, p. 552, in which he explained the action of insects on *Vinca major*.   He was attracted to the periwinkle by the fact that it is not visited by insects and never sets seeds.

information as to the possibility of growing varieties of leguminous plants near each other, and yet keeping them true. It is curious that the Papilionaceæ should not only have been the first flowers which attracted his attention by their obvious adaptation to the visits of insects, but should also have constituted one of his sorest puzzles. The common pea and the sweet pea gave him much difficulty, because, although they are as obviously fitted for insect-visits as the rest of the order, yet their varieties keep true. The fact is that neither of these plants being indigenous, they are not perfectly adapted for fertilisation by British insects. He could not, at this stage of his observations, know that the co-ordination between a flower and the particular insect which fertilises it may be as delicate as that between a lock and its key, so that this explanation was not likely to occur to him.*

Besides observing the Leguminosæ, he had already begun, as shown in the foregoing extracts, to attend to the structure of other flowers in relation to insects. At the beginning of 1860 he worked at Leschenaultia,† which at first puzzled him, but was ultimately made out. A passage in a letter chiefly relating to Leschenaultia seems to show that it was only in the spring of 1860 that he began widely to apply his knowledge to the relation of insects to other flowers. This is somewhat surprising, when we remember that he had read Sprengel many years before. He wrote (May 14) :—

" I should look at this curious contrivance as specially related to visits of insects ; as I begin to think is almost universally the case."

Even in July 1862 he wrote to Dr. Asa Gray :—

" There is no end to the adaptations. Ought not these cases to make one very cautious when one doubts about the

---

* He was of course alive to variety in the habits of insects. He published a short note in the *Entomologists Weekly Intelligencer*, 1860, asking whether the Tineina and other small moths suck flowers.

† He published a short paper on the manner of fertilisation of this flower, in the *Gardeners' Chronicle*, 1871, p. 1166.

use of all parts? I fully believe that the structure of all irregular flowers is governed in relation to insects. Insects are the Lords of the floral (to quote the witty *Athenæum*) world."

He was probably attracted to the study of Orchids by the fact that several kinds are common near Down. The letters of 1860 show that these plants occupied a good deal of his attention; and in 1861 he gave part of the summer and and all the autumn to the subject. He evidently considered himself idle for wasting time on Orchids, which ought to have been given to 'Variation under Domestication.' Thus he wrote :—

"There is to me incomparably more interest in observing than in writing; but I feel quite guilty in trespassing on these subjects, and not sticking to varieties of the confounded cocks, hens and ducks. I hear that Lyell is savage at me. I shall never resist Linum. next summer."

It was in the summer of 1860 that he made out one of the most striking and familiar facts in the book, namely, the manner in which the pollen masses in Orchis are adapted for removal by insects. He wrote to Sir J. D. Hooker July 12 :—

"I have been examining *Orchis pyramidalis*, and it almost equals, perhaps even beats, your Listera case; the sticky glands are congenitally united into a saddle-shaped organ, which has great power of movement, and seizes hold of a bristle (or proboscis) in an admirable manner, and then another movement takes place in the pollen masses, by which they are beautifully adapted to leave pollen on the two *lateral* stigmatic surfaces. I never saw anything so beautiful."

In June of the same year he wrote :—

"You speak of adaptation being rarely *visible*, though present in plants. . I have just recently been looking at the common Orchis, and I declare I think its adaptations in every part of the flower quite as beautiful and plain, or even more beautiful than in the Woodpecker. I have written and

sent a notice for the *Gardeners' Chronicle*,* on a curious difficulty in the Bee Orchis, and should much like to hear what
you think of the case.   In this article I have incidentally
touched on adaptation to visits of insects ; but the contrivance to keep the sticky glands fresh and sticky beats almost
everything in nature.   I never remember having seen it described, but it must have been, and, as I ought not in my book
to give the observation as my own, I should be very glad to
know where this beautiful contrivance is described."

He wrote also to Dr. Gray, June 8, 1860 : —

" Talking of adaptation, I have lately been looking at our
common orchids, and I dare say the facts are as old and well-
known as the hills, but I have been so struck with admiration
at the contrivances, that I have sent a notice to the *Gardeners' Chronicle*.   The *Ophrys apifera*, offers, as you will see, a
curious contradiction in structure."

Besides attending to the fertilisation of the flowers he was
already, in 1860, busy with the homologies of the parts, a
subject of which he made good use in the Orchid book.   He
wrote to Sir Joseph Hooker (July) :—

" It is a real good joke my discussing homologies of Orchids with you, after examining only three or four genera;
and this very fact makes me feel positive I am right !   I do
not quite understand some of your terms; but sometime I
must get you to explain the homologies ; for I am intensely
interested on the subject, just as at a game of chess."

This work was valuable from a systematic point of view.
In 1880 he wrote to Mr. Bentham :—

" It was very kind in you to write to me about the Or-
chideæ, for it has pleased me to an extreme degree that I
could have been of the *least* use to you about the nature of
the parts."

The pleasure which his early observations on Orchids gave

---

* June 9, 1860. This seems to have attracted some attention, especially among entomologists, as it was reprinted in the *Entomologists Weekly
Intelligencer*, 1860.

him is shown in such extracts as the following from a letter
to Sir J. D. Hooker (July 27, 1861) :—

"You cannot conceive how the Orchids have delighted
me. They came safe, but box rather smashed ; cylindrical
old cocoa- or snuff-canister much safer. I enclose postage.
As an account of the movement, I shall allude to what I suppose is Oncidium, to make *certain*,—is the enclosed flower
with crumpled petals this genus ?   Also I most specially want
to know what the enclosed little globular brown Orchid is.
I have only seen pollen of a Cattleya on a bee, but surely
have you not unintentionally sent me what I wanted most
(after Catasetum or Mormodes), viz. one of the Epidendreæ ? !
I *particularly* want (and will presently tell you why) another
spike of this little Orchid, with older flowers, some even almost withered."

His delight in observation is again shown in a letter to
Dr. Gray (1863).   Referring to Crüger's letters from Trinidad, he wrote :—" Happy man, he has actually seen crowds of
bees flying round Catasetum, with the pollinia sticking to
their backs ! "

The following extracts of letters to Sir J. D. Hooker illustrate further the interest which his work excited in him :—

"Veitch sent me a grand lot this morning.   What wonderful structures !

"I have now seen enough, and you must not send me more,
for though I enjoy looking at them *much*, and it has been
very useful to me, seeing so many different forms, it is idle-
ness.   For my object each species requires studying for
days.   I wish you had time to take up the group.   I would
give a good deal to know what the rostellum is, of which I
have traced so many curious modifications.   I suppose it
cannot be one of the stigmas,* there seems a great tendency
for two lateral stigmas to appear.   My paper, though touching on only subordinate points will run, I fear, to 100 MS.
folio pages !   The beauty of the adaptation of parts seems

---

* It is a modification of the upper stigma.

to me unparalleled. I should think or guess waxy pollen was most differentiated. In Cypripedium which seems least modified, and a much exterminated group, the grains are single. In *all others*, as far as I have seen, they are in packets of four; and these packets cohere into many wedge-formed masses in Orchis ; into eight, four, and finally two. It seems curious that a flower should exist, which could *at most* fertilise only two other flowers, seeing how abundant pollen generally is ; this fact I look at as explaining the perfection of the contrivance by which the pollen, so important from its fewness, is carried from flower to flower " (1861).

" I was thinking of writing to you to-day, when your note with the Orchids came. What frightful trouble you have taken about Vanilla ; you really must not take an atom more ; for the Orchids are more play than real work. I have been much interested by Epidendrum, and have worked all morning at them ; for heaven's sake, do not corrupt me by any more " (August 30, 1861).

He originally intended to publish his notes on Orchids as a paper in the Linnean Society's Journal, but it soon became evident that a separate volume would be a more suitable form of publication. In a letter to Sir J. D. Hooker, Sept. 24, 1861, he writes :—

"I have been acting, I fear that you will think, like a goose ; and perhaps in truth I have. When I finished a few days ago my Orchis paper, which turns out 140 folio pages ! ! and thought of the expense of woodcuts, I said to myself, I will offer the Linnean Society to withdraw it, and publish it in a pamphlet. It then flashed on me that perhaps Murray would publish it, so I gave him a cautious description, and offered to share risks and profits. This morning he writes that he will publish and take all risks, and share profits and pay for all illustrations. It is a risk, and heaven knows whether it will not be a dead failure, but I have not deceived Murray, and [have] told him that it would interest those alone who cared much for natural history. I hope I do not exaggerate the curiosity of the many special contrivances."

He wrote the two following letters to Mr. Murray about the publication of the book :]

Down, Sept. 21 [1861].

MY DEAR SIR,—Will you have the kindness to give me your opinion, which I shall implicitly follow. I have just finished a very long paper intended for Linnean Society (the title is enclosed), and yesterday for the first time it occurred to me that *possibly* it might be worth publishing separately which would save me trouble and delay. The facts are new, and have been collected during twenty years and strike me as curious. Like a Bridgewater treatise, the chief object is to show the perfection of the many contrivances in Orchids. The subject of propagation is interesting to most people, and is treated in my paper so that any woman could read it. Parts are dry and purely scientific ; but I think my paper would interest a good many of such persons who care for Natural History, but no others.

. . . It would be a very little book, and I believe you think very little books objectionable. I have myself *great* doubts on the subject. I am very apt to think that my geese are swans ; but the subject seems to me curious and interesting.

I beg you not to be guided in the least in order to oblige me, but as far as you can judge, please give me your opinion. If I were to publish separately, I would agree to any terms, such as half risk and half profit, or what you liked ; but I would not publish on my sole risk, for to be frank, I have been told that no publisher whatever, under such circumstances, cares for the success of a book.

C. Darwin to J. Murray.

Down, Sept. 24 [1861].

MY DEAR SIR,—I am very much obliged for your note and very liberal offer. I have had some qualms and fears. All that I can feel sure of is that the MS. contains many new and curious facts, and I am sure the Essay would have interested me, and will interest those who feel lively interest in the wonders of nature ; but how far the public will care for such minute details, I cannot at all tell. It is a bold experiment ; and at worst, cannot entail much loss ; as a certain amount of sale will, I think, be pretty certain. A large sale is out of the question. As far as I can judge, generally the points which interest me I find interest others ; but I make the experiment with fear and trembling,—not for my own sake, but for yours. . . .

[On Sept. 28th he wrote to Sir J. D. Hooker :—

"What a good soul you are not to sneer at me, but to pat me on the back. I have the greatest doubt whether I am not going to do, in publishing my paper, a most ridiculous thing. It would annoy me much, but only for Murray's sake, if the publication were a dead failure."

There was still much work to be done, and in October he was still receiving Orchids from Kew, and wrote to Hooker :—

"It is impossible to thank you enough. I was almost mad at the wealth of Orchids." And again—

"Mr. Veitch most generously has sent me two splendid buds of Mormodes, which will be capital for dissection, but I fear will never be irritable ; so for the sake of charity and love of heaven do, I beseech you, observe what movement takes place in Cychnoches, and what part must be touched. Mr. V. has also sent me one splendid flower of Catasetum, the most wonderful Orchid I have seen."

On Oct. 13th he wrote to Sir Joseph Hooker :—

"It seems that I cannot exhaust your good nature. I have had the hardest day's work at Catasetum and buds of Mormodes, and believe I understand at last the mechanism of movements and the functions. Catasetum is a beautiful case of slight modification of structure leading to new functions. I never was more interested in any subject in my life than in this of Orchids. I owe very much to you."

Again to the same friend, Nov. 1, 1861 :—

"If you really can spare another Catasetum, when nearly ready, I shall be most grateful ; had I not better send for it ? The case is truly marvellous ; the (so-called) sensation, or stimulus from a light touch is certainly transmitted through the antennæ for more than one inch *instantaneously.* . . . A cursed insect or something let my last flower off last night."

Professor de Candolle has remarked * of my father, " Ce n'est pas lui qui aurait demandé de construire des palais pour y loger des laboratoires." This was singularly true of his orchid work, or rather it would be nearer the truth to say that he had no laboratory, for it was only after the publication of the 'Fertilisation of Orchids,' that he built himself a greenhouse. He wrote to Sir J. D. Hooker (Dec. 24th, 1862) :—

"And now I am going to tell you a *most* important piece of news!! I have almost resolved to build a small hot-house; my neighbour's really first-rate gardener has suggested it, and offered to make me plans, and see that it is well done, and he is really a clever fellow, who wins lots of prizes, and is very observant. He believes that we should succeed with a little patience ; it will be a grand amusement for me to experiment with plants."

Again he wrote (Feb. 15th, 1863) :—

"I write now because the new hot-house is ready, and I long to stock it, just like a schoolboy. Could you tell me pretty soon what plants you can give me ; and then I shall know what to order ? And do advise me how I had better get such plants as you can *spare.* Would it do to send my tax-cart early in the morning, on a day that was not frosty, lining the cart with mats, and arriving here before night ? I have no idea whether this degree of exposure (and of course the cart would be cold) could injure stove-plants ; they would be about five hours (with bait) on the journey home."

A week later he wrote :—

"You cannot imagine what pleasure your plants give me

---

* 'Darwin considéré, &c.,' 'Archives des Sciences Physiques et Naturelles,' 3ème période. Tome vii. 481, 1882 (May).

(far more than your dead Wedgwood ware can give you);
and I go and gloat over them, but we privately confessed to
each other, that if they were not our own, perhaps we should
not see such transcendent beauty in each leaf."

And in March, when he was extremely unwell he wrote:—

"A few words about the Stove-plants; they do so amuse
me. I have crawled to see them two or three times. Will
you correct and answer, and return enclosed. I have hunted
in all my books and cannot find these names,* and I like
much to know the family."

The book was published May 15th, 1862. Of its reception
he writes to Murray, June 13th and 18th:—

"The Botanists praise my Orchid-book to the skies. Some
one sent me (perhaps you) the 'Parthenon,' with a good review. The *Athenæum* † treats me with very kind pity and
contempt; but the reviewer knew nothing of his subject."

"There is a superb, but I fear exaggerated, review in the
'London Review.' ‡ But I have not been a fool, as I thought
I was, to publish; # for Asa Gray, about the most competent
judge in the world, thinks almost as highly of the book as
does the 'London Review.' The *Athenæum* will hinder the
sale greatly."

The Rev. M. J. Berkeley was the author of the notice in
the 'London Review,' as my father learned from Sir J. D.

---

* His difficulty with regard to the names of plants is illustrated, with
regard to a Lupine on which he was at work, in an extract from a letter
(July 21, 1866) to Sir J. D. Hooker: "I sent to the nursery garden, whence
I bought the seed, and could only hear that it was 'the common blue Lupine,' the man saying 'he was no scholard, and did not know Latin, and
that parties who make experiments ought to find out the names.'"

† May 24, 1862.

‡ June 14, 1862.

Doubts on this point still, however, occurred to him about this time.
He wrote to Prof. Oliver (June 8): "I am glad that you have read my
Orchis-book and seem to approve of it; for I never published anything
which I so much doubted whether it was worth publishing, and indeed I
still doubt. The subject interested me beyond what, I suppose, it is
worth."

Hooker, who added, "I thought it very well done indeed. I have read a good deal of the Orchid-book, and echo all he says."

To this my father replied (June 30th, 1862):—

"MY DEAR OLD FRIEND,—You speak of my warming the cockles of your heart, but you will never know how often you have warmed mine. It is not your approbation of my scientific work (though I care for that more than for any one's): it is something deeper. To this day I remember keenly a letter you wrote to me from Oxford, when I was at the Water-cure, and how it cheered me when I was utterly weary of life. Well, my Orchis-book is a success (but I do not know whether it sells)."

In another letter to the same friend, he wrote:—

"You have pleased me much by what you say in regard to Bentham and Oliver approving of my book; for I had got a sort of nervousness, and doubted whether I had not made an egregious fool of myself, and concocted pleasant little stinging remarks for reviews, such as 'Mr. Darwin's head seems to have been turned by a certain degree of success, and he thinks that the most trifling observations are worth publication.'"

Mr. Bentham's approval was given in his Presidential Address to the Linnean Society, May 24, 1862, and was all the more valuable because it came from one who was by no means supposed to be favourable to evolutionary doctrines.]

C. Darwin to Asa Gray.

Down, June 10 [1862].

MY DEAR GRAY,—Your generous sympathy makes you overestimate what you have read of my Orchid-book. But your letter of May 18th and 26th has given me an almost foolish amount of satisfaction. The subject interested me, I knew, beyond its real value; but I had lately got to think that I had made myself a complete fool by publishing in a semi-popular form. Now I shall confidently defy the world.

I have heard that Bentham and Oliver approve of it; but I have heard the opinion of no one else whose opinion is worth a farthing. . . . No doubt my volume contains much error: how curiously difficult it is to be accurate, though I try my utmost. Your notes have interested me beyond measure. I can now afford to d— my critics with ineffable complacency of mind. Cordial thanks for this benefit. It is surprising to me that you should have strength of mind to care for science, amidst the awful events daily occurring in your country. I daily look at the *Times* with almost as much interest as an American could do. When will peace come? it is dreadful to think of the desolation of large parts of your magnificent country; and all the speechless misery suffered by many. I hope and think it not unlikely that we English are wrong in concluding that it will take a long time for prosperity to return to you. It is an awful subject to reflect on. . . .

[Dr. Asa Gray reviewed the book in 'Silliman's Journal,'* where he speaks, in strong terms, of the fascination which it must have for even slightly instructed readers. He made, too, some original observations on an American orchid, and these first-fruits of the subject, sent in MS. or proof sheet to my father, were welcomed by him in a letter (July 23rd) :—

"Last night, after writing the above, I read the great bundle of notes. Little did I think what I had to read. What admirable observations! You have distanced me on my own hobby-horse! I have not had for weeks such a glow of pleasure as your observations gave me."

The next letter refers to the publication of the review :]

---

* 'Silliman's Journal,' vol. xxiv. p. 138. Here is given an account of the fertilisation of *Platanthera Hookeri*. *P. hyperborea* is discussed in Dr. Gray's 'Enumeration' in the same volume, p. 259; also, with other species, in a second notice of the Orchid-book at p. 420.

C. Darwin to Asa Gray.

Down, July 28 [1862].

MY DEAR GRAY,—I hardly know what to thank for first. Your stamps gave infinite satisfaction. I took him * first one lot, and then an hour afterwards another lot. He actually raised himself on one elbow to look at them. It was the first animation he showed. He said only: "You must thank Professor Gray awfully." In the evening after a long silence, there came out the oracular sentence: "He is awfully kind." And indeed you are, overworked as you are, to take so much trouble for our poor dear little man.—And now I must begin the "awfullys" on my own account: what a capital notice you have published on the orchids! It could not have been better; but I fear that you overrate it. I am very sure that I had not the least idea that you or any one would approve of it so much. I return your last note for the chance of your publishing any notice on the subject; but after all perhaps you may not think it worth while; yet in my judgment *several* of your facts, especially *Platanthera hyperborea*, are *much* too good to be merged in a review. But I have always noticed that you are prodigal in originality in your reviews. . . .

[Sir Joseph Hooker reviewed the book in the *Gardeners' Chronicle*, writing in a successful imitation of the style of Lindley, the Editor. My father wrote to Sir Joseph (Nov. 12, 1862) :—

"So you did write the review in the *Gardeners' Chronicle*. Once or twice I doubted whether it was Lindley; but when I came to a little slap at R. Brown, I doubted no longer. You arch-rogue! I do not wonder you have deceived others also. Perhaps I am a conceited dog; but if so, you have much to answer for; I never received so much praise, and coming from you I value it much more than from any other."

With regard to botanical opinion generally, he wrote to

---

* One of his boys who was ill.

Dr. Gray, " I am fairly astonished at the success of my book with botanists." Among naturalists who were not botanists, Lyell was pre-eminent in his appreciation of the book. I have no means of knowing when he read it, but in later life, as I learn from Professor Judd, he was enthusiastic in praise of the 'Fertilisation of Orchids,' which he considered " next to the ' Origin,' as the most valuable of all Darwin's works." Among the general public the author did not at first hear of many disciples, thus he wrote to his cousin Fox in September 1862 : " Hardly any one not a botanist, except yourself, as far as I know, has cared for it."

A favourable notice appeared in the *Saturday Review,* October 18th, 1862 ; the reviewer points out that the book would escape the angry polemics aroused by the ' Origin.' * This is illustrated by a review in the *Literary Churchman,* in which only one fault found, namely, that Mr. Darwin's expression of admiration at the contrivances in orchids is too indirect a way of saying, " O Lord, how manifold are Thy works ! "

A somewhat similar criticism occurs in the ' Edinburgh Review ' (October 1862). The writer points out that Mr. Darwin constantly uses phrases, such as " beautiful contrivance," " the labellum is . . . *in order* to attract," " the nectar is *purposely* lodged." The Reviewer concludes his discussion thus : " We know, too, that these purposes and ideas are not our own, but the ideas and purposes of Another."

The ' Edinburgh ' reviewer's treatment of this subject was criticised in the *Saturday Review,* November 15th, 1862 : With reference to this article my father wrote to Sir Joseph Hooker (December 29th, 1862) :—

" Here is an odd chance ; my nephew Henry Parker, an Oxford Classic, and Fellow of Oriel, came here this evening ;

---

* Dr. Gray pointed out that if the Orchid-book (with a few trifling omissions) had appeared before the ' Origin,' the author would have been canonised rather than anathematised by the natural theologians.

and I asked him whether he knew who had written the little article in the *Saturday*, smashing the [Edinburgh reviewer], which we liked ; and after a little hesitation he owned he had. I never knew that he wrote in the *Saturday ;* and was it not an odd chance ? ".

The 'Edinburgh' article was written by the Duke of Argyll, and has since been made use of in his 'Reign of Law,' 1867. Mr. Wallace replied * to the Duke's criticisms, making some specially good remarks on those which refer to orchids. He shows how, by a "beautiful self-acting adjustment," the nectary of the orchid Angræcum (from 10 to 14 inches in length), and the proboscis of a moth sufficiently long to reach the nectar, might be developed by natural selection. He goes on to point out that on any other theory we must suppose that the flower was created with an enormously long nectary, and that then by a special act, an insect was created fitted to visit the flower, which would otherwise remain sterile. With regard to this point my father wrote (October 12 or 13, 1867) :—

"I forgot to remark how capitally you turn the tables on the Duke, when you make him create the Angræcum and Moth by special creation."

If we examine the literature relating to the fertilisation of flowers, we do not find that this new branch of study showed any great activity immediately after the publication of the Orchid-book. There are a few papers by Asa Gray, in 1862 and 1863, by Hildebrand in 1864, and by Moggridge in 1865, but the great mass of work by Axell, Delpino, Hildebrand, and the Müllers, did not begin to appear until about 1867. The period during which the new views were being assimilated, and before they became thoroughly fruitful, was, however, surprisingly short. The later activity in this department may be roughly gauged by the fact that the valuable ' Bibliography,' given by Prof. D'Arcy Thompson in his translation

---

* 'Quarterly Journal of Science,' October 1867. Republished in 'Natural Selection,' 1871.

of Müller's 'Befruchtung' (1883), contains references to 814 papers.

Besides the book on Orchids, my father wrote two or three papers on the subject, which will be found mentioned in the Appendix. The earliest of these, on the three sexual forms of Catasetum, was published in 1862 ; it is an anticipation of part of the Orchid-book, and was merely published in the Linnean Society's Journal, in acknowledgment of the use made of a specimen in the Society's possession. The possibility of apparently distinct species being merely sexual forms of a single species, suggested a characteristic experiment, which is alluded to in the following letter to one of his earliest disciples in the study of the fertilisation of flowers :]

C. Darwin to J. Traherne Moggridge. *

Down, October 13 [1865].

MY DEAR SIR,—I am especially obliged to you for your beautiful plates and letter-press ; for no single point in natural history interests and perplexes me so much as the self-fertilisation † of the Bee-orchis. You have already thrown some light on the subject, and your present observations promise to throw more.

I formed two conjectures: first, that some insect during certain seasons might cross the plants, but I have almost given up this; nevertheless, pray have a look at the flowers next season. Secondly, I conjectured that the Spider and Bee-orchids might be a crossing and self-fertile form of the same species. Accordingly I wrote some years ago to an acquaintance, asking him to mark some Spider-orchids, and observe

---

* The late Mr. Moggridge, author of ' Harvesting Ants and Trap-door Spiders,' ' Flora of Mentone,' &c.

† He once remarked to Dr. Norman Moore that one of the things that made him wish to live a few thousand years, was his desire to see the extinction of the Bee-orchis,—an end to which he believed its self-fertilising habit was leading.

whether they retained the same character; but he evidently thought the request as foolish as if I had asked him to mark one of his cows with a ribbon, to see if it would turn next spring into a horse. Now will you be so kind as to tie a string round the stem of a half-a-dozen Spider-orchids, and when you leave Mentone dig them up, and I would try and cultivate them and see if they kept constant; but I should require to know in what sort of soil and situations they grow. It would be indispensable to mark the plant so that there could be no mistake about the individual. It is also just possible that the same plant would throw up, at different seasons different flower-scapes, and the marked plants would serve as evidence.

With many thanks, my dear sir,
Yours sincerely,
Ch. Darwin.

P.S.—I send by this post my paper on climbing plants, parts of which you might like to read.

[Sir Thomas Farrer and Dr. W. Ogle were also guided and encouraged by my father in their observations. The following refers to a paper by Sir Thomas Farrer, in the 'Annals and Magazine of Natural History,' 1868, on the fertilisation of the Scarlet Runner:]

C. Darwin to T. H. Farrer.

Down, Sept. 15, 1868.

My dear Mr. Farrer,—I grieve to say that the *main* features of your case are known. I am the sinner and described them some ten years ago. But I overlooked many details, as the appendage to the single stamen, and several other points. I send my notes, but I must beg for their return, as I have *no other copy.* I quite agree, the facts are most striking, especially as you put them. Are you sure that the Hive-bee is the cutter? it is against my experience. If sure, make the point more prominent, or if not sure, erase it. I do not think the subject is quite new enough for the Linnean Society; but I dare say the 'Annals and Magazine of Natural History,' or *Gardeners' Chronicle* would gladly publish your observations, and it is a great pity they should be lost. If you like I would send your paper to either quarter with a note. In this case you must give a title, and your name, and perhaps it would be well to premise your remarks with a line of reference to my paper stating that you had observed independently and more fully.

I have read my own paper over after an interval of several years, and am amused at the caution with which I put the case that the final end was for crossing distinct individuals, of which I was then as fully convinced as now, but I knew that the doctrine would shock all botanists. Now the opinion is becoming familiar.

To see penetration of pollen-tubes is not difficult, but in most cases requires some practice with dissecting under a one-tenth of an inch focal distance single lens; and just at first this will seem to you extremely difficult.

What a capital observer you are—a first-rate Naturalist has been sacrificed, or partly sacrificed to Public life.

Believe me, yours very sincerely,
CH. DARWIN.

P.S.—If you come across any large Salvia, look at it—the contrivance is admirable. It went to my heart to tell a man who came here a few weeks ago with splendid drawings and MS. on Salvia, that the work had been all done in Germany.*

[The following extract is from a letter, November 26th, 1868, to Sir Thomas Farrer, written as I learn from him, " in answer to a request for some advice as to the best modes of observation."

---

* Dr. W. Ogle, the observer of the fertilisation of Salvia here alluded to, published his results in the ' Pop. Science Review,' 1869.

He refers both gracefully and gratefully to his relationship with my father in the introduction to his translation of Kerner's ' Flowers and their Unbidden Guests.'

"In my opinion the best plan is to go on working and making copious notes, without much thought of publication, and then if the results turn out striking publish them. It is my impression, but I do not feel sure that I am right, that the best and most novel plan would be, instead of describing the means of fertilisation in particular plants, to investigate the part which certain structures play with all plants or throughout certain orders; for instance, the brush of hairs on the style, or the diadelphous condition of the stamens, in the Leguminosæ, or the hairs within the corolla, &c. &c. Looking to your note, I think that this is perhaps the plan which you suggest.

"It is well to remember that Naturalists value observations far more than reasoning ; therefore your conclusions should be as often as possible fortified by noticing how insects actually do the work."

In 1869, Sir Thomas Farrer corresponded with my father on the fertilisation of Passiflora and of Tacsonia. He has given me his impressions of the correspondence :—

"I had suggested that the elaborate series of *chevaux-de-frise*, by which the nectary of the common Passiflora is guarded, were specially calculated to protect the flower from the stiff-beaked humming birds which would not fertilise it, and to facilitate the access of the little proboscis of the humble bee, which would do so ; whilst, on the other hand, the long pendent tube and flexible valve-like corona which retains the nectar of Tacsonia would shut out the bee, which would not, and admit the humming bird which would, fertilise that flower. The suggestion is very possibly worthless, and could only be verified or refuted by examination of flowers in the countries where they grow naturally. . . . What interested me was to see that on this as on almost any other point of detailed observation, Mr. Darwin could always say, 'Yes; but at one time I made some observations myself on this particular point ; and I think you will find, &c. &c.' That he should after years of interval remember that he had noticed the peculiar structure to which I was referring in the

Passiflora princeps struck me at the time as very remarkable."

With regard to the spread of a belief in the adaptation of flowers for cross-fertilisation, my father wrote to Mr. Bentham April 22, 1868:

"Most of the criticisms which I sometimes meet with in French works against the frequency of crossing, I am certain are the result of mere ignorance. I have never hitherto found the rule to fail that when an author describes the structure of a flower as specially adapted for self-fertilisation, it is really adapted for crossing. The Fumariaceæ offer a good instance of this, and Treviranus threw this order in my teeth; but in Corydalis, Hildebrand shows how utterly false the idea of self-fertilisation is. This author's paper on Salvia is really worth reading, and I have observed some species, and know that he is accurate."

The next letter refers to Professor Hildebrand's paper on Corydalis, published in the 'Proc. Internat. Hort. Congress,' London, 1866, and in Pringsheim's 'Jahrbücher,' vol. v. The memoir on Salvia alluded to is contained in the previous volume of the same Journal :]

C. Darwin to F. Hildebrand.*

Down, May 16 [1866].

MY DEAR SIR,—The state of my health prevents my attending the Hort. Congress; but I forwarded yesterday your paper to the secretary, and if they are not overwhelmed with papers, yours will be gladly received. I have made many observations on the Fumariaceæ, and convinced myself that they were adapted for insect agency; but I never observed anything nearly so curious as your most interesting facts. I hope you will repeat your experiments on the Corydalis on a larger scale, and especially on several distinct plants; for your plant might have been individually peculiar, like certain indi-

---

* Professor of Botany at Freiburg.

vidual plants of Lobelia, &c., described by Gartner, and of Passiflora and Orchids described by Mr. Scott. . . .

Since writing to you before, I have read your admirable memoir on Salvia, and it has interested me almost as much as when I first investigated the structure of Orchids. Your paper illustrates several points in my 'Origin of Species,' especially the transition of organs. Knowing only two or three species in the genus, I had often marvelled how one cell of the anther could have been transformed into the movable plate or spoon ; and how well you show the gradations ; but I am surprised that you did not more strongly insist on this point.

I shall be still more surprised if you do not ultimately come to the same belief with me, as shown by so many beautiful contrivances, that all plants require, from some unknown cause, to be occasionally fertilized by pollen from a distinct individual. With sincere respect, believe me, my dear Sir,

Yours very faithfully,

CH. DARWIN.

[The following letter refers to the late Hermann Müller's 'Befruchtung der Blumen,' by far the most valuable of the mass of literature originating in the 'Fertilisation of Orchids.' An English translation, by Prof. D'Arcy Thompson was published in 1883. My father's "Prefatory Notice" to this work is dated February 6, 1882, and is therefore almost the last of his writings :]

C. Darwin to H. Müller.

Down, May 5, 1873.

MY DEAR SIR,—Owing to all sorts of interruptions and to my reading German so slowly, I have read only to p. 88 of your book ; but I must have the pleasure of telling you how very valuable a work it appears to me. Independently of the many original observations, which of course form the most important part, the work will be of the highest use as a means of reference to all that has been done on the subject. I am

fairly astonished at the number of species of insects, the visits
of which to different flowers you have recorded.   You must
have worked in the most indefatigable manner.   About half
a year ago the editor of 'Nature' suggested that it would be
a grand undertaking if a number of naturalists were to do
what you have already done on so large a scale with respect
to the visits of insects.   I have been particularly glad to read
your historical sketch, for I had never before seen all the
references put together.   I have sometimes feared that I was
in error when I said that C. K. Sprengel did not fully perceive that cross-fertilisation was the final end of the structure
of flowers ; but now this fear is relieved, and it is a great
satisfaction to me to believe that I have aided in making his
excellent book more generally known.   Nothing has surprised
me more than to see in your historical sketch how much I
myself have done on the subject, as it never before occurred
to me to think of all my papers as a whole.   But I do not
doubt that your generous appreciation of the labours of others
has led you to over-estimate what I have done.   With very
sincere thanks and respect, believe me,

Yours faithfully,
CHARLES DARWIN.

P.S.—I have mentioned your book to almost every one
who, as far as I know, cares for the subject in England ; and
I have ordered a copy to be sent to our Royal Society.

[The next letter, to Dr. Behrens, refers to the same subject as the last :]

C. Darwin to W. Behrens.

Down, August 29 [1878].

DEAR SIR,—I am very much obliged to you for having
sent me your 'Geschichte der Bestaubungs-Theorie,' * and
which has interested me much.   It has put some things in a

---

* Progr. der K. Gewerbschule zu Elberfeld, 1877, 1878.

new light, and has told me other things which I did not know. I heartily agree with you in your high appreciation of poor old C. Sprengel's work ; and one regrets bitterly that he did not live to see his labours thus valued. It rejoices me also to notice how highly you appreciate H. Müller, who has always seemed to me an admirable observer and reasoner. I am at present endeavoring to persuade an English publisher to bring out a translation of his 'Befruchtung.'

Lastly, permit me to thank you for your very generous remarks on my works. By placing what I have been able to do on this subject in systematic order, you have made me think more highly of my own work than I ever did before ! Nevertheless, I fear that you have done me more than justice.

I remain, dear Sir, yours faithfully and obliged,

CHARLES DARWIN.

[The letter which follows was called forth by Dr. Gray's article in 'Nature,' to which reference has already been made, and which appeared June 4, 1874 :]

C. Darwin to Asa Gray.

Down, June 3 [1874].

MY DEAR GRAY,—I was rejoiced to see your hand-writing again in your note of the 4th, of which more anon. I was astonished to see announced about a week ago that you were going to write in 'Nature' an article on me, and this morning I received an advance copy. It is the grandest thing ever written about me, especially as coming from a man like yourself. It has deeply pleased me, particularly some of your side remarks. It is a wonderful thing to me to live to see my name coupled in any fashion with that of Robert Brown. But you are a bold man, for I am sure that you will be sneered at by not a few botanists. I have never been so honoured before, and I hope it will do me good and make me try to be as careful as possible ; and good heavens, how difficult accuracy is ! I feel a very proud man, but I hope this won't last. . . .

[Fritz Müller has observed that the flowers of Hedychium are so arranged that the pollen is removed by the wings of hovering butterflies. My father's prediction of this observation is given in the following letter:]

C. Darwin to H. Müller.

Down, August 7, 1876.

. . . . I was much interested by your brother's article on Hedychium ; about two years ago I was so convinced that the flowers were fertilized by the tips of the wings of large moths, that I wrote to India to ask a man to observe the flowers and catch the moths at work, and he sent me 20 to 30 Sphinx-moths, but so badly packed that they all arrived in fragments ; and I could make out nothing. . . .

Yours sincerely,

CH. DARWIN.

[The following extract from a letter (Feb. 25, 1864), to Dr. Gray refers to another prediction fulfilled :—.

"I have of course seen no one, and except good dear Hooker, I hear from no one. He, like a good and true friend, though so overworked, often writes to me.

"I have had one letter which has interested me greatly, with a paper, which will appear in the Linnean Journal, by Dr. Crüger of Trinidad, which shows that I am all right about Catasetum, even to the spot where the pollinia adhere to the bees, which visit the flower, as I said, to gnaw the labellum. Crüger's account of Coryanthes and the use of the bucket-like labellum full of water beats everything : I *suspect* that the bees being well wetted flattens their hairs, and allows the viscid disc to adhere."]

C. Darwin to the Marquis de Saporta.

Down, December 24, 1877.

MY DEAR SIR,—I thank you sincerely for your long and most interesting letter, which I should have answered sooner had it not been delayed in London. I had not heard before that I was to be proposed as a Corresponding Member of the Institute. Living so retired a life as I do, such honours affect me very little, and I can say with entire truth that your kind expression of sympathy has given and will give me much more pleasure than the election itself, should I be elected.

Your idea that dicotyledonous plants were not developed in force until sucking insects had been evolved seems to me a splendid one. I am surprised that the idea never occurred to me, but this is always the case when one first hears a new and simple explanation of some mysterious phenomenon. . . . I formerly showed that we might fairly assume that the beauty of flowers, their sweet odour and copious nectar, may be attributed to the existence of flower-haunting insects, but your idea, which I hope you will publish, goes much further and is much more important. With respect to the great development of mammifers in the later Geological periods following from the development of dicotyledons, I think it ought to be proved that such animals as deer, cows, horses, &c. could not flourish if fed exclusively on the gramineæ and other anemophilous monocotyledons; and I do not suppose that any evidence on this head exists.

Your suggestion of studying the manner of fertilisation of the surviving members of the most ancient forms of the dicotyledons is a very good one, and I hope that you will keep it in mind yourself, for I have turned my attention to other subjects. Delpino I think says that Magnolia is fertilised by insects which gnaw the petals, and I should not be surprised if the same fact holds good with Nymphæa. Whenever I have looked at the flowers of these latter plants I have felt inclined to admit the view that petals are modified stamens, and not modified leaves; though Poinsettia seems to show that true leaves might be converted into coloured petals. I grieve to say that I have never been properly grounded in Botany and have studied only special points— therefore I cannot pretend to express any opinion on your remarks on the origin of the flowers of the Coniferæ, Gneta-

ceæ, &c. ; but I have been delighted with what you say on the
conversion of a monœcious species into a hermaphrodite one
by the condensations of the verticils on a branch bearing
female flowers near the summit, and male flowers below.

I expect Hooker to come here before long, and I will then
show him your drawing, and if he makes any important remarks I will communicate with you.   He is very busy at
present in clearing off arrears after his American Expedition,
so that I do not like to trouble him, even with the briefest
note.   I am at present working with my son at some Physiological subjects, and we are arriving at very curious results,
but they are not as yet sufficiently certain to be worth communicating to you. . . .

[In 1877 a second edition of the ‘Fertilisation of Orchids’
was published, the first edition having been for some time out
of print.   The new edition was remodelled and almost re-
written, and a large amount of new matter added, much of
which the author owed to his friend Fritz Müller.

With regard to this edition he wrote to Dr. Gray :—

“I do not suppose I shall ever again touch the book.
After much doubt I have resolved to act in this way with all
my books for the future ; that is to correct them once and
never touch them again, so as to use the small quantity of
work left in me for new matter.”

He may have felt a diminution of his powers of reviewing
large bodies of facts, such as would be needed in the preparation of new editions, but his powers of observation were
certainly not diminished.   He wrote to Mr. Dyer on July 14,
1878 :]

MY DEAR DYER,— *Thalia dealbata* was sent me from Kew :
it has flowered and after looking casually at the flowers, they
have driven me almost mad, and I have worked at them for
a week : it is as grand a case as that of Catasetum.

Pistil vigorously motile (so that whole flower shakes when
pistil suddenly coils up) ; when excited by a touch the two

filaments [are] produced laterally and transversely across the flower (just over the nectar) from one of the petals or modified stamens. It is splendid to watch the phenomenon under a weak power when a bristle is inserted into a *young* flower which no insect has visited. As far as I know Stylidium is the sole case of sensitive pistil and here it is the pistil+stamens. In Thalia * cross-fertilisation is ensured by the wonderful movement, if bees visit several flowers.

I have now relieved my mind and will tell the purport of this note—viz. if any other species of Thalia besides *T. dealbata* should flower with you, for the love of heaven and all the saints, send me a few in *tin box with damp moss.*

Your insane friend,
CH. DARWIN.

[In 1878 Dr. Ogle's translation of Kerner's interesting book, 'Flowers and their Unbidden Guests,' was published. My father, who felt much interest in the translation (as appears in the following letter), contributed some prefatory words of approval :]

C. Darwin to W. Ogle.

Down, December 16 [1878].

. . . . I have now read Kerner's book, which is better even than I anticipated. The translation seems to me as clear as daylight, and written in forcible and good familiar English. I am rather afraid that it is too good for the English public, which seems to like very washy food, unless it be administered by some one whose name is well known, and then I suspect a good deal of the unintelligible is very pleasing to them. I hope to heaven that I may be wrong. Anyhow, you and Mrs. Ogle have done a right good service for Botanical Science. Yours very sincerely,

CH. DARWIN.

---

* Hildebrand has described an explosive arrangement in some of the Maranteæ—the tribe to which Thalia belongs.

P.S.—You have done me much honour in your prefatory remarks.

[One of the latest references to his Orchid-work occurs in a letter to Mr. Bentham, February 16, 1880. It shows the amount of pleasure which this subject gave to my father, and (what is characteristic of him) that his reminiscence of the work was one of delight in the observations which preceded its publication, not to the applause which followed it :—

"They are wonderful creatures, these Orchids, and I sometimes think with a glow of pleasure, when I remember making out some little point in their method of fertilisation."]

CHAPTER XI.

THE 'EFFECTS OF CROSS- AND SELF-FERTILISATION IN THE VEGETABLE KINGDOM.' 1876.

[THIS book, as pointed out in the 'Autobiography,' is a complement to the 'Fertilisation of Orchids,' because it shows how important are the results of cross-fertilisation which are ensured by the mechanisms described in that book. By proving that the offspring of cross-fertilisation are more vigorous than the offspring of self-fertilisation, he showed that one circumstance which influences the fate of young plants in the struggle for life is the degree to which their parents are fitted for cross-fertilisation. He thus convinced himself that the intensity of the struggle (which he had elsewhere shown to exist among young plants) is a measure of the strength of a selective agency perpetually sifting out every modification in the structure of flowers which can effect its capabilities for cross-fertilisation.

The book is also valuable in another respect, because it throws light on the difficult problems of the origin of sexuality. The increased vigour resulting from cross-fertilisation is allied in the closest manner to the advantage gained by change of conditions. So strongly is this the case, that in some instances cross-fertilisation gives no advantage to the offspring, unless the parents have lived under slightly different conditions. So that the really important thing is not that two individuals of different *blood* shall unite, but two individuals which have been subjected to different conditions. We are thus led to believe that sexuality is a means for infusing vigour into the offspring by the coalescence of differentiated elements, an advantage which could not follow if reproductions were entirely asexual.

It is remarkable that this book, the result of eleven years of experimental work, owed its origin to a chance observation. My father had raised two beds of *Linaria vulgaris*—one set being the offspring of cross- and the other of self-fertilisation. These plants were grown for the sake of some observations on inheritance, and not with any view to cross-breeding, and he was astonished to observe that the offspring of self-fertilisation were clearly less vigorous than the others. It seemed incredible to him that this result could be due to a single act of self-fertilisation, and it was only in the following year when precisely the same result occurred in the case of a similar experiment on inheritance in Carnations, that his attention was " thoroughly aroused " and that he determined to make a series of experiments specially directed to the question. The following letters give some account of the work in question :]

C. *Darwin to Asa Gray.*

September 10, [1866?]

. . . . I have just begun a large course of experiments on the germination of the seed, and on the growth of the young plants when raised from a pistil fertilised by pollen from the same flower, and from pollen from a distinct plant of the same, or of some other variety. I have not made sufficient experiments to judge certainly, but in some cases the difference in the growth of the young plants is highly remarkable. I have taken every kind of precaution in getting seed from the same plant, in germinating the seed on my own chimney-piece, in planting the seedlings in the same flower-pot, and under this similar treatment I have seen the young seedlings from the crossed seed exactly twice as tall as the seedlings from the self-fertilised seed ; both seeds having germinated on same day. If I can establish this fact (but perhaps it will all go to the dogs), in some fifty cases, with plants of different orders, I think it will be very important, for then we shall positively know why the structure of every flower permits, or favours, or necessitates an occasional cross with a distinct individual. But all this is rather cooking my hare before I have caught it. But somehow it is a great pleasure to me to tell you what I am about. Believe me, my dear Gray,

Ever yours most truly, and with cordial thanks,

CH. DARWIN.

C. Darwin to G. Bentham.

April 22, 1868.

. . . . I am experimenting on a very large scale on the difference in power of growth between plants raised from self-fertilised and crossed seeds; and it is no exaggeration to say that the difference in growth and vigour is sometimes truly wonderful. Lyell, Huxley and Hooker have seen some of my plants, and been astonished; and I should much like to show them to you. I always supposed until lately that no evil effects would be visible until after several genera-tions of self-fertilisation; but now I see that one generation sometimes suffices; and the existence of dimorphic plants and all the wonderful contrivances of orchids are quite in-telligible to me.

With cordial thanks for your letter, which has pleased me greatly,

Yours very sincerely,

CHARLES DARWIN.

[An extract from a letter to Dr. Gray (March 11, 1873) mentions the progress of the work :—

"I worked last summer hard at Drosera, but could not finish till I got fresh plants, and consequently took up the effects of crossing and self-fertilising plants, and am got so interested that Drosera must go to the dogs till I finish with this, and get it published ; but then I will resume my beloved Drosera, and I heartily apologise for having sent the precious little things even for a moment to the dogs."

The following letters give the author's impression of his own book.]

C. Darwin to J. Murray.

Down, September 16, 1876.

My dear Sir,—I have just received proofs in sheet of five sheets, so you will have to decide soon how many copies will have to be struck off. I do not know what to advise. The greater part of the book is extremely dry, and the whole on a special subject. Nevertheless, I am convinced that the book is of value, and I am convinced that for *many* years copies will be occasionally sold. Judging from the sale of my former books, and from supposing that some persons will purchase it to complete the set of my works, I would suggest 1500. But you must be guided by your larger experience. I will only repeat that I am convinced the book is of some permanent value. . . .

C. Darwin to Victor Carus.

Down, September 27, 1876.

My dear Sir,—I sent by this morning's post the four first perfect sheets of my new book, the title of which you will see on the first page, and which will be published early in November.

I am sorry to say that it is only shorter by a few pages than my 'Insectivorous Plants.' The whole is now in type, though I have corrected finally only half the volume. You will, therefore, rapidly receive the remainder. The book is very dull. Chapters II. to VI., inclusive, are simply a record of experiments. Nevertheless, I believe (though a man can never judge his own books) that the book is valuable. You will have to decide whether it is worth translating. I hope so. It has cost me very great labour, and the results seem to me remarkable and well established.

If you translate it, you could easily get aid for Chapters II. to VI., as there is here endless, but I have thought necessary repetition. I shall be anxious to hear what you decide. . . . . .

I most sincerely hope that your health has been fairly good this summer.

My dear Sir, yours very truly,

CH. DARWIN.

C. Darwin to Asa Gray.

Down, October 28, 1876.

MY DEAR GRAY,—I send by this post all the clean sheets as yet printed, and I hope to send the remainder within a fortnight. Please observe that the first six chapters are not readable, and the six last very dull. Still I believe that the results are valuable. If you review the book, I shall be very curious to see what you think of it, for I care more for your judgment than for that of almost any one else. I know also that you will speak the truth, whether you approve or disapprove. Very few will take the trouble to read the book, and I do not expect you to read the whole, but I hope you will read the latter chapters.

. . . I am so sick of correcting the press and licking my horrid bad style into intelligible English.

[The ' Effects of Cross and Self-fertilisation ' was published on November 10, 1876, and 1500 copies were sold before the end of the year. The following letter refers to a review in ' Nature :' *]

C. Darwin to W. Thiselton Dyer.

Down, February 16, 1877.

DEAR DYER,—I must tell you how greatly I am pleased and honoured by your article in ' Nature,' which I have just read. You are an adept in saying what will please an author, not that I suppose you wrote with this express intention.

---

* February 15, 1877.

I should be very well contented to deserve a fraction of your praise. I have also been much interested, and this is better than mere pleasure, by your argument about the separation of the sexes. I dare say that I am wrong, and will hereafter consider what you say more carefully : but at present I cannot drive out of my head that the sexes must have originated from two individuals, slightly different, which conjugated. But I am aware that some cases of conjugation are opposed to any such views.

With hearty thanks,
Yours sincerely,
CHARLES DARWIN.

CHAPTER XII.

'DIFFERENT FORMS OF FLOWERS ON PLANTS OF THE SAME SPECIES.' 1877.

[THE volume bearing the above title was published in 1877, and was dedicated by the author to Professor Asa Gray, "as a small tribute of respect and affection." It consists of certain earlier papers re-edited, with the addition of a quantity of new matter. The subjects treated in the book are :—

(i.) Heterostyled Plants.

(ii.) Polygamous, Diœcious, and Gynodiœcious Plants.

(iii.) Cleistogamic Flowers.

The nature of heterostyled plants may be illustrated in the primrose, one of the best known examples of the class. If a number of primroses be gathered, it will be found that some plants yield nothing but "pin-eyed" flowers, in which the style (or organ for the transmission of the pollen to the ovule) is long, while the others yield only "thrum-eyed" flowers with short styles. Thus primroses are divided into two sets or castes differing structurally from each other. My father showed that they also differ sexually, and that in fact the bond between the two castes more nearly resembles that between separate sexes than any other known relationship. Thus for example a long-styled primrose, though it can be fertilised by its own pollen, is not *fully* fertile unless it is impregnated by the pollen of a short-styled flower. Heterostyled plants are comparable to hermaphrodite animals, such as snails, which require the concourse of two individuals, although each possesses both the sexual elements. The difference is that in the case of the primrose it is *perfect fertility*, and not simply *fertility*, that depends on the mutual action of the two sets of individuals.

The work on heterostyled plants has a special bearing, to which the author attached much importance, on the problem of origin of species.*

He found that a wonderfully close parallelism exists between hybridisation and certain forms of fertilisation among heterostyled plants. So that it is hardly an exaggeration to say that the "illegitimately" reared seedlings are hybrids, although both their parents belong to identically the same species. In a letter to Professor Huxley, given in the second volume (p. 176), my father writes as if his researches on heterostyled plants tended to make him believe that sterility is a selected or acquired quality. But in his later publications, e.g. in the sixth edition of the 'Origin,' he adheres to the belief that sterility is an incidental rather than a selected quality. The result of his work on heterostyled plants is of importance as showing that sterility is no test of specific distinctness, and that it depends on differentiation of the sexual elements which is independent of any racial difference. I imagine that it was his instinctive love of making out a difficulty which to a great extent kept him at work so patiently on the heterostyled plants. But it was the fact that general conclusions of the above character could be drawn from his results which made him think his results worthy of publication.†

The papers which on this subject preceded and contributed to 'Forms of Flowers' were the following :—

"On the two Forms or Dimorphic Condition in the Species of Primula, and on their remarkable Sexual Relations." Linn. Soc. Journal, 1862.

"On the Existence of Two Forms, and on their Reciprocal Sexual Relations, in several Species of the Genus Linum." Linn. Soc. Journal, 1863.

---

* See 'Autobiography,' vol. i. p. 97.
† See 'Forms of Flowers,' p. 243.

"On the Sexual Relations of the Three Forms of *Lythrum salicaria*," Ibid. 1864.

"On the Character and Hybrid-like Nature of the Offspring from the Illegitimate Unions of Dimorphic and Trimorphic Plants." Ibid. 1869.

"On the Specific Differences between *Primula veris*, Brit. Fl. (var. *officinalis*, Linn.), *P. vulgaris*, Brit. Fl. (var. *acaulis*, Linn.), and *P. elatior*, Jacq. ; and on the Hybrid Nature of the Common Oxlip. With Supplementary Remarks on Naturally Produced Hybrids in the Genus Verbascum." Ibid. 1869.

The following letter shows that he began the work on heterostyled plants with an erroneous view as to the meaning of the facts.]

C. *Darwin to J. D. Hooker.*

Down, May 7 [1860].

. . . . I have this morning been looking at my experimental cowslips, and I find some plants have all flowers with long stamens and short pistils, which I will call "male plants," others with short stamens and long pistils, which I will call "female plants." This I have somewhere seen noticed, I think by Henslow ; but I find (after looking at my two sets of plants) that the stigmas of the male and female are of slightly different shape, and certainly, different degree of roughness, and what has astonished me, the pollen of the so-called female plant, though very abundant, is more transparent, and each granule is exactly only $\frac{2}{3}$ of the size of the pollen of the so-called male plant. Has this been observed? I cannot help suspecting [that] the cowslip is in fact diœcious, but it may turn out all a blunder, but anyhow I will mark with sticks the so-called male and female plants and watch their seeding. It would be a fine case of gradation between an hermaphrodite and unisexual condition. Likewise a sort of case of balancement of long and short pistils and stamens. Likewise perhaps throws light on oxlips. . . .

I have now examined primroses and find exactly the same difference in the size of the pollen, correlated with the same difference in the length of the style and roughness of the stigmas.

C. Darwin to Asa Gray.

June 8 [1860].

. . . . I have been making some little trifling observations which have interested and perplexed me much. I find with primroses and cowslips, that about an equal number of plants are thus characterised.

So-called (by me) *male* plant. Pistil much shorter than stamens ; stigma rather smooth,—*pollen grains large,* throat of corolla short.

So-called female plant. Pistil much longer than stamens, stigma rougher, *pollen-grains smaller,*—throat of corolla long.

I have marked a lot of plants, and expected to find the so-called male plant barren ; but judging from the feel of the capsules, this is not the case, and I am very much surprised at the difference in the size of the pollen. . . . If it should prove that the so-called male plants produce less seed than the so-called females, what a beautiful case of gradation from hermaphrodite to unisexual condition it will be ! If they produce about equal number of seed, how perplexing it will be.

C. Darwin to J. D. Hooker.

Down, December 17, [1860?]

. . . . I have just been ordering a photograph of myself for a friend ; and have ordered one for you, and for heaven's sake oblige me, and burn that now hanging up in your room.—It makes me look atrociously wicked.

. . . . In the spring I must get you to look for long pistils and short pistils in the rarer species of Primula and in some allied Genera. It holds with *P. Sinensis.* You remember all the fuss I made on this subject last spring ; well, the other day at last I had time to weigh the seeds, and by Jove the plants of primroses and cowslip with short pistils and large grained pollen * are rather more fertile than those with long pistils, and small-grained pollen. I find that they require the action of insects to set them, and I never will believe that these differences are without some meaning.

Some of my experiments lead me to suspect that the large-grained pollen suits the long pistils and the small-grained pollen suits the short pistils; but I am determined to see if I cannot make out the mystery next spring.

How does your book on plants brew in your mind? Have you begun it? . . . .

Remember me most kindly to Oliver. He must be astonished at not having a string of questions, I fear he will get out of practice!

[The Primula-work was finished in the autumn of 1861, and on Nov. 8th he wrote to Sir J. D. Hooker :—

"I have sent my paper on dimorphism in Primula to the Linn. Soc. I shall go up and read it whenever it comes on ; I hope you may be able to attend, for I do not suppose many will care a penny for the subject."

With regard to the reading of the paper (on Nov. 21st), he wrote to the same friend :—

"I by no means thought that I produced a "tremendous effect" in the Linn. Soc., but by Jove the Linn. Soc. produced a tremendous effect on me, for I could not get out of bed till late next evening, so that I just crawled home. I fear I must give up trying to read any paper or speak ; it is a horrid bore, I can do nothing like other people."

To Dr. Gray he wrote, (Dec. 1861) :—

"You may rely on it, I will send you a copy of my Primula paper as soon as I can get one ; but I believe it will not be printed till April 1st, and therefore after my Orchid Book. I care more for your and Hooker's opinion than for that of all the rest of the world, and for Lyell's on geological points. Bentham and Hooker thought well of my paper when read ;

---

* Thus the plants which he imagined to be tending towards a male condition were more productive than the supposed females.

but no one can judge of evidence by merely hearing a paper.''

The work on Primula was the means of bringing my father in contact with the late Mr. John Scott, then working as a gardener in the Botanic Gardens at Edinburgh,—an employment which he seems to have chosen in order to gratify his passion for natural history. He wrote one or two excellent botanical papers, and ultimately obtained a post in India.* He died in 1880.

A few phrases may be quoted from letters to Sir J. D. Hooker, showing my father's estimate of Scott :—

"If you know, do please tell me who is John Scott of the Botanical Gardens of Edinburgh; I have been corresponding largely with him; he is no common man."

"If he had leisure he would make a wonderful observer; to my judgment I have come across no one like him."

"He has interested me strangely, and I have formed a very high opinion of his intellect. I hope he will accept pecuniary assistance from me; but he has hitherto refused." (He ultimately succeeded in being allowed to pay for Mr. Scott's passage to India.)

"I know nothing of him excepting from his letters; these show remarkable talent, astonishing perseverance, much modesty, and what I admire, determined difference from me on many points."

So highly did he estimate Scott's abilities that he formed a plan (which however never went beyond an early stage of discussion) of employing him to work out certain problems connected with intercrossing.

The following letter refers to my father's investigations on Lythrum,† a plant which reveals even a more wonderful

---

* While in India he made some admirable observations on expression for my father.

† He was led to this, his first case of trimorphism by Lecoq's 'Géographie Botanique,' and this must have consoled him for the trick this work played him in turning out to be so much larger than he expected. He wrote to Sir J. D. Hooker: " Here is a good joke : I saw an extract

condition of sexual complexity than that of Primula. For in Lythrum there are not merely two, but three castes, differing structurally and physiologically from each other :]

C. Darwin to Asa Gray.

Down, August 9 [1862].

MY DEAR GRAY,—It is late at night, and I am going to write briefly, and of course to beg a favour.

The Mitchella very good, but pollen apparently equal-sized. I have just examined Hottonia, grand difference in pollen. *Echium vulgare*, a humbug, merely a case like Thymus. But I am almost stark staring mad over Lythrum; * if I can prove what I fully believe, it is a grand case of TRIMORPHISM, with three different pollens and three stigmas; I have castrated and fertilised above ninety flowers, trying all the eighteen distinct crosses which are possible within the limits of this one species ! I cannot explain, but I feel sure you would think it a grand case. I have been writing to Botanists to see if I can possibly get *L. hyssopifolia*, and it has just flashed on me that you might have Lythrum in North America, and I have looked to your Manual. For the love of heaven have a look at some of your species, and if you can get me seed, do; I want much to try species with few stamens, if they are dimorphic; *Nesæa verticillata* I should expect to be trimorphic. Seed ! Seed ! Seed ! I should rather like seed of Mitchella. But oh, Lythrum !

Your utterly mad friend,

C. DARWIN.

P.S.—There is reason in my madness, for I can see that to those who already believe in change of species, these facts

---

from Lecoq, 'Géograph. Bot.,' and ordered it and hoped that it was a good sized pamphlet, and nine thick volumes have arrived !"

* On another occasion he wrote (to Dr. Gray) with regard to Lythrum : "I must hold hard, otherwise I shall spend my life over dimorphism."

will modify to a certain extent the whole view of Hybridity.*

[On the same subject he wrote to Sir Joseph Hooker in August 1862 :—

"Is Oliver at Kew? When I am established at Bournemouth I am completely mad to examine any fresh flowers of any Lythraceous plant, and I would write and ask him if any are in bloom."

Again he wrote to the same friend in October :—

"If you ask Oliver, I think he will tell you I have got a real odd case in Lythrum, it interests me extremely, and seems to me the strangest case of propagation recorded amongst plants or animals, viz. a necessary triple alliance between three hermaphrodites. I feel sure I can now prove the truth of the case from a multitude of crosses made this summer."

In an article, 'Dimorphism in the Genitalia of Plants' ('Silliman's Journal,' 1862, vol. xxxiv. p. 419), Dr. Gray pointed out that the structural difference between the two forms of Primula had already been defined in the 'Flora of N. America,' as *diœcio-dimorphism*. The use of this term called forth the following remarks from my father. The letter also alludes to a review of the 'Fertilisation of Orchids' in the same volume of 'Silliman's Journal.']

---

* A letter to Dr. Gray (July, 1862) bears on this point : " A few days ago I made an observation which has surprised me more than it ought to do—it will have to be repeated several times, but I have scarcely a doubt of its accuracy. I stated in my Primula paper that the long-styled form of *Linum grandiflorum* was utterly sterile with its own pollen; I have lately been putting the pollen of the two forms on the stigma of the *same* flower; and it strikes me as truly wonderful, that the stigma distinguishes the pollen; and is penetrated by the tubes of the one and not by those of the other; nor are the tubes exserted. Or (which is the same thing) the stigma of the one form acts on and is acted on by pollen, which produces not the least effect on the stigma of the other form. Taking sexual power as the criterion of difference, the two forms of this one species may be said to be generically distinct."

C. Darwin to Asa Gray.

Down, November 26 [1862].

MY DEAR GRAY,—The very day after my last letter, yours of November 10th, and the review in 'Silliman,' which I feared might have been lost, reached me. We were all very much interested by the political part of your letter; and in some odd way one never feels that information and opinions painted in a newspaper come from a living source; they seem dead, whereas all that you write is full of life. The reviews interested me profoundly; you rashly ask for my opinion, and you must consequently endure a long letter. First for Dimorphism; I do not *at present* like the term "Dioecio-dimorphism;" for I think it gives quite a false notion, that the phenomena are connected with a separation of the sexes. Certainly in Primula there is unequal fertility in the two forms, and I suspect this is the case with Linum; and, therefore I felt bound in the Primula paper to state that it might be a step towards a dioecious condition; though I believe there are no dioecious forms in Primulaceæ or Linaceæ. But the three forms in Lythrum convince me that the phenomenon is in no way necessarily connected with any tendency to separation of sexes. The case seems to me in result or function to be almost identical with what old C. K. Sprengel called "dichogamy," and which is so frequent in truly hermaphrodite groups; namely, the pollen and stigma of each flower being mature at different periods. If I am right, it is very advisable not to use the term "dioecious," as this at once brings notions of separation of sexes.

. . . I was much perplexed by Oliver's remarks in the 'Natural History Review' on the Primula case, on the lower plants having sexes more often separated than in the higher plants,—so exactly the reverse of what takes place in animals. Hooker in his review of the 'Orchids' repeats this remark. There seems to be much truth in what you say,* and it did not occur to me, about no improbability of specialisation in *certain* lines in lowly organised beings. I could hardly doubt that the hermaphrodite state is the aboriginal one. But how is it in the conjugation of Confervæ—is not one of the two individuals here in fact male, and the other female? I have been much puzzled by this contrast in sexual arrangements between plants and animals. Can there be anything in the following consideration : By *roughest* calculation about one-third of the British *genera* of aquatic plants belong to the Linnean classes of Mono and Dicecia; whilst of terrestrial plants (the aquatic genera being subtracted) only one-thirteenth of the genera belong to these two classes. Is there any truth in this fact generally? Can aquatic plants, being confined to a small area or small community of individuals, require more free crossing, and therefore have separate sexes? But to return to our point, does not Alph. de Candolle say that aquatic plants taken as a whole are lowly organised, compared with terrestrial ; and may not Oliver's remark on the separation of the sexes in lowly organised plants stand in some relation to their being frequently aquatic? Or is this all rubbish?

. . . . What a magnificent compliment you end your review with ! You and Hooker seem determined to turn my head with conceit and vanity (if not already turned) and make me an unbearable wretch.

With most cordial thanks, my good and kind friend,

Farewell,

C. DARWIN.

[The following passage from a letter (July 28, 1863), to Prof. Hildebrand, contains a reference to the reception of the dimorphic work in France :—

"I am extremely much pleased to hear that you have been

---

* " Forms which are low in the scale as respects morphological completeness may be high in the scale of rank founded on specialisation of structure and function."—Dr. Gray, in ‘ Silliman's Journal.’

looking at the manner of fertilisation of your native Orchids, and still more pleased to hear that you have been experimenting on Linum. I much hope that you may publish the result of these experiments; because I was told that the most eminent French botanists of Paris said that my paper on Primula was the work of imagination, and that the case was so improbable they did not believe in my results."]

C. Darwin to Asa Gray.

April 19 [1864].

. . . . I received a little time ago a paper with a good account of your Herbarium and Library, and a long time previously your excellent review of Scott's 'Primulaceæ,' and I forwarded it to him in India, as it would much please him. I was very glad to see in it a new case of Dimorphism (I forget just now the name of the plant); I shall be grateful to hear of any other cases, as I still feel an interest in the subject. I should be very glad to get some seed of your dimorphic Plantagos; for I cannot banish the suspicion that they must belong to a very different class like that of the common Thyme.* How could the wind, which is the agent of fertilisation, with Plantago, fertilise "reciprocally dimorphic" flowers like Primula? Theory says this cannot be, and in such cases of one's own theories I follow Agassiz and declare, "that nature never lies." I should even be very glad to examine the two dried forms of Plantago. Indeed, any dried dimorphic plants would be gratefully received. . . .

Did my Lythrum paper interest you? I crawl on at the rate of two hours per diem, with 'Variation under Domestication.'

C. Darwin to J. D. Hooker.

Down, November 26 [1864].

. . . . You do not know how pleased I am that you have read my Lythrum paper; I thought you would not have time,

---

* In this prediction he was right. See 'Forms of Flowers,' p. 307.

and I have for long years looked at you as my Public, and care more for your opinion than that of all the rest of the world. I have done nothing which has interested me so much as Lythrum, since making out the complemental males of Cirripedes. I fear that I have dragged in too much miscellaneous matter into the paper.

. . . I get letters occasionally, which show me that Natural Selection is making *great* progress in Germany, and some amongst the young in France. I have just received a pamphlet from Germany, with the complimentary title of " Darwinische Arten-Enstehung-Humbug " !

Farewell, my best of old friends,

C. DARWIN.

C. Darwin to Asa Gray.

September 10, [1867?]

. . . . The only point which I have made out this summer, which could possibly interest you, is that the common Oxlip found everywhere, more or less commonly in England, is certainly a hybrid between the primrose and cowslip ; whilst the *P. elatior* (Jacq.), found only in the Eastern Counties, is a perfectly distinct and good species ; hardly distinguishable from the common oxlip, except by the length of the seed-capsule relatively to the calyx. This seems to me rather a horrid fact for all systematic botanists. . . .

C. Darwin to F. Hildebrand.

Down, November 16, 1868.

MY DEAR SIR,—I wrote my last note in such a hurry from London, that I quite forgot what I chiefly wished to say, namely to thank you for your excellent notices in the 'Bot. Zeitung' of my paper on the offspring of dimorphic plants. The subject is so obscure that I did not expect that any one would have noticed my paper, and I am accordingly very much pleased that you should have brought the subject before the many excellent naturalists of Germany.

Of all the German authors (but they are not many) whose works I have read, you write by far the clearest style, but whether this is a compliment to a German writer I do not know.

[The two following letters refer to the small bud-like " Cleistogamic " flowers found in the violet and many other plants. They do not open and are necessarily self-fertilised :]

C. Darwin to J. D. Hooker.

Down, May 30 [1862].

. . . . What will become of my book on Variation? I am involved in a multiplicity of experiments. I have been amusing myself by looking at the small flowers of Viola. If Oliver * has had time to study them, he will have seen the curious case (as it seems to me) which I have just made clearly out, viz. that in these flowers, the *few* pollen grains are never shed, or never leave the anther-cells, but emit long pollen tubes, which penetrate the stigma. To-day I got the anther with the included pollen grain (now empty) at one end, and a bundle of tubes penetrating the stigmatic tissue at the other end ; I got the whole under a microscope without breaking the tubes; I wonder whether the stigma pours some fluid into the anther so as to excite the included grains. It is a rather odd case of correlation, that in the double sweet violet the little flowers are double; *i.e.*, have a multitude of minute scales representing the petals. What queer little flowers they are.

Have you had time to read poor dear Henslow's life? it has interested me for the man's sake, and, what I did not think possible, has even exalted his character in my estimation. . . . .

---

* Shortly afterwards he wrote : " Oliver, the omniscient, has sent me a paper in the 'Bot. Zeitung,' with most accurate description of all that I saw in Viola."

[The following is an extract from the letter given in part at p. 477, and refers to Dr. Gray's article on the sexual differences of plants :]

C. Darwin to Asa Gray.

November 26 [1862].

. . . . You will think that. I am in the most unpleasant, contradictory, fractious humour, when I tell you that I do not like your term of "precocious fertilisation" for your second class of dimorphism [*i. e.* for cleistogamic fertilisation]. If I can trust my memory, the state of the corolla, of the stigma, and the pollen-grains is different from the state of the parts in the bud ; that they are in a condition of special modification. But upon my life I am ashamed of myself to differ so much from my betters on this head. The *temporary* theory* which I have formed on this class of dimorphism, just to guide experiment, is that the *perfect* flowers can only be perfectly fertilised by insects, and are in this case abundantly crossed ; but that the flowers are not always, especially in early spring, visited enough by insects, and therefore the little imperfect self-fertilising flowers are developed to ensure a sufficiency of seed for present generations. *Viola canina* is sterile, when not visited by insects, but when so visited forms plenty of seed. I infer from the structure of three or four forms of *Balsamineæ*, that these require insects ; at least there is almost as plain adaptation to insects as in the Orchids. I have *Oxalis acetosella* ready in pots for experiment next spring ; and I fear this will upset my little theory. . . . *Campanula carpathica*, as I found this summer, is absolutely sterile if insects are excluded. *Specularia speculum* is fairly fertile when enclosed ; and this seemed to me to be partially effected by the frequent closing of the flower ; the inward angular folds of the corolla corresponding with the clefts of the open stigma, and in this action pushing pollen

---

* This view is now generally accepted.

from the outside of the stigma on to its surface. Now can you tell me, does *S. perfoliata* close its flower like *S. speculum*, with angular inward folds ? if so, I am smashed without some fearful " wriggling." Are the *imperfect* flowers of your Specularia the early or the later ones ? very early or very late ? It is rather pretty to see the importance of the closing of flowers of *S. speculum*.

['Forms of Flowers' was published in July ; in June, 1877, he wrote to Professor Carus with regard to the translation :—

" My new book is not a long one, viz. 350 pages, chiefly of the larger type, with fifteen simple woodcuts. All the proofs are corrected except the Index, so that it will soon be published.

" . . . . I do not suppose that I shall publish any more books, though perhaps a few more papers. I cannot endure being idle, but heaven knows whether I am capable of any more good work."

The review alluded to in the next letter is at p. 445 of the volume of 'Nature' for 1878 :]

C. Darwin to W. Thiselton Dyer.

Down, April 5, 1878.

MY DEAR DYER,—I have just read in 'Nature' the review of 'Forms of Flowers,' and I am sure that it is by you. I wish with all my heart that it deserved one quarter of the praises which you give it. Some of your remarks have interested me greatly. . . . Hearty thanks for your generous and most kind sympathy, which does a man real good, when he is as dog-tired as I am at this minute with working all day, so good-bye.

C. DARWIN.

CHAPTER XIII.

CLIMBING AND INSECTIVOROUS PLANTS.

[My father mentions in his 'Autobiography' (vol. i. p. 75) that he was led to take up the subject of climbing plants by reading Dr. Gray's paper, "Note on the Coiling of the Tendrils of Plants." * This essay seems to have been read in 1862, but I am only able to guess at the date of the letter in which he asks for a reference to it, so that the precise date of his beginning this work cannot be determined.

In June 1863 he was certainly at work, and wrote to Sir. J. D. Hooker for information as to previous publications on the subject, being then in ignorance of Palm's and H. v. Mohl's works on climbing plants, both of which were published in 1827.]

C. Darwin to J. D. Hooker.

Down [June] 25 [1863].

My dear Hooker,—I have been observing pretty carefully a little fact which has surprised me ; and I want to know from you and Oliver whether it seems new or odd to you, so just tell me whenever you write ; it is a very trifling fact, so do not answer on purpose.

I have got a plant of *Echinocystis lobata* to observe the irritability of the tendrils described by Asa Gray, and which of course, is plain enough. Having the plant in my study, I have been surprised to find that the uppermost part of each branch (*i. e.* the stem between the two uppermost leaves ex-

---

* 'Proc. Amer. Acad. of Arts and Sciences,' 1858.

cluding the growing tip) is *constantly* and slowly twisting round making a circle in from one-half to two hours ; it will sometimes go round two or three times, and then at the same rate untwists and twists in opposite directions. It generally rests half an hour before it retrogrades. The stem does not become permanently twisted. The stem beneath the twisting portion does not move in the least, though not tied. The movement goes on all day and all early night. It has no relation to light for the plant stands in my window and twists from the light just as quickly as towards it. This may be a common phenomenon for what I know, but it confounded me quite, when I began to observe the irritability of the tendrils. I do not say it is the final cause, but the result is pretty, for the plant every one and a half or two hours sweeps a circle (according to the length of the bending shoot and the length of the tendril) of from one foot to twenty inches in diameter, and immediately that the tendril touches any object its sensitiveness causes it immediately to seize it ; a clever gardener, my neighbour, who saw the plant on my table last night, said : "I believe, Sir, the tendrils can see, for wherever I put a plant it finds out any stick near enough." I believe the above is the explanation, viz. that it sweeps slowly round and round. The tendrils have some sense, for they do not grasp each other when young.

Yours affectionately,
C. DARWIN.

C. Darwin to J. D. Hooker.

Down, July 14 [1863].

MY DEAR HOOKER,—I am getting very much amused by my tendrils, it is just the sort of niggling work which suits me, and takes up no time and rather rests me whilst writing. So will you just think whether you know any plant, which you could give or lend me, or I could buy, with tendrils, remarkable in any way for development, for odd or peculiar structure, or even for an odd place in natural arrangement. I have seen or can see Cucurbitaceæ, Passion-flower, Virginian-

creeper, *Cissus discolor*, Common-pea and Everlasting-pea.   It
is really curious the diversification of irritability (I do not
mean the spontaneous movement, about which I wrote before and correctly, as further observation shows) : for instance, I find a slight pinch between the thumb and finger at
the end of the tendril of the Cucurbitaceæ causes prompt
movment, but a pinch excites no movement in Cissus.   The
cause is that one side alone (the concave) is irritable in the
former; whereas both sides are irritable in Cissus, so if you
excite at the same time both *opposite* sides there is no movement, but by touching with a pencil the two branches of the
tendril, in any part whatever, you cause movement towards
that point; so that I can mould, by a mere touch, the two
branches into any shape I like. . .

C. Darwin to Asa Gray.

Down, August 4 [1863].

My present hobby-horse I owe to you, viz. the tendrils :
their irritability is beautiful, as beautiful in all its modifications as anything in Orchids.   About the *spontaneous* movement (independent of touch) of the tendrils and upper internodes, I am rather taken aback by your saying, "is it not
well known?"   I can find nothing in any book which I have.
. . . The spontaneous movement of the tendrils is independent of the movement of the upper internodes, but both work
harmoniously together in sweeping a circle for the tendrils to
grasp a stick.   So with all climbing plants (without tendrils)
as yet examined, the upper internodes go on night and day
sweeping a circle in one fixed direction.   It is surprising to
watch the Apocyneæ with shoots 18 inches long (beyond the
supporting stick), steadily searching for something to climb
up.   When the shoot meets a stick, the motion at that point
is arrested, but in the upper part is continued; so that the
climbing of all plants yet examined is the simple result of the
spontaneous circulatory movement of the upper internodes.
Pray tell me whether anything has been published on this

subject? I hate publishing what is old; but I shall hardly regret my work if it is old, as it has much amused me. . . .

C. Darwin to Asa Gray.

May 28, 1864.

. . . . An Irish nobleman on his death-bed declared that he could conscientiously say that he had never throughout life denied himself any pleasure; and I can conscientiously say that I have never scrupled to trouble you; so here goes. —Have you travelled South, and can you tell me whether the trees, which *Bignonia capreolata* climbs, are covered with moss or filamentous lichen or Tillandsia?* I ask because its tendrils abhor a simple stick, do not much relish rough bark, but delight in wool or moss. They adhere in a curious manner by making little disks, like the Ampelopsis. . . . By the way, I will enclose some specimens, and if you think it worth while, you can put them under the simple microscope. It is remarkable how specially adapted some tendrils are; those of *Eccremocarpus scaber* do not like a stick, will have nothing to say to wool; but give them a bundle of culms of grass, or a bundle of bristles and they seize them well.

C. Darwin to J. D. Hooker.

Down, June 10 [1864].

. . . I have now read two German books, and all I believe that has been written on climbers, and it has stirred me up to find that I have a good deal of new matter. It is strange, but I really think no one has explained simple twining plants. These books have stirred me up, and made me wish for plants specified in them. I shall be very glad of those you mention. I have written to Veitch for young Nepenthes and Vanilla (which I believe will turn out a grand

* He subsequently learned from Dr. Gray that *Polypodium incanum* abounds on the trees in the districts where this species of Bignonia grows See 'Climbing Plants,' p. 103.

case, though a root creeper), and if I cannot buy young Vanilla I will ask you. I have ordered a leaf-climbing fern, Lygodium. All this work about climbers would hurt my conscience, did I think I could do harder work.*

[He continued his observations on climbing plants during the prolonged illness from which he suffered in the autumn of 1863, and in the following spring. He wrote to Sir J. D. Hooker, apparently in March 1864 :—

" For several days I have been decidedly better, and what I lay much stress on (whatever doctors say), my brain feels far stronger, and I have lost many dreadful sensations. The hot-house is such an amusement to me, and my amusement I owe to you, as my delight is to look at the many odd leaves and plants from Kew. . . . The only approach to work which I can do is to look at tendrils and climbers, this does not distress my weakened brain. Ask Oliver to look over the enclosed queries (and do you look) and amuse a broken-down brother naturalist by answering any which he can. If you ever lounge through your houses, remember me and climbing plants."

On October 29, 1864, he wrote to Dr. Gray :—

" I have not been able to resist doing a little more at your godchild, my climbing paper, or rather in size little book, which by Jove I will have copied out, else I shall never stop. This has been new sort of work for me, and I have been pleased to find what a capital guide for observations a full conviction of the change of species is."

On Jan. 19, 1865, he wrote to Sir J. D. Hooker :—

" It is working hours, but I am trying to take a day's holiday, for I finished and despatched yesterday my climbing paper. For the last ten days I have done nothing but correct refractory sentences, and I loathe the whole subject."

A letter to Dr. Gray, April 9, 1865, has a word or two on the subject :—

" I have begun correcting proofs of my paper on ' Climb-

---

* He was much out of health at this time.

ing Plants.' I suppose I shall be able to send you a copy in four or five weeks. I think it contains a good deal new and some curious points, but it is so fearfully long, that no one will ever read it. If, however, you do not *skim* through it, you will be an unnatural parent, for it is your child."

Dr. Gray not only read it but approved of it, to my father's great satisfaction, as the following extracts show:—

"I was much pleased to get your letter of July 24th. Now that I can do nothing, I maunder over old subjects, and your approbation of my climbing paper gives me *very* great satisfaction. I made my observations when I could do nothing else and much enjoyed it, but always doubted whether they were worth publishing. I demur to its not being necessary to explain in detail about the spires in *caught* tendrils running in opposite directions; for the fact for a long time confounded me, and I have found it difficult enough to explain the cause to two or three persons." (Aug. 15, 1865.)

"I received yesterday your article * on climbers, and it has pleased me in an extraordinary and even silly manner. You pay me a superb compliment, and as I have just said to my wife, I think my friends must perceive that I like praise, they give me such hearty doses. I always admire your skill in reviews or abstracts, and you have done this article excellently and given the whole essence of my paper. . . . . I have had a letter from a good Zoologist in S. Brazil, F. Müller, who has been stirred up to observe climbers and gives me some curious cases of *branch*-climbers, in which branches are converted into tendrils, and then continue to grow and throw out leaves and new branches, and then lose their tendril character." (October 1865.)

The paper on Climbing Plants was republished in 1875, as a separate book. The author had been unable to give his customary amount of care to the style of the original essay, owing to the fact that it was written during a period of con-

---

* In the September number of 'Silliman's Journal,' concluded in the January number, 1866.

tinued ill-health, and it was now found to require a great deal of alteration. He wrote to Sir J. D. Hooker (March 3, 1875): "It is lucky for authors in general that they do not require such dreadful work in merely licking what they write into shape." And to Mr. Murray in September he wrote: "The corrections are heavy in 'Climbing Plants,' and yet I deliberately went over the MS. and old sheets three times." The book was published in September 1875, an edition of 1500 copies was struck off; the edition sold fairly well, and 500 additional copies were printed in June of the following year.]

INSECTIVOROUS PLANTS.

[In the summer of 1860 he was staying at the house of his sister-in-law, Miss Wedgwood, in Ashdown Forest, whence he wrote (July 29, 1860), to Sir Joseph Hooker :—

"Latterly I have done nothing here ; but at first I amused myself with a few observations on the insect-catching power of Drosera ; and I must consult you some time whether my 'twaddle' is worth communicating to the Linnean Society."

In August he wrote to the same friend :—

"I will gratefully send my notes on Drosera when copied by my copier : the subject amused me when I had nothing to do."

He has described in the 'Autobiography' (vol. i. p. 77), the general nature of these early experiments. He noticed insects sticking to the leaves, and finding that flies, &c., placed on the adhesive glands were held fast and embraced, he suspected that the leaves were adapted to supply nitrogenous food to the plant. He therefore tried the effect on the leaves of various nitrogenous fluids—with results which, as far as they went, verified his surmise. In September, 1860, he wrote to Dr. Gray :—

"I have been infinitely amused by working at Drosera : the movements are really curious ; and the manner in which the leaves detect certain nitrogenous compounds is marvellous. You will laugh; but it is, at present, my full belief (after endless experiments) that they detect (and move in consequence of) the $\frac{1}{2880}$ part of a single grain of nitrate of ammonia; but the muriate and sulphate of ammonia bother their chemical skill, and they cannot make anything of the nitrogen in these salts! I began this work on Drosera in relation to *gradation* as throwing light on Dionæa."

Later in the autumn he was again obliged to leave home for Eastbourne, where he continued his work on Drosera. The work was so new to him that he found himself in difficulties in the preparation of solutions, and became puzzled over fluid and solid ounces, &c. &c. To a friend, the late Mr. E. Cresy, who came to his help in the matter of weights and measures, he wrote giving an account of the experiments. The extract (November 2, 1860) which follows illustrates the almost superstitious precautions he often applied to his researches :—

"Generally I have scrutinised every gland and hair on the leaf before experimenting; but it occurred to me that I might in some way affect the leaf; though this is almost impossible, as I scrutinised with equal care those that I put into distilled water (the same water being used for dissolving the carbonate of ammonia). I then cut off four leaves (not touching them with my fingers), and put them in plain water, and four other leaves into the weak solution, and after leaving them for an hour and a half, I examined every hair on all eight leaves; no change on the four in water; every gland and hair affected in those in ammonia.

"I had measured the quantity of weak solution, and I counted the glands which had absorbed the ammonia, and were plainly affected; the result convinced me that each gland could not have absorbed more than $\frac{1}{64000}$ or $\frac{1}{65000}$ of a grain. I have tried numbers of other experiments all pointing to the same result. Some experiments lead me to believe that very sensitive leaves are acted on by much smaller doses. Reflect how little ammonia a plant can get growing on poor soil—yet it is nourished. The really sur-

prising part seems to me that the effect should be visible,
and not under very high power ; for after trying a high power, I thought it would be safer not to consider any effect
which was not plainly visible under a two-thirds object glass
and middle eye-piece.   The effect which the carbonate of
ammonia produces is the segregation of the homogeneous
fluid in the cells into a cloud of granules and colourless fluid ;
and subsequently the granules coalesce into larger masses,
and for hours have the oddest movements—coalescing, dividing, coalescing *ad infinitum.*   I do not know whether you will
care for these ill-written details ; but, as you asked, I am
sure I am bound to comply, after all the very kind and great
trouble which you have taken."

On his return home he wrote to Sir J. D. Hooker (November 21, 1860) :—

"I have been working like a madman at Drosera.   Here
is a fact for you which is certain as you stand where you are,
though you won't believe it, that a bit of hair $\frac{1}{78000}$ of one
grain in weight placed on gland, will cause *one* of the gland-
bearing hairs of Drosera to curve inwards, and will alter the
condition of the contents of every cell in the foot-stalk of
the gland."

And a few days later to Lyell :—

"I will and must finish my Drosera MS., which will take
me a week, for, at the present moment, I care more about
Drosera than the origin of all the species in the world.   But
I will not publish on Drosera till next year, for I am frightened and astounded at my results.   I declare it is a certain
fact, that one organ is so sensitive to touch, that a weight
seventy-eight times less than that, viz., $\frac{1}{1000}$ of a grain, which
will move the best chemical balance, suffices to cause a conspicuous movement.   Is it not curious that a plant should be
far more sensitive to the touch than any nerve in the human
body?   Yet I am perfectly sure that this is true.   When I
am on my hobby-horse, I never can resist telling my friends
how well my hobby goes, so you must forgive the rider."

The work was continued, as a holiday task, at Bournemouth, where he stayed during the autumn of 1862. The discussion in the following letter on "nervous matter" in Drosera is of interest in relation to recent researches on the continuity of protoplasm from cell to cell :]

C. Darwin to J. D. Hooker.

Cliff Cottage, Bournemouth.
September 26 [1862].

My dear Hooker,—Do not read this till you have leisure. If that blessed moment ever comes, I should be very glad to have your opinion on the subject of this letter. I am led to the opinion that Drosera must have diffused matter in organic connection, closely analogous to the nervous matter of animals. When the glands of one of the papillæ or tentacles, in its natural position is supplied with nitrogenised fluid and certain other stimulants, or when loaded with an extremely slight weight, or when struck several times with a needle, the pedicel bends near its base in under one minute. These varied stimulants are conveyed down the pedicel by some means ; it cannot be vibration, for drops of fluid put on quite quietly cause the movement ; it cannot be absorption of the fluid from cell to cell, for I can see the rate of absorption, which though quick, is far slower, and in Dionæa the transmission is instantaneous ; analogy from animals would point to transmission through nervous matter. Reflecting on the rapid power of absorption in the glands, the extreme sensibility of the whole organ, and the conspicuous movement caused by varied stimulants, I have tried a number of substances which are not caustic or corrosive, ... but most of which are known to have a remarkable action on the nervous matter of animals. You will see the results in the enclosed paper. As the nervous matter of different animals are differently acted on by the same poisons, one would not expect the same action on plants and animals ; only, if plants have diffused nervous matter, some degree of analogous action. And this is partially the case. Considering these experiments, together with the previously made remarks on the functions of the parts, I cannot avoid the conclusion, that Drosera possesses matter at least in some degree analo- gous in constitution and function to nervous matter. Now do tell me what you think, as far as you can judge from my abstract; of course many more experiments would have to be tried; but in former years I tried on the whole leaf, instead of on separate glands, a number of innocuous* substances, such as sugar, gum, starch, &c., and they produced no effect. Your opinion will aid me in deciding some future year in going on with this subject. I should not have thought it worth attempting, but I had nothing on earth to do.

My dear Hooker, Yours very sincerely,
CH. DARWIN.

P.S.—We return home on Monday 28th.   Thank Heaven !

[A long break now ensued in his work on insectivorous plants, and it was not till 1872 that the subject seriously oc- cupied him again. A passage in a letter to Dr. Asa Gray, written in 1863 or 1864, shows, however, that the question was not altogether absent from his mind in the interim :—

" Depend on it you are unjust on the merits of my beloved Drosera ; it is a wonderful plant, or rather a most sagacious animal. I will stick up for Drosera to the day of my death. Heaven knows whether I shall ever publish my pile of experi- ments on it."

He notes in his diary that the last proof of the ' Expres- sion of the Emotions' was finished on August 22, 1872, and that he began to work on Drosera on the following day.]

---

* This line of investigation made him wish for information on the ac- tion of poisons on plants ; as in many other cases he applied to Professor Oliver, and in reference to the result wrote to Hooker : " Pray thank Oli- ver heartily for his heap of references on poisons."

C. Darwin to Asa Gray.

[Sevenoaks], October 22 [1872].

. . . I have worked pretty hard for four or five weeks on Drosera, and then broke down ; so that we took a house near Sevenoaks for three weeks (where I now am) to get complete rest. I have very little power of working now, and must put off the rest of the work on Drosera till next spring, as my plants are dying. It is an endless subject, and I must cut it short, and for this reason shall not do much on Dionæa. The point which has interested me most is tracing the *nerves !* which follow the vascular bundles. By a prick with a sharp lancet at a certain point, I can paralyse one-half the leaf, so that a stimulus to the other half causes no movement. It is just like dividing the spinal marrow of a frog :—no stimulus can be sent from the brain or anterior part of the spine to the hind legs; but if these latter are stimulated, they move by reflex action. I find my old results about the astonishing sensitiveness of the nervous system (! ?) of Drosera to various stimulants fully confirmed and extended. . . .

[His work on digestion in Drosera and other points in the physiology of the plant soon led him into regions where his knowledge was defective, and here the advice and assistance which he received from Dr. Burdon Sanderson was of much value :]

C. Darwin to J. Burdon Sanderson.

Down, July 25, 1873.

MY DEAR DR. SANDERSON,—I should like to tell you a little about my recent work with Drosera, to show that I have profited by your suggestions, and to ask a question or two.

1. It is really beautiful how quickly and well Drosera and Dionæa dissolve little cubes of albumen and gelatine. I kept the same sized cubes on wet moss for comparison. When you were here I forgot that I had tried gelatine, but albumen is far better for watching its dissolution and absorption. Frankland has told me how to test in a rough way for pep-

sin ; and in the autumn he will discover what acid the digestive juice contains.

2. A decoction of cabbage-leaves and green peas causes as much inflection as an infusion of raw meat ; a decoction of grass is less powerful. Though I hear that the chemists try to precipitate all albumen from the extract of belladonna, I think they must fail, as the extract causes inflection, whereas a new lot of atropine, as well as the valerianate [of atropine], produce no effect.

3. I have been trying a good many experiments with heated water. . . . Should you not call the following case one of heat rigor ? Two leaves were heated to 130°, and had every tentacle closely inflected ; one was taken out and placed in cold water, and it re-expanded ; the other was heated to 145°, and had not the least power of re-expansion. Is not this latter case heat rigor ? If you can inform me, I should very much like to hear at what temperature cold-blooded and invertebrate animals are killed.

4. I must tell you my final result, of which I am sure, [as to] the sensitiveness of Drosera. I made a solution of one part of phosphate of ammonia by weight to 218,750 of water; of this solution I gave so much that a leaf got $\frac{1}{8000}$ of a grain of the phosphate. I then counted the glands, and each could have got only $\frac{1}{1552000}$ of a grain ; this being absorbed by the glands, sufficed to cause the tentacles bearing these glands to bend through an angle of 180°. Such sensitiveness requires hot weather, and carefully selected young yet mature leaves. It strikes me as a wonderful fact. I must add that I took every precaution, by trying numerous leaves at the same time in the solution and in the same water which was used for making the solution.

5. If you can persuade your friend to try the effects of carbonate of ammonia on the aggregation of the white blood corpuscles, I should very much like to hear the result.

I hope this letter will not have wearied you.

Believe me, yours very sincerely,
CHARLES DARWIN.

C. Darwin to W. Thiselton Dyer.

Down, 24 [December 1873 ?]

MY DEAR MR. DYER,—I fear that you will think me a great bore, but I cannot resist telling you that I have just found out that the leaves of Pinguicula possess a beautifully adapted power of movement. Last night I put on a row of little flies near one edge of two *youngish* leaves ; and after 14 hours these edges are beautifully folded over so as to clasp the flies, thus bringing the glands into contact with the upper surfaces of the flies, and they are now secreting copiously above and below the flies and no doubt absorbing. The acid secretion has run down the channelled edge and has collected in the spoon-shaped extremity, where no doubt the glands are absorbing the delicious soup. The leaf on one side looks just like the helix of a human ear, if you were to stuff flies within the fold. Yours most sincerely,

CH. DARWIN.

C. Darwin to Asa Gray.

Down, June 3 [1874].

. . . . I am now hard at work getting my book on Drosera & Co. ready for the printers, but it will take some time, for I am always finding out new points to observe. I think you will be interested by my observations on the digestive process in Drosera ; the secretion contains an acid of the acetic series, and some ferment closely analogous to, but not identical with, pepsin ; for I have been making a long series of comparative trials. No human being will believe what I shall publish about the smallness of the doses of phosphate of ammonia which act.

. . . . I began reading the Madagascar squib * quite gravely, and when I found it stated that Felis and Bos inhabited Madagascar, I thought it was a false story, and did not perceive it was a hoax till I came to the woman. . . .

---

* A description of a carnivorous plant supposed to subsist on human beings.

C. Darwin to F. C. Donders.[*]

Down, July 7, 1874.

MY DEAR PROFESSOR DONDERS,—My son George writes to me that he has seen you, and that you have been very kind to him, for which I return to you my cordial thanks. He tells me on your authority, of a fact which interests me in the highest degree, and which I much wish to be allowed to quote. It relates to the action of one millionth of a grain of atropine on the eye. Now will you be so kind, whenever you can find a little leisure, to tell me whether you yourself have observed this fact, or believe it on good authority. I also wish to know what proportion by weight the atropine bore to the water solution, and how much of the solution was applied to the eye. The reason why I am so anxious on this head is that it gives some support to certain facts repeatedly observed by me with respect to the action of phosphate of ammonia on Drosera. The $\frac{1}{4000000}$ of a grain absorbed by a gland clearly makes the tentacle which bears this gland become inflected; and I am fully convinced that $\frac{1}{20000000}$ of a grain of the crystallised salt (*i.e.* containing about one-third of its weight of water of crystallisation) does the same. Now I am quite unhappy at the thought of having to publish such a statement. It will be of great value to me to be able to give any analogous facts in support. The case of Drosera is all the more interesting as the absorption of the salt or any other stimulant applied to the gland causes it to transmit a motor influence to the base of the tentacle which bears the gland.

Pray forgive me for troubling you, and do not trouble yourself to answer this until your health is fully re-established.

Pray believe me,

Yours very sincerely,

CHARLES DARWIN.

---

[*] Professor Donders, the well-known physiologist of Utrecht.

[During the summer of 1874 he was at work on the genus Utricularia, and he wrote (July 16th) to Sir J. D. Hooker giving some account of the progress of his work :—

"I am rather glad you have not been able to send Utricularia, for the common species has driven F. and me almost mad. The structure is *most* complex. The bladders catch a multitude of Entomostraca, and larvæ of insects. The mechanism for capture is excellent. But there is much that we cannot understand. From what I have seen to-day, I strongly suspect that it is necrophagous, *i.e.* that it cannot digest, but absorbs decaying matter."

He was indebted to Lady Dorothy Nevill for specimens of the curious *Utricularia montana*, which is not aquatic like the European species, but grows among the moss and *débris* on the branches of trees. To this species the following letter refers :]

C. Darwin to Lady Dorothy Nevill.

Down September 18 [1874].

DEAR LADY DOROTHY NEVILL,—I am so much obliged to you. I was so convinced that the bladders were with the leaves that I never thought of removing the moss, and this was very stupid of me. The great solid bladder-like swellings almost on the surface are wonderful objects, but are not the true bladders. These I found on the roots near the surface, and down to a depth of two inches in the sand. They are as transparent as glass, from $\frac{1}{20}$ to $\frac{1}{100}$ of an inch in size, and hollow. They have all the important points of structure of the bladders of the floating English species, and I felt confident I should find captured prey. And so I have to my delight in two bladders, with clear proof that they had absorbed food from the decaying mass. For Utricularia is a carrion-feeder, and not strictly carnivorous like Drosera.

The great solid bladder-like bodies, I believe, are reservoirs of water like a camel's stomach. As soon as I have made a few more observations, I mean to be so cruel as to give your plant no water, and observe whether the great bladders shrink and contain air instead of water; I shall then also wash all earth from all roots, and see whether there are true bladders for capturing subterranean insects down to the very bottom of the pot. Now shall you think me very greedy, if I say that supposing the species is not very precious, and you have several, will you give me one more plant, and if so, please to send it to " Orpington Station, S. E. R., to be forwarded by foot messenger."

I have hardly ever enjoyed a day more in my life than I have this day's work; and this I owe to your Ladyship's great kindness.

The seeds are very curious monsters; I fancy of some plant allied to Medicago, but I will show them to Dr. Hooker.

Your Ladyship's very gratefully,

CH. DARWIN.

C. Darwin to J. D. Hooker.

Down, September 30, 1874.

MY DEAR H.,—Your magnificent present of Aldrovanda has arrived quite safe. I have enjoyed greatly a good look at the shut leaves, one of which I cut open. It is an aquatic Dionæa, which has acquired some structures identical with those of Utricularia !

If the leaves open and I can transfer them open under the microscope, I will try some experiments, for mortal man cannot resist the temptation. If I cannot transfer, I will do nothing, for otherwise it would require hundreds of leaves.

You are a good man to give me such pleasure.

Yours affectionately,

C. DARWIN.

[The manuscript of 'Insectivorous Plants' was finished in March 1875. He seems to have been more than usually oppressed by the writing of this book, thus he wrote to Sir J. D. Hooker in February :—

" You ask about my book, and all that I can say is that I am ready to commit suicide ; I thought it was decently written, but find so much wants rewriting, that it will not be ready to go to printers for two months, and will then make a confoundedly big book.   Murray will say that it is no use publishing in the middle of summer, so I do not know what will be the upshot ; but I begin to think that every one who publishes a book is a fool."

The book was published on July 2nd, 1875, and 2700 copies were sold out of the edition of 3000.]

CHAPTER XIV.

THE 'POWER OF MOVEMENT IN PLANTS.' 1880.

[THE few sentences in the autobiographical chapter give with sufficient clearness the connection between the 'Power of Movement,' and one of the author's earlier books, that on 'Climbing Plants.' The central idea of the book is that the movements of plants in relation to light, gravitation, &c., are modifications of a spontaneous tendency to revolve or circumnutate, which is widely inherent in the growing parts of plants. This conception has not been generally adopted, and has not taken a place among the canons of orthodox physiology. The book has been treated by Professor Sachs with a few words of professorial contempt; and by Professor Wiesner it has been honoured by careful and generously expressed criticism.

Mr. Thiselton Dyer * has well said: "Whether this masterly conception of the unity of what has hitherto seemed a chaos of unrelated phenomena will be sustained, time alone will show. But no one can doubt the importance of what Mr. Darwin has done, in showing that for the future the phenomena of plant movement can and indeed must be studied from a single point of view."

The work was begun in the summer of 1877, after the publication of 'Different Forms of Flowers,' and by the autumn his enthusiasm for the subject was thoroughly established, and he wrote to Mr. Dyer: "I am all on fire at the work." At this time he was studying the movements of

---

* 'Charles Darwin' ('Nature' Series), p. 41.

cotyledons, in which the sleep of plants is to be observed in its simplest form ; in the following spring he was trying to discover what useful purpose these sleep-movements could serve, and wrote to Sir Joseph Hooker (March 25th, 1878) :—

"I think we have *proved* that the sleep of plants is to lessen the injury to the leaves from radiation. This has interested me much, and has cost us great labor, as it has been a problem since the time of Linnæus. But we have killed or badly injured a multitude of plants : N. B.—*Oxalis carnosa* was most valuable, but last night was killed."

His letters of this period do not give any connected account of the progress of the work. The two following are given as being characteristic of the author :]

C. Darwin to W. Thiselton Dyer.

Down, June 2, 1878.

MY DEAR DYER,—I remember saying that I should die a disgraced man if I did not observe a seedling Cactus and Cycas, and you have saved me from this horrible fate, as they move splendidly and normally. But I have two questions to ask : the Cycas observed was a huge seed in a broad and very shallow pot with cocoa-nut fibre as I suppose. It was named only Cycas. Was it *Cycas pectinata ?* I suppose that I cannot be wrong in believing that what first appears above ground is a true leaf, for I can see no stem or axis. Lastly, you may remember that I said that we could not raise *Opuntia nigricans ;* now I must confess to a piece of stupidity ; one did come up, but my gardener and self stared at it, and concluded that it could not be a seedling Opuntia, but now that I have seen one of *O. basilaris*, I am sure it was ; I observed it only casually, and saw movements, which makes me wish to observe carefully another. If you have any fruit, will Mr. Lynch * be so kind as to send one more ?

I am working away like a slave at radicles [roots] and at

---

* Mr. R. I. Lynch, now Curator of the Botanic Garden at Cambridge, was at this time in the Royal Gardens, Kew.

movements of true leaves, for I have pretty well done with cotyledons. . . .

That was an *excellent* letter about the Gardens :* I had hoped that the agitation was over. Politicians are a poor truckling lot, for [they] must see the wretched effects of keeping the gardens open all day long.

Your ever troublesome friend,
CH. DARWIN.

C. Darwin to W. Thiselton Dyer.

4 Bryanston St., Portman Square,
November 21 [1878].

MY DEAR DYER,—I must thank you for all the wonderful trouble which you have taken about the seeds of *Impatiens*, and on scores of other occasions. It in truth makes me feel ashamed of myself, and I cannot help thinking : " Oh Lord, when he sees our book he will cry out, is this all for which I have helped so much ! " In seriousness, I hope that we have made out some points, but I fear that we have done very little for the labour which we have expended on our work. We are here for a week for a little rest, which I needed.

If I remember right, November 30th, is the anniversary at the Royal, and I fear Sir Joseph must be almost at the last gasp. I shall be glad when he is no longer President.

Yours very sincerely,
CH. DARWIN.

[In the spring of the following year, 1879, when he was engaged in putting his results together, he wrote somewhat despondingly to Mr. Dyer : " I am overwhelmed with my notes, and almost too old to undertake the job which I have in hand—*i.e.*, movements of all kinds. Yet it is worse to be idle."

Later on in the year, when the work was approaching

---

* This refers to an attempt to induce the Government to open the Royal Gardens at Kew in the morning.

completion, he wrote to Prof. Carus (July 17, 1879), with respect to a translation :—

"Together with my son Francis, I am preparing a rather large volume on the general movements of Plants, and I think that we have made out a good many new points and views.

"I fear that our views will meet a good deal of opposition in Germany ; but we have been working very hard for some years at the subject.

"I shall be *much* pleased if you think the book worth translating, and proof-sheets shall be sent you, whenever they are ready."

In the autumn he was hard at work on the manuscript, and wrote to Dr. Gray (October 24, 1879) :—

"I have written a rather big book—more is the pity—on the movements of plants, and I am now just beginning to go over the MS. for the second time, which is a horrid bore."

Only the concluding part of the next letter refers to the 'Power of Movements':]

C. Darwin to A. De Candolle.

May 28, 1880.

MY DEAR SIR,—I am particularly obliged to you for having so kindly sent me your 'Phytographie;'* for if I had merely seen it advertised, I should not have supposed that it could have concerned me. As it is, I have read with very great interest about a quarter, but will not delay longer thanking you. All that you say seems to me very clear and convincing, and as in all your writings I find a large number of philosophical remarks new to me, and no doubt shall find many more. They have recalled many a puzzle through which I passed when monographing the Cirripedia ; and your book in those days would have been quite invaluable to me. It has pleased me to find that I have always followed your

---

* A book on the methods of botanical research, more especially of systematic work.

plan of making notes on separate pieces of paper; I keep several scores of large portfolios, arranged on very thin shelves about two inches apart, fastened to the walls of my study, and each shelf has its proper name or title; and I can thus put at once every memorandum into its proper place. Your book will, I am sure, be very useful to many young students, and I shall beg my son Francis (who intends to devote himself to the physiology of plants) to read it carefully.

As for myself I am taking a fortnight's rest, after sending a pile of MS. to the printers, and it was a piece of good fortune that your book arrived as I was getting into my carriage, for I wanted something to read whilst away from home. My MS. relates to the movements of plants, and I think that I have succeeded in showing that all the more important great classes of movements are due to the modification of a kind of movement common to all parts of all plants from their earliest youth.

Pray give my kind remembrances to your son, and with my highest respect and best thanks,

Believe me, my dear Sir, yours very sincerely,

CHARLES DARWIN.

P.S.—It always pleases me to exalt plants in the organic scale, and if you will take the trouble to read my last chapter when my book (which will be sadly too big) is published and sent to you, I hope and think that you also will admire some of the beautiful adaptations by which seedling plants are enabled to perform their proper functions.

[The book was published on November 6, 1880, and 1500 copies were disposed of at Mr. Murray's sale. With regard to it he wrote to Sir J. D. Hooker (November 23) :—

" Your note has pleased me much—for I did not expect that you would have had time to read *any* of it. Read the last chapter, and you will know the whole result, but without the evidence. The case, however, of radicles bending after exposure for an hour to geotropism, with their tips (or brains)

cut off is, I think, worth your reading (bottom of p. 525); it astounded me. The next most remarkable fact, as it appeared to me (p. 148), is the discrimination of the tip of the radicle between a slightly harder and softer object affixed on opposite sides of tip. But I will bother you no more about my book. The sensitiveness of seedlings to light is marvellous."

To another friend, Mr. Thiselton Dyer, he wrote (November 28, 1880) :—

"Very many thanks for your most kind note, but you think too highly of our work, not but what this is very pleasant. . . . . Many of the Germans are very contemptuous about making out the use of organs; but they may sneer the souls out of their bodies, and I for one shall think it the most interesting part of Natural History. Indeed you are greatly mistaken if you doubt for one moment on the very great value of your constant and most kind assistance to us."

The book was widely reviewed, and excited much interest among the general public. The following letter refers to a leading article in the *Times*, November 20, 1880 :]

C. Darwin to Mrs. Haliburton.*

Down, November 22. 1880.

MY DEAR SARAH,—You see how audaciously I begin; but I have always loved and shall ever love this name. Your letter has done more than please me, for its kindness has touched my heart. I often think of old days and of the delight of my visits to Woodhouse, and of the deep debt of gratitude which I owe to your father. It was very good of you to write. I had quite forgotten my old ambition about the Shrewsbury newspaper;† but I remember the pride

---

* Mrs. Haliburton was a daughter of my father's early friend, the late Mr. Owen, of Woodhouse.

† Mrs. Haliburton had reminded him of his saying as a boy that if Eddowes' newspaper ever alluded to him as " our deserving fellow-townsman," his ambition would be amply gratified.

which I felt when I saw in a book about beetles the impressive words "captured by C. Darwin." Captured sounded so grand compared with caught. This seemed to me glory enough for any man! I do not know in the least what made the *Times* glorify me,* for it has sometimes pitched into me ferociously.

I should very much like to see you again, but you would find a visit here very dull, for we feel very old and have no amusement, and lead a solitary life. But we intend in a few weeks to spend a few days in London, and then if you have anything else to do in London, you would perhaps come and lunch with us. †

Believe me, my dear Sarah,

Yours gratefully and affectionately,

CHARLES DARWIN.

[The following letter was called forth by the publication of a volume devoted to the criticism of the 'Power of Movement in Plants' by an accomplished botanist, Dr. Julius Wiesner, Professor of Botany in the University of Vienna :]

C. Darwin to Julius Wiesner.

Down, October 25th, 1881.

MY DEAR SIR,—I have now finished your book, ‡ and have understood the whole except a very few passages. In the first place, let me thank you cordially for the manner in which you have everywhere treated me. You have shown how a man may differ from another in the most decided manner, and yet express his difference with the most perfect courtesy. Not a few English and German naturalists might learn a useful lesson from your example; for the coarse language

---

* The following is the opening sentence of the leading article :—" Of all our living men of science none have laboured longer and to more splendid purpose than Mr. Darwin."

† My father had the pleasure of seeing Mrs. Haliburton at his brother's house in Queen Anne Street.

‡ ' Das Bewegungsvermögen der Pflanzen.'   Vienna, 1881.

often used by scientific men towards each other does no good, and only degrades science.

I have been profoundly interested by your book, and some of your experiments are so beautiful, that I actually felt pleasure while being vivisected. It would take up too much space to discuss all the important topics in your book. I fear that you have quite upset the interpretation which I have given of the effects of cutting off the tips of horizontally extended roots, and of those laterally exposed to moisture ; but I cannot persuade myself that the horizontal position of lateral branches and roots is due simply to their lessened power of growth. Nor when I think of my experiments with the cotyledons of *Phalaris*, can I give up the belief of the transmission of some stimulus due to light from the upper to the lower part. At p. 60 you have misunderstood my meaning, when you say that I believe that the effects from light are transmitted to a part which is not itself heliotropic. I never considered whether or not the short part beneath the ground was heliotropic ; but I believe that with young seed-lings the part which bends *near*, but *above* the ground is heliotropic, and I believe so from this part bending only moderately when the light is oblique, and bending rectangularly when the light is horizontal. Nevertheless the bending of this lower part, as I conclude from my experiments with opaque caps, is influenced by the action of light on the upper part. My opinion, however, on the above and many other points, signifies very little, for I have no doubt that your book will convince most botanists that I am wrong in all the points on which we differ.

Independently of the question of transmission, my mind is so full of facts leading me to believe that light, gravity, &c., act not in a direct manner on growth, but as stimuli, that I am quite unable to modify my judgment on this head. I could not understand the passage at p. 78, until I consulted my son George, who is a mathematician. He supposes that your objection is founded on the diffused light from the lamp illuminating both sides of the object, and not being reduced, with increasing distance in the same ratio as the direct light; but he doubts whether this *necessary* correction will account for the very little difference in the heliotropic curvature of the plants in the successive pots.

With respect to the sensitiveness of the tips of roots to contact, I cannot admit your view until it is proved that I am in error about bits of card attached by liquid gum causing movement; whereas no movement was caused if the card remained separated from the tip by a layer of the liquid gum. The fact also of thicker and thinner bits of card attached on opposite sides of the same root by shellac, causing movement in one direction, has to be explained. You often speak of the tip having been injured; but externally there was no sign of injury: and when the tip was plainly injured, the extreme part became curved *towards* the injured side. I can no more believe that the tip was injured by the bits of card, at least when attached by gum-water, than that the glands of Drosera are injured by a particle of thread or hair placed on it, or that the human tongue [is so] when it feels any such object.

About the most important subject in my book, namely circumnutation, I can only say that I feel utterly bewildered at the difference in our conclusions; but I could not fully understand some parts which my son Francis will be able to translate to me when he returns home. The greater part of your book is beautifully clear.

Finally, I wish that I had enough strength and spirit to commence a fresh set of experiments, and publish the results, with a full recantation of my errors when convinced of them; but I am too old for such an undertaking, nor do I suppose that I shall be able to do much, or any more, original work. I imagine that I see one possible source of error in your beautiful experiment of a plant rotating and exposed to a lateral light.

With high respect and with sincere thanks for the kind manner in which you have treated me and my mistakes, I remain, my dear Sir, yours sincerely,

CHARLES DARWIN.

CHAPTER XV.

MISCELLANEOUS BOTANICAL LETTERS.

1873–1882.

[THE present chapter contains a series of miscellaneous letters on botanical subjects. Some of them show my father's varied interests in botanical science, and others give account of researches which never reached completion.]

BLOOM ON LEAVES AND FRUIT.

[His researches into the meaning of the "bloom," or waxy coating found on many leaves, was one of those inquiries which remained unfinished at the time of his death. He amassed a quantity of notes on the subject, part of which I hope to publish at no distant date.*

One of his earliest letters on this subject was addressed in August, 1873, to Sir Joseph Hooker :—

" I want a little information from you, and if you do not yourself know, please to enquire of some of the wise men of Kew.

" Why are the leaves and fruit of so many plants protected by a thin layer of waxy matter (like the common cabbage), or with fine hair, so that when such leaves or fruit are im-

---

* A small instalment on the relation between bloom and the distribution of the stomata on leaves has appeared in the 'Journal of the Linnean Society,' 1886. Tschirsch (*Linnæa*, 1881) has published results identical with some which my father and myself obtained, viz. that bloom diminishes transpiration. The same fact was previously published by Garreau in 1850.

mersed in water they appear as if encased in thin glass? It is really a pretty sight to put a pod of the common pea, or a raspberry into water. I find several leaves are thus protected on the under surface and not on the upper.

"How can water injure the leaves if indeed this is at all the case?"

On this latter point he wrote to Sir Thomas Farrer :—

"I am now become mad about drops of water injuring leaves. Please ask Mr. Paine * whether he believes, *from his own experience*, that drops of water injure leaves or fruit in his conservatories. It is said that the drops act as burning-glasses ; if this is true, they would not be at all injurious on cloudy days. As he is so acute a man, I should very much like to hear his opinion. I remember when I grew hot-house orchids I was cautioned not to wet their leaves; but I never then thought on the subject.

"I enjoyed my visit greatly with you, and I am very sure that all England could not afford a kinder and pleasanter host."

Some years later he took up the subject again, and wrote to Sir Joseph Hooker (May 25, 1877) :—

"I have been looking over my old notes about the "bloom" on plants, and I think that the subject is well worth pursuing, though I am very doubtful of any success. Are you inclined to aid me on the mere chance of success, for without your aid I could do hardly anything?"]

C. Darwin to Asa Gray.

Down, June 4 [1877].

. . . . I am now trying to make out the use or function of "bloom," or the waxy secretion on the leaves and fruit of plants, but am *very* doubtful whether I shall succeed. Can you give me any light? Are such plants commoner in warm than in colder climates? I ask because I often walk out in

---

* Sir Thomas Farrer's gardener.

heavy rain, and the leaves of very few wild dicotyledons can be here seen with drops of water rolling off them like quick-silver.   Whereas in my flower garden, greenhouse, and hot-houses there are several.   Again, are bloom-protected plants common on your *dry* western plains?   Hooker *thinks* that they are common at the Cape of Good Hope.   It is a puzzle to me if they are common under very dry climates, and I find bloom very common on the Acacias and Eucalypti of Australia. Some of the Eucalypti which do not appear to be covered with bloom have the epidermis protected by a layer of some substance which is dissolved in boiling alcohol.   Are there any bloom-protected leaves or fruit in the Arctic regions? If you can illuminate me, as you so often have done, pray do so ; but otherwise do not bother yourself by answering.

Yours affectionately,

C. DARWIN.

C. Darwin to W. Thiselton Dyer.

Down, September 5 [1877].

MY DEAR DYER,—One word to thank you. I declare had it not been for your kindness, we should have broken down.   As it is we have made out clearly that with some plants (chiefly succulent) the bloom checks evaporation— with some certainly prevents attacks of insects; with *some* sea-shore plants prevents injury from salt-water, and, I be-lieve, with a few prevents injury from pure water resting on the leaves.   This latter is as yet the most doubtful and the most interesting point in relation to the movements of plants. . . .

C. Darwin to F. Müller.

Down, July 4 [1881].

MY DEAR SIR,—Your kindness is unbounded, and I can-not tell you how much your last letter (May 31) has inter-ested me.   I have piles of notes about the effect of water resting on leaves, and their movements (as I supposed) to shake off the drops.   But I have not looked over these notes for a long time, and had come to think that perhaps my notion was mere fancy, but I had intended to begin experimenting as soon as I returned home ; and now with your *invaluable* letter about the position of the leaves of various plants during rain (I have one analogous case with Acacia from South Africa), I shall be stimulated to work in earnest.

VARIABILITY.

[The following letter refers to a subject on which my father felt the strongest interest :—the experimental investigation of the causes of variability. The experiments alluded to were to some extent planned out, and some preliminary work was begun in the direction indicated below, but the research was ultimately abandoned.]

*C. Darwin to J. H. Gilbert.**

Down, February 16, 1876.

MY DEAR SIR,—When I met you at the Linnean Society, you were so kind as to say that you would aid me with advice, and this will be of the utmost value to me and my son. I will first state my object, and hope that you will excuse a long letter. It is admitted by all naturalists that no problem is so perplexing as what causes almost every cultivated plant to vary, and no experiments as yet tried have thrown any light on the subject. Now for the last ten years I have been experimenting in crossing and self-fertilising plants ; and one indirect result has surprised me much ; namely, that by taking pains to cultivate plants in pots under glass during several successive generations, under nearly similar conditions, and by self-fertilising them in each generation, the color of the flowers often changes, and, what is very remarkable, they became in some of the most variable species, such as Mimulus, Carnation, &c., quite constant, like those of a wild species.

---

* Dr. Gilbert, F.R.S., joint author with Sir John Bennett Lawes of a long series of valuable researches in Scientific Agriculture.

1876.] MISCELLANEOUS BOTANICAL LETTERS.

This fact and several others have led me to the suspicion that the cause of variation must be in different substances absorbed from the soil by these plants when their powers of absorption are not interfered with by other plants with which they grow mingled in a state of nature. Therefore my son and I wish to grow plants in pots in soil entirely, or as nearly entirely as is possible, destitute of all matter which plants absorb, and then to give during several successive generations to several plants of the same species as different solutions as may be compatible with their life and health. And now, can you advise me how to make soil approximately free of all the substances which plants naturally absorb? I suppose white silver sand, sold for cleaning harness, &c., is nearly pure silica, but what am I to do for alumina? Without some alumina I imagine that it would be impossible to keep the soil damp and fit for the growth of plants. I presume that clay washed over and over again in water would still yield mineral matter to the carbonic acid secreted by the roots. I should want a good deal of soil, for it would be useless to experimentise unless we could fill from twenty to thirty moderately sized flower-pots every year. Can you suggest any plan? for unless you can it would, I fear, be useless for us to commence an attempt to discover whether variability depends at all on matter absorbed from the soil. After obtaining the requisite kind of soil, my notion is to water one set of plants with nitrate of potassium, another set with nitrate of sodium, and another with nitrate of lime, giving all as much phosphate of ammonia as they seemed to support, for I wish the plants to grow as luxuriantly as possible. The plants watered with nitrate of Na and of Ca would require, I suppose, some K; but perhaps they would get what is absolutely necessary from such soil as I should be forced to employ, and from the rain-water collected in tanks. I could use hard water from a deep well in the chalk, but then all the plants would get lime. If the plants to which I give Nitrate of Na and of Ca would not grow I might give them a little alum.

I am well aware how very ignorant I am, and how crude

my notions are ; and if you could suggest any other solutions by which plants would be likely to be affected it would be a very great kindness.   I suppose that there are no organic fluids which plants would absorb, and which I could procure ?

I must trust to your kindness to excuse me for troubling you at such length, and,

I remain, dear Sir, yours sincerely,

CHARLES DARWIN.

[The next letter to Professor Semper* bears on the same subject :]

From C. Darwin to K. Semper.

Down, July 19, 1881.

MY DEAR PROFESSOR SEMPER,—I have been much pleased to receive your letter, but I did not expect you to answer my former one. . . . . I cannot remember what I wrote to you, but I am sure that it must have expressed the interest which I felt in reading your book.† I thought that you attributed too much weight to the *direct* action of the environment ; but whether I said so I know not, for without being asked I should have thought it presumptuous to have criticised your book, nor should I now say so had I not during the last few days been struck with Professor Hoffmann's review of his own work in the ' Botanische Zeitung,' on the variability of plants ; and it is really surprising how little effect he produced by cultivating certain plants under unnatural conditions, as the presence of salt, lime, zinc, &c., &c., during *several* generations.   Plants, moreover, were selected which were the most likely to vary under such conditions, judging from the existence of closely-allied forms adapted for these conditions.   No doubt I originally attributed too little weight

---

* Professor of Zoology at Würzburg.

† Published in the ' International Scientific Series,' in 1881, under the title, ' The Natural Conditions of Existence as they affect Animal Life.'

to the direct action of conditions, but Hoffmann's paper has staggered me. Perhaps hundreds of generations of exposure are necessary. It is a most perplexing subject. I wish I was not so old, and had more strength, for I see lines of research to follow. Hoffmann even doubts whether plants vary more under cultivation than in their native home and under their natural conditions. If so, the astonishing variations of almost all cultivated plants must be due to selection and breeding from the varying individuals. This idea crossed my mind many years ago, but I was afraid to publish it, as I thought that people would say, "how he does exaggerate the importance of selection."

I still *must* believe that changed conditions give the impulse to variability, but that they act *in most cases* in a very indirect manner. But, as I said, it is a most perplexing problem. Pray forgive me for writing at such length ; I had no intention of doing so when I sat down to write.

I am extremely sorry to hear, for your own sake and for that of Science, that you are so hard worked, and that so much of your time is consumed in official labour.

Pray believe me, dear Professor Semper,

Yours sincerely,

CHARLES DARWIN.

GALLS.

[Shortly before his death, my father began to experimentise on the possibility of producing galls artificially. A letter to Sir J. D. Hooker (Nov. 3, 1880) shows the interest which he felt in the question :—

"I was delighted with Paget's Essay ; * I hear that he has occasionally attended to this subject from his youth . . . . I am very glad he has called attention to galls : this has always seemed to me a profoundly interesting subject ; and if I had been younger would take it up."

His interest in this subject was connected with his ever-

---

* 'Disease in Plants,' by Sir James Paget.—See *Gardeners' Chronicle.* 1880.

present wish to learn something of the causes of variation. He imagined to himself wonderful galls caused to appear on the ovaries of plants, and by these means he thought it possible that the seed might be influenced, and thus new varieties arise. He made a considerable number of experiments by injecting various reagents into the tissues of leaves, and with some slight indications of success.]

AGGREGATION.

[The following letter gives an idea of the subject of the last of ·his published papers.* The appearances which he observed in leaves and roots attracted him, on account of their relation to the phenomena of aggregation which had so deeply interested him when he was at work on Drosera :]

C. Darwin to S. H. Vines.†

Down, November 1, 1881.

MY DEAR MR. VINES,—As I know how busy you are, it is a great shame to trouble you. But you are so rich in chemical knowledge about plants, and I am so poor, that I appeal to your charity as a pauper. My question is—Do you know of any solid substance in the cells of plants which glycerine and water dissolves? But you will understand my perplexity better if I give you the facts : I mentioned to you that if a plant of *Euphorbia peplus* is gently dug up and the roots placed for a short time in a weak solution (1 to 10,000 of water, suffices in 24 hours) of carbonate of ammonia the (generally) alternate longitudinal rows of cells in every rootlet, from the root-cap up to the very top of the root (but not as far as I have yet seen in the green stem) become filled with translucent, brownish grains of matter. These rounded grains often cohere and even become confluent. Pure phosphate and nitrate of ammonia produce (though more slowly) the same effect, as does pure carbonate of soda.

---

* 'Journal of the Linnean Society.' Vol. xix., 1882, pp. 239 and 262.
† Reader in Botany in the University of Cambridge.

Now, if slices of root under a cover-glass are irrigated with glycerine and water, every one of the innumerable grains in the cells disappear after some hours. What am I to think of this ? . . . .

Forgive me for bothering you to such an extent; but I must mention that if the roots are dipped in boiling water there is no deposition of matter, and carbonate of ammonia afterwards produces no effect. I should state that I now find that the granular matter is formed in the cells immediately beneath the thin epidermis, and a few other cells near the vascular tissue. If the granules consisted of living protoplasm (but I can see no traces of movement in them), then I should infer that the glycerine killed them and aggregation ceased with the diffusion of invisibly minute particles, for I have seen an analogous phenomenon in Drosera.

If you can aid me, pray do so, and anyhow forgive me.

Yours very sincerely.

CH. DARWIN.

MR. TORBITT'S EXPERIMENTS ON THE POTATO-DISEASE.

[Mr. James Torbitt, of Belfast, has been engaged for the last twelve years in the difficult undertaking, in which he has been to a large extent successful, of raising fungus-proof varieties of the potato. My father felt great interest in Mr. Torbitt's work, and corresponded with him from 1876 onwards. The following letter, giving a clear account of Mr. Torbitt's method and of my father's opinion of the probability of its success, was written with the idea that Government aid for the work might possibly be obtainable :]

C. Darwin to T. H. Farrer.

Down, March 2, 1878.

MY DEAR FARRER,—Mr. Torbitt's plan of overcoming the potato-disease seems to me by far the best which has ever been suggested. It consists, as you know from his printed letter, of rearing a vast number of seedlings from cross-fertilised parents, exposing them to infection, ruthlessly destroying all that suffer, saving those which resist best, and repeating the process in successive seminal generations. My belief in the probability of good results from this process rests on the fact of all characters whatever occasionally varying. It is known, for instance, that certain species and varieties of the vine resist phylloxera better than others. Andrew Knight found in one variety or species of the apple which was not in the least attacked by coccus, and another variety has been observed in South Australia. Certain varieties of the peach resist mildew, and several other such cases could be given. Therefore there is no great improbability in a new variety of potato arising which would resist the fungus completely, or at least much better than any existing variety. With respect to the cross-fertilisation of two distinct seedling plants, it has been ascertained that the offspring thus raised inherit much more vigorous constitutions and generally are more prolific than seedlings from self-fertilised parents. It is also probable that cross-fertilisation would be especially valuable in the case of the potato, as there is reason to believe that the flowers are seldom crossed by our native insects ; and some varieties are absolutely sterile unless fertilised with pollen from a distinct variety. There is some evidence that the good effects from a cross are transmitted for several generations ; it would not, therefore be necessary to cross-fertilise the seedlings in each generation, though this would be desirable, as it is almost certain that a greater number of seeds would thus be obtained. It should be remembered that a cross between plants raised from the tubers of the same plant, though growing on distinct roots, does no more good than a cross between flowers on the same individual. Considering the whole subject, it appears to me that it would be a national misfortune if the cross-fertilised seeds in Mr. Torbitt's possession produced by parents which have already shown some power of resisting the disease, are not utilised by the Government, or some public body, and the process of selection continued during several more generations.

Should the Agricultural Society undertake the work, Mr. Torbitt's knowledge gained by experience would be especially valuable ; and an outline of the plan is given in his printed letter. It would be necessary that all the tubers produced by each plant should be collected separately, and carefully examined in each succeeding generation.

It would be advisable that some kind of potato eminently liable to the disease should be planted in considerable numbers near the seedlings so as to infect them.

Altogether the trial would be one requiring much care and extreme patience, as I know from experience with analogous work, and it may be feared that it would be difficult to find any one who would pursue the experiment with sufficient energy. It seems, therefore, to me highly desirable that Mr. Torbitt should be aided with some small grant so as to continue the work himself.

Judging from his reports, his efforts have already been crowned in so short a time with more success than could have been anticipated ; and I think you will agree with me, that any one who raises a fungus-proof potato will be a public benefactor of no common kind.

My dear Farrer, yours sincerely,

CHARLES DARWIN.

[After further consultation with Sir Thomas Farrer and with Mr. Caird, my father became convinced that it was hopeless to attempt to obtain Government aid. He wrote to Mr. Torbitt to this effect, adding, "it would be less trouble to get up a subscription from a few rich leading agriculturists than from Government. This plan I think you cannot object to, as you have asked nothing, and will have nothing whatever to do with the subscription. In fact, the affair is, in my opinion, a compliment to you." The idea here broached was carried out, and Mr. Torbitt was enabled to continue his work by the aid of a sum to which Sir T. Farrer, Mr. Caird, my father, and a few friends, subscribed.

My father's sympathy and encouragement were highly valued by Mr. Torbitt, who tells me that without them he should long ago have given up his attempt. A few extracts will illustrate my father's fellow feeling with Mr. Torbitt's energy and perseverance :—

"I admire your indomitable spirit. If any one ever deserved success, you do so, and I keep to my original opinion that you have a very good chance of raising a fungus-proof variety of the potato.

"A pioneer in a new undertaking is sure to meet with many disappointments, so I hope that you will keep up your courage, though we have done so very little for you."

Mr. Torbitt tells me that he still (1887) succeeds in raising varieties possessing well-marked powers of resisting disease; but this immunity is not permanent, and, after some years, the varieties become liable to the attacks of the fungus.]

The Kew Index of Plant-Names, or 'Nomenclator Darwinianus'.

[Some account of my father's connection with the Index of Plant-names now (1887) in course of preparation at Kew will be found in Mr. B. Daydon Jackson's paper in the 'Journal of Botany,' 1887, p. 151. Mr. Jackson quotes the following statement by Sir J. D. Hooker :—

"Shortly before his death, Mr. Charles Darwin informed Sir Joseph Hooker that it was his intention to devote a considerable sum of money annually for some years in aid or furtherance of some work or works of practical utility to biological science, and to make provisions in his will in the event of these not being completed during his lifetime.

"Amongst other objects connected with botanical science, Mr. Darwin regarded with especial interest the importance of a complete index to the names and authors of the genera and species of plants known to botanists, together with their native countries. Steudel's 'Nomenclator' is the only existing work of this nature, and although now nearly half a century old, Mr. Darwin had found it of great aid in his own researches. It has been indispensable to every botanical institution, whether as a list of all known flowering plants, as an indication of their authors, or as a digest of botanical geography."

Since 1840, when the 'Nomenclator' was published, the number of described plants may be said to have doubled, so that the 'Nomenclator' is now seriously below the requirements of botanical work. To remedy this want, the 'Nomenclator' has been from time to time posted up in an interleaved copy in the Herbarium at Kew, by the help of "funds supplied by private liberality." *

My father, like other botanists, had as Sir Joseph Hooker points out, experienced the value of Steudel's work. He obtained plants from all sorts of sources, which were often incorrectly named, and he felt the necessity of adhering to the accepted nomenclature, so that he might convey to other workers precise indications as to the plants which he had studied. It was also frequently a matter of importance to him to know the native country of his experimental plants. Thus it was natural that he should recognize the desirability of completing and publishing the interleaved volume at Kew. The wish to help in this object was heightened by the admiration he felt for the results for which the world has to thank the Royal Gardens at Kew, and by his gratitude for the invaluable aid which for so many years he received from its Director and his staff. He expressly stated that it was his wish "to aid in some way the scientific work carried on at the Royal Gardens" †—which induced him to offer to supply funds for the completion of the Kew 'Nomenclator.'

---

* Kew Gardens Report, 1881, p. 62.
† See 'Nature,' January 5, 1882.

The following passage, for which I am indebted to Professor Judd, is of much interest, as illustrating the motives that actuated my father in this matter. Professor Judd writes :—

"On the occasion of my last visit to him, he told me that his income having recently greatly increased, while his wants remained the same, he was most anxious to devote what he could spare to the advancement of Geology or Biology. He dwelt in the most touching manner on the fact that he owed so much happiness and fame to the natural-history sciences, which had been the solace of what might have been a painful existence ;—and he begged me, if I knew of any research which could be aided by a grant of a few hundreds of pounds, to let him know, as it would be a delight to him to feel that he was helping in promoting the progress of science. He informed me at the same time that he was making the same suggestion to Sir Joseph Hooker and Professor Huxley with respect to Botany and Zoology respectively. I was much impressed by the earnestness, and, indeed, deep emotion, with which he spoke of his indebtedness to Science, and his desire to promote its interests."

Sir Joseph Hooker was asked by my father "to take into consideration, with the aid of the botanical staff at Kew and the late Mr. Bentham, the extent and scope of the proposed work, and to suggest the best means of having it executed. In doing this, Sir Joseph had further the advantage of the great knowledge and experience of Professor Asa Gray, of Cambridge, U.S.A., and of Mr. John Ball, F.R.S." *

The plan of the proposed work having been carefully considered, Sir Joseph Hooker was able to confide its elaboration in detail to Mr. B. Daydon Jackson, Secretary of the Linnean Society, whose extensive knowledge of botanical literature qualifies him for the task. My father's original idea of producing a modern edition of Steudel's 'Nomenclator' has been practically abandoned, the aim now kept in

---

* 'Journal of Botany,' *loc. cit.*

view is rather to construct a list of genera and species (with references) founded on Bentham and Hooker's 'Genera Plantarum.' The colossal nature of the work in progress at Kew may be estimated by the fact that the manuscript of the 'Index' is at the present time (1887) believed to weigh more than a ton. Under Sir Joseph Hooker's supervision the work goes steadily forward, being carried out with admirable zeal by Mr. Jackson, who devotes himself unsparingly to the enterprise, in which, too, he has the advantage of the active interest in the work felt by Professor Oliver and Mr. Thiselton Dyer.

The Kew 'Index,' which will, in all probability, be ready to go to press in four or five years, will be a fitting memorial of my father : and his share in its completion illustrates a part of his character—his ready sympathy with work outside his own lines of investigation—and his respect for minute and patient labour in all branches of science.]

CHAPTER XVI.

CONCLUSION.

SOME idea of the general course of my father's health may have been gathered from the letters given in the preceding pages. The subject of health appears more prominently than is often necessary in a Biography, because it was, unfortunately, so real an element in determining the outward form of his life.

During the last ten years of his life the condition of his health was a cause of satisfaction and hope to his family. His condition showed signs of amendment in several particulars. He suffered less distress and discomfort, and was able to work more steadily. Something has been already said of Dr. Bence Jones's treatment, from which my father certainly derived benefit. In later years he became a patient of Sir Andrew Clark, under whose care he improved greatly in general health. It was not only for his generously rendered service that my father felt a debt of gratitude towards Sir Andrew Clark. He owed to his cheering personal influence an often-repeated encouragement, which latterly added something real to his happiness, and he found sincere pleasure in Sir Andrew's friendship and kindness towards himself and his children.

Scattered through the past pages are one or two references to pain or uneasiness felt in the region of the heart. How far these indicate that the heart was affected early in life, I cannot pretend to say; in any case it is certain that he had no serious or permanent trouble of this nature until shortly before his death. In spite of the general improvement in his health, which has been above alluded to, there was a certain loss of physical vigour occasionally apparent during the last few years of his life. This is illustrated by a sentence in a letter to his old friend Sir James Sullivan, written on January 10, 1879 : "My scientific work tires me more than it used to do, but I have nothing else to do, and whether one is worn out a year or two sooner or later signifies but little."

A similar feeling is shown in a letter to Sir J. D. Hooker of June 15, 1881. My father was staying at Patterdale, and wrote : "I am rather despondent about myself . . . . I have not the heart or strength to begin any investigation lasting years, which is the only thing which I enjoy, and I have no little jobs which I can do."

In July, 1881, he wrote to Mr. Wallace, "We have just returned home after spending five weeks on Ullswater; the scenery is quite charming, but I cannot walk, and everything tires me, even seeing scenery . . . . What I shall do with my few remaining years of life I can hardly tell. I have everything to make me happy and contented, but life has become very wearisome to me." He was, however, able to do a good deal of work, and that of a trying sort,[*] during the autumn of 1881, but towards the end of the year he was clearly in need of rest ; and during the winter was in a lower condition than was usual with him.

On December 13 he went for a week to his daughter's house in Bryanston Street. During his stay in London he went to call on Mr. Romanes, and was seized when on the door-step with an attack apparently of the same kind as those which afterwards became so frequent. The rest of the incident, which I give in Mr. Romanes' words, is interesting too from a different point of view, as giving one more illustration of my father's scrupulous consideration for others :—

---

[*] On the action of carbonate of ammonia on roots and leaves.

"I happened to be out, but my butler, observing that Mr. Darwin was ill, asked him to come in. He said he would prefer going home, and although the butler urged him to wait at least until a cab could be fetched, he said he would rather not give so much trouble. For the same reason he refused to allow the butler to accompany him. Accordingly he watched him walking with difficulty towards the direction in which cabs were to be met with, and saw that, when he had got about three hundred yards from the house, he staggered and caught hold of the park-railings as if to prevent himself from falling. The butler therefore hastened to his assistance, but after a few seconds saw him turn round with the evident purpose of retracing his steps to my house. However, after he had returned part of the way he seems to have felt better, for he again changed his mind, and proceeded to find a cab."

During the last week of February and in the beginning of March, attacks of pain in the region of the heart, with irregularity of the pulse, became frequent, coming on indeed nearly every afternoon. A seizure of this sort occurred about March 7, when he was walking alone at a short distance from the house; he got home with difficulty, and this was the last time that he was able to reach his favourite 'Sand-walk.' Shortly after this, his illness became obviously more serious and alarming, and he was seen by Sir Andrew Clark, whose treatment was continued by Dr. Norman Moore, of St. Bartholomew's Hospital, and Mr. Alfrey, of St. Mary Cray. He suffered from distressing sensations of exhaustion and faintness, and seemed to recognise with deep depression the fact that his working days were over. He gradually recovered from this condition, and became more cheerful and hopeful, as is shown in the following letter to Mr. Huxley, who was anxious that my father should have closer medical supervision than the existing arrangements allowed:

Down, March 27, 1882.

"My dear Huxley,—Your most kind letter has been a real cordial to me. I have felt better to-day than for three weeks, and have felt as yet no pain. Your plan seems an excellent one, and I will probably act upon it, unless I get very much better. Dr. Clark's kindness is unbounded to me, but he is too busy to come here. Once again, accept my cordial thanks, my dear old friend. I wish to God there were more automata * in the world like you.

Ever yours,
Ch. Darwin."

The allusion to Sir Andrew Clark requires a word of explanation. Sir Andrew Clark himself was ever ready to devote himself to my father, who, however, could not endure the thought of sending for him, knowing how severely his great practice taxed his strength.

No especial change occurred during the beginning of April, but on Saturday 15th he was seized with giddiness while sitting at dinner in the evening, and fainted in an attempt to reach his sofa. On the 17th he was again better, and in my temporary absence recorded for me the progress of an experiment in which I was engaged. During the night of April 18th, about a quarter to twelve, he had a severe attack and passed into a faint, from which he was brought back to consciousness with great difficulty. He seemed to recognise the approach of death, and said, "I am not the least afraid to die." All the next morning he suffered from terrible nausea and faintness, and hardly rallied before the end came.

He died at about four o'clock on Wednesday, April 19th, 1882, in the seventy-fourth year of his age.

I close the record of my father's life with a few words of

---

* The allusion is to Mr. Huxley's address 'On the Hypothesis that Animals are Automata, and its History,' given at the Belfast meeting of the British Association in 1874, and republished in 'Science and Culture.'

retrospect added to the manuscript of his ' Autobiography'
in 1879 :—

"As for myself, I believe that I have acted rightly in
steadily following, and devoting my life to Science. I feel no
remorse from having committed any great sin, but have often
and often regretted that I have not done more direct good to
my fellow creatures."

APPENDIX I.

THE FUNERAL IN WESTMINSTER ABBEY.

ON the Friday succeeding my father's death, the following letter, signed by twenty members of Parliament, was addressed to Dr. Bradley, Dean of Westminster :—

HOUSE OF COMMONS, April 21, 1882.

VERY REV. SIR,—We hope you will not think we are taking a liberty if we venture to suggest that it would be acceptable to a very large number of our fellow-countrymen of all classes and opinions that our illustrious countryman, Mr. Darwin, should be buried in Westminster Abbey.

We remain, your obedient servants,

JOHN LUBBOCK,	RICHARD B. MARTIN,
NEVIL STOREY MASKELYNE,	FRANCIS W. BUXTON,
A. J. MUNDELLA,	E. L. STANLEY,
G. O. TREVELYAN,	HENRY BROADHURST,
LYON PLAYFAIR,	JOHN BARRAN,
CHARLES W. DILKE,	J. F. CHEETHAM,
DAVID WEDDERBURN,	H. S. HOLLAND,
ARTHUR RUSSEL,	H. CAMPBELL-BANNERMAN,
HORACE DAVEY,	CHARLES BRUCE,
BENJAMIN ARMITAGE,	RICHARD FORT.

The Dean was abroad at the time, and telegraphed his cordial acquiescence.

The family had desired that my father should be buried at **Down:** with regard to their wishes, Sir John Lubbock wrote :—

House of Commons, April 25, 1882.

My dear Darwin,—I quite sympathise with your feeling, and personally I should greatly have preferred that your father should have rested in Down amongst us all. It is, I am sure, quite understood that the initiative was not taken by you. Still, from a national point of view, it is clearly right that he should be buried in the Abbey. I esteem it a great privilege to be allowed to accompany my dear master to the grave.

Believe me, yours most sincerely,

JOHN LUBBOCK.

W. E. DARWIN, Esq.

The family gave up their first-formed plans, and the funeral took place in Westminster Abbey on April 26th. The pall-bearers were:—

SIR JOHN LUBBOCK,	CANON FARRAR,
Mr. HUXLEY,	SIR J. D. HOOKER,
Mr. JAMES RUSSELL LOWELL (American Minister),	Mr. WM. SPOTTISWOODE (President of the Royal Society),
Mr. A. R. WALLACE,	The EARL OF DERBY,
The DUKE OF DEVONSHIRE,	The DUKE OF ARGYLL.

The funeral was attended by the representatives of France, Germany, Italy, Spain, Russia, and by those of the Universities, and learned Societies, as well as by large numbers of personal friends and distinguished men.

The grave is in the North aisle of the Nave, close to the angle of the choir-screen, and a few feet from the grave of Sir Isaac Newton. The stone bears the inscription—

CHARLES ROBERT DARWIN.

Born 12 February, 1809.

Died 19 April, 1882.

APPENDIX II.

I.—LIST OF WORKS BY C. DARWIN.

Narrative of the Surveying Voyages of Her Majesty's Ships 'Adventure' and 'Beagle' between the years 1826 and 1836, describing their examination of the Southern shores of South America, and the 'Beagle's' circumnavigation of the globe. Vol. iii. Journal and Remarks, 1832–1836. By Charles Darwin. 8vo. London, 1839.

Journal of Researches into the Natural History and Geology of the countries visited during the Voyage of H.M.S. 'Beagle' round the world, under the command of Capt. Fitz-Roy, R.N. 2nd edition, corrected, with additions. 8vo. London, 1845. (Colonial and Home Library.)

A Naturalist's Voyage. Journal of Researches, &c. 8vo. London, 1860. [Contains a postscript dated Feb. 1, 1860.]

Zoology of the Voyage of H.M.S. 'Beagle.' Edited and superintended by Charles Darwin. Part I. Fossil Mammalia, by Richard Owen. With a Geological Introduction, by Charles Darwin. 4to. London, 1840.

——Part II. Mammalia, by George R. Waterhouse. With a notice of their habits and ranges, by Charles Darwin. 4to. London, 1839.

—— Part III. Birds, by John Gould. An "Advertisement" (2 pp.) states that in consequence of Mr. Gould's having left England for Australia, many descriptions were supplied by Mr. G. R. Gray of the British Museum. 4to. London, 1841.

—— Part IV. Fish, by Rev. Leonard Jenyns. 4to. London, 1842.

—— Part V. Reptiles, by Thomas Bell. 4to. London, 1843.

The Structure and Distribution of Coral Reefs. Being the First Part of the Geology of the Voyage of the 'Beagle.' 8vo. London, 1842.

The Structure and Distribution of Coral Reefs. 2nd edition. 8vo. London, 1874.

Geological Observations on the Volcanic Islands, visited during the Voyage of H.M.S. 'Beagle.' Being the Second Part of the Geology of the Voyage of the 'Beagle.' 8vo. London, 1844.

Geological Observations on South America. Being the Third Part of the Geology of the Voyage of the 'Beagle.' 8vo. London, 1846.

Geological Observations on the Volcanic Islands and parts of South America visited during the Voyage of H.M.S. 'Beagle.' 2nd edition. 8vo. London, 1876.

A Monograph of the Fossil Lepadidæ; or, Pedunculated Cirripedes of Great Britain. 4to. London, 1851. (Palæontographical Society.)

A Monograph of the Sub-class Cirripedia, with Figures of all the Species. The Lepadidæ; or, Pedunculated Cirripedes. 8vo. London, 1851. (Ray Society.)

—— The Balanidæ (or Sessile Cirripedes); the Verrucidæ, &c. 8vo. London, 1854. (Ray Society.)

A Monograph of the Fossil Balanidæ and Verrucidæ of Great Britain. 4to. London, 1854. (Palæontographical Society.)

On the Origin of Species by means of Natural Selection, or the Preservation of Favoured Races in the Struggle for Life. 8vo. London, 1859. (Dated Oct. 1st, 1859, published Nov. 24, 1859.)

—— Fifth thousand. 8vo. London, 1860.

—— Third edition, with additions and corrections. (Seventh thousand.) 8vo. London, 1861. (Dated March, 1861.)

—— Fourth edition, with additions and corrections. (Eighth thousand.) 8vo. London, 1866. (Dated June, 1866.)

—— Fifth edition, with additions and corrections. (Tenth thousand.) 8vo. London, 1869. (Dated May, 1869.)

—— Sixth edition, with additions and corrections to 1872. (Twenty-fourth thousand.) 8vo. London, 1882. (Dated Jan., 1872.)

On the various contrivances by which Orchids are fertilised by Insects. 8vo. London, 1862.

—— Second edition. 8vo. London, 1877. [In the second edition the word "On" is omitted from the title.]

The Movements and Habits of Climbing Plants. Second edition. 8vo. London, 1875. [First appeared in the ninth volume of the 'Journal of the Linnean Society.']

The Variation of Animals and Plants under Domestication. 2 vols. 8vo. London, 1868.

—— Second edition, revised. 2 vols. 8vo. London, 1875.

The Descent of Man, and Selection in Relation to Sex. 2 vols. 8vo. London, 1871.

—— Second edition. 8vo. London, 1874. (In 1 vol.)

The Expression of the Emotions in Man and Animals. 8vo. London, 1872.

Insectivorous Plants. 8vo. London, 1875.

The Effects of Cross and Self Fertilisation in the Vegetable Kingdom. 8vo. London, 1876.

—— Second edition. 8vo. London, 1878.

The different Forms of Flowers on Plants of the same Species. 8vo. London, 1877.

—— Second edition. 8vo. London, 1880.

The Power of Movement in Plants. By Charles Darwin, assisted by Francis Darwin. 8vo. London, 1880.

The Formation of Vegetable Mould, through the Action of Worms, with Observations on their Habits. 8vo. London, 1881.

II.—LIST OF BOOKS CONTAINING CONTRIBUTIONS BY C. DARWIN.

A Manual of scientific enquiry; prepared for the use of Her Majesty's Navy: and adapted for travellers in general. Ed. by Sir John F. W. Herschel, Bart. 8vo. London, 1849. (Section VI. Geology. By Charles Darwin.)

Memoir of the Rev. John Stevens Henslow. By the Rev. Leonard Jenyns. 8vo. London, 1862. [In Chapter III., Recollections by C. Darwin.]

A letter (1876) on the 'Drift' near Southampton, published in Prof. J. Geikie's 'Prehistoric Europe.'

Flowers and their unbidden guests. By A. Kerner. With a Prefatory Letter by Charles Darwin. The translation revised and edited by W. Ogle. 8vo. London, 1878.

Erasmus Darwin. By Ernst Krause. Translated from the German by W. S. Dallas. With a preliminary notice by Charles Darwin. 8vo. London, 1879.

Studies in the Theory of Descent. By Aug. Weismann. Translated and edited by Raphael Meldola. With a Prefatory Notice by Charles Darwin. 8vo. London, 1880—.

The Fertilisation of Flowers. By Hermann Müller. Translated and edited by D'Arcy W. Thompson. With a Preface by Charles Darwin. 8vo. London, 1883.

Mental Evolution in Animals. By G. J. Romanes. With a posthumous essay on instinct by Charles Darwin, 1883. [Also published in the Journal of the Linnean Society.]

Some Notes on a curious habit of male humble bees were sent to Prof. Hermann Müller, of Lippstadt, who had permission from Mr. Darwin to make what use he pleased of them. After Müller's death the Notes were given by his son to Dr. E. Krause, who published them under the title, " Ueber die Wege der Hummel-Männchen " in his book, ' Gesammelte kleinere Schriften von Charles Darwin ' (1886).

III.—LIST OF SCIENTIFIC PAPERS, INCLUDING A SELECTION OF LETTERS AND SHORT COMMUNICATIONS TO SCIENTIFIC JOURNALS.

Letters to Professor Henslow, read by him at the meeting of the Cambridge Philosophical Society, held Nov. 16, 1835. 31 pp. 8vo. Privately printed for distribution among the members of the Society.

Geological Notes made during a survey of the East and West Coasts of South America in the years 1832, 1833, 1834, and 1835; with an account of a transverse section of the Cordilleras of the Andes between Valparaiso and Mendoza. [Read Nov. 18, 1835.] Geol. Soc. Proc. ii. 1838, pp. 210–212. [This Paper is incorrectly described in Geol. Soc. Proc. ii., p. 210 as follows :—" Geological notes, &c., by F. Darwin, Esq., of St. John's College, Cambridge: communicated by Prof. Sedgwick." It is Indexed under C. Darwin.]

Notes upon the Rhea Americana. Zool. Soc. Proc., Part v. 1837, pp. 35–36.

Observations of proofs of recent elevation on the coast of Chili, made during the survey of H.M.S. " Beagle," commanded by Capt. FitzRoy. [1837.] Geol. Soc. Proc. ii. 1838, pp. 446–449.

A sketch of the deposits containing extinct Mammalia in the neighbourhood of the Plata. [1837.] Geol. Soc. Proc. ii. 1838, pp. 542–544.

On certain areas of elevation and subsidence in the Pacific and Indian oceans, as deduced from the study of coral formations. [1837.] Geol. Soc. Proc. ii. 1838, pp. 552-554.

On the Formation of Mould. [Read Nov. 1, 1837.] Geol. Soc. Proc. ii. 1838, pp. 574-576 ; Geol. Soc. Trans. v. 1840, pp. 505-510.

On the Connexion of certain Volcanic Phenomena and on the formation of mountain-chains and the effects of continental elevations. [Read March 7, 1838.] Geol. Soc. Proc. ii. 1838, pp. 654-660; Geol. Soc. Trans. v. 1840, pp. 601-632. [In the Society's Transactions the wording of the title is slightly different.]

Origin of saliferous deposits. Salt Lakes of Patagonia and La Plata. Geol. Soc. Journ. ii. (Part ii.), 1838, pp. 127-128.

Note on a Rock seen on an Iceberg in 16° South Latitude. Geogr. Soc. Journ. ix. 1839, pp. 528-529.

Observations on the Parallel Roads of Glen Roy, and of other parts of Lochaber in Scotland, with an attempt to prove that they are of marine origin. Phil. Trans. 1839, pp. 39-82.

On a remarkable Bar of Sandstone off Pernambuco, on the Coast of Brazil. Phil. Mag. xix. 1841, pp. 257-260.

On the Distribution of the Erratic Boulders and on the Contemporaneous Unstratified Deposits of South America. [1841.] Geol. Soc. Proc. iii. 1842, pp. 425-430 ; Geol. Soc. Trans. vi. 1842, pp. 415-432.

Notes on the Effects produced by the Ancient Glaciers of Caernarvonshire, and on the Boulders transported by Floating Ice. London Philosoph. Mag. vol. xxi. p. 180. 1842.

Remarks on the preceding paper, in a Letter from Charles Darwin, Esq., to Mr. Maclaren. Edinb. New Phil. Journ. xxxiv. 1843, pp. 47-50. [The "preceding" paper is : "On Coral Islands and Reefs as described by Mr. Darwin. By Charles Maclaren, Esq., F.R.S.E."]

Observations on the Structure and Propagation of the genus *Sagitta*. Ann. and Mag. Nat. Hist. xiii. 1844, pp. 1-6.

Brief Descriptions of several Terrestrial *Planariæ*, and of some remarkable Marine Species, with an Account of their Habits. Ann. and Mag. Nat. Hist. xiv. 1844, pp. 241-251.

An account of the Fine Dust which often falls on Vessels in the Atlantic Ocean. Geol. Soc. Journ. ii. 1846, pp. 26-30.

On the Geology of the Falkland Islands. Geol. Soc. Journ. ii. 1846, pp. 267-274.

A review of Waterhouse's ' Natural History of the Mammalia.' [Not signed.] Ann. and Mag. of Nat. Hist. 1847. Vol. xix. p. 53.

On the Transportal of Erratic Boulders from a lower to a higher level.
Geol. Soc. Journ. iv. 1848, pp. 315-323.

On British fossil Lepadidæ. Geol. Soc. Journ. vi. 1850, pp. 439-440.
[The G. S. J. says, " This paper was withdrawn by the author with
the permission of the Council."]

Analogy of the Structure of some Volcanic Rocks with that of
Glaciers. Edinb. Roy. Soc. Proc. ii. 1851, pp. 17-18.

On the power of Icebergs to make rectilinear, uniformly-directed
Grooves across a Submarine Undulatory Surface. Phil. Mag. x.
1855, pp. 96-98.

Vitality of Seeds. *Gardeners' Chronicle*, Nov. 17, 1855, p. 758.

On the action of Sea-water on the Germination of Seeds. [1856.]
Linn. Soc. Journ. i. 1857 (*Botany*), pp. 130-140.

On the Agency of Bees in the Fertilisation of Papilionaceous Flowers.
Gardeners' Chronicle, p. 725, 1857.

On the Tendency of Species to form Varieties ; and on the Per-
petuation of Varieties and Species by Natural Means of Selection.
By Charles Darwin, Esq., F.R.S., F.L.S., and F.G.S., and Alfred
Wallace, Esq. [Read July 1st, 1858.] Journ. Linn. Soc. 1859,
vol. iii. (*Zoology*), p. 45.

> Special titles of C. Darwin's contributions to the foregoing :—
> (i) Extract from an unpublished work on Species by C. Dar-
> win, Esq., consisting of a portion of a chapter entitled, " On
> the Variation of Organic Beings in a State of Nature ; on the
> Natural Means of Selection ; on the Comparison of Domestic
> Races and true Species." (ii) Abstract of a Letter from C.
> Darwin, Esq., to Professor Asa Gray, of Boston, U. S., dated
> Sept. 5, 1857.

On the Agency of Bees in the Fertilisation of Papilionaceous Flowers, and on the Crossing of Kidney Beans. *Gardeners' Chronicle*,
1858, p. 828 and Ann. Nat. Hist. 3rd series ii. 1858, pp. 459-465.

Do the Tineina or other small Moths suck Flowers, and if so what
Flowers? *Entom. Weekly Intell.* vol. viii. 1860, p. 103.

Note on the achenia of *Pumilio Argyrolepis*. *Gardeners' Chronicle*,
Jan. 5, 1861, p. 4.

Fertilisation of Vincas. *Gardeners' Chronicle*, pp. 552, 831, 832.
1861.

On the Two Forms, or Dimorphic Condition, in the species of *Primula*, and on their remarkable Sexual Relations. Linn. Soc. Journ.
vi. 1862 (*Botany*), pp. 77-96.

On the Three remarkable Sexual Forms of *Catasetum tridentatum*, an Orchid in the possession of the Linnean Society. Linn. Soc. Journ. vi. 1862 (*Botany*), pp. 151-157.

Yellow Rain. *Gardeners' Chronicle*, July 18, 1863, p. 675.

On the thickness of the Pampean formation near Buenos Ayres. Geol. Soc. Journ. xix. 1863. pp. 68-71.

On the so-called " Auditory-sac " of Cirripedes. Nat. Hist. Review, 1863, pp. 115-116.

A review of Mr. Bates' paper on 'Mimetic Butterflies.' Nat. Hist. Review, 1863, p. 221 —. [Not signed.]

On the existence of two forms, and on their reciprocal sexual relation, in several species of the genus *Linum*. Linn. Soc. Journ. vii. 1864 (*Botany*), pp. 69-83.

On the Sexual Relations of the Three Forms of *Lythrum salicaria*. [1864.] Linn. Soc. Journ. viii. 1865 (*Botany*), pp. 169-196.

On the Movement and Habits of Climbing Plants. [1865.] Linn. Soc. Journ. ix. 1867 (*Botany*), pp. 1-118.

Note on the Common Broom (*Cytisus scoparius*). [1866.] Linn. Soc. Journ. ix. 1867 (*Botany*), p. 358.

Notes on the Fertilization of Orchids. Ann. and Mag. Nat. Hist. 4th series, iv. 1869, pp. 141-159.

On the Character and Hybrid-like Nature of the Offspring from the Illegitimate Unions of Dimorphic and Trimorphic Plants. [1868.] Linn. Soc. Jour. x. 1869 (*Botany*), pp. 393-437.

On the Specific Difference between *Primula veris*, Brit. Fl. (var. *officinalis*, of Linn.), *P. vulgaris*, Brit. Fl. (var. *acaulis*, Linn.), and *P. elatior*, Jacq.; and on the Hybrid Nature of the common Oxslip. With Supplementary Remarks on naturally produced Hybrids in the genus *Verbascum*. [1868.] Linn. Soc. Journ. x. 1869 (*Botany*), pp. 437-454.

Note on the Habits of the Pampas Woodpecker (*Colaptes campestris*). Zool. Soc. Proc. Nov. 1, 1870, pp. 705-706.

Fertilisation of *Leschenaultia*. *Gardeners' Chronicle*, p. 1166, 1871.

The Fertilisation of Winter-flowering Plants. 'Nature,' Nov. 18, 1869, vol. i. p. 85.

Pangenesis. 'Nature,' April 27, 1871, vol. iii. p. 502.

A new view of Darwinism. 'Nature,' July 6, 1871, vol. iv. p. 180.

Bree on Darwinism. 'Nature,' Aug. 8, 1872, vol. vi. p. 279.

Inherited Instinct. 'Nature,' Feb. 13, 1873, vol. vii. p. 281.

Perception in the Lower Animals. 'Nature,' March 13, 1873, vol. vii. p. 360.

Origin of certain instincts. 'Nature,' April 3, 1873, vol. vii. p. 417.

Habits of Ants. 'Nature,' July 24, 1873, vol. viii. p. 244.

On the Males and Complemental Males of Certain Cirripedes, and on Rudimentary Structures. 'Nature,' Sept. 25, 1873, vol. viii. p. 431.

Recent researches on Termites and Honey-bees. 'Nature,' Feb. 19, 1874, vol. ix. p. 308.

Fertilisation of the Fumariaceæ. 'Nature,' April 16, 1874, vol. ix. p. 460.

Flowers of the Primrose destroyed by Birds. 'Nature,' April 23, 1874, vol. ix. p. 482; May 14, 1874, vol. x. p. 24.

Cherry Blossoms. 'Nature,' May 11, 1876, vol. xiv. p. 28.

Sexual Selection in relation to Monkeys. 'Nature,' Nov. 2, 1876, vol. xv. p. 18. Reprinted as a supplement to the 'Descent of Man,' 18..

Fritz Müller on Flowers and Insects. 'Nature,' Nov. 29, 1877, vol. xvii. p. 78.

The Scarcity of Holly Berries and Bees. *Gardeners' Chronicle*, Jan. 20, 1877, p. 83.

Note on Fertilization of Plants. *Gardeners' Chronicle*, vol. vii. p. 246, 1877.

A biographical sketch of an infant. 'Mind,' No. 7, July, 1877.

Transplantation of Shells. 'Nature,' May 30, 1878, vol. xviii. p. 120.

Fritz Müller on a Frog having Eggs on its back—on the abortion of the hairs on the legs of certain Caddis-Flies, &c. 'Nature,' March 20, 1879, vol. xix. p. 462.

Rats and Water-Casks. 'Nature,' March 27, 1879, vol. xix. p. 481.

Fertility of Hybrids from the common and Chinese Goose. 'Nature,' Jan. 1, 1880, vol. xxi. p. 207.

The Sexual Colours of certain Butterflies. 'Nature,' Jan. 8, 1880, vol. xxi. p. 237.

The Omori Shell Mounds. 'Nature,' April 15, 1880, vol. xxi. p. 561.

Sir Wyville Thomson and Natural Selection. 'Nature,' Nov. 11, 1880, vol. xxiii. p. 32.

Black Sheep. 'Nature,' Dec. 30, 1880, vol. xxiii. p. 193.

Movements of Plants. 'Nature,' March 3, 1881, vol. xxiii. p. 409.

The Movements of Leaves. 'Nature,' April 28, 1881, vol. xxiii. p. 603.

Inheritance. 'Nature,' July 21, 1881, vol. xxiv. p. 257.

Leaves injured at Night by Free Radiation. 'Nature,' Sept. 15, 1881. vol. xxiv. p. 459.

The Parasitic Habits of Molothrus. 'Nature,' Nov. 17, 1881, vol. xxv. p. 51.

On the Dispersal of Freshwater Bivalves. 'Nature,' April 6, 1882, vol. xxv. p. 529.

The Action of Carbonate of Ammonia on the Roots of certain Plants. [Read March 16, 1882.] Linn. Soc. Journ. (*Botany*), vol. xix. 1882, pp. 239–261.

The Action of Carbonate of Ammonia on Chlorophyll-bodies. [Read March 6, 1882.] Linn. Soc. Journ. (*Botany*), vol. xix. 1882, pp. 262–284.

On the modification of a Race of Syrian Street-Dogs by means of Sexual Selection. By W. Van Dyck. With a preliminary notice by Charles Darwin. [Read April 18, 1882.] Proc. Zoolog. Soc. 1882, pp. 367–370.

APPENDIX III.

PORTRAITS.

Date.	Description.	Artist.	In the Possession of
1838	Water-colour .	G. Richmond	The Family.
1851	Lithograph . .	Ipswich British Assn. Series.	
1853	Chalk Drawing .	Samuel Lawrence	The Family.
1853?	Chalk Drawing*	Samuel Lawrence	Prof. Hughes, Cambridge.
1869	Bust, marble .	T. Woolner, R. A.	The Family.
1875	Oil Painting† .	W. Ouless, R. A.	The Family.
	Etched by	P. Rajon.	
1879	Oil Painting .	W. B. Richmond.	The University of Cambridge.
1881	Oil Painting‡ .	Hon. John Collier	The Linnæan Society.
	Etched by	Leopold Flameng	

CHIEF PORTRAITS AND MEMORIALS NOT TAKEN FROM LIFE.

	Statue	Joseph Boehm, R. A.	Museum, South Kensington.
	Bust	Chr. Lehr, Junr.	
	Plaque	T. Woolner, R. A., and Josiah Wedgwood and Sons.	Christ's College, in Charles Darwin's Room.
	Deep Medallion .	J. Boehm, R. A.	To be placed in Westminster Abbey.

* Probably a sketch made at one of the sittings for the last-mentioned.

† A *replica* by the artist is in the possession of Christ's College, Cambridge.

‡ A *replica* by the artist is in the possession of W. E. Darwin, Esq., Southampton.

Chief Engravings from Photographs.

* 1854? By Messrs. Maull and Fox, engraved on wood for ' Harper's Magazine' (Oct. 1884).

* 1870? By O. J. Rejlander, engraved on steel by C. H. Jeens for ' Nature' (June 4, 1874).

* 1874? By Capt. Darwin, R. E., engraved on wood for the ' Century Magazine' (Jan. 1883). Frontispiece, vol. i.

1881   By Messrs. Elliott and Fry, engraved on wood by G. Kruells, for vol. ii. of the present work.

---

* The dates of these photographs must, from various causes, remain uncertain. Owing to a loss of books by fire, Messrs. Maull and Fox can give only an approximate date. Mr. Rejlander died some years ago, and his business was broken up. My brother, Captain Darwin, has no record of the date at which his photograph was taken.

APPENDIX IV.*

HONOURS, DEGREES, SOCIETIES, &c.

Order.—Prussian Order, 'Pour le Mérite.' 1867.

Office.—County Magistrate. 1857.

Degrees.—Cambridge {
B.A.   1831 [1832].†
M.A.   1837.
Hon. LL.D.   1877.
}

Breslau . Hon. Doctor in Medicine and Surgery.   1862.

Bonn . . Hon. Doctor in Medicine and Surgery.   1868.

Leyden . Hon. M.D.   1875.

Societies.—London . Zoological.   Corresp. Member.   1831.‡

Entomological.   1833, Orig. Member.

Geological.   1836.   Wollaston Medal, 1859.

Royal Geographical.   1838.

Royal.   1839.   Royal Medal, 1853.   Copley Medal, 1864.

Linnean.   1854.

Ethnological.   1861.

Medico-Chirurgical.   Hon. Member.   1868.

Baly Medal of the Royal College of Physicians, 1879.

---

* The list has been compiled from the diplomas and letters in my father's possession, and is no doubt incomplete, as he seems to have lost or mislaid some of the papers received from foreign Societies. Where the name of a foreign Society (excluding those in the United States) is given in English, it is a translation of the Latin (or in one case Russian) of the original Diploma.

† See vol. i. p. 139.

‡ He afterwards became a Fellow of the Society.

Societies.—PROVINCIAL, COLONIAL AND INDIAN.

Royal Society of Edinburgh, 1865.
Royal Medical Society of Edinburgh, 1826. Hon. Member, 1861.
Royal Irish Academy. Hon. Member, 1866.
Literary and Philosophical Society of Manchester. Hon. Member, 1868.
Watford Nat. Hist. Society. Hon. Member, 1877.
Asiatic Society of Bengal. Hon. Member, 1871.
Royal Society of New South Wales. Hon. Member, 1879.
Philosophical Institute of Canterbury, New Zealand. Hon. Member, 1863.
New Zealand Institute. Hon. Member, 1872.

Foreign Societies.

AMERICA.

Sociedad Científica Argentina. Hon. Member 1877.
Academia Nacional de Ciencias, Argentine Republic. . Hon. Member, 1878.
Sociedad Zoolójica Arjentina. Hon. Member, 1874.
Boston Society of Natural History. Hon. Member, 1873.
American Academy of Arts and Sciences (Boston). Foreign Hon. Member, 1874.
California Academy of Sciences. Hon. Member, 1872.
California State Geological Society. Corresp. Member, 1877.
Franklin Literary Society, Indiana. Hon. Member, 1878.
Sociedad de Naturalistas Neo-Granadinos. Hon. Member, 1860.
New York Academy of Sciences. Hon. Member, 1879.
Gabinete Portuguez de Leitura em Pernambuco. Corresp. Member, 1879.
Academy of Natural Sciences of Philadelphia. Correspondent, 1860.
American Philosophical Society, Philadelphia. Member, 1869.

AUSTRIA-HUNGARY.

Imperial Academy of Sciences of Vienna. Foreign Corresponding Member, 1871; Hon. Foreign Member, 1875.
Anthropologische Gesellschaft in Wien. Hon..Member, 1872.
K. k. Zoologisch‑botanische Gesellschaft in Wien. Member, 1867.
Magyar Tudományos Akadémia, Pest, 1872.

BELGIUM.

Société Royale des Sciences Médicales et Naturelles de Bruxelles. Hon. Member, 1878.
Société Royale de Botanique de Belgique. 'Membre Associé,' 1881.
Académie Royale des Sciences, &c., de Belgique. 'Associé de la Classe des Sciences.' 1870.

DENMARK.

Royal Society of Copenhagen. Fellow, 1879.

FRANCE.

Société d'Anthropologie de Paris. Foreign Member, 1871.
Société Entomologique de France. Hon. Member, 1874.
Société Géologique de France (Life Member), 1837.
Institut de France. 'Correspondant' Section of Botany, 1878.

GERMANY.

Royal Prussian Academy of Sciences (Berlin). Corresponding Member, 1863; Fellow, 1878.
Berliner Gesellschaft für Anthropologie, &c. Corresponding Member, 1877.
Schlesische Gesellschaft für Vaterländische Cultur (Breslau). Hon. Member, 1878.
Cæsarea Leopoldino-Carolina Academia Naturæ Curiosorum (Dresden).* 1857.
Senkenbergische Naturforschende Gesellschaft zu Frankfurt am Main. Corresponding Member, 1873.
Naturforschende Gesellschaft zu Halle. Member 1879.
Siebenbürgische Verein für Naturwissenschaften (Hermannstadt). Hon. Member, 1877.
Medicinisch - naturwissenschaftliche Gesellschaft zu Jena. Hon. Member, 1878.

---

* The diploma contains the words "accipe . . . ex antiqua nostra consuetudine cognomen Forster." It was formerly the custom in the *Cæsarea Leopoldino-Carolina Academia*, that each new member should receive as a 'cognomen,' a name celebrated in that branch of science to which he belonged. Thus a physician might be christened Boerhave, or an astronomer, Kepler. My father seems to have been named after the traveler John Reinhold Forster.

Royal Bavarian Academy of Literature and Science (Munich). Foreign Member, 1878.

HOLLAND.

Koninklijke Natuurkundige Vereeniging in Nederlandsch - Indie (Batavia). Corresponding Member, 1880.

Société Hollandaise des Sciences à Harlem. Foreign Member, 1877.

Zeeuwsch Genootschap der Wetenschappen te Middleburg. Foreign Member, 1877.

ITALY.

Società Geografica Italiana (Florence). 1870.

Società Italiana di Antropologia e di Etnologia (Florence). Hon. Member, 1872.

Società dei Naturalisti in Modena. Hon. Member, 1875.

Academia de' Lincei di Roma. Foreign Member, 1875.

La Scuola Italica, Academia Pitagorica, Reale ed Imp. Società (Rome). "Presidente Onoraria degli Anziani Pitagorici," 1880.

Royal Academy of Turin. 1873. *Bressa* Prize, 1879.

PORTUGAL.

Sociedade de Geographia de Lisboa (Lisbon). Corresponding Member, 1877.

RUSSIA.

Society of Naturalists of the Imperial Kazan University. Hon. Member, 1875.

Societas Cæsarea Naturæ Curiosorum (Moscow). Hon. Member, 1870.

Imperial Academy of Sciences (St. Petersburg). Corresponding Member, 1867.

SPAIN.

Institucion Libre de Enseñanza (Madrid). Hon. Professor, 1877.

SWEDEN.

Royal Swedish Acad. of Sciences (Stockholm). Foreign Member, 1865.

Royal Society of Sciences (Upsala). Fellow, 1860.

SWITZERLAND.

Société des Sciences Naturelles de Neuchatel. Corresponding Member, 1863.

INDEX.

72

THE END.